Organizing Audiovisual and Electronic Resources for Access

A Cataloging Guide

Second Edition

INGRID HSIEH-YEE

Library and Information Science Text Series

LIBRARIES
UNLIMITED
A Member of the Greenwood Publishing Group
Westport, Connecticut • London

Library of Congress Cataloging-in-Publication Data

Hsieh-Yee, Ingrid.
  Organizing audiovisual and electronic resources for access : a cataloging
guide / by Ingrid Hsieh-Yee—2nd ed.
      p.   cm.—(Library and information science text series)
  Includes bibliographical references and index.
  ISBN 1–59158–051–X (pbk. : alk. paper)
  1. Cataloging of audio-visual materials.   2. Cataloging of electronic
information resources.   3. Anglo-American cataloging rules.
  I. Title.   II. Series.
Z695.66H75   2006
025.3'44—dc22   2005036160

British Library Cataloguing in Publication Data is available.

Library of Congress Catalog Card Number: 2005036160
ISBN: 1–59158–051–X

First published in 2006

Libraries Unlimited, 88 Post Road West, Westport, CT 06881
A Member of the Greenwood Publishing Group, Inc.
www.lu.com

Printed in the United States of America

The paper used in this book complies with the
Permanent Paper Standard issued by the National
Information Standards Organization (Z39.48–1984).

10 9 8 7 6 5 4 3 2 1

Organizing Audiovisual
and Electronic Resources for Access

To Cordell and Corinna,
who broaden my perspective

Contents

Illustrations

Preface to the
Second Edition

This work began in 2001 and evolved as digital resources became abundant, the Internet became users' favorite place for information, and the cataloging community developed and revised cataloging rules and practices to accommodate new formats of resources. The journey was stimulating and overwhelming. The amended Chapter 9 was published in 2001, the new Chapter 12 for continuing resources became available in 2002, and the 2002 edition of the *Anglo-American Cataloguing Rules (AACR)* has been updated several times. The Library of Congress issued guidelines for cataloging electronic resources and rule interpretations for describing integrating resources, electronic serials, and other types of materials. Its Network Development and MARC Standards Office has actively provided support for libraries to operate in the XML environment. OCLC has provided guidelines and Web-based instructions on cataloging Internet resources. And numerous workshops and presentations have covered the treatment of DVDs, digital resources, and Web resources. At the same time, metadata gained acceptance inside and outside the library profession as a means for describing information resources, and strong interests in creating and using digital collections resulted in the development of numerous metadata schemas, some with input from librarians, and many without.

This is a challenging time for libraries and catalogers. As libraries incorporate new formats of sound recordings, videos, and digital resources into their services, catalogers have to learn and apply new rules to catalog these materials. This book draws on rule interpretations, guidelines, the literature, and the author's teaching experience to clarify the treatments of CDs, DVDs, MP3s, streaming videos, electronic books and other files, Web resources, and remote access electronic serials. The book illustrates the latest standards with examples and uses fully cataloged records to explain cataloging issues specific to each type of material. The objective is to help students, librarians, educators, and anyone new to these media to gain competency in cataloging them. The book is designed for self-study and classroom use. Readers can study the subjects at their own pace, and educators may find the text and examples useful for courses on media cataloging, advanced cataloging, and the cataloging of Internet resources.

Changes in this edition reflect the 2002 revision of the *Anglo-American Cataloguing Rules* and its 2004 update, the latest version of the *Library of Congress Rule Interpretations,* and the *CONSER Module 31.* Chapter 1 explains the relationship between information organization and cataloging and discusses how librarians have organized audio and electronic resources. The effort of the Joint Steering Committee for Revision of the Anglo-American Cataloguing Rules (JSC) to develop "AACR3" and its recent decision to develop *Resources Description and Access (RDA)* are incorporated into Chapter 1 to give readers an update on rule development and changes. Chapter 2 provides an overview of the cataloging process to prepare readers for the rest of the book. The MARC section was expanded to provide more details on fixed-field elements, the 006 field, and the coding of the variable fields. Chapter 3 ("Sound Recordings") and Chapter 4 ("Videorecordings") were substantially revised to reflect the latest rules, new examples of CDs and DVDs are included, and all records include fixed-field elements.

Chapter 5 ("Electronic Resources"), Chapter 6 ("Integrating Resources"), and Chapter 7 ("Remote Access Electronic Serials") are new and reflect the latest practice in cataloging these types of materials. The second edition includes more than thirty-five new examples of full bibliographic records, and all examples from the first edition were revised and updated. Each of these chapters begins with an introduction—followed by a discussion, with examples, of current standards for descriptive cataloging, choice of access points, and subject analysis—and concludes with analyses of ten bibliographic records. Options for arranging audiovisual and electronic resources are included whenever appropriate. Items cataloged for this book came from public, school, academic, and special libraries. The author created records according to the current standards and presented the records in the MARC format. All access points were checked against the Library of Congress name and subject authority files. New names were established according to the 2002 revision of AACR.

Chapter 8 was updated and expanded to include metadata. In addition to discussing the changing information environment and its implications for cataloging, it clarifies the relationship between metadata and cataloging, presents examples of metadata schemas that are used more often in library environments, and explains the process of metadata implementation.

The bibliography includes cataloging standards in print and in electronic format, selected resources on metadata and cataloging, and a group of handbooks and guidebooks. To facilitate access to important cataloging tools and literature on the Web and update readers on the latest developments in the treatment of audiovisual and electronic resources, a Web site has been created. The author will maintain the site continuously (http://slis.cua.edu/ihy/aver.htm) and the Libraries Unlimited Web site will provide a link to this site.

As a teacher of cataloging for more than fifteen years, I firmly believe in the value of cataloging and the need for information organization. My goal has always been to give students enough practical details to perform original cataloging and to provide them with the principles of cataloging to adapt to a changing information environment. In addition to the immediate goal of helping readers gain some competency in cataloging selected types of material, I hope to underscore the importance of the information organization principles, because the future of the library profession depends on them. Recent popularity of metadata has unfortunately led to an erroneous view that cataloging is no longer needed. The fact is cataloging is an application of the metadata concept in the library environment, and the metadata/cataloging data that catalogers provide has proven to be critical for information discovery and access in the digital age. I hope catalogers and prospective catalogers will take heart in knowing that information organization is sorely needed, and the knowledge of cataloging principles and standards will help them deal with many changes ahead. The future of our profession depends on lifelong learning and collaboration with other information professionals. Librarians have successfully integrated sound recordings and videorecordings into their services. If history is our guide, catalogers will turn the challenges posed by electronic resources into opportunities and help make libraries an essential player in the future information environment.

Ingrid Hsieh-Yee

Acknowledgments

Many individuals have written about the description and organization of sound recordings, video recordings, computer files, Web resources, and electronic serials. Professional groups such as ALCTS, CONSER, and OLAC have provided guidelines and informative workshops on rule changes and treatments of electronic and other types of resources. These works contribute to my understanding of the subjects and the development of this book. Besides the rich content, I am impressed by these individuals' generosity in sharing their knowledge and experience, and the spirit of cooperation that is the trademark of library professionals. To these colleagues in this invisible college, all of them listed in the references, I am immeasurably grateful.

All of my students at the Catholic University of America in Washington, D.C. have a part in this book. Their questions, comments, and insights on issues related to information organization often provide fresh perspectives and stimulate my thinking. Several assistants worked on this project, doing literature searches, preparing bibliographies, and verifying cataloging rules. A most sincere thank you goes to them. Colleagues, past and present, at the School of Library and Information Science of the Catholic University of America, provided much needed moral support.

I also would like to acknowledge the staff at Libraries Unlimited, Shelley Yeager, and the personnel at Westchester Book Group for editing and designing this book. Ron Maas and Sue Easun were most patient and accommodating. They made the process much easier for me.

I am deeply grateful to my husband for his faith in me. His unwavering support is amazing in light of what he had to endure during the creation of this work. He not only took care of the family and mundane business in life, but also gave me the courage and determination to press on. He and our daughter, Corinna, bring much joy to my life and give meaning to my effort. Their love, patience, and sacrifice make this book possible.

1

Organization of Information and Cataloging

Cataloging is the cornerstone of librarianship. Some people perceive it narrowly as a subject that involves rigid rules and forced logic. But it is through cataloging that library information professionals enable patrons to search, browse, access, and obtain information. Cataloging also provides the bibliographic infrastructure needed to support reference services and facilitate efficient collection management. As digital resources proliferate and users' interest in electronic resources increases, an understanding of cataloging and how it relates to information organization will enable library information professionals to be more effective in serving users.

The Information Transfer Cycle

Cataloging is a method of information organization and a critical part of the information transfer cycle. As Figure 1.1 illustrates, information transfer is cyclical. A potential author could begin at the **search and access** stage by researching for materials for a project. The author may consult print and computerized information resources as well as human resources, such as colleagues or librarians, to locate known items, search for works on selected subjects, and learn what has been published in an area of interest. At the **evaluation and synthesis** stage, the author may take time to review those items, discard irrelevant ones, synthesize relevant literature, develop theses and antitheses, add personal insight, and move on to the **creation** stage to produce a new work. When the work is completed, it is submitted for peer review. When the work passes review, it becomes available to the public. The **information organization** stage begins next. The work could be included in a directory such as *Books in Print*. It could be indexed by an abstracting and indexing service or listed in a bibliography. In a library, the

1

work is most likely to be cataloged. Descriptive information, access points, subject information (descriptors, subject headings, classification, or similar devices) would be provided, and the item would be placed on the shelf for access. After such treatment the item is ready for the search and access stage, and the cycle continues.

Figure 1.1. The information transfer cycle

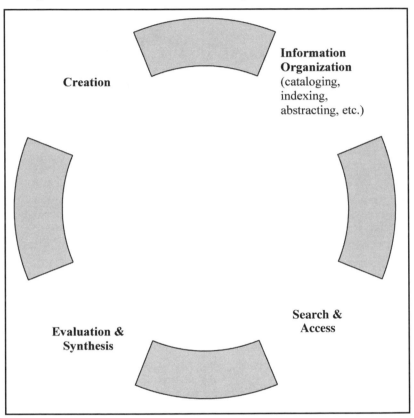

Different approaches to information organization result in different outputs—a directory, an index, a bibliography, or a catalog. But the objectives of these tools are similar: to find, identify, select, and obtain needed information. If information organization were removed from this cycle, the gap between creators and users of information would become very costly to bridge. Patrons would have to spend much time and energy determining what information is available, searching for the desired items, and evaluating the relevancy of everything they happen to find. This is, in fact, the challenge facing Internet users today. Although search engines like Google support keyword searches and give the impression that Internet searches are easy, it is common for users to receive a large number of hits. Some users are willing to scan the first couple of screens of search results and make do with what they find. But serious researchers usually need to sift through a lot of material to find something satisfactory. The lack of systematic and well-coordinated information organization on the Internet means doing serious research on the Internet will remain challenging.

The Principles of Information Organization

Organizing information for access is a major concern of library and information professionals. They have applied many approaches to organizing analog, digital, and mixed-format materials for access, resulting in tools such as catalogs, indexes (print and online), abstracts, finding aids, bibliographies, pathfinders, and digital directories or databases. The large number of information tools gives the impression that these methods cover separate parts of the information universe and are quite different in their design and purpose. But these approaches share common goals that were first advocated by Charles A. Cutter in his *Rules for a Dictionary Catalog* (1904): they identify, collocate, evaluate, and locate information. The importance of these functions was underscored by the IFLA report that specifies finding, identifying, selecting, and obtaining access as the functional requirements of bibliographic records (IFLA Study Group, 1998). While the procedures for building these tools may be different, these bibliographic tools, in fact, follow the same principles. These principles have been applied but rarely articulated. Taylor (1994) and Hagler (1997) are probably the first writers to successfully describe the important principles of information organization. Svenonious (2000) provides a conceptual framework for organizing information and articulates a set of principles of bibliographic description and access that is particularly relevant in the digital environment. The following section draws on these authors' ideas.

Principle One: Definition of Scope and Selection Criteria

The first principle for organizing information, regardless of the approach an organizer takes, is defining the scope of the information system. While it is desirable to have a system that organizes the entire information universe, the reality is every information system is constrained by time and resources (financial and human). Specifying the types of materials a system will organize and how materials will be selected is therefore a necessary first task in information organization. Information organizers can focus on the holdings of a library or an archive, the materials on a subject, the resources of special interest to a particular user community, and so on. Among the factors to consider, the most critical is the users' information needs.

With an understanding of user needs, the organizer then can develop selection criteria and begin to search the information universe for appropriate resources for the user community. In a library, activities entailed by the first principle are usually in the domain of the collection development department. Dramatic growth of electronic resources in recent years, however, has resulted in the increased participation of reference and cataloging staff in this stage.

Principle Two: Creation of Representation

Once resources have been specified for coverage, the next concern is the creation of a representation, or surrogate. This step is necessary because it is understood that a representation, that is, a description of a resource, is more efficient than the original source material for searching and browsing purposes. For example, although it is possible to provide a full-text search on many documents, good descriptions of these documents would reduce search time and effort and collocate documents that are related by author, subject, and other bibliographic elements. Such collocation gives users a better picture of the range of materials in their topic of interest and enables them to select relevant materials more quickly.

The procedure for creating a representation varies according to tool, but two objectives are common to all. First, the representation should contain enough detail to identify a resource. Second, it should include sufficient information to distinguish one resource from another.

To ensure consistency in representation creation, various standards have been created. Indexing agencies have guidelines on how to describe resources, and citation style manuals offer similar advice. For cataloging purposes, the key content standard is the *Anglo-American Cataloguing Rules*, second edition, 2002 revision (*AACR2r*), and the most popular standard for encoding cataloging records is the MARC 21 standards.

Principle Three: Analysis for Access

Related to resource description is the analysis of a resource for access purposes. The goal of this principle is to ensure that a tool serves the evaluation and collocation functions. Information organizers typically identify individuals or organizations that are responsible for, or have contributed substantially to, the intellectual content of a work. Depending on the tools, authors, co-authors, and editors are likely to be selected as access points. Series titles, journal titles, and titles of related works can also be used as non-subject access points.

In addition, information organizers analyze the subjects, or the "aboutness," of a work to inform users of its contents. Indexers assign descriptors, abstractors create abstracts, bibliography compilers prepare annotations, and catalogers assign subject headings. Some tools also make use of classification codes or product codes. The objective is to enable users to conduct subject searches, determine the relevancy of retrieved items, and select the most useful items for their purposes.

For effective retrieval, authority control needs to be performed on all access points, subject and non-subject. Most tools strive to control synonyms, homographs, and variant spellings, and to represent the relationships between concepts in their subject authority lists. But not all tools make an effort to control non-subject access points. The lack of consistency in non-subject access points, as experienced in some online databases, means searchers have to shoulder the burden of multiple name searches if they want to retrieve all publications by an author who has published under different names.

In creating bibliographic descriptions of resources and assigning access points, information organizers will want to keep in mind the need of the users and the need for accurate and standardized records for materials in all formats. One of the key principles of the *Library of Congress Subject Headings* states that users should be the focus, and the terminology used for subject access should be familiar to the majority of users (Chan 1995). Similarly, Svenonius (2000) recommends that information organizers follow the "principle of user convenience" by keeping users in mind when they describe resources and select name forms for access, and follow the "principle of common usage" by choosing the most familiar vocabulary for access. She also emphasizes that bibliographic descriptions and controlled forms of names for access should be **representative** (i.e., based on the way a resource describes itself), **accurate** (i.e., accurately reflect the resource), **sufficient**

and necessary (i.e., include elements that are bibliographically significant only), and **standardized** (i.e., used according to consistent rules and applications). In information environments that offer various types of materials to users, she recommends an integrated approach so that a common set of rules is followed, to the extent possible, to describe all the materials.

Principle Four: Organization of Resources and Their Representations

The final principle concerns how resources and their representations are organized for access. If resources are owned locally, some kind of location notation such as a call number is desirable. The objective is to facilitate retrieval of the needed item and provide collocation on the shelf so that users, especially shelf browsers, can select from similar items.

If resources are located remotely such as electronic journals or books, some mechanism such as a hypertext link should be provided for online access. Many online services have well-established document delivery services and some have made full-text documents available online by request, too.

This principle also applies to the organization of representations (or bibliographic descriptions). This step is critical because it affects access to resources, especially in an online environment. Unlike the manual environment where a user can thumb through pages or drawers of cards, online tools provide few physical cues to users. The screen display of representations informs the user of what is available. It is therefore critical that the order of the elements in a representation and the screen display of multiple items be carefully designed. A successful design presents collocation on the screen and enables users to make good use of the resources covered by the tool.

The Principles and Cataloging

As one of the many approaches for information organization, cataloging closely follows the principles described above. To prepare users who are new to cataloging for the work in the next few chapters, this section discusses how catalogers apply these principles and describes standard cataloging procedures. Users with some cataloging knowledge and background may find this section useful for refreshing their memory of this subject.

The scope of a library catalog is guided by the library's mission and goals, and the catalog's organization is designed to serve its user communities. Most libraries have collection development policies and procedures in place, and staff in the collection development unit is responsible for the selection and acquisition of resources for users. So the first principle of information organization in a library setting is usually applied by collection development specialists. Some libraries have streamlined their operation, and collection development staff may create preliminary records for items that have been ordered. Serious cataloging work begins when the resources arrive.

In many libraries newly arrived materials are searched in bibliographic utilities such as Online Computer Library Center (OCLC) or Research Library Information Network (RLIN) to determine if bibliographic records exist. If records are found, catalogers perform copy cataloging. Otherwise, they create original catalog records for the materials. There are several major steps in original cataloging, including description, assignment of access points, subject analysis, authority control, MARC encoding (or tagging), and contributing records to a bibliographic utility. The purpose of descriptive cataloging is to

Figure 1.2. Cataloging workflow

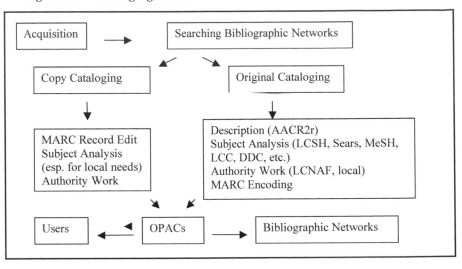

create a representation for an item. The representation must contain enough details for an item to be identified and to be distinguished from others. The principle of record creation is applied in descriptive cataloging.

Catalogers apply the third principle, the principle of analyzing materials for access, by examining the materials for potential non-subject and subject access points. Part II of the *Anglo-American Cataloguing Rules (AACR)* provides guidelines for selecting non-subject access points and determining the proper forms of names for access. Subject authority lists such as *Library of Congress Subject Headings, Sears Subject Headings*, and *Medical Subject Headings* provide controlled terms for catalogers to indicate the subjects of materials. To ensure consistency in access points and facilitate searching and browsing in the catalog, catalogers perform authority work on all access points.

When these tasks are completed, the original materials and their surrogates are processed for access. They are assigned call numbers and placed on shelves, while bibliographic records for them are put into machine-readable format and parsed for further manipulation. Catalogers and system designers make decisions on how to display elements of the representations, and how to sort multiple items and display them on computer screen (Yee and Layne 1998). This is how catalogers put Principle Four into practice.

Organizing Audiovisual and Electronic Materials

Figure 1.2 illustrates the cataloging work flow that libraries have always organized, provided access to, and preserved materials that are relevant to the needs of users. The format of resources has expanded from analog to digital, and sometimes the same resource can be accessed physically as well as virtually. But the focus of library information professionals continues to be on organizing information for access. Recent studies have reported the proliferation of nonprint collections in libraries. In a survey of Canadian libraries, Weihs and Howarth (1995) found that 93.7 percent of responding libraries have collected one or more types of nonprint media. Videorecordings were the most frequently collected medium, followed by microforms, sound recordings, cartographic material, computer software, and film, all owned by more than 50 percent of the libraries surveyed. A survey of the largest 100 American academic and public libraries also found videorecordings to be the most popular medium (collected by 99.3 percent of responding libraries) and sound recordings are close behind (98.6 percent). Computer files are popular as well (96.6 percent) and Internet resources are making an inroad (77.2 percent) (Hsieh-Yee 1999). Regarding the method for organization, the Canadian study reported 75.1 percent of libraries with nonbook collections used *AACR2r* to catalog all or part of their collections. The U.S. study found a higher percentage of full cataloging activities among the large libraries owning media—97.9 percent of the responding libraries fully cataloged their sound recording collections, 95.1 percent fully cataloged videos, 88.6 percent fully cataloged computer files, and 61.6 percent fully cataloged Internet resources. A 2004 study (Hsieh-Yee) investigated how libraries in the Washington Metropolitan Area have organized free Web resources, digital collections, electronic journals, and databases for access. Data show that 73 percent of responding libraries catalog databases and electronic journals, 69 percent catalog free Web resources, and 48 percent catalog digital collections. These studies suggest that *AACR2r* rules for sound recordings, videorecordings, and computer files are accepted as the standards for cataloging such materials.

The latest additions to library collections are Internet resources. Their organization remains a work in progress. Many librarians believe libraries should integrate Internet resources into their collection because users demand access (Hill 1996) and some valuable materials are available only on the Internet. Internet resources are of varying quality, but librarians can add value to such resources through careful selection and organization (Chepesiuk 1999; Morgan 1996). From bookmarking to full cataloging, librarians have attempted to impose order over parts of the Internet. Some rely on simple grouping of resources, while others provide resource annotations (e.g., A Guide to Social Policy Resources, 2005) or employ control vocabularies for better access—for example, INFOMINE (1994) organizes resources with modified LC subject headings, The Scout Report Archives (2004) classifies resources by LC subject headings, and Beyond Bookmarks (2001) includes many projects that use classification schemes. Some projects focus on a particular audience or a subject area (e.g., KidsClick!, 2003 and SunSite's Digital Library, 2005) while others have a broader scope (e.g., Sailor, 2005). Scholars have also created digital collections or archives to increase access to resources on various subjects. The William Blake Archive (2004) and the James Joyce Scholars' Collection are good examples. An effort that has the potential for organizing Internet resources on a larger scale is cooperative cataloging. It is true that the dynamic nature, volatility, and large number of Internet resources have caused many to question the validity of cataloging Internet resources (e.g., Tennant 1998). Some catalogers have worried that Internet resources would be difficult to catalog for a variety of reasons (e.g., Banerjee 1997; Weihs 1996). But if evaluation criteria are applied, the number of resources to be cataloged will become manageable (Hillmann 1996), and new technology and techniques such as PURL (Persistent Uniform Resource Locator, 2005) will alleviate the challenge of link maintenance.

OCLC's InterCat project (Dillon and Jul 1996) created an experimental catalog to show that cataloging is a feasible solution to the management of Internet resources if the resources are carefully selected and if libraries cooperate in this venture. The Cooperative Online Resource Catalog (CORC) project (1999) further demonstrated the benefit of using technology to integrate various tools and standards for the creation of MARC records and Dublin Core records. While Internet resources are different from print resources, the principles of bibliographic description and access can be applied to them. Mandel and Wolven have discussed how these principles can be applied with the help of the latest technology and techniques, such as Z39.50, field 856, encoding standards, and metadata (Mandel and Wolven 1996). Projects such as InterCat and CORC demonstrate that cataloging Internet resources is feasible. The Joint Steering Committee for the Revision of AACR has published new Chapters 9 and 12 for the description of direct access and remote access electronic resources and integrating resources. And in 2002, OCLC incorporated all the features of the CORC prototype into OCLC Connexion (2005), a Web-based integrated cataloging service to facilitate resource description and access for catalogers. As more and more libraries actively including Internet resources in their services and catalogs, librarians are likely to draw on their previous experience in handling new material formats to control Internet resources. In the 1960s and 1970s, the concern was about new nonprint resources such as sound recordings and videorecordings. In the 1980s microcomputer files dominated catalogers' attention. In the 1990s Internet resources have presented catalogers with challenges and opportunities.

Purpose of This Book

This book was developed to meet the strong interest in cataloging sound recordings, videorecordings, computer files, Internet resources, and electronic journals. While the *AACR2r* rules for sound recordings and videorecordings remain fairly stable, *AACR* has provided new guidelines for the description of electronic resources (Chapter 9) and continuing resources (Chapter 12) in recent years. This book offers examples to illustrate the current standards and analyzes fully cataloged records to explain cataloging considerations specific to each type of material. The objective is to help students, catalogers, educators, and anyone new to these media gain competency in describing and providing access to them. In addition, to demystify metadata, the final chapter examines cataloging and metadata as methods for information organization in the digital age, discusses the relationship between these two approaches, provides recommendations for implementing and managing metadata projects, and considers the role of cataloging in future information organization.

This book is designed for self-study and classroom use. Readers can study the subjects at their own pace, and educators may find the text useful for courses on media cataloging, advanced cataloging, and the cataloging of Internet resources. Chapter 2 provides an overview of the cataloging process to prepare students new to cataloging for the description and access of nonprint materials. Students and catalogers with some knowledge of monograph cataloging can use this material to refresh their memory of the subject. Those familiar with monograph cataloging can skip ahead to the chapters covering the specific media. Chapters 3 to 7 are devoted to the cataloging of sound recordings, videorecordings, direct access electronic resources (often referred to as "computer files" in the literature), Internet resources, and electronic journals. Because of changes in *AACR* rules, interactive multimedia are included in the chapter on direct access electronic resources, instead of comprising a chapter of its own. To address the strong interest in remote access electronic serials, a new chapter addresses the description and access of this type of materials. Each chapter begins with an introduction, followed by a discussion of current standards and examples for descriptive cataloging, choice of access points, and subject analysis. Each chapter concludes with analyses of ten bibliographic records created according to Level 2 of *AACR2r*. The records were created according to the current standards for descriptive cataloging and subject analysis. All the access points were checked against the name and subject authority files on Connexion (http://connexion.oclc.org) or LC authority files (http://authorities.loc.gov). New names were established according to *AACR2r*.

Conclusion

Libraries have successfully integrated new formats of material into their collections by developing sensible solutions to organize such materials. The best way to organize sound recordings, videorecordings, electronic resources, Internet resources, and electronic journals is to become familiar with the standards. As catalogers become experienced in describing these resources they will also encounter problems and think of new solutions. Then the standards can be informed by such experience. Technology will continue to advance and that will make the task of information organization both challenging and exciting. To operate well in a changing information environment, librarians can take comfort in knowing they have the proven principles of information organization. Those principles, if applied intelligently and coupled with new technology and techniques, will help them manage and organize information in all formats.

References

Banerjee, Kyle. (1997). Describing remote electronic documents in the online catalog: Current issues. *Cataloging & Classification Quarterly* 25 (1): 5–20.

Berkeley digital library sunsite. (2005). http://sunsite.berkeley.edu/ (accessed June 1, 2005).

Beyond bookmarks: Schemes for organizing the Web. (2001). http://www.public .iastate.edu/~CYBERSTACKS/CTW.htm (accessed June 1, 2005).

Chan, Lois Mai. (1995). *Library of Congress subject headings: Principles and application*. Englewood, Colo.: Libraries Unlimited.

Chepesiuk, Ron. (1999, January). Organizing the Internet. *American Libraries* 30: 60–63.

Cooperative Online Resource Catalog (CORC) project. (1998–1999). http://www.oclc .org/research/projects/archive/default.htm (accessed June 1, 2005).

Cutter, Charles A. (1904). *Rules for a dictionary catalog* (4th ed.). Washington, D.C.: U.S. Government Printing Office.

Dillon, Martin, and Jul, Erik. (1996). Cataloging Internet resources: The convergence of libraries and Internet resources. *Cataloging & Classification Quarterly* 22 (3/4): 197–238.

Eaves, Morris, Essick, Robert, and Viscomi, Joseph (Eds.). (2004). *William Blake archive*. http://www.blakearchive.org/ (accessed June 1, 2005).

A guide to social policy resources. (2005). http://libraries.cua.edu/instruct/irsocpol .html (accessed June 1, 2005).

Hagler, Ronald. (1997). *The bibliographic record and information technology* (3rd ed.). Chicago: American Library Association.

Hayman, David (Ed.). *The James Joyce scholars' collection*. http://digicoll.library
.wisc.edu/JoyceColl/ (accessed June 1, 2005).

Hill, Janet Swan. (1996). The elephant in the catalog: Cataloging animals you can't
see or touch. *Serials Librarian* 23: 6–7.

Hillmann, Diane I. (1996). "Parallel universes" or meaningful relationships: En-
visioning a future for the OPAC and the Net. *Cataloging & Classification
Quarterly* 22 (3/4): 97–103.

Hsieh-Yee, Ingrid. (1999, May 30). Organization of nonprint resources in public and
academic libraries. Unpublished report.

Hsieh-Yee, Ingrid. (2004, December 20). How libraries provide access to digital resources. Unpublished report.

IFLA Study Group on the Functional Requirements for Bibliographic Records.
(1998). *Functional requirements for bibliographic records: Final report*.
München: K. G. Saur. http://www.ifla.org/VII/s13/frbr/frbr.pdf (accessed June
1, 2005).

INFOMINE. (1994–). http://infomine.ucr.edu/ (accessed June 1, 2005).

Kids Click! (2003). http://sunsite.berkeley.edu/KidsClick!/ (accessed June 1, 2005).

Mandel, Carol A., and Wolven, Robert. (1996). Intellectual access to digital documents: Joining proven principles with new technologies. *Cataloging & Classification Quarterly* 22 (3/4): 25–42.

Morgan, Eric Lease. (1996). Possible solutions for incorporating digital information
mediums into traditional library cataloging services. *Cataloging & Classification Quarterly* 22 (3/4): 143–170.

OCLC Connexion. (2005). http://www.oclc.org/connexion/ (accessed June 1, 2005).

PURLS. (2005). http://purl.oclc.org/ (accessed June 1, 2005).

Sailor. (2005). http://www.sailor.lib.md.us (accessed June 1, 2005).

The Scout Report archives. (2004). http://scout.wisc.edu/Archives/index.php (accessed June 1, 2005).

Svenonius, Elaine. (2000). *The intellectual foundation of information organization*.
Cambridge, Mass.: MIT Press.

Taylor, Arlene G. (1994, July/August). The information universe: Will we have chaos
or control? *American Libraries* 25: 629–632.

Tennant, Roy. (1998, October 15). The art and science of digital bibliography. *Library Journal* 123: 28, 30.

Weihs, Jean. (1996, April). Solving the Internet cataloging nightmare. *Technicalities*
16: 4–8.

Weihs, Jean, and Howarth, Lynne C. (1995, April). Nonbook materials: Their occurrence and bibliographic description in Canadian libraries. *Library Resources and Technical Services* 39: 184–197.

Yee, Martha M., and Layne, Sara Shatford. (1998). *Improving online public access
catalogs*. Chicago: American Library Association.

Suggested Readings

Hagler, Ronald. (1997). Principles of bibliographic control. In *The bibliographic record and information technology* (3rd ed.). Chicago: American Library Association.

IFLA Study Group on the Functional Requirements for Bibliographic Records. (1998). *Functional requirements for bibliographic records: Final report.* München: K. G. Saur. http://www.ifla.org/VII/s13/frbr/frbr.pdf (accessed June 1, 2005).

Mandel, Carol A., and Wolven, Robert. (1996). Intellectual access to digital documents: Joining proven principles with new technologies. *Cataloging & Classification Quarterly* 22 (3/4): 25–42.

Svenonius, Elaine. (2000). *The intellectual foundation of information organization.* Cambridge, Mass.: MIT Press.

Taylor, Arlene G. (2004). *The organization of information* (2nd ed.). Westport, Conn.: Libraries Unlimited.

2

Cataloging: An Overview

Treatment of Nonprint Resources

The cataloging of nonprint resources has evolved over time. Weihs presented a historical perspective on bibliographic control of nonbook materials (1987), Intner (1984) and Frost (1989) detailed the development of cataloging rules for nonprints, and Maillet (1991) described efforts to provide subject access to film and video. Among the issues debated, uniformity in bibliographic access and equality in physical access were the most critical. Uniformity in bibliographic access refers to the application of the same cataloging rules to all types of material. This is consistent with the principle of integration advocated by Svenonius that descriptions for all types of materials should be based on a common set of rules, to the extent possible (2000). This practice results in an integrated catalog where users can retrieve items of interest regardless of their format. Advocates of this **omnimedia** approach believe it would make retrieval easier for users and encourage the use of nonprint resources (e.g., Weihs, Lewis, and Macdonald 1979; Kaye 1991; Weihs 1991). But opponents have cited the unique characteristics of nonprints and recommended special treatment (Daily 1972). The cost of full cataloging has also caused concern and led libraries to adopt the departmentalized approach, which separates nonprint items from the book collection and from the catalog. After several major changes, acceptable cataloging rules have emerged and most libraries have adopted the omnimedia approach. A 1989 survey, for instance, reported that 73 percent of American libraries serving a population of over 25,000 fully cataloged their nonprint items (Pitman). A 1995 report of the cataloging practice of Canadian libraries of various types found 89.7 percent of libraries owning sound recordings cataloged them, with 72.6 percent of them following *Anglo-American Cataloguing Rules*, second edition (*AACR2*); 89.3 percent of libraries owning videorecordings cataloged them, with 72.1 percent of them follow *AACR2*; and 70.9 percent of libraries owning computer files cataloged them, with 63.4 percent using *AACR2* (Weihs and Howarth). A 1998 study of the largest 100 public and academic libraries found more than 95 percent of responding libraries fully cataloged sound recordings and videorecordings (Hsieh-Yee 1999). A 2004 study investigated how libraries in the Washington Metropolitan Area organize free Web resources, digital collections, electronic journals, and databases for access (Hsieh-Yee). Data show that 73 percent of responding libraries catalog databases and electronic journals, 69 percent catalog free Web resources, and 48 percent catalog digital collections. The integrated approach seems to have been prevalent among large libraries, especially where sound recordings and videorecordings were concerned. The omnimedia approach has been endorsed by many practitioners and researchers (e.g., Intner and Weihs 1998; Kaye 1991; Mason-Robinson 1996; Scholtz 1995).

Equality in physical access is a less settled issue. The goal is to provide the same access to print and nonprint resources, and one major approach is intershelving all types of material. Patrons benefit from this approach because all materials are organized under one system, and all works on the same subject are collocated on the shelf or in the online catalog. This approach may also attract new patrons and increase use of the library (Weihs 1991). Concerns for security, maintenance, and space, however, have led some libraries to adopt other methods for arranging nonprint resources. For instance, Scholtz indicated that genre classification, not classification by *Dewey Decimal Classification* or *Library of Congress Classification*, was popular among public libraries (1995). A 1998 study of the top 100 public and academic libraries found that public librarians expressed a commitment to browsing and 99 percent shelved sound recordings by format, while 94 percent shelved videorecordings by format (Hsieh-Yee 1999).

Description

Current cataloging rules reflect a strong interest among librarians to integrate various types of resources into the catalog. This chapter presents descriptive cataloging rules and subject analysis approaches applicable to sound recordings, videorecordings, direct access electronic resources, remote access electronic resources, and integrating resources. Treatment of remote access electronic serials is not summarized here because of the special characteristics of this type of materials. MARC elements that are important to all of these formats are explained. Special issues related to these types of material are discussed in the chapters devoted to the specific media.

To ensure consistency in record creation and support international sharing of bibliographic records, catalogers follow the *Anglo-American Cataloguing Rules* (*AACR*), which are based on the International Standard Bibliographic Description (ISBD) and the Paris Principles. The current standard is the revised edition of the second edition of *AACR*, commonly known as *AACR2r*. *AACR2r* incorporates many changes to *AACR2* and the Library of Congress's interpretations for the rules. Because of the emergence of new types of resources, new guidelines were developed to describe interactive multimedia (*Guidelines for Bibliographic Description* 1994) and Internet resources (Olson 1997). The 2002 revision of *AACR2r* presents important changes to the chapter on computer files (Chapter 9) and a new chapter on continuing resources (Chapter 12). The Joint Steering Committee has published annual updates to bring new changes to the attention of the cataloging community. The new Chapter 9 is entitled "Electronic Resources" and covers direct and remote access electronic resources, including interactive multimedia. The *ALA Guidelines* for interactive multimedia are no longer in use. The new Chapter 12 is entitled "Continuing Resources" to cover materials that exhibit seriality, that is, materials that are updated periodically or continuously, including loose-leaf publications, serials (print and electronic), updating databases, and Internet resources that are updated. As major changes are incorporated into *AACR2r*, *Library of Congress Rule Interpretations* continues to be an important tool for clarifying the application of *AACR2r* rules.

The Joint Steering Committee (JSC) of *AACR* has been working on "AACR3" since 2002 and decided in April 2005 that a new approach is needed to organize digital resources more effectively in the digital era. As a result, a new code, Resource Description and Access (RDA), is being developed. RDA will be based on the conceptual framework of FRBR (Functional Requirements of Bibliographic Records) and make explicit the importance of authority control for information access.[1] Principles of bibliographic description and access recommended by Svenonius will be followed closely. These principles (Svenonius 2000) are paraphrased here to illustrate that the user has always been the focus of cataloging effort and that accurate description and access, prepared in a consistent way across formats, continues to be the concern of catalogers. Here are the principles:

- User convenience: Decisions on description and access should be made with users in mind.

- Common usage: Vocabulary used in description and access should be consistent with user vocabulary.

- Representation: Description and form of access points should reflect how information is presented in the resource.

- Accuracy: Description and form of access points should faithfully reflect the resource.

- Sufficiency and necessity: Only elements that are bibliographically significant should be included in description and used for access.

- Standardization: Description and form of access points should be standardized.

- Integration: A common set of rules should be used to describe all types of materials.

Details on the Joint Steering Committee for Revision of Anglo-American Cataloguing Rules and its progress are available at http://www .collectionscanada.ca/jsc/index.html.

MARC 21 continues to be the dominant format for encoding bibliographic records in libraries in spite of Miller's call for catalogers to use MARC XML (2000) and Tennant's declaration that MARC must die (2002). Yee's article effectively addresses these criticisms and points out how MARC may need to change to stay effective in the twenty-first century (2004). The Network Development and MARC Standards Office has developed a framework for libraries and vendors who wish to use MARC data in an XML environment (2005). Bibliographic utilities have developed their own MARC guidelines and validation systems to increase the quality of records entering their databases. Drawing on its experiments in InterCat and CORC, OCLC (Online Computer Library Center) unveiled its Connexion system in the summer of 2002, which integrates OCLC's input standards for bibliographic records and authority files into the record creation process, enables users to create records in MARC and Dublin Core formats, and provides options for record output in MARC and Dublin Core. In addition, Connexion (2005) supports conversion of bibliographic records between MARC and Dublin Core. Because of the large number of libraries using OCLC and Connexion, MARC records in this book are presented in OCLC screen display, and OCLC input standards are used to explain the coding of records.

The goal of descriptive cataloging is to create a bibliographic record with sufficient detail for an item to be identified and distinguished from other items. Part I of *AACR2r* is devoted to this effort. Chapter 1 of *AACR2r* presents general rules that apply to materials of all formats, followed by chapters on specific media. The structure of Chapter 1 is repeated in the rest of the chapters in Part I. For example, Chapter 1 stipulates eight areas for description:

Area 1. Title and Statement of Responsibility (MARC Field 245)

Area 2. Edition (MARC Field 250)

Area 3. Material Specific Details

Area 4. Publication, Distribution, Etc. (MARC Field 260)

Area 5. Physical Description (MARC Field 300)

Area 6. Series (MARC Field 4XX)

Area 7. Notes (MARC Field 5XX)

Area 8. International Standard Numbers (MARC Fields 020 or 022)

Rule 1.1 covers the description of Area 1, rule 1.2, the recording of edition information, and so on. The number before the period in the rule number refers to the chapter, while the number after the period refers to the area of description. The parallel structure in Part I means that while rule 1.4 is about publication information, rule 2.4 covers the recording of publication information for monographs, and rule 6.4 instructs catalogers to record the place, name, and date related to the publication of sound recordings. Catalogers usually need to consult Chapter 1 and the chapter devoted to the specific medium being cataloged. This parallel structure is designed to simplify the use of *AACR2r* and encourage consistency in record creation.

The following section summarizes Chapter 1 and Chapter 2 of *AACR2r* to provide readers with an overview of the basics of cataloging.

Rules for Descriptive Cataloging

Levels of Description

Following Charles A. Cutter's model, *AACR2r* recommends three levels of description. The first level records basic elements to identify an item and is often quite brief (see 1.0D1 of *AACR2r* for example). Libraries with limited resources sometimes adopt this level of description to make their collections known to users. The second level of description is considered the standard level of cataloging. It includes elements of the eight areas stipulated by 1.0B1 (see 1.0D2 for example). Most libraries catalog their materials at this level of specification. The third level of description includes all elements specified by *AACR2r* rules that are applicable to the work being cataloged. Libraries often choose this level to describe materials of local significance or rare materials.

Chief Source and Prescribed Sources of Information

In describing any type of publication, the cataloger looks for the chief source of information first. The chief source is specified at the beginning of each chapter in Part I of *AACR2r* to ensure consistency in cataloging. Information from this source is preferred to information from other areas of the item. For each area of the description, *AACR2r* prescribes one or more sources. The cataloger should use square brackets for information taken from outside the prescribed sources.

In the following discussion of *AACR2r* rules, examples are presented in the MARC format without the first subfield $a because that is the way OCLC presents MARC records. Users of other bibliographic information systems will need to include the first subfield $a if their systems require it.

Area 1. Title and Statement of Responsibility (MARC Field 245)

245	_ _	Title proper $h [GMD] : $b other title information / $c statement of responsibility ; subsequent statement of responsibility.

Area 1 records the title proper, general material designation if appropriate, other title information, and statement(s) of responsibility. The order of these elements, the punctuation pattern, and the MARC field and subfields for this area are shown above. In this area the main objective is to record the title proper faithfully by following exactly its wording, order, and spelling, but not necessarily its punctuation or capitalization (rule 1.1B1). The objective is to show users how the title information is presented in the chief source.

If a general material designation (GMD) is needed to describe an item, it follows the title proper immediately in square brackets and is encoded in subfield $h. A GMD is useful for indicating the medium of nonprint materials. Libraries in Australia, Canada, and the United States use List 2 provided in *AACR2r*, and the Library of Congress makes use of only a small number of these terms, including electronic resource, filmstrip, kit, microform, motion picture, slide, sound recording, transparency, and videorecording (CSB 44: 10).

Other title information is transcribed according to the same rules for the title proper. If an item contains more than one other title information, the first other title information is entered under subfield $b, while each subsequent one is preceded with a colon but without a subfield code in the MARC format because subfield $b is not repeatable in the 245 field. Statements of responsibility presented prominently are transcribed in subfield $c, and individuals with different responsibilities for the item, such as authors and editors, are separated by semicolons. Subfield $c is not repeatable in the 245 field.

Area 2. Edition (MARC Field 250)

> 250   Edition statement / $b statement of responsibility
>   relating to the edition.

If an edition statement is found on the item, it is transcribed using abbreviations in Appendix B and numerals in Appendix C of *AACR2r*. If a statement of responsibility is related to only one particular edition, it is transcribed after the edition statement in subfield $b of the 250 field. The punctuation pattern is the same as that for Area 1.

> 250   Definitive ed. / $b edited, with an introduction, by
>   Susan Sontag.

The edition statement should be a formal statement found on the item. Expressions such as edition, version, or issues are evidence of the presence of an edition statement. Catalogers should be careful not to infer an edition statement. For example, "first published in America in 1998" should not be interpreted as the first American edition.

If an editor has been involved in all editions of a work, the editor's name is recorded in subfield $c of the 245 field instead of the 250 field.

Area 3. Material Specific Details

This area applies to only three types of materials: cartographic materials, music, and continuing resources. In some cases, descriptions of microforms may include elements for this area. This area will be discussed in detail in Chapter 7 of this book on electronic serials.

Area 4. Publication, Distribution, Etc. (MARC Field 260)

> 260   Place of publication : $b Name of publisher, $c Date
>   of publication.

The place of publication is transcribed as found on the item. The first place of publication is always transcribed, and state names, if used, are abbreviated according to Appendix B of *AACR2r*. The name of country, state, province, and so on is added in square brackets if it is necessary to distinguish between places or to identify a place.

In the prescribed source: DeKalb, Illinois	Transcribed as: DeKalb, Ill.
In the prescribed source: Madison	Transcribed as: Madison, [S.D.]

If the name of a larger jurisdiction appears with a place name in the prescribed source, the Library of Congress instructs catalogers to add it to Area 4 even though it may not be necessary for identification purpose.

In the prescribed source: Universal City, CA 91608
Transcribed per LC practice: Universal City, CA

If the first place of publication is not in the home country of the cataloging agency or if the layout or typography suggests another place to be more important, a second place of publication should be added. Subfield $a for the 260 field is repeatable and each place of publication is entered under its own subfield $a.

In the prescribed source: Toronto   London   Chicago
An America library will transcribe it as follows:
260   Toronto ; $a Chicago

The name of the publisher is recorded in subfield $b of the 260 field and should be recorded in the shortest possible form that is recognizable internationally. Reference tools such as *Books in Print* are good sources to determine to what extent the name of a publisher can be shortened. Initial articles and terms such as "limited" and "incorporated" are dropped. If in doubt, however, the cataloger should not shorten a publisher's name.

If a publisher responsible for an item is a subordinate unit of a parent organization, the name of the division responsible for the publication, not that of the parent organization, is recorded as the publisher.

In the prescribed source: Beginners Books, a division of MacMillan
Transcribed as: Beginners Books

Phrases indicating the function or responsibility of the publisher other than publishing should be recorded. This is typical of association publications that are contracted out to commercial publishers.

In the prescribed source: Published for the American Society
for Information Science by John Wiley.
Transcribed as: Published for the American Society for
Information Science by J. Wiley.

The publication date of the edition in hand is the third element for Area 4 and is entered in subfield $c. If an item contains multiple dates, publication date is preferred to copyright date or printing date. If a publication date is not available, the cataloger will use the copyright date. If a copyright date is not available, a printing date is used. *AACR2r* offers an option to include both the publication date and the copyright date if they are different. The Library of Congress decided in 1989 that it would not apply this option to monographs or print serials.

260   Toronto ; $a Chicago : $b Beginners Books, $c 1990.

Area 5. Physical Description (MARC Field 300)

> 300   Extent : $b Other details ; $c Dimensions + $e Accompanying material.

The extent of an item is recorded as the number of physical units in arabic numerals and the specific material designation. For books, the cataloger records the number of pages, such as "320 p." For nonprint materials, the cataloger should consult the .5B subrules in the relevant chapter. For example, for sound recordings (covered in Chapter 6 of *AACR2r*), rule 6.5B provides guidance for describing the physical carriers of sound information.

If playing time is available, it is included in parentheses after the physical units description.

> 300   2 sound cassettes (60 min.)

If other physical details of an item are available, they are included as the second element, subfield $b, in the 300 field. Examples include number of sound tracks, recording methods, and playing speed. For dimensions of the item (subfield $c), chapters devoted to specific formats provide details for recording such information. For example, no dimensions are recorded for standard sound cassettes, but CDs will be described as $4\frac{3}{4}$ in.

> 300   1 sound disc (62 min.) : $b digital, stereo. ; $c 4 3/4 in.

Accompanying material can be included in the record in two ways in Area 5. A popular approach is to provide the number of physical units in arabic numerals and a descriptive term of the material at the end of Area 5, using subfield $e. If catalogers choose to provide more detail, the physical description is entered in parentheses following the number of physical units, but no subfields are used.

> 300   1 sound disc (62 min.) : $b digital, stereo ; $c 4 3/4 in. + $e 1 booklet.
> 300   245 p. : $b ill.; $c 22 cm. + $e 1 CD (1 computer optical disc : sd., col. ; 4 3/4 in.)

Area 6. Series (Field 4XX)

> 440   –   Series title, $x ; $v
> 490   0   Series title. [not used as an added entry]
> 490   1   Series title as found in the item [not to be used for added entry]
> 830   –   Authorized form of series title as added entry.

Series titles are usually found in the chief source, the series title page, or other prescribed sources. It is transcribed according to the same rules for transcribing title proper. If the International Standard Serial Number (ISSN) is readily available, it is transcribed in Area 6, using subfield $x. The numbering of an item within a series is recorded in arabic form in subfield $v, and abbreviations in Appendix B are used when appropriate.

Other title information of a series is rarely transcribed unless it provides useful identifying information. Similarly, the statement of responsibility for a series is usually not included unless it is needed to identify the series. The Library of Congress interprets this to mean adding statements to titles which are vague or generic (CSB 22: 16). For example, the series, Occasional papers, from the National Geological Society will be transcribed as: Occasional papers / National Geological Society.

Series information is entered in the 440 field, if it is to serve as an added entry; otherwise field 490 is used. When a series title is chosen to be an added entry, but in a form different from that found on the item, both fields 490 and 830 are used. In such cases, the series title on the item is recorded in field 490 (using indicator value "1" to specify the series is to be traced), and the authorized form of the series title is recorded in field 830. If the authorized form is established under a personal name, the series title is recorded in field 800 subfield $t.

440	0	Contribution to information science studies ; $v 25
490	0	Penguin classics [series title not traced]
490	1	Series of unfortunate events [series title to be traced but in a different form that is recorded in the 8XX field]
800	1	Snicket, Lemony. $t Series of unfortunate events

Area 7. Notes (Field 5XX)

Notes supplement information formally presented in the first six areas of a record. Some notes provide identifying detail, some indicate the nature of an item, while others give background information such as publishing history or the intended audience. Rules under 1.7 cover various types of notes applicable to materials of all formats. In addition, catalogers should consult individual chapters of Part I of *AACR2r* to prepare notes for specific types of media. For example, a note on cast members is important for videos, a note on performers is appropriate for sound recordings, and a note on system requirements is essential for electronic resources.

Notes serve at least two major purposes:

1. They offer additional information about an item that cannot be recorded in one of the first six areas of a bibliographic record.

2. They justify the provision of additional access points.

Information for notes can be taken from any source. Quotations can be used in notes to simplify the provision of notes. For quotations that are not taken from the chief source of information, the cataloger will need to indicate the source:

> "Proceedings of the Symposium on Hypertension"—T.p. verso.

Notes providing general information about an item as a whole are presented first. The rest of the notes are presented in the order of the eight areas specified by *AACR2r*. Some of the more popular notes and their MARC fields are:

1.7B1. Nature, scope, or artistic form (field 500)

1.7B2. Language of the item and/or translation or adaptation (field 546)

1.7B3. Source of title proper (field 500)

1.7B4. Variations in title (field 246)

1.7B6. Statements of responsibility (field 500)

1.7B7. Edition and history (fields 500, 518, etc.)

1.7B13. Dissertation (field 502)

1.7B14. Audience (field 521)

1.7B16. Other formats (field 530)

1.7B17. Summary (field 520)

1.7B18. Contents (fields 504, 500, and 505)

1.7B19. Numbers borne by the item (fields 023–030, 036, 037)

AACR2r recommends that notes be entered in the order specified in rules .7 of each chapter. As a result, in the MARC record the notes may not appear in numerical sequence. To reduce the time and agony over the order of notes, CONSER recommends that notes be entered in numerical order. Most libraries follow the order of notes specified by *AACR2r*, but the order of notes is a local decision. Catalogers should consult the vendor of their online catalog system to determine whether notes can be presented in the order they prefer.

Area 8. International Standard Numbers (MARC Field 020 or 022)

> 020   Ten digits without hyphens (qualifier) $c availability

The International Standard Book Number (ISBN) or International Standard Serial Number (ISSN) should be recorded in Area 8. If an item contains more than one standard number (one ISBN for the paperback version and another for the hard copy), the number on the item in hand should be recorded first. Both *AACR2r* and the Library of Congress allow the option for including additional standard numbers with qualifiers. Although *AACR2r* presents standard numbers in the last area of a bibliographic record, the MARC format presents them early in the record. The ISBN is entered in the 020 field and the ISSN in the 022 field for serial records. OCLC guidelines advise libraries other than the National Serials Data Program (NSDP) and ISSN Canada to use "blank" for the first indicator of the 022 field. The ISSN of a serial title is entered in the 4XX field in subfield $x. Sound recordings and videos often contain publisher's numbers and such information is recorded in the 028 field. The Universal Product Number is recorded in the 024 field. ISBN and UPC numbers are transcribed without hyphens or spaces.

020		0262032554 (hardcover: alk. paper) $c $42.50
022		0010-0870
440	0	Yesterday's music, $x 4344-1277 ; $v 50
028	42	21116 $b Universal Studios
024	1	608628316642

Assignment of Access Points

Part II of *AACR2r* is based on the Paris Principles. Chapter 21 stipulates how access points should be selected, and Chapters 22 to 25 provide guidance for creating authorized form for headings. The chief source of information of the item being cataloged is the main source for potential access points. Other statements that appear prominently (i.e., in the prescribed sources for the first two areas of the type of materials cataloged) should be considered as well.

Personal authorship: *AACR2r* defines a personal author as "the person chiefly responsible for the creation of the intellectual or artistic content of a work" (21.1A1). The choice of access points follows the tradition that honors individuals responsible for a work, and catalogers' "rule of three" is followed in selecting access points. That is, if there are no more than three authors involved in the creation of a work, all three authors will be assigned access points, with the first one as the main access point unless the principal author is identified. If more than three authors contribute to a work, the main access point is the title and only the first named author is used as an additional access point. The rule of three applies to editors as well.

Corporate bodies: *AACR2r* defines a corporate body as "an organization or a group of persons that is identified by a particular name and that acts, or may act, as an entity" (21.1B1). The rules for using corporate bodies as the main access point have evolved and become more stringent. A work must emanate from one or more corporate bodies and must belong to one of the six categories of materials identified in rule 21.1B2 for it to be entered under a corporate body. In case of doubt, *AACR2r* encourages catalogers not to use a corporate body as the main access point.

Title as the main access point: There are four occasions when title is used as the main access point.

1. When there are more than three authors (see 21.6C2) or when the authorship is unknown (see 21.5).

2. When the item being cataloged is a collection of works by many people or corporate bodies (see 21.7).

3. When the item emanates from a corporate body but does not belong to any of the six categories stipulated by rule 21.1B2.

4. When the item is a sacred scripture of a religious group (see 21.37).

AACR2r also stipulates how adapters, illustrators, revisers, commentators, translators, and persons being honored by a work should be used as access points (see 21.9–21.15). In addition, it offers guidelines for determining access points for artworks, musical works, and sound recordings (see 21.23). Rules under 21.29 provide general rules for added entries, and rules under 21.30 provide specific instructions on when to assign individuals, corporate bodies, titles, and series as added entries. Rule 21.29C gives catalogers the authority to make an added entry "if some catalogue users might suppose that the description of an item would be found" under the added entry. Rule 21.29F also states that if the description does not clearly indicate why an added entry is made, a note should be provided. *AACR2r does not* specify the order of added entries in a description, but an LC (Library of Congress) interpretation (21.29: CSB 12) gives the order of added entries:

1. Personal name;

2. Personal name/title;

3. Corporate name;

4. Corporate name/title;

5. Uniform title (all instances of works entered under title);

6. Title traced as Title-period;

7. Title traced as Title-colon, followed by a title;

8. Series.

Within each group the added entries should follow the order in which the data appear in the bibliographic description. Nonprint materials are often the result of many individuals' efforts, and it is not unusual for a work to have many added entries. Rules relevant to the selected formats covered in this book and the Library of Congress's interpretations to those rules are discussed in later chapters of this book.

Chapters 22 to 26 in *AACR2r* cover headings for persons, corporate bodies, uniform titles, and references. With the help of the Library of Congress Name Authority Files (LCNAF), catalogers can simplify authority work substantially. For names not found in LCNAF, catalogers will need to consult Chapters 22 to 26 to establish headings. Many libraries follow the "no conflict" policy in such situations. That is, the cataloger would accept a new name as found on the item with the assumption that the name does not conflict with any names in the collection. If conflict is discovered later, the form of the name is adjusted according to *AACR2r* to render it a unique heading.

Subject Analysis

Catalogers analyze the content of materials to enable users to search and evaluate these materials. Subject analysis can be performed using controlled vocabulary or natural language. In the library environment, controlled vocabulary such as subject headings or descriptors are regularly assigned to indicate the aboutness of materials. In addition, catalogers have used other forms of controlled vocabulary—classification numbers or codes—for this purpose. No matter which form of controlled vocabulary they use, catalogers must perform authority control on the indexing terms to control for synonyms, homographs, and variant spellings, and to represent the relationships among authorized terms.

The objectives of subject analysis are to indicate the content of a work and to collocate works on the same subject. Before choosing the language for subject indexing and deciding the depth of subject analysis, the cataloger needs to know the intended users of the catalog. Serious researchers may appreciate scientific language and in-depth indexing, while public library users will prefer less technical terminology and less exhaustive indexing. Because the *Library of Congress Subject Headings* covers a wide range of subjects and contains many headings, research, academic, and large public libraries have used it for subject analysis. *Sears List of Subject Headings* is more popular in small and medium-sized public libraries and school libraries. Regardless of the differences between these authority lists, the same principles of subject cataloging apply. David Judson Haykin (1951), a well-regarded chief of the Library of Congress's subject division in the 1950s, has discussed these principles, and Lois Mai Chan (1995) has elaborated on the subject cataloging principles and practices of the Library of Congress. These principles include user and usage, literary warrant, uniform heading, unique heading, specific entry and co-extensiveness, internal consistency, and stability. If these principles are followed when one develops subject headings or terms for a local information system, the result is likely to be of great service to users. This is because the principles will guide catalogers to keep users in mind, using the terminology appropriate to the users' intellectual level. In addition, catalogers will make sure one subject is represented by one heading, and synonyms, variant spellings, different phrasings, and homographs are controlled within the system. Catalogers will create headings that are specific to the subjects represented in the information resources, and the headings will be easily accessible for users. For example, if the cataloger needs to establish a heading for a particular kind of flower such as lilies that is discussed in a work, then "lilies," as a direct and most specific heading for this topic, will be created, instead of something less direct such as "Botany—Flower—Lilies." In addition, catalogers will strive to maintain form and structural consistency among analogous headings and keep them stable within a subject system.

The first step in subject analysis is to determine the subject of a work. Catalogers examine the title, preface, introduction, table of contents, and the bibliography, if necessary. The containers, accompanying materials, and "README" files (for electronic resources) often provide useful information on the subjects of sound recordings, videorecordings, electronic resources, and Web resources. For Internet resources, meta tags in the HTML header and links for "About this page," "About us," or "About this site" often shed light on the purposes and subjects of a Web site. After the subjects are identified, the next step is to translate the subjects into authorized headings. The procedures for subject cataloging are detailed in the *Library of Congress Subject Cataloging Manual* (2004), and section H180 in particular offers specific instructions. The guidelines can be summarized as follows:

> *Summative approach*: Catalogers should identify topics of a work and try to find headings that will summarize the contents. This practice has a long tradition in cataloging and is rooted in the manual environment. Due to advances in technology, many catalogers

have urged the Library of Congress to provide more in-depth analysis. Their guideline now allows catalogers to assign up to ten subject headings.

Substantial treatment required: Only topics treated substantially in a work should be assigned subject headings. The general rule is if a topic takes up at least 20 percent of a work, then it should be represented by a heading.

Specific and direct headings: Following the principle of coextensiveness, catalogers should assign specific and direct headings to represent the content of a work. For a work about dolphins, the most specific and direct heading is "dolphins." For a work about mammals, the most specific and direct heading is "mammals." The Library of Congress also discourages catalogers from assigning specific headings and general headings at the same time, with few exceptions. So catalogers should not assign both mammals and dolphins to either of the works above.

Aspects of a topic: Because LC subject headings are highly precoordinated, catalogers are urged to find appropriate phrase headings or subdivisions to represent aspects of a topic. In addition to the subdivisions listed in the authority list, there are pattern headings to follow and free-floating subdivisions to use. If two or more topics are in a work, catalogers should consider the relationship of these topics in choosing headings. If more than three topics are in a work and they constitute the whole of a broader subject, a heading for the broad subject is used. But if these topics do not constitute the whole of a broader subject, then catalogers should assign a heading for each topic. Assigning subject headings takes practice. Various handbooks provide good exercises (e.g., Chan 1994; Saye 2000).

Another method to represent the result of subject analysis is through classification number. The *Library of Congress Classification* scheme (*LCC*) and the *Dewey Decimal Classification* scheme (*DDC*) are two popular classification systems. Both systems are discipline-based, hierarchical, and enumerative. Based on the principle of literary warrant, *LCC* reflects the collection of the Library of Congress and continues to expand as the collection grows. *DDC* was initially based on a classification of W. T. Harris, which was based on an inverted order of Francis Bacon's classification of knowledge (Chan 1994), but has evolved to accommodate new subjects—for instance, the expansion of numbers, 004–006, for computer science. With more than twenty major classes, *LCC* has been popular in research, academic, and large public libraries in the United States. *DDC* has a more compact structure and contains only ten major classes, but its history, reputation, and structure have made it the most popular classification system worldwide.

The procedure for assigning classification number is the same regardless of the format of the material being cataloged. The cataloger identifies the main thrust of the work (e.g., teaching ecology in elementary schools), determines the discipline in which the topic is treated (e.g., education [300]), then focuses on the corresponding class (e.g., elementary education in specific subjects [372.3–372.8]) to find the most specific classification number for a work (e.g., natural study [372.357]). The Library of Congress does not assign class numbers to audiovisual media and special instructional materials but has provided alternate class numbers in brackets to films, sound recordings, slide sets, and so on to aid catalogers outside of LC (Chan 1990). Nonprint materials are classified in the same manner as print materials. Table 1 of *DDC* includes provisions for some formats (e.g., encyclopedias, periodicals, handbooks) but *DDC* numbers usually do not represent the form of a work. Rather, information on the format is recorded elsewhere in the bibliographic record (Chan 1996). After the classification number has been assigned, the cataloger usually assigns an author number to provide further subdivision within the same subject class. This author number is often called the Cutter number because the numbers are from Cutter tables. *LCC* has its own Cutter table, while *DDC* can be used with any Cutter tables. Some libraries develop their own author numbering system to sub-arrange materials in the same subject class. Date of publication is usually added to make the call number complete. Call numbers in most American libraries serve as the addresses for works on the shelves.

MARC Format

After the cataloger creates bibliographic records according to *AACR2r* and assigns subject headings and classification numbers, he or she will encode the records in the Machine-Readable Cataloging (MARC) format to support searching and manipulation of these records. The Library of Congress developed the LC MARC formats in the 1960s (Avram 1975), which evolved into the USMARC in the 1980s, and were harmonized with Canadian MARC formats into MARC 21 in 1997 (MARC FAQ 2005). MARC 21 includes five formats for the encoding of five types of data—bibliographic, authority, holdings, community information, and classification data. The Library of Congress maintains these standards and provides documentation. The format catalogers use most frequently is the bibliographic format. Bibliographic utilities, such as the Online Computer Library Center (OCLC) and the Research Library Information Network (RLIN), have also developed guidelines specific to their environment, and catalogers will need to consult those guidelines to conform to their input standards.

A MARC 21 record consists of many fields. It includes a leader, a record directory, control fields, variable control fields, and variable fields (Furrie 2003). The **leader** consists of the first twenty-four characters of the record, and each position encodes information necessary for computer processing. The elements encoded include record status, type of record, bibliographic level, encoding level, and others. The **record directory** refers to a block of data following the leader that lists the tags in the record and their respective starting positions. The computer compiles a record directory from information in a bibliographic record. All control fields begin with the digit 0 (0XX) and encode information such as Library of Congress control numbers (010), International Standard Book Numbers (020), and classification numbers (082, 050, etc.). **Variable control fields** are tagged 00X. They can contain a single data or a series of data. For instance, the 007 field for sound recording has more than ten subfields. Field 008, the field of "Fixed-Length Data Elements," is quite valuable because its forty characters can be used to identify and retrieve records that meet the search criteria of the user. Field 008 is format specific and not repeatable. Bibliographic utilities like OCLC have added labels to the fixed field elements and place the block of information at the top of their bibliographic records to make it easier for human readers to understand the records, but other systems may display the same information differently. **Variable fields** contain descriptive cataloging data and access points and are the parts most users see on their online catalogs, often with labels supplied by the system vendors. Each variable field begins with a three-digit tag, followed by two indicators and subfields specifically designated for that field. The variable fields correspond closely to elements and areas specified by *AACR2r*. The following scheme illustrates the relationship of MARC fields to areas in *AACR2r*:

Variable fields	AACR2r
1XX	Main entry (except for title main entry)
245	Area 1. Title and statement of responsibility
250	Area 2. Edition statement
260	Area 4. Publication place, publisher, date
300	Area 5. Extent of item
4XX	Area 6. Series
5XX	Area 7. Notes
6XX	Subject added entries
7XX	Non-subject added entries

The tags are displayed according to the first digit, but within each group (2XX, 4XX, 5XX, etc.), the order of the tags is stipulated by *AACR2r*. The MARC 21 standard provides the scheme for content designation, but it is *AACR2r* that specifies the data elements (the content) and the order of the elements in the bibliographic record. The MARC 21 format for monograph is presented here to provide an introduction to this format. In individual chapters of this book, the 008 field used for a particular type of materials (such as the 008 field for sound recording), and the necessary variable control field (such as the 006 field for electronic resources and the 007 field for videorecording), are discussed in depth.

The MARC bibliographic format for monographs has an 008 field as follows.

Type	a	ELvl	__	Srce	__	Audn	__	Ctrl		Lang	__
BLvl	m	Form		Conf	__	Biog	__	Mrec		Ctry	__
		Cont	__	Gpub		Fict		Indx			
Desc	a	Ills	__	Fest		DtSt	__	Dates	Date 1, Date 2		

The Network Development and MARC Standards Office provides documentation on these elements (see http://www.loc.gov/MARC/) and OCLC's input standards document the usage of these elements and the code values defined for these elements (see http://www.oclc.org/bibformats/). Here is a summary of the mandatory elements for the book format, according to OCLC, "Input standards for fixed-field elements and 006":

Mandatory Elements	Commonly Used Codes
BLvl Bibliographic level	Code "m" is the default value. It indicates a work is complete in one part or intended to complete in a finite number of parts.
Conf Conference publication	Code "0" = not a conference publication; code "1" = a conference publication.
Dates Date 1 and Date 2	Date 1 is based on subfield $c of field 260 and can be system-supplied. The element is coordinated with the DtSt element.
Desc Descriptive cataloging form	Code "a" indicates the item is cataloged according to *AACR2*
DtSt Type of date	Code "s" represents a single date of distribution, publication, release, production, execution, or writing. Code "m" indicates multiple dates of publication and should be coordinated with DATES, using Date 1 for the initial year and Date 2 for the terminal year. This code is appropriate for multipart monographic publications. Code "r" stands for reprint/reissue date and should be coordinated with DATES, with Date 1 for the reprint/reissue date and Date 2 for the date of original release.
ELvl Encoding level	Code "I" indicates full-level input by OCLC participants and represents full cataloging. Code "K" indicates less-than-full input by OCLC participants and represents less-than-full cataloging.
Fest Festschrift	Code "0" = not a festschrift; code "1" = a festschrift
GPub Government publication	Code "0" = not a government publication; code "f" = a federal/national publication; code "s" = state publication; etc.
Lang Language code	For the language of the work. MARC Code Lists for Languages (http://www.loc.gov/marc/languages/langhome.html) is the source for language codes.
Srce Cataloging source	Code "blank" is for users at an authorized national bibliographic agency. Code "c" is for participants of a cooperative cataloging program such as BIBCO (the monographic bibliographic record component of the Program for Cooperative Cataloging) and CONSER (Cooperative Online Serials). Code "d" is for all other OCLC users.
Type Type of record	Code "a" is for language material and is most often used with monographic publications.

Commonly used variable fields for monographs include the following fields:

Variable Field	Indicators	Commonly Used Subfields
020 ISBN	Indicators not defined	$a ISBN $c availability
1XX Main entry heading, not for title main entry	— 1st indicator = nature of the name 2nd indicator not defined	$a for personal name or corporate name. $b for subordinate unit, $d for year(s) of birth and/or death. $c for title $q for qualifier, usually the full form of the initials
245 Title and statement of responsibility	— — 1st indicator = title as added entry or not 2nd indicator = non-filing characters	$a Title proper : $b other title information / $c statement of responsibility ; subsequent statement of responsibility.
246 Variant title	— — 1st indicator = whether a note and an added entry area are to be generated 2nd indicator = nature of the variant title	$a variant title $i display text
250 Edition statement	Indicators not defined	$a edition statement / $b statement of responsibility.
260 Publication information	Indicators not defined	$a Place of publication : $b publisher, $c year of publication.
300 Physical description	Indicators not defined	$a Extent : $b Other physical details ; $c Dimensions.
4XX Series statements	Indicators vary, depending on whether the series is traced	$a Series title, $x ISSN ; $v numbering
5XX Note fields	Indicators vary, depending on the nature of the 5XX notes	$a note information.
6XX Subject added entries	— — 1st indicator = definition varies by field 2nd indicator = source of the authority terms	$a main heading $x topical subdivision $y period subdivision $z geographical subdivision $v form subdivision Order of subdivisions depends on how the subject heading string is formed

| 7XX
Non-subject
added entries | —
1st indicator = nature of
the name
2nd indicator = not defined | $a personal name or
corporate name.
$b for subordinate unit,
$d for year(s) of birth
and/or death.
$c for title
$q for qualifier, usually the
full form of the initials |
| 8XX (800, 830,
and 856 are
used often) | Indicators vary, depending on
the nature of the field | Subfields vary, depending
on the nature of the field. |

Prior to format integration, catalogers had seven MARC bibliographic formats for encoding cataloging records. Based on the primary characteristics of a work, the cataloger selected the appropriate format to encode the item, and secondary but important characteristics could not be represented. For instance, when cataloging a videorecording serial, the cataloger had to choose between a serials format and a videorecording format. The Library of Congress and the MARBI (Machine-Readable Bibliographic Information) Committee of the American Library Association began exploring the integration process in the early 1980s to address problems like this, as well as to increase consistency in description of resources regardless of formats, reduce the cost of maintaining seven bibliographic formats, and remove the need to create new formats whenever new forms of intellectual expression appear (Coyle 1993). When format integration was completed in March of 1996, many fields and values became obsolete and new ones were added to make most of the fields and codes valid for all forms of material. Many of the changes affect serials catalogers, but changes such as the creation of field 006, "field-length data element—additional material characteristics," and the use of field 246 for variant titles affect the entire cataloging community. Update no. 1 to the *USMARC Format for Bibliographic Data* summarizes the changes (http:// www.loc.gov/today/pr/1995/95-156.html).

Field 006 is probably one of the most important results of format integration. By using several 006 fields, catalogers are able to represent multiple aspects of a work and the characteristics of accompanying material. There are seven types of 006 fields, including 006 for books, serials, maps, music, visual materials, electronic resources, and archival materials. This field has eighteen character positions and is optional and repeatable. Field 006 has a tree structure by which the form of the material (the first code) determines what other data elements are allowed for subsequent character positions. For instance, if the first element is coded "a" for monographs, then the following data elements are allowed:

Books Format 006 Information					
T006: a	Ills:	Audn:	Form:	Cont:	Gpub:
Conf: 0	Fest: 0	Indx: 0	Fict: 0	Biog:	

OCLC provides prompts for data input for this field and the example above shows that in the 006 field OCLC makes use of the same elements used in the 008 field. Field 006 has no indicators or subfields, and data elements are identified by their position. In the OCLC system, brackets are used to present this field. For example, if a Web page is textual, the book format workform is used to create a record, and the 008 field for the book format will be used (with the "Type" coded as "a"). To reflect the fact that the work is a Web page, the cataloger who uses OCLC's Connexion system will pull down the menu for 006 fields to select the "computer files" option. The following data elements will appear for the cataloger to enter appropriate codes:

```
006 field for Computer Files
Audn: File: u GPub:
```

When the cataloger enters the appropriate codes—using "m" for the first element to specify computer file, and "d" for File to specify this is primarily a text file—field 006 will appear on the record this way (*OCLC Technical Bulletin* 212, 1996):

```
006    [m    d    ]
```

In creating a MARC record, the first decision catalogers must make is about the appropriate 008 field for the item being cataloged. Catalogers may find it helpful to follow the next model when they select the 008 field for describing a work.[2]

Figure 2.1. Model for selecting 008 fields

	Text Content	*Computer Content*	*Other Nontext Content*
TYPE	**a** (language material) **p** (mixed material) **t** (manuscript language material)	**m** (computer files/ electronic resources)	**c** (printed music) **d** (manuscript music) **e** (printed map) **f** (manuscript map) **g** (projected medium) **i** (nonmusical sound recording) **j** (musical sound recording) **k** (two-dimensional nonprojectable graphic) **o** (kit) **r** (three-dimensional artifact or naturally occurring object)
BLvl	Any valid code	Any valid code	Any valid code
008	Book, Serial, or Mixed material	Computer files/ Electronic resources	Music, Map, Visual material
006	Any applicable 006 fields to main item or accompanying material	No computer file/ electronic resource 006 Any other applicable 006 fields to main item or accompanying material	Any applicable 006 fields to main item or accompanying material

According to this model, a book accompanied by a computer disk will be coded as follows:

> Type of record = a   Bibliographic level = m
> 008 for the Book format will be used
> 006 for electronic resources will be used to represent the accompanying disk.

A computer program accompanied by a manual, however, will be coded as follows:

> Type of record = m   Bibliographic level = m
> 008 for the Computer File/Electronic Resource format will be used
> 006 for the book format will be used to cover the accompanying manual.

The use of 006 fields is further discussed in Chapters 5 ("Electronic Resources"), 6 ("Internet Resources"), and 7 ("Remote Access Electronic Serials"), where 006 fields are more likely to be needed to bring out important aspects of a work. Readers should know that 006 and 007 fields serve different purposes. Field 006 describes additional characteristics of an item or the characteristics of accompanying material, while field 007 describes the physical characteristics of the item or the material accompanying it. The use of field 007 is discussed in Chapters 3 ("Sound Recordings"), 4 ("Videorecordings"), 5, 6, and 7 of this book.

Other important changes of format integration include the addition of field 856 (Electronic Location and Access) for remote access electronic resources, and the use of subfield $v (form subdivision) to designate specific kinds or genres of material. Details of field 856 are presented in Chapters 6 ("Internet Resources") and 7 ("Remote Access Electronic Serials"). The objective of form subdivision is to enable online catalogs to provide better display of records and assist users in searching. Subfield $v became valid after format integration in 1996, and the Library of Congress issued guidelines on form subdivisions and the use of subfield code $v in the fall of 1998 (1998 update no. 2). The guidelines instruct catalogers to code a subdivision as $v (form subdivision) when it indicates what an item *is*, and to code it as $x (topical subdivision) when it characterizes what an item is *about*. See, for example:

> 650   0   Biology $v Periodicals.
> [assigned to a journal on biology. $v indicates the form of this publication.]
> 650   0   Biology $x Periodicals.
> [assigned to a work that discusses journals on biology.]

The Library of Congress began implementing subfield $v in February 1999 and has created authority records for subdivisions. All records include usage instruction, and two records are created for subdivisions that can be used as topical and form subdivisions. Taylor presented an educational forum on subdivision $v at the 1999 ALA midwinter meeting (2000) and has maintained a site on the implementation of form subdivisions on behalf of the ALCTS/CCS/SAC Subcommittee (2000).

Arrangement

The physical arrangement of nonprint materials, especially electronic resources, may not necessarily follow the order of the call numbers. While many libraries assign subject headings to nonprint materials to support subject collocation in their online catalog systems, not all of them assign call numbers to these materials. In fact, many of them have developed in-house systems to shelve nonprint resources, some by the material's format, others by the materials' nature. These systems are designed to address the concerns for security and preservation of nonprint resources. With the growth of electronic resources, the demand for easy access to these resources from users has increased. It is clearly challenging to organize sound recordings, videorecordings, computer programs, multimedia, and Internet resources for easy local and remote access. Factors to consider in organizing and arranging audiovisual and electronic resources will be discussed in the chapters on these media.

Notes

1. For background information and the latest presentations on "AACR3" and RDA, see "Current Activities" on the Web site of the Joint Steering Committee for Revision of Anglo-American Cataloguing Rules at http://www.collectionscanada.ca/jsc/current.html#AACR3.

2. This model was derived from a handout for Sally McCallum's presentations at a workshop on "USMARC Format Integration: Implementation Issues and Strategies," Monday, October 18, 1993, Washington, D.C. An earlier model appeared in Network Development and MARC Standards Office, *Format integration and its effect on the USMARC bibliographic format* (Washington, D.C.: 1992), 9.

References

ALCTS/CCS/SAC Subcommittee on Form Headings/Subdivisions Implementation, 1996–2000. (2000). http://www.pitt.edu/~agtaylor/ala/implem.htm (accessed June 1, 2005).

Avram, Henriette D. (1975). *MARC: Its history and implications*. Washington, D.C.: Library of Congress.

Chan, Lois Mai. (1990). *Immroth's guide to the Library of Congress classification* (4th ed.). Englewood, Colo.: Libraries Unlimited.

Chan, Lois Mai. (1994). *Cataloging and classification: An introduction*. New York: McGraw-Hill.

Chan, Lois Mai. (1995). *Library of Congress subject headings: Principles and application* (3rd ed.). Englewood, Colo.: Libraries Unlimited.

Chan, Lois Mai. (1996). *Dewey decimal classification: A practical guide* (2nd ed., rev. for *DDC* 21). Albany, N.Y.: Forest Press.

Connexion. (2005). http://connexion.oclc.org/ (accessed June 1, 2005). (Username and password required for login.)

Coyle, Karen (Ed.). (1993). *Format integration and its effect on cataloging, training, and systems*. Chicago: American Library Association.

Daily, Jay E. (1972). *Organizing nonprint materials*. New York: Marcel Dekker.

Frost, Carolyn O. (1989). *Media access and organization: A cataloging and reference sources guide for nonbook materials*. Englewood, Colo.: Libraries Unlimited.

Furrie, Betty. (2003). Understanding MARC bibliographic. Washington, D.C.: Library of Congress, Cataloging Distribution Service. http://www.loc.gov/marc/umb/ (accessed June 1, 2005).

Guidelines for bibliographic description of interactive multimedia. (1994). Chicago: American Library Association.

Haykin, David Judson. (1951). *Subject headings: A practical guide.* Washington, D.C.: U.S. Government Printing Office.

Hsieh-Yee, Ingrid. (1999, May 30). Organization of nonprint resources in public and academic libraries. Unpublished report.

Hsieh-Yee, Ingrid. (2004, December 20). How libraries provide access to digital resources. Unpublished report.

Input standards for fixed-field elements and 006. http://www.oclc.org/bibformats/en/fixedfield/ (accessed June 1, 2005).

Intner, Sheila S. (1984). *Access to media: A guide to integrating and computerizing catalogs.* New York: Neal-Schuman.

Intner, Sheila S., and Weihs, Jean. (1998). *Special libraries: A cataloging guide.* Englewood, Colo.: Libraries Unlimited.

Kaye, Alan L. (1991). *Video and other nonprint resources in the small library.* Chicago: Library Administration and Management Association, American Library Association.

Library of Congress. Cataloging Policy and Support Office. (2004). *Subject cataloging manual: Subject headings* (5th ed.). Washington, D.C.: Cataloging Distribution Service, Library of Congress.

Library of Congress rule interpretations. (1990). (2nd ed.). Washington, D.C.: Cataloging Distribution Service, Library of Congress.

Maillet, Lucienne. (1991). *Subject control of film and video: A comparison of three methods.* Chicago: American Library Association.

MARC 21 frequently asked questions. (2005). http://www.loc.gov/marc/faq.html#definition (accessed June 1, 2005).

MARC 21 XML schema. (2005). http://www.loc.gov/standards/marcxml/// (accessed June 1, 2005).

Mason-Robinson, Sally. (1996). *Developing and managing video collections.* New York: Neal-Schuman.

Miller, Dick R. (2000, Summer). XML: Libraries' strategic opportunity. *School Library Journal*: 18–22.

1998 update number 2 to the subject cataloging manual: Subject headings. (1998). Washington, D.C.: Cataloging Distribution Service, Library of Congress.

OCLC. (1996). *OCLC technical bulletin 212, Format integration phase 2.* Dublin, Ohio: OCLC.

Olson, Nancy B. (Ed.). (1997). *Cataloging Internet resources: A manual and practical guide* (2nd ed.). Dublin, Ohio: OCLC. http://www.oclc.org/support/documentation/worldcat/cataloging/internetguide/ (accessed June 1, 2005).

Pitman, Randy. (1989, June 30). Rockefeller Foundation Videocassette Distribution Task Force, Final report: Library market. Unpublished report.

Saye, Jerry D. (2000). *Manheimer's cataloging and classification* (4th ed., rev. and expanded). New York: Marcel Dekker.

Scholtz, James C. (1995). *Video acquisitions and cataloging: A handbook*. Westport, Conn.: Greenwood.

Svenonius, Elaine. (2000). *The intellectual foundation of information organization*. Cambridge, Mass.: MIT Press.

Taylor, Arlene G. (2000). Educational forum: LCSH and subfield v. http://www.pitt.edu/~agtaylor/ala/edforum.htm (accessed June 1, 2005).

Tennant, Roy. (2002, October 15). MARC must die. *Library Journal* 127: 26, 28.

Weihs, Jean. (1987). A taste of nonbook history: Historical background and review of the state of the art of bibliographic control of nonbook materials. In S. Intner and R. Smiraglia (Eds.) *Policy and practice in bibliographic control of nonbook media*, 3–14. Chicago: American Library Association.

Weihs, Jean. (1991). *The integrated library*. Phoenix, Ariz.: Oryx Press.

Weihs, Jean, and Howarth, Lynne C. (1995, April). Nonbook materials: Their occurrence and bibliographic description in Canadian libraries. *Library Resources and Technical Services* 39: 184–197.

Weihs, Jean, with Lewis, Shirley, and Macdonald, Janet. (1979). *Nonbook materials: The organization of integrated collections* (2nd ed.). Ottawa: Canadian Library Association.

Yee, Martha M. (2004). New perspectives on the shared cataloging environment and a MARC 21 shopping list. *Library Resources and Technical Services* 48 (3): 165–178.

Suggested Readings

Chan, Lois Mai, and Hodges, Theodora; revised by Martin, Giles. (1998). Subject cataloguing and classification. In *Technical services today and tomorrow* (2nd ed.). Englewood, Colo.: Libraries Unlimited.

Furrie, Betty. (2003). *Understanding MARC bibliographic: Machine-readable cataloging* (7th ed.). Washington, D.C.: Library of Congress, Cataloging Distribution Service. http://www.loc.gov/marc/umb/ (accessed June 1, 2005).

McCallum, Sally. (2001). Extending MARC for bibliographic control in the Web environment: Challenges and alternatives. *Proceedings of the Bicentennial Conference on Bibliographic Control for the New Millennium (2001)*. Washington, D.C.: Library of Congress, Cataloging Distribution Service. http://www.loc.gov/catdir/bibcontrol/mccallum_paper.html (accessed June 1, 2005).

Thomas, Sarah E. (2001). The catalog as portal to the Internet. *Proceedings of the Bicentennial Conference on Bibliographic Control for the New Millennium (2001)*. Washington, D.C.: Library of Congress, Cataloging Distribution Service. http://www.loc.gov/catdir/bibcontrol/thomas_paper.html (accessed June 1, 2005).

Yee, Martha M. (2004). New perspectives on the shared cataloging environment and a MARC 21 shopping list. *Library Resources and Technical Services* 48 (3): 165–178.

3

Sound Recordings

Sound recordings are available in various formats. Technology has improved the quality of recorded sound and made random access of sound tracks possible on CDs and DVDs. New formats such as MP3 and Audio DVD continue to emerge. Chapter 6 of *AACR2r* covers sound recordings in various formats, including disc (long-playing records and compact discs), tape (open reel-to-reel, cassettes, cartridges), rolls, and sound recordings on film (excluding those designed to accompany films). And practitioners have offered their treatment of new formats such as MP3 to guide the description and access for these materials (Freeborn 2002). At the beginning of the twenty-first century, sound cassettes remain a popular format, especially for audio books, but CDs have become the dominant format for musical recordings, and many fictional and nonfictional works are now available in both CDs and cassettes. For this reason this chapter focuses on the description and access of these two formats. In addition, it discusses the treatment of Enhanced CDs, a favorite format among musicians, and MP3 files, which have been growing dramatically on the Internet.

Sound recordings on CDs and DVDs pose several challenges for catalogers:

1. Unlike print publishers, who have a fairly standard pattern for presenting information on the title page, publishers of sound recordings tend to vary in their presentation of information on the item and its label, which are designated the chief source of information by *AACR2r*.

2. Most sound recordings come in a container and are frequently accompanied by textual materials. Information on composers, performers, producers, sound engineers, and so on often appear differently in different parts of a sound recording package, making it difficult for novice catalogers to determine which information to transcribe.

3. Description of sound recordings' physical characteristics is more involved than that of print publications and the MARC 007 field for sound recording is required to encode physical characteristics of the recording.

4. The place of publication is often not present in sound recordings, making it necessary for the cataloger to consult reference works to fill in the gap.

5. The full names of composers and performers, especially for classical musical recordings, may not be readily available, and catalogers often need to consult reference works for guidance.

Decision on access points can also be challenging because of the large number of people involved in the creation of a sound recording. Fortunately *AACR2r* offers specific guidelines for this task in Chapter 21. Several good tools are available on the Web:

- *Authority Tools for Audiovisual and Music Catalogers: An Annotated List of Useful Resources* (http://www.olacinc.org/capc/authtools.html)

- *Reference Works Used For Music Cataloging* (http://www.music .indiana.edu/tech_s/mla/reflist99.html)

- *Source of Authority Work for Cataloging Popular Music* (http:// www.music.indiana.edu/tech_s/mla/wgpms/wgpms.htm)

MARC Fields for Sound Recordings

The MARC 21 *Concise Format for Bibliographic Data* (2004) and OCLC's *Bibliographic Formats and Standards* (2003) provide details on tags and codes for encoding *AACR2r* records and are valuable resources for creating MARC records. For sound recordings the fixed field includes the following elements:

Type	_	ELvl	_	Srce	_	Audn	_	Ctrl	Lang	_
BLvl	m	Form		Comp	_	AccM	_	MRec	Ctry	_
Desc	a	FMus	_	LTxt	_	DtSt	_	Dates	Date 1, Date 2	

Mandatory elements and frequently used optional elements are highlighted on pages 39 and 40.

Sound Recording 007 Field

The sound recording 007 field is required for sound recordings. It consists of thirteen subfields, many of them mandatory. Subfield $a is coded "s" for sound recording, codes for the rest of the subfields are listed in OCLC's *Bibliographic Formats and Standards*. Three subfields (j, k, and l) are for archival cataloging of sound recordings. Information in field 300 is the basis for coding field 007, so it is important to record field 300 correctly according

Mandatory Elements	Commonly Used Codes
BLvl Bibliographic level	Code "m" is the default value. It indicates an item is complete in one part or intended to complete in a finite number of parts.
Dates Date 1 and Date 2	Date 1 is the same as the value recorded in subfield $c of field 260 and can be system-supplied. The element is coordinated with the DtSt element. If a recording contains materials issued earlier, the earlier publication date is recorded as Date 2, and the latest release date is recorded as Date 1.
Desc Descriptive cataloging form	Code "a" indicates the item is cataloged according to *AACR2*.
DtSt Type of date	Code "s" represents a single date of distribution, publication, release, production, execution, or writing. Code "p" means the date of distribution/release/ issue and the date of production are different by at least one year. If DtSt is coded "p", catalogers will use Date 1 for the latest publication year and Date 2 for the year of production for the DATES element. The publication date is recorded in subfield $c of field 260 while the date of recording is recorded in the 518 note. Code "m" indicates multiple dates of publication and should be coordinated with DATES, using Date 1 for the initial year and Date 2 for the terminal year. Code "r" stands for reprint/reissue date and should be coordinated with DATES, with Date 1 for the reprint/reissue date and Date 2 for the date of original. Code "r" is for reissues of sound recordings **in the same medium or different medium**. When a recording consists of previously released materials from numerous sources, code "r" is appropriate.
ELvl Encoding level	"I" indicates full-level input by OCLC participants and represents full cataloging. "K" indicates less-than-full input by OCLC participants and represents less-than-full cataloging.
Lang Language code	For the language of the work. MARC Code Lists for Languages (http://www.loc.gov/marc/languages/ langhome.html) is the source for language codes.
Srce Cataloging source	Code "blank" is for catalogers at an authorized national bibliographic agency. Code "c" is for participants of a cooperative cataloging program such as BIBCO (the monographic bibliographic record component of the Program for Cooperative Cataloging) and CONSER (Cooperative Online Serials). Code "d" is for all other OCLC users.
Type Type of record	Code "i" is for nonmusical sound recordings. Code "j" is for musical sound recordings.

Optional Elements	Commonly Used Codes
AccM accompanying material	This code refers to the contents of program notes and other materials accompanying sound recordings. It is used only for materials that are substantial or unique and are usually not available in reference works. Up to six codes may be used. Code "blank" (no accompanying materials) and code "d" (for libretto or text of the verbal contents of a sound recording) are often used.
Audn Target audience	For musical recordings this code identifies music used or performed by a specific audience group. For nonmusical recordings the code represents the reading grade or interest age information recorded in field 521. If both types of information are present in field 521, the code should represent the interest-age information. When a work is appropriate for more than one target audience, the code will stand for the primary audience group.
Comp Form of composition	This element is used for **print music, manuscript music, and musical sound recordings**. Codes are based on LC subject headings and should be assigned when they apply to the work as a whole. Examples include "bg" for bluegrass music, "hy" for hymns, "jz" for jazz, and "op" for operas.
FMus Format of music	A system-supplied code. The default value for sound recording is "n" because it is not a music manuscript or printed music.
LText Literary text for sound recordings	Up to two one-character codes can be used. Code "blank" is for musical recordings. Other examples include "b" for biography, "p" for poetry, and "t" for interviews.

to *AACR2r*. Because sound cassettes and compact discs are popular media for sound recordings, the following examples present subfields common to these two formats.

Sound recording 007 subfields:
007   $a s $b specific material designation $d speed $e playback channels $f groove width $g dimensions $h tape width $i tape configuration $m special playback characteristics $n capture and storage technique

Subfields of standard cassettes

007 $a s $b s $d l $e _ $f n $g j $h l $i c $n _

($a s = sound recording, $b s = sound cassette, $d l = 1 7/8 ips (speed), $e s = stereophonic, u = unknown configuration of playback channels, $f n = no grooves, $g j = cassette dimensions 3 7/8 × 2 1/2 in., $h l = tape width 1/8 in., $i c = 4 tracks, $m c = Dolby-B encoded, $n e = analog electrical storage)

007	s $b s $d l $e u $f n $g j $h l $i c $m c $n e
300	1 sound cassette : $b analog, Dolby processed
007	s $b s $d l $e s $f n $g j $h l $i c $n e
300	1 sound cassette: $b analog, stereo

Subfields of standard CDs

007   s $b d $d f $e_$f n $g g $h n $i n $m e $n_

($a s = sound recording, $b d = sound disc, $d f = speed of
compact digital discs, $e s = stereophonic, u = unknown
configuration of playback channels, $f n = no grooves,
$g g = compact disc dimensions 4 3/4 in., $h n = tape width
not applicable, $i n = tape configuration not applicable,
$m e = digital recording, $n d =digital storage)

007	s $b d $d f $e s $f n $g g $h n $i n $m e $n d
300	1 sound disc (63 min., 13 sec.) : $b digital, stereo ; $c 4 3/4 in.
007	s $b d $d f $e u $f n $g g $h n $i n $m e $n d
300	1 sound disc (50 min., 55 sec.) : $b digital ; $c 4 3/4 in.

MARC fields commonly used to code sound recordings are:

Field	Indicators	Subfields
028	__ __	Publisher's stock number $b publisher's label name
100	__	Author, composer, artist, etc., $d date. (If title is not the main entry)
240	__ __	Uniform title for musical work or literary work
245	__ __	Title proper $h [sound recording] : $b other title information / $c statement of responsibility ; subsequent statement of responsibility.
246	__ __	Variant title Subfield $i is used to generate special display text
250		Edition statement.
260		Place of publication : $b Publisher, $c Date of publication.
300		Number of specific material designation (total playing time) : $b other details ; $c dimensions + $e Accompanying material.
4XX	__ __	Series statement, $x ; $v numbering
511	__	Performer, instrument ; performer, instrument.
518		History of recording.
500		Location of accompanying material.

520		Summary for nonmusical recordings.
521	—	Audience note.
6XX	— —	Subject headings.
655	—	Genre headings.
700	—	Performer(s).
710	—	Performing group(s).
730	— —	Uniform title added entry.
740	— 2	Analytical title added entry.

Description

Rules for Descriptive Cataloging

Chief Source and Prescribed Sources of Information

AACR2r stipulates the same chief source of information for all types of sound recordings: the physical item (the disc, the reel, the cassette, the cartridge, etc.) and the "label" that is permanently affixed to the item. If an item has labels on both sides, both labels should be treated as part of the chief source.

If no information can be found from the chief source, catalogers may take information, in this order of preference, from accompanying textual material, container, or other sources. If sound data and textual data are both available, the cataloger should use textual data.

The same eight areas of bibliographic description for print materials are used in describing sound recordings. The prescribed sources of information for each area (rule 6.0B2) are as follows:

Areas	*Prescribed sources of information*
Area 1 (245 field)	Chief source of information
Area 2 (250 field)	Chief source of information
Area 4 (260 field)	accompanying textual information and
Area 6 (4XX field)	container
Area 5 (300 field)	Any source
Area 7 (5XX fields)	
Area 8 (020)	

6.1. Title and Statement of Responsibility (MARC Field 245)

Rule 6.1B1 states that the title of a sound recording should be transcribed exactly as to wording, spelling, and order, but the punctuation and capitalization may vary. This rule is the same as rule 1.1B1. A few examples illustrate this practice:

Men are from Mars, women are from Venus
Morning aire
James Joyce's Chamber music [a book of poems by Joyce]
Diana Ross greatest hits
6 sonatas, BWV 1030–1035

The first word of the title proper must be capitalized but not necessarily the rest of the title. Proper names should be capitalized and the first word of another title, such as "Chamber music" above, should be capitalized.

General Material Designation (GMD): For sound recordings in all formats, except remote access sound files, the GMD is "sound recording." Terms such as CD, sound cassette, enhanced CD, read-along CD, and LP are not the official GMD of *AACR2r*. In the physical description area, the cataloger provides more details on the format, using terms for specific material designation (SMD).

When audio files are compressed to reduce their size for easy download, they are called digital sound files. According to Freeborn (2002), MP3 (MPEG [Motion Picture Entertainment Group] 1, Layer III), AAC (MPEG-2 AAC [Advanced Audio Coding]), RealAudio, and WMA (Windows Media Audio) are popular file formats for digital sound files. In cataloging digital sound files, catalogers will need to consult Chapter 6 ("Sound Recordings") and Chapter 9 ("Electronic Resources") of *AACR2r*. Freeborn reminds catalogers that remote access digital sound files are electronic files that will have "electronic resource" instead of "sound recording" as GMD. Direct access digital sound files that require the use of a computerized device or a peripheral attached to a computerized device, such as iPod or PalmPilot, will also have "electronic resource" as GMD. The treatment of MP3 digital sound files is discussed later in this chapter.

Statement of responsibility: For this element, *AACR2r* instructs the cataloger to record only writers, composers, and collectors of field materials if these names appear prominently. "Prominently" means the names must appear in the chief source, accompanying textual materials, or container of a sound recording. Performers of popular, rock, and jazz music, who do more than perform or interpret a piece of music (e.g., who also compose or arrange it), are recorded in the statement of responsibility. But performers of classical music or narrators are usually recorded in the note area. The Library of Congress has strict guidelines about this: "The rule allows performers who do more than perform to be named in the statement of responsibility. Accept only the most obvious cases as qualifying for the statement of responsibility" (CSB 11). If performers are listed on the item or its label, the information is recorded in the 511 note field for performers instead of the statement of responsibility area. Here are a few examples:

Disc label:	DIANA ROSS	
	DIANA ROSS GREATEST HITS	
Transcribed as:		
245	10	Diana Ross greatest hits $h [sound recording]/ $c Diana Ross

Disc label:	BACH	
	6 Sonatas, BWV 1030–1035	
	Michala Petri, recorder	
	Keith Jarrett, harpsichord	
Transcribed as:		
245	10	6 sonatas, BWV 1030–1035 $h [sound recording] / $c Bach.
511	0	Michala Petri, recorder; Keith Jarrett, harpsichord.

Cassette label: FUNNY PAPERS
          by Elaine Scott Narrated by Norman Dietz
Transcribed as:
245   10   Funny papers $h [sound recording] / $c by
                 Elaine Scott.
511   0   Narrated by Norman Dietz.

CD label: Meg Ryan/Art Lande
               RED RIDING HOOD & GOLDILOCKS
               (Narration and Music)
1. Red Riding Hood 14:17
2. Goldilocks 11:27 ...
Transcribed as:
245   00   Red Riding Hood & Goldilocks $h [sound
                 recording].
511   0   Narration by Meg Ryan.
500   Story adapted by Tom Roberts; music and lyrics
                 by Art Lande.

Some sound recordings contain several works but lack a collective title. *AACR2r* allows catalogers to describe the item as a unit or create separate records for each titled work (6.1G). The Library of Congress instructs its catalogers to describe the item as a unit (CSB 11) and not to apply the other option (CSB 47).

In describing an item without a collective title, if all the works are by the same person, the cataloger should transcribe the works in the order in which they appear in the chief source and separate them with semicolons (6.1G and 1.1G3). For instance,

---

Disc label: Ludwig van Beethoven
              Sonata No. 8 in C minor,
              Op. 13 "Pathetique"
              Sonata No. 23 in F minor,
              Op. 57 "Appassionata"
              Sonata No. 14 in C sharp minor,
              Op. 27 No. 2 "Moonlight"
              CLAUDIO ARRAU, piano
Transcribed as:
100   1   Beethoven, Ludwig van, $d 1770–1827.
245   10   Sonata no. 8 in C minor, op. 13 $h [sound
                recording] : $b pathetique ; sonata no. 23 in F
                minor, op. 57 : appasionata ; sonata no. 14 in C
                sharp minor, op. 27 no. 2 : moonlight / $c Ludwig
                van Beethoven.
511   0   Claudio Arrau, piano.

6.2. Edition (MARC Field 250)

The edition statement of sound recordings should be recorded according to rule 1.2B. Abbreviations and numerical notations in Appendices B and C of *AACR2r* should be consulted.

250	Remastered original sound track ed.

6.3. Material Specific Details

This area does not apply to sound recordings.

6.4. Publication, Distribution, Etc. (MARC Field 260)

The prescribed sources for this area are, in the order of preference, the chief source of information, accompanying textual material, and container. Information taken from other sources must be placed in brackets. Because many sound recordings lack the place of publication, the cataloger often needs to consult reference sources for this information. The following titles are good starting points:

> *Billboard International Buyer's Guide.* New York: Billboard Publications, 1970–
> *Rolling Stone Encyclopedia of Rock & Roll.* 3rd ed., rev. and updated for the 21st century. New York : Fireside, c2001.
> Music Publishers' Association online directories of publishers at http://www.mpaorg/index.html

Rule 1.4 states that the name of a larger jurisdiction may be added to identify the name of a city if necessary. When the name of a larger jurisdiction appears with a place name in the prescribed source, the Library of Congress adds it to Area 4 even though it may not be necessary for identification purpose.

Cassette label: Transcribed as: 260	Prince Frederick, MD 20678 Prince Frederick, MD

The name of the publisher is transcribed in the shortest form possible so long as no confusion would be caused. If the publisher's name on the item is different from that on the container, the cataloger should prefer the information on the label. If a sound recording contains a company's name and its subdivision, rule 6.4D2 instructs catalogers to record the subdivision as the publisher. Rule 6.4D3 states that when a recording contains a trade name that seems to be a series, it should be transcribed as a series title.

Disc label: Transcribed as: 260	Electra Entertainment Group, A Division of Warner Communications, Inc. 1996 Beverly Hills, CA : $b Elektra Entertainment Group, $c p1996.

The date of publication is recorded as instructed in 1.4F. Sound recordings sometimes carry two copyright dates. Dates preceded by © are the copyright dates of textual data, while dates preceded by (p) are the copyright dates of sound data. Current practice is to use "p" as the date of publication. *LCRI* 6.4F1 specifies that catalogers should not treat © date as the copyright date of the sound recording, but may use it to estimate a date of publication if no "p" date is available. If the recording date is different from the publishing date, the cataloger records the publishing date in the 260 field and the recording date in a note in field 518.

260	New York, N.Y. : $b RCA Victor, $c p1988.
518	Recorded in September 1987 in London, England.

6.5. Physical Description (MARC Field 300)

300	Number of specific material designation (total playing time) : $b other details ; $c dimension. + $e accompanying material.

The prescribed source of this area is the entire work. Catalogers record the number of physical parts by giving the number of parts in arabic numerals, followed by a specific material designation. *AACR2r* gives catalogers several terms for specific material designation: sound cartridge, sound cassette, sound disc, sound tape reel, and sound track film. Cassette and reel can be added to "sound track film," and the name of an instrument can be added to roll (such as "piano rolls"). The 2004 update to *AACR2r*, which allows catalogers to use conventional terminology such as CD and DVD as specific material designations (rule 6.5B1), brings this in line with the practice for recording physical characteristics of electronic resources (rule 9.5B).

Rule 6.5B2 instructs catalogers to record the playing time according to rule 1.5B4, giving time in hours, minutes, and seconds as it appears on the work and using abbreviations for hours (hr.), minutes (min.), and seconds (sec.). *LCRI* 6.5B2 indicates that if the total playing time is not on the sound recording but the times of all parts are, catalogers may add all the times to record a total time, rounding up to the next minute if the total exceeds five minutes. Times for individual parts can be recorded as they appear on the item in a contents note (505 field). An estimated duration is preceded by "ca." If no playing time is readily available, do not record it.

245	14	The Beatles book $h [sound recording].
300		1 sound cassette (60 min.)
505	00	Eleanor Rigby (2:09) — Here, there and everywhere (2:35) — In my life (2:55) — And I love her (2:06) . . .

If a recording contains two or more works and is without a collective title, the individual titles are recorded in field 245 but the playing time of each title is recorded in the 500 note. Optionally, catalogers may also enter playing times in the 306 field. This field has six character positions to represent duration in hours, minutes, and seconds.

100	1	Beethoven, Ludwig van, $d 1770–1827.
245	10	Sonata no. 8 in C minor, op. 13 $h [sound recording] : $b pathetique ; sonata no. 23 in F minor, op. 57 : appasionata ; sonata no. 14 in C sharp minor, op. 27 no. 2 : moonlight / $c Ludwig van Beethoven.

```
300        1 sound disc.
306        001412 $a 001256 $a 001105 [optional note]
500        Durations: 14:12; 12:56; 11:05
```

The second element of Area 5, other physical details, includes several subelements (rule 6.5C1): (1) type of recording (analog or digital), (2) playing speed, (3) groove characteristics (of analog discs), (4) track configuration (of sound track films), (5) number of tracks (on tapes), (6) number of sound channels, and (7) recording and reproduction characteristics.

"Type of recording" refers to the way the sound is encoded during mastering and the type of playback equipment needed. It is a critical element. Older recordings such as long-playing records tend to be analog, while more recent recordings on CDs and DVDs are usually digital. This element should match subfield $m of the 007 field for sound recordings.

Playing speed, groove characteristics, and number of tracks are not recorded if the information is standard for a medium. The standard speed is $1\frac{7}{8}$ inches per second for analog tape cassette and 1.4 meters per second for a digital disc. The number of sound channels, however, is always transcribed if the information is readily available. "Mono," "stereo," and "quad" are the three most common terms for this sub-element (rule 6.5C7).

LCRI 6.5C8 advises catalogers to record the recording and reproduction characteristics whenever the information is necessary for selecting playback equipment. "Dolby processed" is one of the most common terms recorded for this subelement. Many CDs have notations such as ADD or DDD that indicate the type of recording, the type of equipment used in mixing and editing, and the type of equipment used in mastering the disc. Such information is not recorded in the 300 field. As these CDs become more prevalent, some libraries have included this type of information in a 500 note that describes the physical carrier of the recording.

```
300    1 sound disc : $b stereo, $c 4 3/4 in.
500    Compact disc (ADD).
```

Dimensions for rolls, cartridges, and cassettes are not recorded if they are standard. Discs are measured in inches, according to the standard measurement of the recording industry. An analog disc is usually 12 inches, while a CD is $4\frac{3}{4}$ inches. A note may be provided when a sound disc is a CD (see the 500 note above), unless the cataloger chooses to use CD as the specific material designation in the 300 field, a practice the 2004 update allows.

Details of accompanying material are added to the end of Area 5 in $e. The location of the accompanying material, however, is usually recorded in a 500 note. If the accompanying material is substantial or unique, the cataloger should provide a note for it and code the content in the AccM element in the fixed field.

```
300    2 sound cassettes (60 min., 20 sec.) : $b analog,
       stereo. + $e 1 booklet (20 p. : ill. (some col.) ; 8 cm.)

300    1 sound disc (52 min.) : $b digital ; $c 4 3/4 in.
500    Program notes on container.
500    Compact disc (DDD).
```

6.6. Series (MARC Field 4XX)

Details for this area can be taken, in the order of preference, from the chief source of information, accompanying textual material, or the container. Series title should be recorded as instructed in 1.1B1. Wording, spelling, and order of the title should be followed, but not necessarily punctuation or capitalization. Field 440 records the series title to be traced (i.e., used as an access point), while field 490 usually records a series title that is not traced. If a series is traced in a form different from the title on the item, catalogers will use field 490 to record the series title as found and field 830 to record the authorized form for the series. Occasionally, a series may be entered under a personal name, using a 800 field. In the popular Lemony Snicket series, for example, the series information is recorded as follows

490	1	A series of unfortunate events ; $v bk. 3
800	1	Snicket, Lemony. $t Series of unfortunate events ; $v bk. 3

When a series is made available by several publishers, several authorized series statements are established to distinguish different versions, and catalogers will choose the authorized form that matches the item in hand as the access point.

800	1	Snicket, Lemony. $t Series of unfortunate events.
800	1	Snicket, Lemony. $t Series of unfortunate events (Harper Audio (Firm))
800	1	Snicket, Lemony. $t Series of unfortunate events (Listening Library)
800	1	Snicket, Lemony. $t Series of unfortunate events (Recorded Books, Inc.)

6.7. Notes (MARC 5XX Fields)

Notes serve two purposes for bibliographic descriptions and access:

1. They provide additional information about a work that cannot be recorded elsewhere in the record.

2. They justify the provision of additional access points.

Notes are to be recorded in the order specified in rule 6.7B, but at the discretion of the cataloger, notes of special significance to users could be presented first. Generally speaking, notes on the nature and scope of the sound recording as a whole are presented first, followed by other types of notes in the order of the eight areas of bibliographic description.

Rule 6.7B covers many types of notes that are common to sound recordings. They include notes on language, title variations, performers, time and/or place of recording, additional physical descriptions, location of accompanying material, audience, other available formats, summary, contents, publisher's numbers, and Universal Product Codes.

Language (MARC Fields 546 and 041): A language note (Field 546) is provided when a sound recording contains more than one language, when it includes a translation, or when the language of a sung or spoken text and the language of any accompanying text are different. In such cases, catalogers should code the languages in the 041 field and the language in $d of the 041 field will be coordinated with the Lang element in the fixed field. For musical sound recordings the language of the work is entered in subfield $d, not subfield $a. Subfields that are often used for sound recordings are presented in the following table.

Subfield	Usage
$d	for the language of the sung or spoken text
$e	for the language of librettos
$g	for the language of accompanying material other than librettos
$h	for the original language of sung or spoken text translated for a sound recording
$2	source of language code used

Catalogers consult MARC Code List for Languages (http://lcweb.loc.gov/marc/languages) to code this field. When a subfield has multiple codes, the codes are entered under separate subfields. For example, a sound recording in French with program notes in English, French, and German will be coded

Lang:	fre	
041	0	$d fre $g eng $g fre $g ger
546		Recording in French and program notes in English, French, and German.

Variant title (MARC Field 246): Titles that are different from the title proper and are likely to be used by searchers are recorded in field 246 to generate a note and a title added entry. The first indicator specifies if a note and an added entry should be produced, and the second indicator specifies the type of variant title.

245	10	Concertos for cello.
246	18	Cello concertos

["1" and "8" will create a title added entry and a note: Spine title: Cello concertos.]

245	14	The tailor of Gloucester $h [sound recording] : $b narration and music.
246	1_	$i Container title: $a Meryl Streep reads The tailor of Gloucester

[Indicator "1" will generate a note from subfields $i and $a and make a title added entry for the title in subfield $a]

Performers (MARC Field 511): Performers not named in the statement of responsibility area are recorded in the note area if the information is considered necessary. *AACR2r* instructs catalogers to record the names of performers, the role they play, or the medium in which they perform. This information is entered in field 511 and the first indicator value is "0".

245	14	The wide window $h [sound recording] / $c written by Lemony Snicket.
511	0	Read by the author; original music by the Gothic Archies.
511	0	Seiji Ozawa, conductor; Boston Symphony Orchestra.
511	0	Read by Meryl Streep; music performed by The Chieftains.

History of Recording (MARC Field 518): Information about the recording session is usually found on the sound recording, the container, or the accompanying material and recorded in field 518. In addition, catalogers may code such information in the 033 field. This is an optional field for recording the date, time, or place of recording, filming, broacasting, or finding sound. OCLC input guidelines at http://www.oclc.org/bibformats/en/0xx/033.shtm explain the use of this field.

518	Recorded April 6 and 7, 1987, at St. Timothy Church, Toronto.
260	Stanford, CA : $b Windham Hill Productions, $c p1988.
518	Music recorded at Windmill Lane Studios, Dublin, Ireland; narration recorded at ServiSound, Inc., NYC.

Physical description (MARC Field 500): *AACR2r* allows a note of "analog recording" for a digital disc that is made from an analog original, and a note of "digital recording" for an analog disc made from a digital original. Many CDs bear the three-letter codes such as ADD and DDD, especially classical music recordings, and libraries have developed a practice of including such information with the "compact disc" note in the 500 field.

| 500 | Compact disc (ADD). |
| 500 | CD read-along. |

Other formats (MARC Field 530): If a sound recording is known to be available in other formats, the information is recorded in field 530. Such information may appear in the package, or catalogers may consult the publisher's Web site or Schwann catalog to find this information, but they should not do extensive research to find such information.

| 530 | Also available in CD. |

Summary (MARC Field 520): Summary notes are usually provided for nonmusical recordings because it gives users a good idea of the item without playing it. Summary notes are to be objective and succinct and are entered in field 520.

Contents (MARC Field 505): Contents of a sound recording are frequently recorded for music recordings and some nonmusical recordings. By listing the works of a recording, the cataloger informs users of the contents of a recording and enables them to evaluate and select the item. If duration of each titled work is available, it is recorded as it appears on the item.

505	0	The tailor of Gloucester (24:11) — Theme for The tailor of Glouceseter (2:39) — The tailor of Gloucester at work (3:03) — Simpkin the cat/mice to the rescue (3:16) — Closing theme music (2:20).

Publisher's number (MARC Field 028): Publisher's numbers for sound recordings are useful identifiers. Although it is listed as the last type of note in *AACR2r*, this information appears as the first note in printed catalog cards. Subfield $b is used for the name of the publisher. The following 028 field with a second indicator 2 will generate a note: "Publisher no.: RCA Victor 7774-2-RC."

028	02	7774-2-RC $b RCA Victor

When the publisher's numbers are not in one sequence, catalogers may repeat the 028 field to record the information. For example, in an audio box set of stories on Winnie-the-Pooh, the publisher's numbers on the four cassettes are recorded as follows to generate four notes:

028	02	BBC 047A $b BDD Audio
028	02	BBC 047B $b BDD Audio
028	02	BBC 068A $b BDD Audio
028	02	BBC 068B $b BDD Audio

Alternatively, catalogers may use code "0" for the second indicator to suppress the generation of notes and add a 500 note to list these numbers in one field (see the James Joyce example later).

Universal Product Codes (MARC Field 024): Universal Product Code (UPC) is another useful identifier for sound recordings. UPC appears as a barcode symbol with a twelve-digit code below the parallel bars. The code is recorded in field 024 without spaces or hyphens. Catalogers should use value "1" for the first indicator to specify the nature of the number.

024	1	724353208820

6.8. Standard Number and Terms of Availability Area (MARC Field 020 or 022)

The cataloger should record international standard numbers such as International Standard Book Number (ISBN) or International Standard Serial Number (ISSN) in field 020 or 022, if the information is readily available. Other numbers should be recorded in the note area.

Enhanced CDs

Many musicians have combined video or multimedia in their recordings to present information about their songs, concerts, and personal interests. A standard practice is to create an "Enhanced CD," which is a regular audio CD with a multimedia CD-ROM track. To play an Enhanced CD, one needs an audio CD player for the audio portion of the disc and a computer for the multimedia CD-ROM track. An enhanced CD is considered a sound recording, and a 538 field for system requirements is used to record the set up needed to play the multimedia track. The cataloging of Enhanced CDs is the same as that of regular CDs, except for the following steps:

- The cataloger provides a note to indicate the item is an Enhanced CD. It can be a 500 note (e.g., An Enhanced CD), a 520 note (An Enhanced CD of ten songs and a CD-ROM multimedia presentation), or a 505 note (1. CD-ROM Multimedia presentation — 2. Elsewhere — 3. Plenty).

- The cataloger records the system requirements of the multimedia track in a 538 field, following rule 9.7B1b.

- The cataloger records the characteristics of the multimedia CD-ROM track in an electronic resource 006 field so that the item can be retrieved as a computer file.

- The cataloger uses an electronic resource 007 field to record the physical characteristics of the multimedia CD-ROM. Field 007 is required for all electronic resources.

Type	j	ELvl	I	Srce	d	Audn		Ctrl		Lang	eng
BLvl	m	Form		Comp	rc	AccM		MRec		Ctry	nyu
Desc	a	FMus	n	LTxt		DtSt	s	Dates	1997,		

006		[m h]	
007		s $b d $d f $e u $f n $g g $h n $i n $m e $n d	
007		c $b o $d c $e g $f a	
028	02	07822-18970-2 $b Arista	
100	1	McLachlan, Sarah.	
245	10	Surfacing $h [sound recording] / $c Sarah McLachlan.	
260		New York : $b Arista, $c p1997.	
300		1 sound disc (41 min.) : $b digital ; $c 4 3/4 in.	
511	0	Sarah McLachlan, vocals, piano, keys, acoustic and electric guitar ; with vocal and instrumental accompaniment.	

508		Recorded, mixed and produced by Pierre Marchand.
500		Enhanced CD.
500		Program notes on container insert.
538		System requirements for CD-ROM multimedia presentation: Macintosh System 7.0 or greater or Windows 95 compatible computer; 6 MB of available RAM; monitor capable of displaying 640x480 screen resolution and at east 256 colors; double speed or faster CD-ROM drive that is multisession enabled.
505	0	Building a mystery / Sarah McLachlan ; Pierre Marchand (4:07) — I love you / Sarah McLachlan (4:44) — Sweet surrender / Sarah McLachlan (4:40) — Angel / Sarah McLachlan (4:30) — Witness / Sarah McLachlan ; Pierre Marchand (4:45) — Do what you have to do / Sarah McLachlan (3:47) — Adia / Sarah McLachlan ; Pierre Marchand (4:05) — Black & white / Sarah McLachlan (5:02) — Full of grace / Sarah McLachlan (3:41) — Last dance / Sarah McLachlan (2:33).
650	0	Rock music $y 1991–2000.

Because this is a musical CD, "Type" is coded "j" for "musical sound recording" and "BLvl" is coded "m" for a nonserial item. The musical sound recording 008 field is used to create the record. "Comp" is coded "rc" for Rock music. The 006 field is added to represent the computer characteristics of this item, with "m" specifying this is a computer file, and code "h" in "File" indicating sound file. The presence of this field makes it possible for users to retrieve this item as a computer file. The first 007 field is a sound recording 007 field that records the characteristics of the sound recording, and the second one is an electronic resource 007 field that describes the physical characteristics. A 500 note identifies the item as an enhanced CD. Field 538 records the system requirements, listing the elements according to the order specified by rule 9.7B1b—model, memory, operating system, software, and peripherals.

Read-Along CDs

Another type of sound recording that blurs the line between audio CDs and electronic files is the "Read-Along CD" that readers can read along using computers as well as regular CD players. This type of CDs is treated as sound recordings, using the sound recording format, with the 007 field for sound recording added. To inform users that the CDs can play on computers, catalogers will add a field 538 to record the system requirements for playing this type of recordings. For example, a CD read-along that can be played on a CD player or a computer will be described as follows

Type	i	ELvl	I	Srce	d	Audn		Ctrl		Lang	eng
BLvl	m	Form		Comp	nn	AccM		MRec		Ctry	cau
Desc	a	FMus	n	Ltxt	f	DtSt	s	Dates	2001		

007		s $b d $d f $e s $f n $g g $h n $i n $m e $n d
245	00	Monsters, Inc. $h [sound recording] / $c Disney-Pixar.

260		Burbank, CA : $b Walt Disney Records: $b Pixar Animated Studios, $c c2001.
300		1 sound disc : $b digital ; $c 4 3/4 in. + $e 1 book (32 p. : ill. ; 18 cm.) + 1 sound cassette.
500		CD read-along.
500		Title from disc label.
500		CD may be played on a CD player while users read along in the accompanying storybook, or played on a computer while users read along by watching the storybook on the computer screen.
538		System requirements: PC; 166 MHz Pentium processor; Windows 95 or later; 32MB RAM; 4X CD-ROM drive; 16-bit sound card; 16-bit compatible video card; standard keyboard and mouse.
538		System requirements: Macintosh; 120 MHz PPC processor; System 8.1; 32MB RAM; 4X CD-ROM drive; standard keyboard and mouse.
511	0	Narrated by Dom DeLuise.
650	0	Monsters $v Juvenile fiction.
700	1	DeLuise, Dom.
710	2	Walt Disney Records.
710	2	Pixar Animation Studios.
730	0	Monsters, Inc. (Motion picture)

For the 007 field subfield $a is "s" for sound recordings; subfield $b is "d" for sound discs; subfield $d is "f" (1.4 m. per sec.) for compact digital discs; subfield $e is "s" for stereo; subfield $f (groove width) is "n" for not applicable; subfield $g is "g" (4 ¾ in.) for the dimensions of CDs; subfield $h (tape width) and subfield $i (tape configuration) are "n" for not applicable; subfield $m is "e" for digital recording that requires digital playback equipment; and subfield $n is "d" for an item that is captured and stored using digital techniques. The third 500 note explains the use of this item. The two 538 fields specify the requirements for playing this item. Narrator and the publishers are traced, and a uniform title used in 730 to link this item to the original movie.

MP3: Digital Sound Files for Remote Access

Digital sound files can be accessed directly from the Internet or downloaded and saved for later access on devices such as iPod or PalmPilot. They can also be packaged on CD-ROM for desktop access. MP3 files are one of the most popular formats for digitized music files on the Internet. In recent years many MP3 files have been put on CD-ROM for sale. When digital sound files are on CD-ROMs or for remote access via a network, their bibliographic records will have [electronic resource] as the general material designation (GMD). But if digital sound files are stored on standard CD, Enhanced CDs, or Read-along CDs, [sound recording] will be the GMD. In describing remote access digital sound files such as streaming audio files, catalogers will use the sound recording format (Type "i" for nonmusic recording and Type "j" for music recording). In addition, the following fields will be used to describe the sound and computer aspects of the files:

- Electronic resource 006 field: Because Type is not coded "m" for electronic resources, this field is used to represent the electronic resource aspect of this item. The presence of this 006 field will enable users to retrieve the digital sound file when their search focuses on electronic resources.

- Sound recording 007 field: This 007 field is required for all sound recordings.

- Electronic resource 007 field: This 007 is required for all electronic resources.

- No 300 field will be provided for remote-access files.

- 500 field: The 500 field can be produced as a general note to explain the nature of the file.

- 538 fields: Two separate 538 fields will be used to record the system requirements and the mode of access, if the item is a remote-access files.

- 500 field: A general note should be provided to indicate the source of the title; this note is required for all electronic resources.

- If appropriate, additional physical characteristics of the item can be recorded in the 500 field.

- 530 field: If the item is known to be available in other formats, the information is recorded in the 530 field.

- 856 field: If the item is a remote access digital sound file, the URL is recorded in the 856 field to facilitate access.

Assignment of Access Points

Three chapters of *AACR2r* provide guidelines for assigning access points to sound recordings. Chapter 21 of *AACR2r* presents rules on how to select access points, and rule 21.23 is devoted to sound recordings. Chapter 22 covers the construction of proper headings, and Chapter 25 focuses on formulating uniformed titles, which are commonly assigned to musical works.

21.23A. The Work of One Person

The principles of authorship specified in Chapter 21 apply to sound recordings. Rule 21.23A states that the sound recording of a work by a single person (composer, writer, artist) should be entered under that person. Performers, readers, or narrators are assigned as additional access points.

100	1	Moyers, Bill.
245	10	Healing and the mind $h [sound recording] / $c Bill Moyers.
100	1	Brown, Dan, $d 1964-
245	14	The Da Vinci code $h [sound recording] / $c by Dan Brown.
511	0	Read by Paul Michael.
700	1	Michael, Paul. $4 nrt.

21.23B. Two or More Works by the Same Person(s) or Body (Bodies)

Two or more works by the same person will be entered under the name of the person. Recordings of music may need uniform titles to bring various renditions of the work together. Chapter 25 focuses on uniform title and the cataloger should search OCLC Authority File to ensure proper form is used. Added entries are usually provided for principal performers.

100	1	Bach, Johann Sebastian, $d 1685–1750.
240	10	Sonatas. $k Selections. $o arr.
245	10	6 sonatas, BWV 1030–1035 $h [sound recording] / $c Bach.
511	0	Michala Petri, recorder; Keith Jarrett, harpsichord.
700	1	Petri, Michala.
700	1	Jarrett, Keith.

21.23C. Collections with Collective Title

A sound recording containing the works by two or more people is entered under the principal performer. *LCRI* 21.23C (CBS 45) clarifies that "performer" refers to a person or corporate body whose performance is on the sound recording. It also states that a conductor is not a member of the group he or she conducts, and a member of a performing group should not be considered a separate performer.

Disc label:

THE PHILHARMONIC ORCHESTRA LESLEY GARRETT **PRIMA DONNA** CONDUCTED BY IVOR BOLTON [A collection of 15 songs by various composers.]

Transcribed as:

100	1	Garrett, Lesley, $d 1955-
245	10	Prima donna $h [sound recording] / $c Lesley Garrett.
511	0	Lesley Garrett, soprano; Philharmonic Orchestra; Ivor Bolton, conductor.

If a sound recording of this type has a collective title, but no principal performer can be identified or there are more than three principal performers, the item will be entered under the title.

Cassette label:

Frost, Williams, Stevens, Eberhart, Pound & Wilbur THE CAEDMON TREASURY OF MODERN POETS Read by Each Respective Author

Transcribed as:

```
245     04      The Caedmon treasury of modern poets $h [sound
                recording].
```

21.23D. Collections Without Collective Title

If a sound recording contains the works by two or more people and lacks a collective title, the main access point depends on the participation of the performers. If the performer goes beyond performance, execution, and interpretation, the item should be entered under the heading of the principal performer. Rock, jazz, and popular music recordings tend to belong to this category.

But if the performer's participation is limited to performance, execution, and interpretation, the item should be entered under the heading appropriate to the first work. Added entries are made for other works and performers.

21.29D. Added Entries

LCRI 21.29D (CBS 45) provides guidelines for the selection of added entries for sound recordings. It recommends that catalogers make added entries for all named performers, with six exceptions:

1. If a corporate body is selected as an access point, no added entries should be provided for individual members of the group. A conductor and accompanist should not be considered members of the body he or she conducts or accompanies, so it is acceptable to select conductors and accompanists as added entries. If a person's name appears with a corporate body, the cataloger needs to determine if the corporate name includes this person's name. If so, no added entry should be assigned. Otherwise, this person can be selected as an added entry.

2. If the chorus and the orchestra of an opera company perform in an opera and are named along with the name of the parent body, only the parent body should be selected as the added entry.

3. No added entry should be made for a performer whose role is minor or a performer who is chosen as the main entry.

4. If many performers perform the same function (e.g., actors in a drama), only those given prominence in the chief source are selected as added entries.

5. If number four does not apply, performers given prominence in other parts of the work should be selected.

6. If number five also does not apply, performers given the most important functions (the principal roles) should be selected as added entries.

Subject Analysis

In assigning subject headings, Library of Congress treats all works on the same subject in the same way regardless of their medium. Catalogers analyze sound recordings in the same way they analyze print materials and assign headings—according to the general guidelines provided by the Library of Congress's *Subject Cataloging Manual* (H 180). Because nonprint materials are much harder to browse and users tend to rely on the catalog for subject information about them, catalogers tend to assign more subject headings to them. But no special form subdivision is assigned to bring out the format.

Juvenile Sound Recordings

The only exception is juvenile materials, which include materials intended for children and young adults from preschool through age sixteen. For materials with the intellectual level code "a," "b," or "c" in "Audn" in the fixed field, subdivision "Juvenile sound recordings" is added to the topical headings. For instance, a sound cassette on nutrition for teenagers will be assigned a heading: Nutrition—Juvenile sound recordings. If a work is coded "f" for special audiences and is clearly juvenile in nature, this subdivision can be assigned also. This subdivision can be used for fictional or factual treatment of a topic.

Sound recordings cover all types of topics, and music and literature are two of the more popular subject areas. So the subject cataloging practices for works of literature and works of music are briefly introduced here. The following discussion is based on the *Subject Cataloging Manual* and Chan's description of these topics (1995).

Music

Many valid music headings are not listed in *Library of Congress Subject Headings* because the Library of Congress has issued standard citation patterns for catalogers to establish music headings appropriate for the item being cataloged. Catalogers should consult H1160 of the *Subject Cataloging Manual (SCM)* for the citation patterns. Library of Congress also designates the phrase heading "Medium or form for instrumental music, arranged" as a pattern to cover a wide range of music (e.g., Piano music, Arranged). Free-floating subdivisions can be found under "Operas" (e.g., the pattern for music composition, including musical form, medium, style, music for special occasions, and others) and "Piano" (e.g., the pattern for musical instruments). (See H1161.) Section H1160 includes free-floating period subdivisions for headings for music compositions and explains the assignment of these subdivisions.

The practice of the Library of Congress is to treat musical sound recordings in the same way as other musical works. For instrumental music, headings are usually assigned for musical form (e.g., Sonatas; Suites), medium of performance (e.g., Flute music; Piano music), and performing group (e.g., Orchestra music; Quintets). For vocal music, headings are assigned for form (e.g., Chants; Operas), voice range (e.g., High voice; Men's voices), number of vocal parts (e.g., 4 parts), and accompanying medium (e.g., Piano). If topical headings are appropriate, they can be assigned with music subdivisions. "Keats, John, 1795–1821—Musical settings," for instance, is assigned to a work in which the writings of Keats have been set to music.

If a sound recording includes works in different musical forms, a heading is assigned to represent the form of each work. A recording of

Vivaldi's concertos for cello that includes two forms of concertos will be assigned a heading for each form: "Concertos (Violoncello with string orchestra)," and "Concertos (Bassoon, violoncello with string orchestra)."

A musical work for a specific dance form is assigned a heading for the dance form (e.g., Tangos) and headings for the medium and other appropriate topics. *SCM* H1917 details the treatment of music of ethnic groups, national groups, and non-Western art music.

Literature

Library of Congress Subject Headings lists four types of headings for works of and about literature, including literary form headings (e.g., Poetry), topical headings for themes, characters, or features in literary works (e.g., Peace—Fiction), headings with form and topic combined (e.g., Mystery and detective stories), and other topical headings. Sound recordings of literature tend to include collections of literary works or individual literary works. For collections of two or more independent works by different authors, literary form headings are assigned. If a collection has a theme, a topical heading with a form subdivision is also assigned. For instance, American poetry—19th century; and Love—Poetry are assigned to a collection of several nineteenth century American poets' works. Although subdivision "—Collected works" is free-floating, it *cannot* be used with literary form headings. Subdivision "—Collections" is not free-floating and can be used with very few literary form headings, including Drama, Fiction, Literature, and Poetry.

For collected works by an individual literary author, the practice is to assign *no* literary form heading unless the literary form headings combine form and topic (e.g., War poetry) or the form heading is highly specific (e.g., Radio stories). Topical headings with a literary form subdivision, if appropriate, are assigned.

For individual works of poetry or drama by an individual literary author, the practice is to assign no major literary forms (e.g., English poetry), but form headings that include a topic (e.g., War poetry) or highly specific form headings (e.g., Nursery rhymes) can be assigned. Topical headings with subdivisions "—Poetry" or "—Drama" can be assigned if appropriate. Children's poems or plays are assigned literary form headings for children's literature (e.g., Children's plays).

For individual works of adult fiction, children's fiction, or young adult fiction, no form headings are assigned. Topical headings with subdivision "—Fiction" are assigned to only three types of fiction: biographical fiction (e.g., Joyce, James, 1882–1941—Fiction), historical fiction (e.g., Holocaust—Fiction), and animal stories (e.g., Animals—Fiction; Pigs—Fiction).

The August 1998 version of *SCM* H1790 indicates that Library of Congress has begun a cooperative program with OCLC to provide increased subject access to fiction as recommended by ALA's *Guidelines on Subject Access to Individual Works of Fiction, Drama, Etc.* (1990). Under this program OCLC adds headings for topic, setting, characters, and genre to update LC records. Genre and form headings taken from the *Guidelines* are coded "gsafd" in subfield $2.

Both *Library of Congress Classification* and *Dewey Decimal Classification* classify topical sound recordings for adults and those for juveniles in the same manner as other topical materials. The most specific class number should be assigned, and Cutter numbers are used to subarrange materials.

In *LCC* juvenile materials are classed with a number for "Juvenile works" under the appropriate heading, if it is available. Otherwise, the number for "General works" is used. *DDC*'s Table 1 has a provision for intended audience, but the audience aspect is usually not represented by the class number.

LCC places juvenile belles lettres in PZ5-90 and juvenile fiction, folklore, and so on in English are placed in PZ5-PZ10.3, with unique Cutter numbers assigned to authors. If necessary, work letters from the title are used to subarrange works by the same author (e.g., the work letters for *Freddy the Detective* are "Fr"). The work letters include a capital letter and one or more lowercase letters. The same class number is assigned to editions of the same work, and the publication date is used to distinguish the editions. Work letters are not used if a work has a title main entry and if a work is not written in English. Except for collections of juvenile literature that are classed in 808.899282, *DDC* does not have specific numbers for juvenile belles lettres. Cutter numbers from the Cutter tables and work marks from the title are often used to subarrange materials assigned the same *DDC* number.

Arrangement

While subject headings provide collocation on the catalog, call numbers provide a reasonable extent of collocation on the shelves. The assignment of classification number, however, is not directly related to how sound recordings are shelved. If a library is committed to an integrated catalog, sound recordings should be shelved with other types of material. But intershelving works of different media is challenging. Weihs offers detailed instructions on intershelving, but she also acknowledges the cost of such an effort (Weihs 1991). Preservation and security concerns also make intershelving all media less appealing. For these reasons libraries have developed many ways to organize sound recordings (Kaye 1991). Major factors the organizer must consider are ease of browsing, ease of access, security, preservation, and equipment. Four methods and their strengths and limitations are described below.

Intershelving with Dummies

Because sound recordings come in several formats and publishers do not have standards for packaging these works, intershelving sound recordings can be difficult. One solution is to create dummies for the recordings and place them on the shelves with the rest of the collection. When a user finds the dummy, he or she can bring it to the librarian to exchange for the recording. This approach has several benefits. It collocates works on the same subject on the shelves for easy browsing. It uses only one shelving system and should cause little confusion for users. The sound recordings are less likely to be damaged because they are kept in a place only librarians can access. If special equipment is needed to play a recording, the librarian will be able to point that out to the user or provide the equipment if the library has it. As with any system, intershelving has some drawbacks. One is that the user will not have the opportunity to examine the physical item before asking for it. Another drawback is that the user will not be able to browse the entire sound recording collection. A more serious drawback is that when access to items is mediated through a librarian, full access to items may be discouraged, especially items of more controversial topics.

Case Display for Browsing

To encourage browsing, some public libraries have tried displaying cassette and CD cases without their contents. When a user desires an item, he or she will give the librarian the number on the case. This method of organization is not strongly tied to the catalog, supports browsing, and allows users to examine the cases. It also has advantages for security and preservation reasons. But the library will need to have more storage space for sound recordings—an area for the case display and an area for storing the physical items. Another challenge is that the arrangement of the cases must be logical to facilitate browsing. Because sound recordings can be arranged by title, author, composer, principal performer, type of music, and so on, it is not a simple task to arrange these materials or to maintain the order of cases in the display area. Some libraries have resorted to placing cases in a locked display case to maintain the order of the cases. That method, however, limits the user's access to the cases.

Shelving by Format

Another popular approach is to shelve sound recordings by the medium, with sound cassettes in one area and CDs in another. Within each category the items are subarranged according to the nature or type. For example, music CDs are stored together and color-coded by music type (red for rock music, green for jazz, and so on); musical cassettes are similarly treated and stored in a separate area; while nonmusical cassettes are subarranged by type with "B" designating biography and subdivided by Cutter number, and other codes for different categories. This arrangement is very good for browsing and encourages direct access. The limitations are that the items tend to be touched by many users, the subgroupings within the same medium may not be very explicit, and users interested in various presentations of the same subject will have to check several media areas. Security and preservation of the items will present difficulties as well.

Shelving by Size

Although this may sound impractical, shelving by size has been used in closed stacks with success. Works are shelved according to their size and assigned an accession number. The benefits of this arrangement include space saving, easy shelf maintenance, and quick retrieval once the access number is found in the catalog. The drawback is the collection becomes unusable without the catalog. Subject collocation on the shelves and browsing are impossible, and no users can access the stacks. This approach favors the security and preservation of sound recordings at the expense of direct user access.

Each of these methods has its strengths and limitations. In devising ways to organize sound recordings for access, the organizer will need to consider the needs of the intended users first. Is browsing important to these users? Is it likely they will want to examine the physical items? Are they likely to search the catalog first? How good is the online catalog? Does the library expect heavy use of sound recordings? Can the library afford to replace damaged items frequently? Answers to these questions should guide the decision on how to organize sound recordings for access.

Cataloging Examples

Figure 3.1. The sound of your voice

Cassette label:

THE SOUND OF YOUR VOICE
DR. CAROL FLEMING

TAPE 1   [Dolby System symbol]
SIDE A   79665-8
SIMON & SCHUSTER   © 1988 Carol Fleming. All rights reserved p
AUDIO   1992 Simon & Schuster Inc. All rights Reserve
                          SOUND IDEAS is an imprint of Simon &
                          Schuster Audio Division Simon & Schuster
                          Inc.

[The same label appears on three other sound cassettes.]

Type	i	ELvl	I	Srce	d	Audn		Ctrl		Lang	eng
BLvl	m	Form		Comp	nn	AccM		MRec		Ctry	nyu
Desc	a	FMus	n	LTxt	i	DtSt	s	Dates	1992,		

007		s $b s $d l $e s $f n $g j $h l $i c $m c $n e
020		0671796658
028	02	79665-8 $b Simon & Schuster Sound Ideas
090		PN4162
092		808.5
100	1	Fleming, Carol.
245	14	The sound of your voice $h [sound recording] / $c Carol Fleming.
260		New York, NY: $b Simon & Schuster Sound Ideas, $c p1992.
300		4 sound cassettes (ca. 4 hrs.) : $b analog, stereo, Dolby Processed.
500		"The essential program for communicating confidently and clearly"—Container.
511	0	Featuring the author.
520		The author takes the listener step-by-step through the fundamentals of good, confident vocal technique. Uses real-life speaking situations to demonstrate various voice characteristics.
650	0	Voice culture.

Discussion for Figure 3.1

- Fixed field: Code "i" for Type stands for a nonmusical sound recording; code "m" for BLvl indicates this is a monographic item; because this is not a print music or music manuscript, FMus (format of music) is coded "n", and Comp (form of composition) is coded "nn" for nonmusical recording. LTxt (literary text) is "i" because this work is about how to use your voice effectively. The item has a single publication date of 1992.

- 007: 007 field is required for sound recording. Subfields common to sound cassettes are included. $a is "s" for sound recordings; $b is "s" for cassettes; $d is "l" ($1\frac{7}{8}$ ips) for the standard speed of cassettes; $e is "s" for stereo; $f "groove width" is "n" for not applicable to CD or tapes; $g is "j" ($3\frac{7}{8} \times 2\frac{1}{2}$ in.) for the standard dimensions of a cassette; $h is "l" for $\frac{1}{8}$ inch, the standard tape width for cassettes; $i is "c" for quarter track used for standard cassettes; $m is "c" for standard Dolby encoding; $n is "e" for analog recording.

- 020: The ISBN is from the container. It is recorded without the hyphens.

- 028: Publisher's number is entered in subfield $a, subfield $b is for the label name. The second indicator "2" will produce a note for this number.

- 100: The work of a single author is entered under the author.

- 260: Although "Simon & Schuster" and "Sound Ideas" do not appear right next to each other on the cassette label, their relationship is made clear on the label. The phrase "Simon & Schuster Sound Ideas" appears with the publisher's number on the container. "Simon & Schuster Sound Ideas" is therefore used as the name of the publisher. The copyright date of the sound recording (1992) is transcribed in subfield $c.

- 300: The approximate running time, sound channel information, and the recording characteristics are on the container. Because the dimension of the cassettes is standard, subfield $c is not used.

- 500: This text appears prominently on the container. Because the quotation is not from the chief source, its source is indicated.

- 511: Even though the narrator is the same as the author, this note is necessary to identify the narrator. Since the author is the main entry, no added entry needs to be created for her.

- 520: Summary note is usually provided for nonmusical recordings to inform users of the content of the work.

- 650: A topical heading for the subject content of this work. No special form subdivision is assigned to bring out the format.

Figure 3.2. Touch sensitive

Disc label:

TANGENT
STANLEY JORDAN
TOUCH SENSITIVE

SIDE 1   1001
33 1/3 RPM   STEREO

1. Renaissance Man 8:12   3. All The Children 4:38
2. Touch of Blue 4:12   4. Jumpin' Jack 2:14

All selections composed by Stanley Jordan and published
by Manifold Music (BMI) with the exception of
Havah Nagilah, which is in the public domain.
© 1982 Manifold Music
p1982 Tangent Records, Inc.
134 Evergreen Place
Suite 700
E. Orange, N.J. 07018
All Rights Reserved

[Side 2 has exactly the same information except the following contents:
1. I Have A Dream 8:45   3. Orb 4:00
2. Havah Nagilah 5:22   4. A-flat Purple 5:51]

Type	j	ELvl	I	Srce	d	Audn		Ctrl		Lang	eng
BLvl	m	Form		Comp	pp	AccM		MRec		Ctry	nju
Desc	a	FMus	n	LTxt		DtSt	s	Dates	1982,		

007			s $b d $d b $e s $f m $g e $h n $i n $n e
028	02		1001 $b Tangent
090			M126
092			787.87
100	1		Jordan, Stanley.
245	10		Touch sensitive $h [sound recording] / $c Stanley Jordan.
260			East Orange, N.J. : $b Tangent Records, $c p1982.
300			1 sound disc : $b analog, 33 1/3 rmp, stereo ; $c 12 in.
505	0		Renaissance man (8:12) — Touch of blue (4:12) —All the children (4:38) — Jump' Jack (2:14) — I have a dream (8:45) — Havah nagilah (5:22) — Orb (4:00) — A-flat purple (5:51)
650	0		Guitar music.

Discussion for Figure 3.2

- Chief source of information: Both sides of the disc constitute the chief source.

- Fixed field: Code "j" for Type indicates this is a musical recording; FMus (format of music) is "n" because this is not a music manuscript or print music; Comp (form of composition) is "pp" for popular music because there is no code for guitar music; LTxt (literary text) is blank for a musical recording; the item has a single publication date of 1982.

- 007: Subfields common to sound discs are included. $e is "s" for stereo sound; $f is "m" for "33 ⅓ rpm"; $g is "e" for 12 inches, the dimensions a sound disc; $h (tape width) is "n" for not applicable; $1 (tape configuration) is "n" for not applicable; $n is "e" for analog recording.

- 028: Publisher's number is entered in subfield $a, and label name is in subfield $b.

- 260: The copyright date for the music and the copyright date for the recording are both present, but only the one for the sound recording is transcribed for subfield $c.

- 505: The duration of each piece is listed on the labels, so the durations are recorded in the contents note. Only the first words of the titles are capitalized.

- 650: For instrumental music, the LC practice is to assign headings for the musical form, medium of performance, and/or performing group. Guitar music specifies the medium of performance for this work.

Figure 3.3. The wide window

Cassette label

A Series of Unfortunate Events: THE WIDE WINDOW
WRITTEN AND READ BY LEMONY SNICKET

Harper   Tape One
Audio   SIDE 1
UAO   34:18
69(3)

© 2000 Lemony Snicket   **DOLBY B NR**
(p)2001 HarperCollinsPublishers, Inc.
10 E. 53rd St., New York, NY 10022.
All rights reserved. Made in the USA.

Container label (front)

HARPER CHILDREN'S AUDIO
A Series of Unfortunate Events

Written and Read by LEMONY SNICKET
* THE WIDE WINDOW *
Original Music by The Gothic Archives
UNABRIDGED

Container label (back)
Copyright © 2000 by Lemony Snicket
Produced and directed by Rick Harris
Mixed by Richard Romaniello   **3 ½ hours / 3 cassettes**
                                               Unabridged

Music performed by The Gothic Archives, written by Stephin Merritt
(p) & © 2001 Stephen Merritt
Published by Gay and Loud (ASCAP)
Cover illustration © 2000 by Brett Helquist
(p) & © 2001 HarperCollinsPublishers, Inc.
All rights reserved.
DOLBY B NR   [upc code] 9 780694 525423
                                            ISBN: 0-694-52542-1

Type	1	ELvl	1	Srce	d	Audn		Ctrl		Lang	eng
BLvl	m	Form		Comp	nn	AccM		MRec		Ctry	nyu
Desc	a	FMus	n	LTxt	f	DtSt	s	Dates		2001,	

007		s $b s $d l $e u $f n $g j $h l $i c $m c $n e
020		0694525421
024	3	9780694525423
028	0 2	UAO 69(3) $b Harper Children's Audio
090		PZ7
092		813
100	1	Snicket, Lemony.
245	14	The wide window $h [sound recording] / $c written and read by Lemony Snicket.
260		New York, N.Y. : $b Harper Children's Audio, $c p2001.
300		3 sound cassettes (3 hrs., 30 min.) : $b analog, Dolby processed.
306		033000.
490	1	A series of unfortunate events
511	0	Read by the author; original music by The Gothic Archies.
500		Unabridged.
520		Catastrophes and misfortunes continue to plague the Baudelaire orphans after they are sent to live with fearful Aunt Josephine, who offers little protection against Count Olaf's treachery.
650	0	Baudelaire, Violet (Fictitious character) $v Juvenile sound recordings.
650	0	Baudelaire, Klaus (Fictitious character) $v Juvenile sound recordings.
650	0	Baudelaire, Sunny (Fictitious character) $v Juvenile sound recordings.
650	0	Orphans $v Juvenile sound recordings.
650	0	Brothers and sisters $v Juvenile sound recordings.
650	0	Children's audiobooks.
710	2	Gothic Archies.
800	1	Snicket, Lemony. $t Series of unfortunate events (Harper Audio (Firm)); $v bk. 3

Discussion for Figure 3.3

- Fixed field: Code "i" for Type indicates this is a nonmusical recording; code "m" for BLvl stands for a nonserial recording; FMus (format of music) has the default value of "n" because this item is not a print music or music manuscript; Comp (form of composition) is "nn" for nonmusical recordings; LTxt (literary text) is "f" for fiction. The item has one publication date, 2001.

- 007 field is required for sound recording. $a is "s" for sound recordings; $b is "s" for cassettes; $d is "l" ($1\frac{7}{8}$ ips) for the standard speed of cassettes; $e is "u" for no information about the playback channels; $f "groove width" is "n" for not applicable to CD or tapes; $g is "j" ($3\frac{7}{8} \times 2\frac{1}{2}$ in.) for the standard dimensions of a cassette; $h is "l" for $\frac{1}{8}$ inch, the standard tape width for cassettes; $i is "c" for quarter track used for standard cassettes; $m is "c" for standard Dolby encoding; $n is "e" for analog recording.

- 090 & 092: PZ7 is the *LCC* number for general juvenile belle lettres. Individual literary works for children are placed here and further subarranged by the Cutter number based on Snicket. 813 is for American fiction in English.

- 100: Lemony Snicket is the pseudonym of Daniel Handler and it is chosen as the main access point, according to rule 22.2B1. If desired, the cataloger may provide a cross reference from the real name to the pseudonym. The information on author is transcribed in subfield $c of the 245 field.

- 260: Harper Children's Audio is a division of HarperCollins and is transcribed as the publisher.

- 300: The number of specific material designation and the sound quality are recorded, but the dimensions of the item are not transcribed because the size is standard.

- 490 and 800: The series information is important for identification and access purposes. The LC authority file shows the authorized form for this series is under the author, so the series title found in the item is entered in field 490, while the authorized form of the series is transcribed in the 800 field, with subfield $v added to indicate the number of this item in the series.

- 500: The term, "Unabridged", is important but it is not accompanied by words such as edition or version, so it is transcribed as a 500 note, not as an edition statement in the 250 field.

- 511: Information on the narrator and the musicians are recorded in the 511 field, separated by a semicolon.

- 520: A summary note is always provided for children's literature and for nonmusical recordings.

- 650s: For a literary work for children, a topical heading with a form subdivision, "Juvenile sound recordings", is appropriate. The three Baudelaire children are fictitious characters that are important access points for this work, so they are entered as topical headings, not personal headings. In addition, a form heading, "Children's audiobooks" is used to facilitate access, and main themes of the book are added as topical headings.

Figure 3.4. *Ulysses*

Disc label:

James Joyce
ULYSSES
p 1994 NAXOS AudioBooks Ltd. © 1994 NAXOS AudioBooks Ltd.
DIGITAL AUDI   CD 1
GEMA Read by Jim Norton
            with Marcella Riordan
            NA 401112
            DDD
[CD 2 has NA 401122, CD 3 has NA 401132, and CD4 has NA 402242.]
*Information on the container:
    Abridged and produced by Roger Marsh.
    CD1: 70:25; CD 2: 60:52; CD 3: 79:30; CD4: 79:30
    Total time: 4:49:17

Type	i	ELvl	I	Srce	d	Audn		Ctrl	Lang	eng
BLvl	m	Form		Comp	nn	AccM		MRec	Ctry	ger
Desc	a	FMus	n	LTxt	f	DtSt	s	Dates	1994,	

007:		s $b d $d f $e s $f n $g g $h n $i n $m e $n d
020		9626340118
028	00	NA 401112 $b NAXOS AudioBooks
028	00	NA 401122 $b NAXOS AudioBooks
028	00	NA 401132 $b NAXOS AudioBooks
028	00	NA 401142 $b NAXOS AudioBooks
090		PR6019.O9 $b U42 1994
092		823.912
100	1	Joyce, James, $d 1882–1941.
245	10	Ulysses $h [sound recording] / $c James Joyce.
260		Germany : $b NAXOS AudioBooks, $c p1994.
300		4 sound discs (4 hr., 49 min., 17 sec.) : $b digital, stereo ; $c 4 3/4 in. + $e 1 pamphlet ([12] p.: ill. ; 12 cm.)
500		Abridged and produced by Roger Marsh.
511	0	Read by Jim Norton with Marcella Riordan.
500		Compact disc.
500		Pamphlet in container.
520		Leopold Bloom wanders through Dublin on June 16, 1904, talking to people, observing life in Dublin, and thinking of his passionate wife, Molly.
500		NAXOS AudioBooks: NA 401112, NA 401122, NA 401132, NA 401142.
650	0	Bloom, Leopold (Fictitious character) $v Fiction.
650	0	Bloom, Molly (Fictitious character) $v Fiction.
650	0	Men $z Ireland $z Dublin $v Fiction.
700	1	Marsh, Roger.
700	1	Norton, Jim.
700	1	Riordan, Marcella.

Discussion for Figure 3.4

- Fixed field: Code "i" for Type indicates this is a nonmusical recording; code "m" for BLvl stands for a nonserial recording; FMus (format of music) has the default value of "n" because this item is not a print music or music manuscript; Comp (form of composition) is "nn" for nonmusical recordings; LTxt (literary text) is "f" for fiction. The item has one publication date, 1994. The item was published in Germany, so Ctry (country of publication) is coded "ger", according to the *MARC Code List of Countries* (http://www.loc.gov/marc/countries/).

- 007: Subfields common to compact discs are included. $a is "s" for sound recordings; $b is "d" for sound discs; $d is "f" (1.4 m. per sec.) for compact digital discs; $e is "s" for stereo; $f (groove width) is "n" for not applicable; $g is "g" (4 ¾ in.) for the dimensions of CD; $h (tape width) and $1 (tape configuration) are "n" for not applicable; $m is "e" for digital recording indicating the item needs digital playback equipment; and $n is "d" for an item that is captured and stored using digital techniques.

- 028: Normally the second indicator for field 028 is used to generate a note for the publisher's number, but when the publisher's numbers are non-consecutive, each number is recorded in a separate 028 field. "0" is used for the second indicator to indicate that no note will be produced from the 028 field. The numbers are entered in field 500 so that all numbers will be included in one note. Notice the connection between the 028 fields and the last 500 field.

- 090 and 092: PR6019.O9 is the number for James Joyce, and U4-79 is for Ulysses. 823 is for English fiction, and 912 refers to the twentieth century.

- 100: The original author of a literary work is used as the main access point.

- 300: The total time is on the back of the container.

- 500: A note on statement of responsibility is listed first.

- 511: Performers are recorded in the 511 field.

- 500: The nature of the sound disc is specified in a note. An alternate approach is to remove this note and use "4 CDs" in the 300 field for specific material designation.

- 500: This note indicates the location of the accompanying pamphlet.

- 520: A summary of the contents of a nonmusical recording is usually provided to help users understand the subject of the item.

- 650: For a literary work, no form headings are assigned, but topical headings with the subdivision "—Fiction" are appropriate. Both characters are fictitious ones and are listed in *Library of Congress Subject Headings*. No form subdivision is used to bring out the format.

- 700s: The producer and the readers are traced.

Figure 3.5. *Concertos for cello*

Disc label: [a red label "RCA VICTOR Red Seal" appears on the left side of the disc]
Vivaldi
Concertos for Cello
Ofra Harnoy, Cello
Toronto Chamber Orchestra
Paul Robinson, Conductor
7774-2-RC

COMPACT DISC
DIGITAL AUDIO
1988 BMG Music
TMK(S) RCA Corp.
& BMG Music
Made in U.S.A.

1-3 Concerto in D Minor, RV 405
4-6 Concerto in C Minor, RV 401
7-9 Concerto in B-Flat, RV 423
10-12 Concerto in C, RV 399
13-15 Concerto for Cello and Bassoon in E Minor, RV 409 James McKay, Bassoon
16 Concerto Movement in D Minor, RV 538

Type	j	ELvl	I	Srce	d	Audn	Ctrl	Lang	eng
BLvl	m	Form		Comp	co	AccM	MRec	Ctry	nyu
Desc	a	FMus	n	LTxt		DtSt	s	Dates	1988,

007:		s $b d $d f $e s $f n $g g $h n $i n $m e $n d
028	02	7774-2-RC $b RCA Victor Red Seal
090		M1117
092		784.274
100	1	Vivaldi, Antonio, $d 1678–1741.
240	10	Concertos $k Selections
245	10	Concertos for cello $h [sound recording] / $c Vivaldi.
246	1	$i Title on container: $a Cello concertos
260		New York, NY : $b BMG Music, $c p1988.
300		1 sound disc (53 min., 53 sec.) : $b digital, stereo ; $c 4 3/4 in.
546		Program notes in English, German, French and Italian in container.
511	0	Ofra Harnoy, cello; James McKay, bassoon; Toronto Chamber Orchestra; Paul Robinson, conductor.
518		Recorded April 6 and 7, 1987, at St. Timothy Church, Toronto.
500		Compact disc.
505	0	D minor, RV 405 (10:18) — C minor, RV 401 (12:07) — B-flat, RV 423 (10:02) — C, RV 399 (8:27) — E minor, RV 409 (8:52) — D minor, RV 538 (3:37).
650	0	Concertos (Violoncello with string orchestra).
650	0	Concertos (Bassoon, violoncello with string orchestra).
700	1	Harnoy, Ofra, $d 1965-
700	1	McKay, James, $d 1944-
700	1	Robinson, Paul, $d 1940-
700	12	Vivaldi, Antonio, $d 1678–1741. $t Concertos, $m violoncello, string orchestra, $n RV 405, $r D minor. $f 1988.
700	12	Vivaldi, Antonio, $d 1678–1741. $t Concertos, $m violoncello, string orchestra, $n RV 401 $r C minor. $f 1988.
700	12	Vivaldi, Antonio, $d 1678–1741. $t Concertos, $m violoncello, string orchestra, $n RV 423, $r B-flat major. $f 1988.
700	12	Vivaldi, Antonio, $d 1678–1741. $t Concertos, $m violoncello, string orchestra, $n RV 399, $r C major. $f 1988.
700	12	Vivaldi, Antonio, $d 1678–1741. $t Concertos, $m violoncello, bassoon, string orchestra, $n RV 409, $r E minor. $f 1988.
700	12	Vivaldi, Antonio, $d 1678–1741. $t Concertos, $m violoncello, string orchestra, $n RV 538, $r D minor. $f 1988.
710	2	Toronto Chamber Orchestra.

Discussion for Figure 3.5

- Fixed field: Code "j" for Type indicates a musical recording; code "m" for BLvl stands for a nonserial recording; FMus (format of music) has the default value of "n" because this item is not a print music or music manuscript; Comp (form of composition) is "co" for concertos; LTxt (literary text) is "blank" for musical recordings. The item has one publication date, 1988.

- 007: Subfields common to compact discs are included. $a is "s" for sound recordings; $b is "d" for sound discs; $d is "f" (1.4 m. per sec.) for compact digital discs; $e is "s" for stereo; $f (groove width) is "n" for not applicable; $g is "g" (4¾ in.) for the dimensions of CD; $h (tape width) and $i (tape configuration) are "n" for not applicable; $m is "e" for digital recording indicating the item needs digital playback equipment; and $n is "d" for an item that is captured and stored using digital techniques.

- 028: Publisher's number is entered in subfield $a, and the label is in subfield $b.

- 090 and 092: M1117 is for string orchestra with a single instrument. 784.274 is for violoncello with orchestra.

- 100: Vivaldi is the composer of these musical works and is therefore selected as the main entry.

- 240: A uniform title is created to bring recordings of various selections of Vivaldi's cello concertos together.

- 246: The source of the variant title is entered in subfield $i and the variant title is entered in subfield $a. The first indicator, "1", specifies a note and a title added entry will be generated from this field, and the blank second indicator is used to display the text in subfield $i Title on container:

- 300: The total playing time is from the container and recorded here, but the playing time of each piece is recorded in the 505 content note below.

- 511: Performers are recorded and separated by semicolons.

- 518: The date and place of recording are recorded.

- 505: The contents note lists titles included in this work and includes playing time for each piece.

- 650: For instrumental music, subject headings are assigned for musical form, medium of performance, and performing group. When a recording includes more than one form, each form of presentation is assigned a heading.

- 700s: Added entries are created for principal performers. Following *LCRI* 21.29, the entries are arranged in the order in which the names appear in the bibliographic description.

- 700s: The name-title added analytical added entries are provided for each work in this collection. The uniform titles are created according to Chapter 25 of *AACR2r*, and rule 25.30 in particular. For musical work the typical pattern is: title, medium of performance, numerical identifying element, key. "Date" is the last element. The subfield codes can be found in *OCLC-MARC Code List*.

- 710: An added entry for the chamber music group, which is treated as a corporate body.

Figure 3.6. *Beauty and the beast*

Disc label:

Walt Disney PICTURES PRESENTS
Beauty and the Beast
Original Motion Picture Sound track

60618-2   Walt Disney
Music by Alan Menken   Records
Lyrics by Howard Ashman   p 1991 Buena Vista Pictures Distribution, Inc.
                                           ©1991 Walt Disney Music Company (ASCAP)/
                                           Wonderland Music Company, Inc.
Total time: 50:55   (BMI)

1. Prologue (2:27) 2. Belle (5:07) 3. Belle (reprise) (1:03) 4. Gaston (3:37) 5. Gaston (reprise) (2:01) 6. Be our guest (3:42) 7. Something there (2:16) 8. The mob song (3:28) 9. Beauty and the beast (2:44) 10. To the fair (1:55) 11. West wing (4:22) 12. The beast lets Belle go (2:19) 13. Battle on the tower (5:26) 14. Transformation (5:47) 15. Beauty and the beast (duet) (4:03).

II ©The Walt Disney company
Printed in U.S.A.

Type	j	ELvl	I	Srce	d	Audn		Ctrl	Lang	eng
BLvl	m	Form		Comp	mp	AccM		MRec	Ctry	cau
Desc	a	FMus	n	LTxt		DtSt	s	Dates	1991,	

007:		s $b d $d f $e u $f n $g g $h n $i n $m e $n d
028	02	60618-2 $b Walt Disney Records
090		M1505
092		782.14
100	1	Menken, Alan.
245	10	Walt Disney Pictures presents Beauty and the beast $h [sound recording] : $b original motion picture soundtrack / $c music by Alan Menken ; lyrics by Howard Ashman.
246	30	Beauty and the beast
260		Burbank, CA : $b Walt Disney Records : $b [distributed by] Buena Vista Pictures, $c p1991.
300		1 sound disc (50 min., 55 sec.) : $b digital ; $c 4 3/4 in.
511	0	Robby Benson as Beast; Paige O'Hara as Belle; end title duet "Beauty and the beast" performed by Celine Dion and Peabo Bryson.
500		Compact disc.
500		Program notes on insert.
505	0	Prologue (2:27) — Belle (5:07) — Belle (reprise) (1:03) — Gaston (3:37) — Gaston (reprise) (2:01) — Be our guest (3:42) — Something there (2:16) — The mob song (3:28) — Beauty and the beast (2:44) — To the fair (1:55) — West wing (4:22) — The beast lets Belle go (2:19) — Battle on the tower (5:26) — Transformation (5:47) — Beauty and the beast (duet) (4:03).
650	0	Motion picture music $v Excerpts.
700	1	Ashman, Howard.
700	1	Benson, Robby.
700	1	O'Hara, Paige.
700	1	Dion, Celine.
700	1	Bryson, Peabo.
730	0	Beauty and the beast (Motion picture : 1991)

Discussion for Figure 3.6

- Fixed field: Code "j" for Type indicates a musical recording; code "m" for BLvl stands for a nonserial recording; FMus (format of music) has the default value of "n" because this item is not a print music or music manuscript; Comp (form of composition) is "mp" for motion picture music; LTxt (literary text) is "blank" for musical recordings. The item has one publication date, 1991.

- 007: $a is "s" for sound recordings; $b is "d" for sound discs; $d is "f" (1.4 m. per sec.) for compact digital discs; $e is "u" indicating no information on the configuration of playback channels; $f (groove width) is "n" for not applicable; $g is "g" (4 ¾ in.) for the dimensions of CD; $h (tape width) and $i (tape configuration) are "n" for not applicable; $m is "e" for digital recording indicating the item needs digital playback equipment; and $n is "d" for an item that is captured and stored using digital techniques.

- 028: Publisher's number is entered in subfield $a, and the label is in subfield $b.

- 090 and 092: M1505 is for vocal music excerpts for a movie; 782.14 is for musical plays.

- 245: Record the wording of the title proper as presented on the disc label. Separate the first statement of responsibility from the second one by a semicolon.

- 246: A variant title is made because this title is better known than the title proper. Indicator "3" will produce an added entry but not a note, indicator "0" explains the variant title as part of the title proper.

- 260: Place of publication is on the container. Information on the distributor is entered into a separate subfield $b.

- 511: Performers are listed in the program notes; only the principal performers are included.

- 505: The total playing time of the disc is included in field 300, and the duration of each song is listed in the contents note.

- 700s: Personal name added entries are made for all named performers and the entries are arranged in the order in which the names appear in the bibliographic description.

- 730: A uniform title for the motion picture is used to link this work to the original movie for users.

Figure 3.7. Winnie-the-Pooh audio boxed set

Item label:

BBC RADIO PRESENTS:
Winnie-the-Pooh and
The House at Pooh Corner
A. A. Milne

BDD   PART
AUDIO   ONE
....
SIDE
ONE
© 1984 BBC Enterprises, Ltd.   BBC047A
© 1992 BBC Enterprises, Ltd.
All rights reserved
Manufactured in USA   **DOLBY SYSTEM**

Container (front)

_B B C_
AUDIO PRESENTS
Winnie-the-Pooh
Audio Boxed Set

A. A. Milne

Performances by
Alan Bennett, Richard Briers and Felicity Kendal

Container (back)
4 cassettes
$22.00 U.S.
$29.95 IN CANADA
ISBN 0-553-47866-4
[UPC code] 9 780553 478662   DISTRIBUTED UNDER EXCLUSIVE LICENSE
FROM BBC WORLDWIDE LTD.
_B B C_ © **_1988_**
RUNNING TIME: 300 Minutes
© 1992, 1994, 1996 BBC WORLDWIDE LTD.
(p) 1984, 1994, 1996 BBC WORLDWIDE LTD.
BANTAM DOUBLEDAY DELL AUDIO PUBLISHING,
A DIVISION OF BANTAM DOUBLEDAY DELL
PUBLISHING GROUP, INC. 1540 BROADWAY,
NEW YORK, NEW YORK 10036

Type	i	ELvl	I	Srce	d	Audn		Ctrl		Lang	eng
BLvl	m	Form		Comp	nn	AccM		MRec		Ctry	nyu
Desc	a	FMus	n	LTxt	f	DtSt	r	Dates		1996, 1984	

007		s $b s $d l $e u $f n $g j $h l $i c $m c $n e
020		0553478664
024	3	9780553478662
028	00	BBC 047A $b BDD Audio
028	00	BBC 047B $b BDD Audio
028	00	BBC 068A $b BDD Audio
028	00	BBC 068B $b BDD Audio
090		PZ7
092		813
100	1	Milne, A. A. $q (Alan Alexander), $d 1882–1956.
245	10	Winne-the-Pooh audio boxed set $h [sound recording] / $c A.A. Milne.
260		New York, N.Y.: $b BDD Audio, $c p1996.
300		4 sound cassettes (300 min.) : $b analog, Dolby processed.
500		Title from container.
500		At head of title: BBC presents.
505	00	$t Winnie-the-Pooh — $t House at Pooh Corner — $t Party for Pooh — $t When we were very young — $t Now we are six.
511	0	Read by Alan Bennett, Richard Briers, and Felicity Kendal.
500		BDD Audio: BBC 047A, BBC 047B, BBC 068A, BBC 068B
650	0	Winnie-the-Pooh (Fictitious character) $v Juvenile sound recordings.
650	0	Animals $v Juvenile sound recordings.
650	0	Bears $v Juvenile sound recordings.
650	0	Children's audiobooks.
700	1	Bennett, Alan, $d 1934-
700	1	Briers, Richard.
700	1	Kendal, Felicity.

Discussion of Figure 3.7

- Fixed field: Code "i" for Type indicates a nonmusical recording; code "m" for BLvl stands for a nonserial recording; FMus (format of music) has the default value of "n" because this item is not a print music or music manuscript; Comp (form of composition) is "nn" for nonmusical recordings; LTxt (literary text) is "f" for fiction. The item was previously published in 1984, so DtSt (type of date) is "r" for reissue of an item that has a previous published existence. Code "r" is used for reissues of sound recordings in the same medium or different medium. The code has been coordinated with the DATES element, with the reissue date in Date 1 and date of original in Date 2.

- 007 field: Subfields common to sound cassettes are included. $a is "s" for sound recordings; $b is "s" for sound cassettes; $d is "l" (1 $\frac{7}{8}$ ips) for standard cassettes; $e is "u" for no information about the playback channels; $f "groove width" is "n" for not applicable to tapes; $g is "j" (3 $\frac{7}{8}$ × 2 $\frac{1}{2}$ in.) for the standard dimensions of a cassette; $h is "l" for $\frac{1}{8}$ inch, the standard tape width for cassettes; $i is "c" for quarter track used for standard cassettes; $m is "c" for standard Dolby encoding; $n is "e" for analog recording.

- 020, 024, and 028: ISBN and the UPC code are recorded in field 020 and field 024 respectively. Field 028 is for publisher's number. When the numbers are nonconsecutive, the cataloger has the option of repeating the 028 field for the numbers. The second indicator value could be 2 or 0. Value "2" would produce a note, while "0" would suppress the note. If the cataloger chooses to use value "0", then the numbers should be recorded in a 500 note for it to be presented as a note.

- 245: The collective title comes from the container and the source of the title is recorded in a 500 note below.

- 300: The number of special material designation and the sound characteristics are recorded but not the size of the cassettes, which is standard.

- 500: The cassette label and the container label both carry "BBC presents" at the top of title, so it is noted in a 500 field.

- 505: An enhanced contents note is provided by entering each work in a subfield $t. This will enable an online catalog to search these titles if the system administrators and catalogers decide to do so.

- 650s: Winnie-the-Pooh, the fictitious character, and the themes are used as topical headings, followed by the form subdivision "Juvenile sound recordings."

- 700s: Performers are traced by the 700 fields.

- 700s: If the cataloger chooses to, an option is to provide name-title added entries for the six works that are part of this package. The name-title added entry would be presented according to this pattern:

700	12	Milne, A. A. $q (Alan Alexander), $d 1882–1956. $t Winnie-the-Pooh.
700	12	Milne, A. A. $q (Alan Alexander), $d 1882–1956. $t House at Pooh Corner.

Figure 3.8. Trilogy

Disc information:
09026-61228-2

RCA VICTOR
RED SEAL

p 1993, BMG Music
TMK(S) ® G.E. Co., USA
& BMG Music
Made in U.S.A.

BOCCHERINI
1-3 Concerto for Cello and Orchestra
in B-Flat
MYSLIVECEK
4-6 Concerto for Cello
and Orchestra in C
VIOTTI
7-9 Concerto for Cello and
Orchestra in C

OFRA HARNOY
TRILOGY

BOCCHERINI . MYSLIVECEK . VIOTTI
I SOLISTI VENETI
CLAUDIO SCIMONE
conductor

Type	j	ELvl	I	Srce	d	Audn		Ctrl		Lang		eng
BLvl	m	Form		Comp	co	AccM		MRec		Ctry		nyu
Desc	a	FMus	n	LTxt		DtSt	p	Dates	1993, 1991			

007:		s $b d $d f $e s $f n $g g $h n $i n $m e $n d
028	02	09026-61228-2 $b RCA Victor Red Seal
090		M1117
092		784.274
100	1	Harnoy, Ofra, $d 1965-
245	10	Trilogy $h [sound recording] / $c Ofra Harnoy.
260		New York, NY : $b BMG Music, $c p1993.
300		1 sound disc (63 min., 13 sec.) : $b digital, stereo ; $c 4 3/4 in.
511	0	Ofra Harnoy, cello; I Solisti Veniti; Claudio Scimone, conductor.
518		Recorded digitally on June 4, 6 & 7, 1991, in La Chiesa di San Francesco in Schio, Italy.
500		Compact disc.
500		Program notes on insert.
505	0	Concerto for cello and orchestra in B-flat / Boccherini (20:16) — Concerto for cello and orchestra in C / Myslivecek (19:06) — Concerto for cello and orchestra in C / Viotti (23:41).
650	0	Concertos (Violoncello with orchestra).
700	1	Scimone, Claudio.
700	12	Boccherini, Luigi, $d 1743-1805. $t Concertos, $m violoncello, orchestra, $n G. 482, $r B-flat major. $f 1993.
700	12	Myslivecek, Josef, $d 1737-1781. $t Concertos, $m violoncello, orchestra, $r C major. $f 1993.
700	12	Viotti, Giovanni Battista, $d 1755-1824. $t Concertos, $m violoncello, orchestra, $r C major. $f 1993.
710	2	I Solisti Veneti.

Discussion for Figure 3.8

- Fixed field: Code "j" for Type indicates a musical recording; code "m" for BLvl stands for a nonserial recording; FMus (format of music) has the default value of "n" because this item is not a print music or music manuscript; Comp (form of composition) is "co" for concertos; LTxt (literary text) is "blank" for musical recordings. The item became available in 1993 but the recording session took place in 1991, so DtSt is coded "p" and Date 1 of DATES is 1993, while Date 2 is used for the year of recording, 1991.

- 007: Subfields common to compact discs are included. $a is "s" for sound recordings; $b is "d" for sound discs; $d is "f" (1.4 m. per sec.) for compact digital discs; $e is "s" for stereo; $f (groove width) is "n" for not applicable; $g is "g" (4 ¾ in.) for the dimensions of CD; $h (tape width) and $i (tape configuration) are "n" for not applicable; $m is "e" for digital recording indicating the item needs digital playback equipment; and $n is "d" for an item that is captured and stored using digital techniques.

- 100: The recording has a collective title and contains the works of three composers. According to rule 21.23C1, the recording is entered under the principal performer, Ofra Harnoy.

- 300: The total playing time is included in the 300 field. If desired, the cataloger may add a 306 field, with the content "006313", to encode the playing time.

- 511: Performers are noted.

- 518: The recording date and site are from the program notes.

- 505: The duration of each work is from the program notes.

- 650: For instrumental music, a subject heading for the form of music is assigned.

- 700s: An added entry is provided for the conductor. Name-title analytical added entries are provided for the composers to make the individual works searchable. If desired, the cataloger may make the title of each work searchable by presenting each in a 740 field, with an indicator value "2."

- 710: An added entry is provided for the performing group.

Figure 3.9. *Fantasia*

Cassette label:

Walt Disney's FANTASIA
Leopold Stokowski and the Philadelphia Orchestra
REMASTERED ORIGINAL SOUNDTRACK EDITION

VOL. 1   600074
SIDE 1
DOLBY SYSTEM
Printed in U.S.A.

Toccata and Fugue in D Minor (John Sebastian Bach) *
The Sorcerer's Apprentice (Paul Dukas) * The Nutcracker Suite
(Peter Ilich Tchaikovsky)
© The Walt Disney Company p 1990 Buena Vista Pictures
Distribution, Inc.

Type	j	**ELvl**	I	**Srce**	d	**Audn**		**Ctrl**		**Lang**	eng
BLvl	m	**Form**		**Comp**	mp	**AccM**		**MRec**		**Ctry**	cau
Desc	a	**FMus**	n	**LTxt**		**DtSt**	r	**Dates**		1990,1940	

007:		s $b s $d l $e u $f n $g j $h l $i c $m c $n e
090		M1527
092		784.21542
110	2	Philadelphia Orchestra.
245	10	Walt Disney's Fantasia $h [sound recording] / $c Leopold Stokowski and the Philadelphia Orchestra.
246	30	Fantasia
250		Remastered original soundtrack ed.
260		Burbank, CA : $b Buena Vista, $c p1990.
300		2 sound cassettes : $b analog, Dolby processed.
500		Program notes by David R. Smith.
511	0	Philadelphia Orchestra ; Leopold Stokowski, conductor.
500		Originally released in 1940.
505	0	Toccata and fugue in D minor / Bach — The sorcerer's apprentice / Dukas — The nutcracker suite / Tchaikovsky — Symphony no. 6 "Pastoral" / Beethoven — Rite of spring / Stravinsky — Dance of the hours / Ponchielli — A night on Bald Mountain / Moussorgsky — Ave Maria, op. 52, no. 6 / Schubert.
650	0	Motion picture music.
650	0	Orchestra music.
700	1	Stokowski, Leopold, $d 1882-1977.
730	0	Fantasia (Motion picture)

Discussion for Figure 3.9

- Fixed field: Code "j" for Type indicates a musical recording; code "m" for BLvl stands for a nonserial recording; FMus (format of music) has the default value of "n" because this item is not a print music or music manuscript; Comp (form of composition) is "mp" for motion picture music; LTxt (literary text) is "blank" for musical recordings. The item is a re-release of the same information, so DtSt (type of publication date) is "r", the reissue date is recorded as Date 1, and the original release date as Date 2 for the DATES element.

- 007: $a is "s" for sound recordings; $b is "s" for sound cassettes; $d is "l" ($1\frac{7}{8}$ ips) for standard cassettes; $e is "u" for no information about the playback channels; $f "groove width" is "n" for not applicable to tapes; $g is "j" ($3\frac{7}{8} \times 2\frac{1}{2}$ in.) for the standard dimensions of a cassette; $h is "l" for $\frac{1}{8}$ inch, the standard tape width for cassettes; $i is "c" for quarter track used for standard cassettes; $m is "c" for standard Dolby encoding; $n is "e" for analog recording.

- 090 and 092: M1527 is for specific sound track movie. 784.21542 is built from 784.2 for orchestra music and 1542 for film music.

- 110: The orchestra is selected as the main entry, according to rule 21.23C1.

- 245: Record the information as instructed in rule 1.1B1.

- 246: A variant title added entry is provided to lead users to this item. This added entry is necessary because the title proper is not as well known as this variant title.

- 250: Record the exact edition statement except for the use of the abbreviation "ed."

- 511: The performing body and individuals are recorded.

- 500: The history of the movie and the music is from the program notes.

- 505: Contents of the item are taken from the cassettes. The titles are listed in the order of their appearance in the item; only the last names of the composers are included because these are well-known composers.

- 700: Conductor is traced.

- 730: A uniform title added entry link this item to the original movie.

Figure 3.10. *The Caedmon treasury of modern poets*

Cassette label: Frost, Williams, Stevens, Eberhart, Pound & Wilbur
THE CAEDMON TREASURY OF MODERN POETS
Read by Each Respective Author

Caedmon   Side 1
CPN 2006   25:35
© 1957 HarperCollins Publishers, Inc., 10 East 53rd Street,
New York, N.Y. 10022. All rights reserved.
Made in the U.S.A. DOLBY SYSTEM®

[Sides 2-4 have the same information except the durations:
Side 2: 22:50 Side 3: 24:50 Side 4: 22:13]
Case insert: Library of Congress card #: R57-256
Copyright © 1957, 1988 Caedmon, 1995 Broadway, New York,
N.Y. 10023

Type	i	ELvl	I	Srce	d	Audn		Ctrl		Lang	eng
BLvl	m	Form		Comp	nn	AccM		MRec		Ctry	nyu
Desc	a	FMus	n	LTxt	p	DtSt	r	Dates	1988, 1957		

007:		s $b s $d l $e u $f n $g j $h l $i c $m c $n e
010		r57-256
020		0694503703
028	02	CPN 2006 $b Caedmon
090		PR1225
092		821.91
245	04	The Caedmon treasury of modern poets $h [sound recording]
246	1	$i Title on container: $a Modern poets reading their own poetry
260		New York, N.Y. : $b Caedmon, $c c1988.
300		2 sound cassettes (1 hr., 35 min.) : $b analog, Dolby processed..
518		Originally recorded in 1957.
500		In one container.
520		Twenty-seven poems, read by each respective author, by T. S. Eliot, W.B. Yeats, W.H. Auden, Dylan Thomas, Louis MacNeice, Robert Graves, Gertrude Stein, Archibald MacLeish, e.e. cummings, Marianne Moore, William Empson, Stephen Spender, Conrad Aiken, Robert Frost, William Carlos Williams, Wallace Stevens, Richard Eberhart and Ezra Pound.
650	0	American poetry $y 20th century.
650	0	English poetry $y 20th century

Discussion for Figure 3.10

- Fixed field: Code "i" for Type indicates a nonmusical recording; code "m" for BLvl stands for a nonserial recording; FMus (format of music) has the default value of "n" because this item is not a print music or music manuscript; Comp (form of composition) is "nn" for nonmusical recordings; LTxt (literary text) is "p" for poetry. The item was previously released in 1957, so DtSt (date type) is "r", the reissue date is recorded as Date 1 and the original date as Date 2 for the DATES element.

- 007: $a is "s" for sound recordings; $b is "s" for sound cassettes; $d is "l" ($1\frac{7}{8}$ ips) for standard cassettes; $e is "u" for no information about the playback channels; $f "groove width" is "n" for not applicable to tapes; $g is "j" ($3\frac{7}{8} \times 2\frac{1}{2}$ in.) for the standard dimensions of a cassette; $h is "l" for $\frac{1}{8}$ inch, the standard tape width for cassettes; $i is "c" for quarter track used for standard cassettes; $m is "c" for standard Dolby encoding; $n is "e" for analog recording.

- 010: This field is for Library of Congress card number.

- 020: The ISBN is from the back of the container.

- 090 and 092: PR1225 refers to twentieth century English poetry general work. 821.91 is built from 821 (English poetry) and 91 is for the period 1900–1999.

- 245: This item is entered under its title because it contains works by several authors, and no principal author can be identified.

- 246: The title on the container is different from the title proper, so indicator "1" is used to generate a note and a title added entry. Subfield $i indicates the source of this title, and subfield $a records the title.

- 500: This note indicates the two cassettes are in one container.

- 520: This note summarizes the contents and the nature of the recording.

- 650: This is a collection of works, so form headings are assigned. But the subdivision "—Collection" is not used because it is not a free-floating subdivision and can only be used with very few headings such as Drama, Literature, and Poetry.

References

American Library Association. Subcommittee on Subject Access to Individual Works of Fiction, Drama, Etc. (1990). *Guidelines on subject access to individual works of fiction, drama, etc.* Chicago: American Library Association.

Bibliographic Formats and Standards. (2003). http://www.oclc.org/bibformats/ (accessed June 1, 2005).

Chan, Lois Mai. (1995). *Library of Congress subject headings: Principles and applications* (2nd ed.). Englewood, Colo.: Libraries Unlimited.

Freeborn, Robert B. (2002, September 27–29). Cataloging digital sound files: *AACR2* chapters 6 and 9. *OLAC Conference, Electronic and Media Cataloging for the 21st Century.* St. Paul, Minn. http://elibrary.unm.edu/catdept/training/digitalsoundfiles.ppt (accessed June 1, 2005).

Kaye, Alan L. (1991). *Video and other nonprint resources in the small library.* Chicago: Library Administration and Management Association, American Library Association.

MARC 21 concise format. (2004). http://www.loc.gov/marc/bibliographic/ecbdhome.html (accessed June 1, 2005).

Weihs, Jean. (1991). *The integrated library.* Phoenix, Ariz.: Oryx Press.

Suggested Readings

ACRL Media Resources Committee. (1999, April). Guidelines for media resources in academic libraries. *College and Research Libraries News* 60: 294–302.

Freeborn, Robert B. (2001). Cataloging non-music sound recordings. *Cataloging & Classification Quarterly* 31 (2): 37–51.

Freeborn, Robert B. (2002, September 27–29). Cataloging digital sound files: *AACR2* chapters 6 and 2. *OLAC Conference, Electronic and Media Cataloging for the 21st Century.* St. Paul, Minn. http://elibrary.unm.edu/catdept/training/digitalsoundfiles.ppt (accessed June 1, 2005).

Simpkins, Terry. (2001). Cataloging popular music recordings. *Cataloging & Classification Quarterly* 31 (2): 1–35.

4

Videorecordings

Creators of videos have drawn on literature, music, history, science, philosophy, religion, biographies, and many other topics to provide entertainment and enlightenment. A large number of videos are available commercially, many of them based on previously released movies. Another type of video is locally produced, usually in relation to special events or research projects, and intended for local users instead of the mass market. Videos of commencement speeches are an example. Several formats for videos have emerged over the years due to advances in technology. Depending on the purposes of their projects, creators have used U-Matic, VHS, laser disc, CD-ROM, and DVD as video formats. In recent years the DVD has become the dominant format, thanks to promotion by the movie and television industries. It has much more storage capacity than the VHS format, offers the flexibility of random access that allows viewers to select scenes and features of interest, and can be viewed on properly equipped computers or televisions. As a result, DVDs have become part of library collections.

AACR2r Chapter 7 presents rules for the description of motion pictures and videos of all kinds, including complete films, trailers, newscasts, and many others. It covers formats such as film cartridge, film cassette, video cassette, and videodisc. The rules have remained fairly stable over time. An important recent update is the option to use conventional terminology (such as DVD) to describe the physical carrier (rule 7.5B1). The DVD format involves additional technical details and video creators often take advantage of the DVD's storage capacity to include more materials on DVDs than on VHS formats. Catalogers will want to consult an important document from the Online Audiovisual Catalogers, Inc. (OLAC), *Guide to Cataloging DVDs Using AACR2r Chapters 7 and 9* (http://www.olacinc.org/capc/dvd/dvdprimer0.html), which provides helpful explanations and examples for the description of DVDs. For an explanation of DVD technology, readers will find "DVD Frequently Asked Questions (and Answers)" (http://www.dvddemystified.com/dvdfaq.html) helpful. It is part of the DVD Demystified Web site.

The focus of this chapter is on videorecordings on VHS tapes, video-discs, and DVDs. Rule discussion draws on *AACR2r* Chapter 7, the OLAC DVD guidelines, and MARC 21. Examples are of videos often available in public libraries.

Challenges in Describing Videorecordings

Like the treatment of print resources, the cataloging of videos involves taking data from the chief and prescribed sources for the description of eight areas, assigning access points, and the analysis of subject contents. Major challenges for cataloging videos include

1. Video producers do not present information in a standard manner, which often makes it difficult for catalogers to determine where the title frames begin and end. The lack of standard presentation means that catalogers must check beginning frames and closing frames to make sure appropriate information is included in the description.

2. Video production often involves many people. The authorship is so diffuse that it can be difficult to select access points.

3. Containers of videos usually present a great deal of information and some of the information is different from the information on the video, making it necessary for catalogers to determine what to record and how to reconcile the differences.

4. Some videos are now presented on videodiscs or DVDs and require special equipment for viewing. Remote access videos such as streaming videos require special plug-ins that may need to be downloaded from the Internet.

5. Production information is usually provided, and catalogers often have to make a judgment call on what types of notes to provide for this type of information. The subject analysis of videos also requires a slight variation in how subject headings are assigned, which makes it difficult for catalogers not familiar with the use of format and genre headings.

These challenges can be addressed through a careful examination of the video and its container. Videorecordings tend to contain plenty of information. To assist readers in finding information useful for cataloging purposes, the next section describes areas with pertinent information.

Technical Reading of Videorecordings

Title frames and end credits frames: These areas usually provide information on the people involved in the creation of the videorecording, including production firm, title proper, producers, directors, lead actors, supporting actors, and technical staff. *LCRI* 7.1F1 instructs catalogers to keep in mind that only people with "overall responsibility" for the work should be included in the statement of responsibility area (field 245, $c). These people will also be assigned as access points. In addition, lead actors will be recorded in field 511, while important technical staff will be recorded in field 508. These names are usually used as added entry headings.

Container label: This area often presents information on title, production firm, distributor, catalog number, series information, playing time, rating, sound, and copyright information. The information on the label can be useful for fields 245, 028, 260, and 300.

Box or case of the videorecording: Because the box or case is not the preferred chief source of information, information found in these places should be verified in the chief source. Nevertheless, this area usually presents important information about the video that can be used to speed up the cataloging process. For example, for film videos, the lower back of a box/case usually presents information that is almost identical to that presented on the title and credit frames. Producer, distributor, rating, sound, captioning, and playing time are usually included in this area also. In the front of the box/case, lead actors are usually listed. The spine of the box has publisher information and stock number. This information is typically recorded in field 028.

Although the information in this area cannot be transcribed without verification, it does provide catalogers a short list of very important data. If these data are verified in the prescribed sources, they should be transcribed. If there is discrepancy, then the data in the prescribed sources are used.

DVD main menu: The latest medium, DVD, usually has a main menu that presents choices to viewers. The "CAST" entry can be used to verify people responsible for the work. Lead characters, director, screenplay writers, and other key people are usually listed here. Important cast members are recorded in field 511, while technical staff are entered in field 508.

The "Language" entry usually lists the languages in which the video is dubbed, subtitled, or captioned. This information is transcribed in field 546. The main menu often also includes special features such as a documentary about the film, the director's commentary, interviews with lead actors, or games. Such information could be recorded in field 500 or field 505, if considered important.

Similar to the box/case of a film video, the back of a DVD box often has the information presented on the DVD's main menu. This can speed up the process of cataloging. This area tends to include information on rating, color, playing time, sound characteristics, and closed-captioning.

Circumstances for New Records

Because videos are often based on materials that were published or released before, a major issue catalogers need to consider is when to create a new bibliographic record. *Differences Between Changes Within*, an ALCTS (Association for Library Collections and Technical Services) publication, specifies when new records should be prepared (2005). OCLC's input guidelines also offer advice on when to enter new records (2003). Weitz (2001) identifies a number of situations when a new record is appropriate: (1) if the video in hand is a colorized version of a black-and-white original; (2) if the new video has sound added to a silent video; (3) if the recording format is different (e.g., original film vs. VHS); (4) if the new video is a different language version (e.g., an English version vs. a Spanish version of *Wuthering Heights*); (5) if the new video is dubbed or subtitled but the original version is not; and (6) if the new video and the earlier version are different in length (e.g., the version of *The Return of the King* with more than fifty minutes of additional footage). Occasionally, a new video may not list all of the original publishers or distributors who are recorded in an existing bibliographic record for the original work, but if it has at least one of the publishers or distributors in the record, no new record should be created.

MARC Fields for Videorecordings

In creating bibliographic records for videos, catalogers will choose code "g" for Type and use the 008 field for video. The MARC fields commonly used to encode videorecordings are presented below. MARC 21 Web site (2004) and *OCLC Bibliographic Formats and Standards* (2003) explain the usage of these fields.

Field	Indicators	Subfields
007		$a $b $d $e $f $g $h $i
020		ISBN
024	—	Universal Product Number
028	— —	$a numbering $b production firm
041	—	languages $a $b $g $e $h
245	— —	Title $h [videorecording] / $c statement of people responsible for the overall production of the video.
246	— —	Title variation
250		Edition statement.
260		Place of publication : $b Publisher, $c Date of publication.
300		No. of specific material designation (playing time) : $b sound, color ; $c dimensions.
4X0	— —	Series statement
500		Nature and scope.
538		Technical information (e.g., VHS hi-fi)
511	—	Cast members.
508		Creation/production credits.
546		Languages.
521	—	Audience, rating.
520		Summary.
6XX	— —	Subject headings.
700	—	Personal name added entries. Performers, contributors, etc.
710	—	Corporate body added entries. Production firm, distributor, etc.
730	—	Related corporate body (e.g., American experience [Television program])
740	— —	Analytical title added entry.

Fixed Field

The fixed field consists of the following elements:

Type	g	ELvl	—	Srce	—	Audn	—	Ctrl		Lang	—
BLvl	m	Form		GPub	—	Time	—	MRec		Ctry	—
Desc	a	TMat	—	Tech	—	DtSt	—	Dates	Date 1	Date 2	

Mandatory elements include, in alphabetical order, BLvl, Dates, Desc, DtSt, ELvl, GPub, Lang, Srce, Time, TMat, and Type. Required elements, elements that should be provided if appropriate, are Ctrl, Ctry, Form, and MRec. Optional elements include Audn and Tech. The table below clarifies the usage of a few elements that are often used for video recordings.

Elements	*Commonly Used Codes*
Audn	
Target audience	For musical recordings this code identifies music used or performed by a specific audience group. For nonmusical recordings the code represents reading-grade or interest-age information recorded in field 521. If both types of information are in field 521, the code should represent the interest-age information. When a work is appropriate for more than one target audience, the code will stand for the primary audience group.
DtSt	
Type of date	Code "s" represents a single date of distribution, publication, release, production, execution, or writing. If the content of a videorecording has changed, such as change in length or addition of special features, code "s" would be appropriate.
	Code "p" represents the date of distribution/release/issue. A videorecording is coded "p" for DtSt if the content remains the same as that of the original motion picture or TV program. In such cases, catalogers will use Date 1 for the new release and Date 2 for the original release date.
	Code "r" is for reissues of videorecordings in the same medium without any changes in content or addition of special features. Catalogers will coordinate this code with DATES, using Date 1 for the reprint/reissue date and Date 2 for the date of original release.
Dates	
Date1 and Date2	Date 1 is based on subfield $c of field 260 and can be system-supplied. The element is coordinated with the DtSt element.
Tech	
Technique	The technique used to create motion for motion picture and videos. Code "a" is for animation. Code "c" is for animation and live action. Code "l" is for live action. It is also used when technique is NOT stated explicitly and cannot be determined.
Time	
Total playing time	Total running time is entered in a three-digit format. For example, 1 hour 20 minutes will be recorded as 080.
TMat	
Type of material	Code "v" is always used for videorecordings.

007 Videorecording Field

This field is required for all videorecordings. It has eight subfields; code values are available from the MARC 21 site (2004) and OCLC Input Standard site (2003).

007	$a category of material $b specific material designation $d color $e format $f sound $g medium of sound $h dimensions $i playback channel configuration

Examples:

A videocassette in color, VHS format, with stereo sound

007    $a v (video) $b f (cassette) $d c (colored) $e b (VHS) $f a (sound on medium) $g h (videotape) $h o (dimensions) $i s (stereo)

A videodisc in black and white, VHS format, with Dolby surround

007    $a v (video) $b d (videodisc) $d b (B&W) $e b (VHS) $f a (sound on medium) $g i (videodisc) $h z (dimensions) $i q (surround)

Description

Rules for Descriptive Cataloging

Chief Source of Information

AACR2r states that the chief source of information for videos is the item itself (such as the title frames and credit frames), or the container label if the container is an integral part of a video. If the information needed for description does not appear in these sources, catalogers will take it from the following sources, in order of preference: accompanying textual material, container (if not an integral part of the item), and other sources. If any of these sources is used, the source of the title proper should be given in a note (field 500).

[title frame]:   **LENNON** **LEGEND** [accompanying material]: **LENNON** **LEGEND** The Very Best of John Lennon

Transcribed as:

245	10	Lennon legend $h [videorecording] : $b the very best of John Lennon.
246	30	Legend
500		Title from accompanying material.

Since the information on the accompanying material is more complete, it is transcribed for the title field. When the title proper is not taken from the preferred chief source (i.e., title frame), a note is provided to clarify this practice.

Prescribed Sources of Information

The prescribed sources of information for each of the seven areas of the description of videorecordings are as follows:

Area	*Prescribed Sources of Information*
Area 1 (field 245)	Chief source of information
Area 2 (field 250) Area 4 (field 260) Area 6 (field 4X0)	Chief source of information, accompanying material, container
Area 5 (field 300) Area 7 (field 5XX) Area 8 (field 02X)	Any source

Information taken from nonprescribed sources should be recorded in square brackets.

7.1. Title and Statement of Responsibility (MARC Field 245)

The title proper of a video is transcribed in the same way as specified by rule 1.1B1. Catalogers are to copy the wording, spelling, and order of the title proper, but not necessarily the punctuation and capitalization. A common challenge in transcribing the title proper is that the title frames are usually preceded or followed by the names of the production company, producers, performers, and so on. *LCRI* 7.1B1 (CSB 13) recommends that these names not be considered part of the title proper. When the beginning screen of the video looks as follows:

ORION HOME VIDEO

AN ORION PICTURES RELEASE

A STRONG HEART/DEMME PRODUCTION

JODIE FOSTER

ANTHONY HOPKINS

SCOTT GLENN

THE SILENCE OF THE LAMBS

TED LEVINE . . .

SCREENPLAY BY

TED TALLY

PRODUCED BY

EDWARD SAXON

KENNETH UTT

RON BOZMAN

DIRECTED BY

JONATHAN DEMME

The title proper is transcribed as:

| 245 | 04 | The silence of the lambs $h [videorecording] |

Similarly, if a video begins with "So and so present," this phrase is in general not considered part of the title proper.

Warner Home Video

Warner Bros-Seven Arts

present

A Phil Feldman Production

The Wild Bunch

William Holden . . .

Title proper is transcribed as

| 245 | 04 | The wild bunch $h [videorecording] |

If a parallel title appears in the chief source, it is transcribed after the general material designation.

245	00	Como agua para chocolate $h [videorecording] = $b Like water for chocolate

If different titles appear outside the chief source and are considered important, catalogers may use field 246 to generate a note and/or make a variant title added entry. For example,

[on title frame]

Dr. Seuss

Green Eggs and Ham

[DVD case cover and spine]

Green Eggs and Ham PLUS 2 MORE SEUSS STORIES

If the cataloger feels this title is important for access and would like to make the other two stories searchable, the following fields could be used:

246	14	Green eggs and ham plus 2 more Seuss stories [Code "1" for Indicator 1 specifies a note and a title added entry will be generated from this field. Code "4" for Indicator 2 will generate "Cover title:" as the display text for this note. The note will read: **Cover title: Green eggs and ham plus 2 more Seuss stories**]
505	0	Green eggs and ham — Ten apples up on top! — The tooth book. [Contents note list the three stories.]
740	02	Ten apples up on top!
740	42	The tooth book [740 provides analytical title added entries.]

For videos without a collective title, rule 7.1G1 instructs that catalogers can describe the unit as a unit or make a separate description for each separately titled part. *LCRI* recommends that the unit be treated as a unit (*LCRI* 7.1G1). Rule 7.1G2 instructs catalogers to transcribe the titles of the parts per rule 1.1G3, and rule 7.1G3 says catalogers may add a word or short phrase to make clear the relationship between the individual titles and statements of responsibility. For example, on the following video two stories are presented in sequence and the video does not carry a collective title. On the DVD label the following information appears:

WHAT A LOVELY THING TO SEE—

A DOUBLE FEATURE DVD!

Dr. Seuss	**P. D. Eastman**
One fish two fish red fish blue fish	Are You My Mother?

The first title and statement of responsibility will be transcribed as follows, and the second title and the related statement of responsibility are recorded as uncontrolled analytical entry in field 740. Value "0" for the first indicator of field 740 indicates no initial article character positions are disregarded, and value "2" for the second indicator explains the item contains the work represented by the added entry.

100	1	Seuss, $c Dr.
245	10	One fish, two fish, red fish, blue fish $h [videorecording] / Dr. Seuss. Are you my mother? / P.D. Eastman.
740	02	Are you my mother?

General material designation (GMD): The GMD for videos is "videorecording" regardless of the type of physical carrier. So VHS videos and DVDs will have the same GMD. But when the video is accessed remotely, such as streaming video, the item is considered an electronic resource, and its GMD is "electronic resource" instead of "videorecording." This treatment is consistent with the treatment of remote access digitized audio files, which also use "electronic resource" as GMD.

Statement of responsibility: The production of a video usually involves many individuals. *LCRI* 7.1F1 indicates that only person(s) or body(bodies) with *overall responsibility for the work* should be entered in the statement of responsibility area. People in this category typically include producers, directors, and writers. People responsible for one part or aspect of the work are covered by notes. In the *Silence of the Lambs* example below, actors with major roles are recorded in a note, while the screenplay writer, the producers, and the director are entered in Area 1.

Another common practice of film and video producers is to present credit information at the end of the product. That's why it is important that

245	04	The silence of the lambs $h [videorecording] / $c Orion Pictures ; screenplay by Ted Tally ; produced by Edward Saxon, Kenneth Utt, Ron Bozman ; directed by Jonathan Demme.
511	1	Jodie Foster, Anthony Hopkins, Scott Glenn.

catalogers check the beginning and closing frames of a video for relevant credit information.

[Title frame]: **Pathways**

to Better Living with Arthritis

and related conditions

[End credits]

Produced for the

Arthritis Foundation by

MOBILITY LIMITED

Written by

SHOOSH CROTZER

Directed by THOMAS WALTERS ...

Arthritis Foundation

Pittsfield, MA 01202-4284

Transcribed as

245	00	Pathways to better living with arthritis and related conditions $h [videorecording] / $c written by Shoosh Crotzer ; directed by Thomas Walters.
260		Pittsfield, MA : $b Produced for the Arthritis Foundation by Mobility Limited, $c 1997. [In field 245 the transcription of the statement of responsibility follows that of the original to simplify the transcription activity. In field 260, the phrase indicating the function of the producer is also included, following rule 1.4D3.]

When many individuals are listed in the credit area, it can be difficult to determine who has the overall responsibility and should be recorded in Area 1. It can also be challenging to determine which actors play "major roles" in a video. Fortunately the disc label, cassette label, or the container usually provides helpful information by presenting important production people or actors prominently.

[beginning frames]

The X-Files

Starring

DAVID DUCHOVNY

GILLIAN ANDERSON

... [names of other actors]

WRITTEN BY

CHRIS CARTER

DIRECTED BY

ROBERT MANDEL

[container]: STARRING DAVID DUCHOVNY GILLIAN ANDERSON

Transcribed as

245	04	The X-Files $h [videorecording] / $c written by Chris Carter ; directed by Robert Mandel.
511	1	David Duchovny, Gillian Anderson.
700	1	Duchovny, David.
700	1	Anderson, Gillian.

7.2. Edition (MARC Field 250)

The prescribed sources for this area are the chief source, the accompanying material, and the container. Rule 7.2B1 instructs catalogers to transcribe an edition statement according to rule 1.2B, using abbreviations as instructed in *AACR2* Appendix B, and numerals as instructed in Appendix C. Catalogers should look for formal edition statements and should not infer any edition statement. For example, "a video first produced in the U.S. in 1999" should not be interpreted as the first American edition. If uncertain as to whether a statement is an edition statement, rule 1.2B3 states that words such as *edition*, *issue*, or *version* can be considered evidence of an edition statement. Edition statements often appear on the containers of video cassettes and DVDs. *LCRI* 1.2B4 states that if an item has known significant differences from other editions, catalogers may provide a brief statement for the differences.

250	Letterboxed ed.
250	Widescreen ed.
250	Commemorative ed., widescreen version.

7.3. Material Specific Details

AACR2 does not use this area for motion pictures and videorecordings.

7.4. Publication, Distribution, Etc. (MARC Field 260)

The prescribed sources for this area are the chief source, the accompanying material, and the container. Rule 7.4B1 instructs catalogers to record the place, name, and date of publication according to 1.4B. Catalogers will transcribe the first named place of publication and include the name of the country, state, province, and so on, if necessary for identifying a place. When the name of the country, state, province, and so on is used, catalogers should use abbreviations in Appendix B (B.14) if appropriate. If the layout or typography suggests another named place is more prominent, catalogers will record that place as well. If the first named place is not in the country of the cataloging library, catalogers should add the first named place that is. When no place or probable place is found, catalogers provide s.l. (sine loco) in square brackets for this element. For unpublished films or videos, catalogers will not record the place of publication or distribution and should not use [s.l.], either (rules 7.4C2 and 1.4C8).

Rule 7.4D1 instructs catalogers to record the name of the publisher according to rule 1.4D, and gives them the option to record the name of the distributor. *LCRI* 7.4D1 applies this option. Catalogers should record the names of the publisher and the distributor after their locations and supply words to clarify the relationship if necessary.

260	Universal City, Calif. : \$b MCA Universal Home Video, \$c c1996.
260	Alexandria, Va. : \$b Distributed by PBS Home Video, \$c c1995.
260	Boston, Mass. : \$b Blackside ; \$a Alexandria, Va. : \$b PBS Video [distributor], \$c c1989.

They should use the shortest form of the names of the publisher and the distributor as long as the shortened names can be understood and identified internationally (rule 1.4D2). In case of doubt, catalogers will use the original names. If a unit and its parent organization are both present on a video, catalogers will record the specific unit as the publisher (rule 1.4D2 examples). For example, the publisher will be identified as "HBO" based on the following statement:

© 2000 HOME BOX OFFICE, A DIVISION OF TIME WARNER ENTERTAINMENT COMPANY, L.P.

For unpublished films or videos, catalogers will not record the name of the publisher or distributor and should not use [s.n.], either (rules 7.4D2 and 1.4D8). Rule 7.4E1 gives catalogers the option of adding a statement of function to the name of the publisher or the distributor per rule 1.4D3. Such statements usually indicate the intended audience or clarify the role of the distributor.

> 260   Pittsfield, MA : $b Produced for the Arthritis
>   Foundation by Mobility Limited, $c 1997.

Catalogers may find different date information in various parts of a video package—the video itself, label, container, and accompanying materials may present different date information. In such a case catalogers should use a date that covers the entire work, if possible. If this is not possible, the latest date is used. For videos of feature films, catalogers may find the date of original production, the date of the original release as a motion picture, as well as the publication date of the video. In such a case, catalogers will record the publication date of the video in subfield $c of field 260, and record the date of the original film as an edition and history note (rule 7.7B7). Rule 7.4F3 instructs catalogers to record the date of creation of an unedited or unpublished film or video.

The date of publication entered in subfield $c of the 260 field should be coordinated with the DtSt (date type) and the Dates elements in the fixed field. Three situations are typical:

- Code "p" (production date): This applies when the video is the same as the original film or television program but the *medium is different*. For example, the video of *Toy Story 2* will be coded "p" and its date of publication entered in Date 1, while the original movie release date entered in Date 2.

- Code "r" (reissue date): This applies when the video is a reissue of the original in *the same medium without any changes*. The latest release date is entered in Date 1 and the original release date in Date 2.

- Code "s" (single date): This applies when the content of the video is different from that of the original. This may include addition of special features, changes in length, or languages used for subtitle. Creators of DVDs often include additional materials to entice buyers, if these materials are significant (such as a documentary on the making of the film, deleted scenes, or interviews with actors, directors, screen writers), the DVD will be coded "s" for DtSt. For example, a DVD of *Mary Poppins* includes "The making of *Mary Poppins*," "*Mary Poppins* trivia game," "Hollywood goes to a world premiere," and "Original theatrical trailer"; so it is coded "s". Similarly, the DVD of *The Return of the King* that includes fifty minutes more footage than the original will be coded "s" and only one date will be recorded (in Date 1).

7.5. Physical Description (MARC Field 300)

> 300 $a number of specific material designation (playing
>   time or frames for "still images"[see 7.5B2]) : $b
>   sound, color ; $c dimensions. + $e accompanying
>   material.

In addition to videocassettes, other video media include videodisc and DVD. Videodisc has two distinct formats, CAV (constant angular velocity) and CLV (constant linear velocity). CAV is the preferred format for interactive videodisc applications because the frames are laid down in concentric circles and each frame has its own 360-degree track on the videodisc, making it possible for laser readers to randomly access the frames (Dillon and Leonard 1998). Information on CLV is laid down in one continuous spiral, making the format appropriate for long, continuous video plays. DVD stands for digital videodisc and appeared in the market in 1997. It expands the optical storage capacity of CD-ROM into the multigigabyte range to support applications such as digital video. The *DVD Forum* identifies three levels of DVD storage capacity: a 4.7 GB standard for single-layer DVD, an 8.5 GB standard for dual-layer, and a 17 GB standard for floppy disks designed to record on both sides of a dual-layer system (Dillon and Leonard 1998). Major film studios have released feature films on DVD. Encyclopedias and games with video and surround sound are also popular applications of DVD. DVDs require their own player. The attraction of such a player is that it can also read both CD-ROMs and audio CDs.

Data for Area 5 can be taken from any source. The information usually appears on the label or the container. Rule 7.5B1 instructs catalogers to record the number of physical units of a film or video, using arabic numerals and one of the specific material designations given in the rule. For videodiscs (CAV and CLV) and DVD, the specific material designation is "videodisc." The 2004 update to *AACR2r* gives catalogers the option to use conventional terminology such as DVD, but the format still needs to be recorded in the 538 field. This update brings the description of videos in line with that of electronic resources. Rule 7.5B2 instructs catalogers to record the playing time of a film or video according to rule 1.5B4. If the playing time is stated, it is recorded. If it is not stated but the information is "readily ascertainable" (rule 1.5B4b), catalogers will provide the information. The rule gives catalogers the option of providing an approximate time, but *LCRI* does not apply this option. Rule 7.5B2 also states that for videodiscs containing frames of still images, catalogers should record the playing time if available. If the playing time is not stated, catalogers have the option of recording the number of frames if the number is "readily ascertainable." The playing times of special features such as a documentary on the making of the film can be included in the notes for such materials.

Information on the type of aspect ratio and special projection characteristics, sound, color, and project speed is entered in subfield $b of the 300 field. The "sound" element indicates whether a sound track is on a video. The quality of the sound, such as "stereo" or "Dolby surround" is recorded in a 538 note, not in the 300 field. Information on layers, aspect ratio and the pan-and-scan technique is entered in the 500 field. Such information can be combined with the 538 format note (OLAC 2005). Besides the one-sided format, DVDs can be dual-layer or double-sided. A dual layer DVD will play data from one layer to the other, while a double-sided DVD requires the user to turn the DVD over to play data on the other side. Two major types of audio presentations are common on DVDs. Dolby Digital sound tracks contain up to 5.1 channels of discrete audio, while Dolby Surround sound tracks contain up to four channels of encoded audio (Dolby Digital FAQ 2005). By the "pan-and-scan" technique, video producers select a portion of the original screen to fill the television screen. The technique often leaves out important parts and distorts the images (Letterbox 2005). That's why many movie makers advocate the letterboxed presentation that shows the original screen size with black borders on top and bottom of a television screen. Although the borders are not pretty, advocates feel this type of presentation is a faithful rendition of the original.

500	Dual layer.
538	DVD, stereo., Dolby surround, double-layer.
538	DVD, aspect ratio 4:3; DTS 5.1 Surround sound; Dolby Digital 5.1 Surround and LPCM stereo.

Rule 7.5D instructs catalogers to provide the dimensions of a film or video by recording the width of a motion picture in millimeters, the width of a videotape in inches or millimeters, and the diameter of a videodisc in inches. Standard videodiscs is 12 inches in diameter while standard DVD is $4\frac{3}{4}$ inches in diameter.

300	1 videocassette (1 hr., 55 min.) : \$b sd., col. ; \$c 1/2 in.
300	1 videocassette (52 min.) : \$b sd., col. with b&w sequences ; \$c 1/2 in.
300	4 videodiscs (4 hrs.) : \$b sd., col. ; \$c 12 in.
538	CAV, standard play; THX digital sound, Dolby system, stereo.

7.6. Series (MARC Field 4XX)

The prescribed sources for this area are the chief source, the accompanying material, and the container. Rule 7.6B1 instructs catalogers to transcribe the series information according to rule 1.6. The series title should be transcribed exactly as for wording and order, but not necessarily for capitalization and punctuation. If ISSN is available, it is recorded here. If a number is used with the series, the numbering information should be recorded as instructed in Appendix C. Series information usually appears prominently on the container or the first few frames of a video.

440	0	Eyewitness video series
440	0	Storyteller's classics
440	0	Yoga with Linda Arkin
440	0	At time of diagnosis
440	0	Beginner book video
440	0	Angelina ballerina

When an item belongs to a series, a common practice is to create a record for the item and use a series added entry to collocate all items of the series. This practice is sometimes applied to multiple-part items, and should be done according to the library's policy. *Joseph Campbell and the Power of Myth*, for instance, includes six parts, each with its own title. Catalogers have at least two ways to describe these items. One option is to catalog these six items as a set under the collective title, provide a content note listing the six parts, and provide analytical added entries for the six titles. This practice is common for parts with a collective title.

Option One (one record)

245	00	Joseph Campbell and the power of myth $h [videorecording] ...
246	30	Power of myth
505	0	1. The hero's adventure — 2. The message of the myth — 3. The first storytellers — 4. Sacrifice and bliss — 5. Love and the goddess — 6. Masks of eternity.
740	02	Hero's adventure.
740	02	Message of the myth.
740	02	First storytellers.
740	02	Sacrifice and bliss.
740	02	Love and the goddess.
740	02	Masks of eternity.
		[Field 246 is used to record a variant title, and 740 fields are used for analytics. OCLC input guidelines recommend that initial articles not be used in fields 246 and 740.]

A second approach to cataloging this item for libraries that do not own all parts of a work is to create a record for each item and use the collective title as a series title to link the parts owned by the library together. This approach is similar to the treatment of monographic series. While both approaches are acceptable, a rule of thumb is to see if the second approach would result in six records with nearly identical information. If so, the first option may be more economical.

Option Two (each part has its own record)

245	04	The hero's adventure $h [videorecording] ...
440	0	Joseph Campbell and the power of myth ; $v 1

7.7. Notes

Information for Area 7 can be taken from any source. Rule 7.7A instructs catalogers to provide notes according to rule 1.7A. The order of notes parallels the order of the eight areas of a bibliographic record. But if a particular note is considered of primary importance, catalogers may give it as the first note (rule 7.7B). Fields 546, 500, 508, 511, 538, 520, 505, and 521 are frequently used for describing videos.

Language (MARC Field 546): Languages can be associated with videos in a number of ways. Subtitling and closed captioning are common on videos. Some videos include signing or audio description on a second audio track of the video. Such information is usually listed on the container or on the main menu. Such information should be recorded in the 546 field and coordinated with the fixed-field element "Lang" and field 041 (language code), which records full language information in coded form. The 041 field is used when a work is multilingual, involves translation, or contains a sign language. *MARC 21 Code List for Languages* is the source of codes used in the 041 field. Previously, subfields $a, $b, and $h were not repeatable and multiple codes were entered in the same subfield. Current practice is to enter each language code in a subfield. Subtitles and closed captioning languages are recorded in subfield $b. If the language for closed captioning is the same as the language on the sound track, it should be coded in subfield $a and not repeated in subfield $b. When a film or video has closed captioning, it may be stated on the menu, the container or through a "CC" symbol on the label or container. Catalogers will record such information in the 546 field for language and use the subject heading "video recordings for the hearing impaired".

If an item contains several languages, LC practice is to record the code for the predominant language first, if it can be identified, followed by other language codes in English alphabetical order. If the item contains more than six languages, catalogers should record the code for the language of the first title, followed by "mul".

Example: For a bilingual program presented in Italian and English
Transcribed as: Lang: ita
041   0   ita $a eng
546   A bilingual program in Italian and English.

Example: For a DVD video with subtitles in "English, Francais, Espanol" and is closed captioned.
Transcribed as: Lang: eng
041   0   eng $b fre $b spa
546   Subtitles in English, French, and Spanish.
546   Closed-captioned.

Source of title proper (MARC Field 500): If the title proper is not taken from the chief source of information, catalogers will use a note in field 500 to record the source of the title proper.

Variant title (MARC Field 246): Titles other than the title proper are recorded in field 246, and the first indicator can be coded to produce a note and a title added entry.

---

245   00   My first green video $h [videorecording]
246   1 $i Subtitle on cassette and container: $a kids' guide
                 to ecology and environmental activities

Most videos have title frames, but the information on the title frames may not be the same as that on the container labels. When that happens, the title from the title frame is usually preferred and recorded in field 245 and the other titles are recorded in 246 fields.

[title frame]: YOGA

FOR RELAXATION

WITH LINDA ARKIN

[cassette label]: YOGA

WITH LINDA ARKIN

FOR RELAXATION & REJUVENATION

Transcribed as

245	00	Yoga for relaxation with Linda Arkin $h [videorecording]
246	3	Yoga with Linda Arkin for relaxation & rejuvenation
246	3	Yoga for relaxation and rejuvenation [The 245 field reflects the title information on the title frame, the first 246 field provides the title on the cassette label as the added entry, and the second 246 field provides another title variation for access. The cassette container lists other titles in the "Yoga with Linda Arkin Series", so the second variant title may be a useful additional access point for users.]

[title frame]: EYES ON THE PRIZE
AMERICA AT THE RACIAL CROSSROADS
POWER!
1967–1968

[cassette label]:

EYES ON THE PRIZE II: America at the
racial crossroads
Power 1967–1968

Transcribed as

245	00	Eyes on the prize $h [videorecording] : $b America at the racial crossroads. $p Power, 1967–1968.
246	3	Eyes on the prize II
246	3	American at the racial crossroads
246	3	Power, 1967–1968

Statement of responsibility (MARC Fields 511, 508): Two important note fields for statement of responsibility are field 511 (for cast), which records players, performers, narrators, hosts, or presenters of a video; and field 508 (for credits), which records people who contribute to a part or an aspect (often artistic or technical) of the production of a video. Assistants, associates, and people making minor contribution are not recorded. The wording and the order in which names appear in the credit frames usually suggest the importance of these names. Information on the carrier (cassette or videodisc) and the container may be helpful, too.

245	00	High blood pressure $h [videorecording]
508		C. Everett Koop, medical director.
511	0	Host, Boyd Matson.

Edition and history (MARC Field 500): This type of note describes the edition being cataloged or the history of a videorecording. Many videos or feature films contain information on the original release.

500	Originally produced for PBS television in 1986.
500	Based on the Mary Poppins books by P. L. Travers.
500	A 1990 episode of the television series.
500	Videocassette release of the 1982 motion picture.
500	Remake of a 1977 motion picture of the same name.

Physical description (MARC Fields 500, 538): Several physical characteristics of a video should be noted. "Sound characteristics" and color information are typically recorded in field 500, while videorecording system information is recorded in field 538.

500	Dolby stereo.
500	Technicolor.
538	VHS.
538	DVD Read-Along.
538	CAV.

When a video uses different sound systems for different languages such information is best presented in a 538 note.

English: Dolby Digital 5.1 Surround
French: 2.0 Mono
Spanish: 2.0 Mono
Recorded as
538   Dolby digital 5.1 surround (English), 2.0 mono. (French), and 2.0 mono. (Spanish).

Accompanying material (MARC Field 500): This note is mainly used to indicate the location of accompanying material. It is also used to describe accompanying material that is not described elsewhere in the record.

500	Program note on insert.

Audience (MARC Field 521): If the intended audience or the intellectual level of a videorecording is stated in the item, its container, or accompanying material, catalogers will provide an audience note using the 521 field. This field is also used for rating information. If the first indicator is blank, a print constant "Audience" will be displayed; if it is "8", no print constant will be displayed.

521		Suitable for Grades 4–8.
521		For age 8+.
521	8	Rated PG.
521	8	MPAA rating.

Other formats (MARC Field 530): If the item also appears in other physical formats, the information is presented in a 530 note.

530	Also available on videodisc.
530	Also available on VHS.

Summary (MARC Field 520): To inform users of the content of an item, catalogers should prepare a brief, objective summary. The *Subject Cataloging Manual* instructs catalogers to use summaries to determine which topics will be assigned subject headings, so it is important to prepare an informative and unbiased summary for each item cataloged.

Contents (MARC Field 505): The parts included in a videorecording can be presented in a formal note in field 505 or an informal note in field 500. If each part has its own statement of responsibility, the statements can be added. To make the parts searchable, an enhanced contents note could be created, with value "0" for the second indicator, and each title entered under $t.

245	04	Kids' favorite songs $n 2 $h [videorecording]
505	00	$t Elmo's song — $t On top of spaghetti — $t Hey diddle diddle — $t The bear went over the mountain — $t The ants go marching — $t If you're happy and you know it — $t Mary had a little lamb — $t Up and down with Captain Brown — $t Rubber duckie — $t Duermete Mi Nino — $t Itsy bitsy spider.

Numbers (MARC Fields 028, 024): Videos often come with ISBN, publisher's number, UPC code, and other numbers. Rule 7.7B19 instructs catalogers to record important numbers associated with a work. Field 028 is used for publisher's number that usually consists of a publisher's brand name and a stock or inventory number. Value "4" is used for the first indicator for videorecording, and the second indicator is used to specify whether a note or added entry will be generated. The 028 note will print as the last note, following all the 5XX notes. If a multipart set contains a number for the set and numbers for the parts, the former is recorded.

Field 024 is used for the twelve-digit Universal Product Code (UPC) or the thirteen-digit International Article Number/European Article Number

(EAN). Both numbers are recorded without hyphens or spaces between the digits. The first indicator is coded "1" for UPC and "3" for EAN.

028	42	91708 $b HBO Kids Video
028	42	LVD 49347 $b Sony Wonder
024	1	074644934793
024	1	085365310124
024	3	9780838907535

7.8. International Standard Numbers (Fields 020, 022, and 024)

The international standard numbers such as ISBN and ISSN are recorded in field 020 or field 022. Major changes to ISBN will take place in 2007. The ISBN organization has decided to expand ISBN to thirteen digits, using the first three digits to identify the industry, followed by a nine-digit number, and a check digit at the end. The new thirteen-digit ISBN will be identical to the EAN code. Details of the implementation plan are available at http://www.isbn-international.org/en/revision.html and http://www.isbn-international.org/en/download/implementation-guidelines-04.pdf. The Library of Congress planned to begin recording the thireen-digit ISBN in the 020 field in October 2004. OCLC's interim solution is for catalogers contributing original records to record thirteen-digit ISBN in the EAN field—024 field with value "3" for the first indicator (OCLC Interim 2004).

020	1568324928

Music Videos

In choosing access points for music videos, catalogers are to follow the practice for sound recordings, according to the Working Group on Bibliographic Control of Music Video Material of the Music Library Association (1996). It may be appropriate to enter a concert video under the performing group or the individual artist. *Diana Krall Live in Paris*, for example, features her concert performance of several well-known songs by various composers. According to rule 21.23C1, this work will be entered under the singer: "if a sound recording containing works by different persons or bodies has a collective title, enter it under the heading for the person or body represented as principal performer." But if a music video contains works by different persons or bodies and has no collective title, the rule 21.23D should be consulted. If the performer's participation goes beyond execution or interpretation (usually the case in popular music), the work is entered under the principal performer (rule 21.23D1a). *Norah Jones in New Orleans*, for example, features her performance of songs written by her, so it is appropriate to enter the music video under Norah Jones. But in classical and other "serious" musical works the performers' participation usually does not go beyond performance, execution, and interpretation. In such cases the heading appropriate for the first work is the main entry (rule 21.23D1b).

Story music videos, on the other hand, will be treated like regular videos and performers are rarely treated as authors. *Cats*, for example, is based on a work by T. S. Eliot and features the music of Andrew Lloyd Webber and the performance of Elaine Page and other cast members. Because so many people contributed to the creation of the videorecording, this work is entered under title and added entries are provided for Eliot, Lloyd Webber, Page, and other important cast members.

Television Episodes and Series

Many episodes of television series are available to the public in DVD or VHS formats. If a video contains an episode and has a distinctive title, catalogers should record the title as the title proper. If the publisher uses the TV series as a video publisher series, the series title is entered in the 440 field to generate a series added entry. If the TV series is not used as a video publisher series, catalogers will use a note to clarify the relationship between the episode and the TV series and make a 730 title added entry for the TV series.

245	00	Assignment: Earth $n Episode 55 $h [videorecording] Spectre of the gun $n Episode 56.
440	0	Star Trek the original series ; $v v. 28
245	00	The orphan trains $h [videorecording]
500		Originally produced as an episode of the television series: The American experience.
730	0	American experience (Television program)

When a TV series is finite or has a small number of episodes, a common practice is to create a record with a title main entry for each item and use the series name to collocate the episodes. But if the series or program is open-ended, then it is better to present the program or series as a title added entry in the 730 field. The following work is part of the documentary series, *Frontline*:

245	00	China in the red $h [videorecording]
500		Part of public television's public affairs series, Frontline.
730	0	Frontline (Television program)

Streaming Videos

Streaming video is a stream of moving images transmitted in compressed format to users over a network such as the Internet. Because of the compression, file size is usually small and the user can play the video as data arrives. Streaming media is streaming video with sound. Popular streaming media formats include

- RealMedia format (.rm file extension) from RealNetworks
- Windows Media format (.wmv file extension) from Microsoft
- QuickTime format (.mov file extension) from Apple

RealPlayer, Window Media Player, and QuickTime Player are three major players. Streaming video can be sent from prerecorded files or a live broadcast (Streaming Video 2005). In describing these resources, catalogers need to keep in mind that streaming videos are treated as remote access electronic resources, so no physical description (field 300) is used. Because a streaming video is an electronic resource that contains video, catalogers will need to consult both Chapters 6 and 9 of *AACR2r* for the description of the record. The primary content of a streaming video is video, so the video workform is used for record creation but the GMD is **electronic resource**. This treatment is consistent with the treatment of remote access digital sound files such as MP3 files (see Chapter 3). Records for streaming videos usually contain the following elements and fields (Weitz 2002).

Field	*Definition*	*Example*
Type in field 008	"g" for videorecording	Type: g
Form in field 008	"s" for electronic resource	Form: s
Computer file 006	To bring out the electronic aspects of the work	006 m # u # m = computer file, Audn is "#" (blank) for audience not specified, File is "u" for unknown file type, and GPub is "#" (blank) for not a government publication.
Videorecording 007	A required 007 for coding the physical characteristics of video	007 v $b z $d c $e z $f a $g z $h u
Electronic resource 007	An optional but often included 007 for encoding the physical characteristics of the electronic resource	007 c $b r $d c $e n $f a
245	Title proper $h [electronic resource]	245 10 Here comes the sun $h [electronic resource] / $c The Beatles.
500	Nature and file format. Playing time can be included in parentheses.	500 Streaming video (12:08)
538	System requirements, including video player and other requirements for playing the resource	538 System requirements: RealPlayer.
538	Mode of access	538 Mode of access: World Wide Web.
856	URL for each primary access method	856 40 $u http://freestreamingvideo .com

Assignment of Access Points

The assignment of access points to videorecordings is the same as that to print materials, except for musical videorecordings. Videorecordings usually do not have a personal author as the main entry because they tend to include the intellectual and artistic work of many people. In addition, videorecordings tend not to have a corporate body as the main entry because a work will have to be emanated from the body and belong to one of the six categories of material named in rule 21.1B2. Most videorecordings have title as the main entry.

LCRI 21.23C recommends that rules 21.23C1 and 21.23D be applied to videorecordings that are "collections of music performed by a principal performer." *Sarah Brightman in Concert*, for instance, contains performances by Brightman of a selection of songs. Applying rule 21.23C1 to this video, the cataloger will select Sarah Brightman as the main entry. Rule 21.23D covers videos containing works by several people without collective title.

LCRI 21.29 also provides guidance on the selection of added entries for videorecordings. These guidelines are similar to those for sound recordings and are summarized below:

1. Catalogers should make added entries for all openly named persons or corporate bodies that contributed to the creation of the work.

    a. But if a production company, unit, and so on has been made an added entry, no entries should be made for persons such as producers, directors, and writers unless their contributions are significant. If no production company is present, added entries should be made for producers, directors, and writers. Added entries are made for other persons only if they made significant contribution to the work.
    b. If a person is the main entry heading, make no added entries for other people unless they are true collaborators.

2. All corporate bodies named in the "publication, distribution, etc.," area should be traced.

3. All featured players, performers, and narrators should be traced, but not group members. If a person's name appears with a group, do not consider him a member of the group. If several players are involved, make added entries for those given prominence in the chief source. If this criterion does not apply, make added entries for each if there are no more than three.

4. Make added entries for persons serving as interviewers, interviewees, lecturers, and so on who are not selected as the main entry.

Subject Analysis

Library of Congress Subject Headings

Catalogers have been concerned about the limitations of authority lists such as the *Library of Congress Subject Headings (LCSH)* and the *Sears List of Subject Headings* for the subject analysis of nonprint materials. Weihs pointed out in 1987 that *LCSH* did not incorporate new topics fast enough and the terms were not specific enough for the indexing of nonprint materials. Intner and Studwell stated in 1992 that precision and retrieval remained problematic because many *LCSH* terms could be used as topical headings and form headings. Furthermore, LC's principle of literary warrant, a principle to use LC collection as the basis for establishing headings, also precluded LC from adding new terms for works it did not own (Intner and Studwell 1992). The National Moving Image Database Standards Committee of the National Center for Film and Video Preservation at the American Film Institute published *Moving Image Materials: Genre Terms (MIM)* in 1988 (Yee); and Miller described the use of *MIM* and *LCSH* in their catalog to illustrate the compatibility concerns (1992). As Intner and Studwell pointed out, *LCSH* has remained the main source for subject headings because of a strong interest in integrating nonprint resources into the catalog, the benefit of record sharing, LC's effort to revise and augment the tool, and the high cost of developing and maintaining a new list. Intner and Studwell extracted descriptors pertaining to motion pictures, television, and videorecordings from the thirteenth edition of *LCSH* (1990) and made it easier for catalogers to use the terms and to decide if new terms ought to be developed locally.

The cataloging policy has also been a matter of concern. ALA published *Guidelines on Subject Access to Individual Works of Fiction, Drama, Etc.* in 2000. The ALA *Guidelines* recommend four types of subject access that are valuable for searchers, including form/genre access, access for characters or group of characters, access for setting, and topical access. The current Library of Congress policies for visual materials have similar treatments for motion pictures that can be extended to videorecordings. These policies are summarized below.

Fiction Films

Videos that are feature films are assigned:

1. topical headings with the subdivision "—Drama" (use the subdivision "—Juvenile films" for juvenile fiction films),

2. form headings indicating genre (e.g., Western films) or technique (e.g., Silent films), and

3. either the form heading "Feature films" (for films at least forty minutes long) or "Short films" (for films less than forty minutes long).

The first two types of headings are assigned if appropriate, while the third heading is required. If all three types of headings are assigned to a work, the headings should be arranged in the order presented above.

245	00	Get Shorty $h [videorecording]
520		Loan shark Chili Palmer had done his time as a gangster. So when "business" takes him to Los Angeles to collect a debt from down-and-out filmmaker Harry Zimm, Chili pitches Harry a script idea and is immediately swept into the Hollywood scene. All would be smooth for this cool new producer, if it weren't for the drug smugglers and an angry mobster who won't leave him alone.
650	0	Gangsters $z United States $v Drama.
650	0	Motion picture producers and directors $z California $z Los Angeles $v Drama.
650	0	Comedy films.
650	0	Feature films.

Genre terms are recorded in field 655 if the library wants to have the text "Genre:" displayed with the term. In using field 655 catalogers have two options to encode them. One common practice is to use value "7" for the second indicator and subfield $2 for the source of the term (such as "lcsh" or "aat"). Genre terms that are also authorized LC subject headings may be recorded in field 655 with value "0" for the second indicator (*Technical Bulletin* 2003). Alternatively, these terms may be recorded in field 650 with value "0" for the second indicator to indicate the source of the term is an LC subject heading.

655	7	Shorts. $2 mim
655	0	Science fiction films.
or		
650	0	Science fiction films.

Films prepared with captions or sign language for viewing by the hearing impaired should also be assigned the heading, "Films for the hearing impaired" or "Videorecordings for the hearing impaired." But films with subtitles in other languages should not be assigned such headings if the subtitles are meant as translation and not as an aid for the hearing impaired.

Films prepared with audio description for the visually handicapped should be assigned either "Films for the visually handicapped" or "Videorecordings for the visually handicapped."

Nonfiction Films

Topicals: For topical films all important topics mentioned in the summary statement are assigned headings. The form subdivision "—Pictorial works" is never used.

520		Step-by-step video instructions: layout and installation of fence posts and rails; how to build and install a gate; installation of a chain link fence.
650	0	Fences $v Amateurs' manuals.
650	0	Gates $v Amateurs' manuals.

Person and profession: Films about a person as illustrative of a profession are assigned headings for the person and the profession.

520		Alfred I. Maleson, Professor Emeritus of the Suffolk University Law School, discusses his career in legal education, from his first teaching position in Toledo, Ohio to Suffolk University in Boston.
600	10	Maleson, Alfred I., $d 1922–
650	0	Law teachers $z Massachusetts $z Boston.
610	20	Suffolk University. $b Law School. $x Faculty.

Topic and place: Films that present a topic in a particular place are assigned headings for the topic and the place.

520		Follows three international stars Laurent Fignon of France, Pedro Delgado of Spain, and Greg LeMond of the U.S. as they pedal across the French countryside and mountains in a battle for victory in the 1989 Tour de France.
600	10	LeMond, Greg.
650	0	Tour de France (Bicycle race)
650	0	Bicycle racing $z France.
651	0	France $x Description and travel $y 1975-

Commercials: Commercials advertising a particular product are assigned the generic name of the product and a heading for the advertising medium.

520		A commercial for Taster's Choice.
650	0	Instant coffee.
650	0	Television advertising.

Films on foreign-language teaching are assigned, as the first heading, a heading based on the pattern: [Language]—Films for [group] speakers. For example, Japanese—Films for Chinese speakers.

Juvenile works with topical headings should have the free-floating subdivision "—Juvenile films" added to them. "Juvenile videorecordings," however, is not a form subdivision.

245	00	Beating and bleeding
520		Examines and explores the workings of the heart with its lifelong movement of blood.
650	0	Heart $v Juvenile films.
650	0	Blood $v Juvenile films.

Classification Numbers

In assigning numbers from *DDC* and *LCC*, the cataloger should focus on the content of the videorecordings instead of the format. Topical videorecordings should be assigned the most specific number available in the classification schedule for the topics and no special number is assigned to bring out the format. Videorecordings of feature films and literary works intended for entertainment are classed with PN1997 A2-Z8 in *LCC*, and subarranged by Cutter number from title. Special topics for motion pictures are classed under PN 1995.9 A-Z, with .C55 for comedy, .F36 for fantastic films, and .S26 for science fiction films. Videorecordings of juvenile belles lettres are classed in PZ5-PZ90, and those written in English are classed in PZ5-PZ10.3. PZ7 is for American and English juvenile belles lettres,

1870–, PZ8 for fairy tales, PZ8.1 for folklore, PZ8.3 for verses for children and stories in rhyme, and PZ 10.3 for animal stories. PZ5-PZ10.3 includes unique Cutter numbers assigned to literary authors to subarrange materials. Work letters from the title (ignoring the initial article) can be added to subarrange works by the same author (Chan 1990). Date can also be added to distinguish editions of the same work.

In *DDC* topical videorecordings are also assigned the most specific number available in the schedule. Table 1 of *DDC*, the standard subdivision, supports catalogers to add numbers to represent some forms (e.g., dictionaries, directories), but in general the form aspect of a work is usually ignored when one assigns a classification number (Chan 1996). For videorecordings of feature films, *DDC* has a number (791.4372) for single films, which can be subarranged by Cutter number of film title. Videorecordings of literary works are classed in the literature class. Works by and about individual literary authors are grouped together. Class numbers for such works usually consist of numbers for the main class, language, form, and period. For instance, Fitzgerald's *The great Gatsby* will be classed in 813.54 [813.54 = 8 (literature) + 1 (American literature in English) + 3 (Fiction) + 54 (1945–1999)]. Collections for and by specific kinds of persons classified in 808.89. With the help of Table 3-C, catalogers can build a number for collections of juvenile literary works (808.899282).

Arrangement

The use of classification numbers does not necessarily affect the physical arrangement of a video collection. Although shelving videorecordings with the other types of material makes it easier for users to browse and access the collection, security and preservation concerns cause many libraries to separate videorecordings from other types of material. Here are a few popular approaches for arranging videorecordings.

Closed Stacks

The closed-stacks arrangement is popular among academic libraries for several reasons. First, some of the videorecordings are educational materials that would be expensive to replace. Second, the major function of academic media centers is to support curricula, so these centers are strongly interested in ensuring the condition, security, and availability of materials for educators. Many, in fact, do not circulate videorecordings to students because of licensing restrictions. In closed stacks, because materials are stored in a secure and controlled environment, it becomes easier to inventory the collection, to maintain and preserve the materials, and to control access. But users cannot browse the stacks, and the collection cannot be used without the catalog.

Libraries using *DDC* or *LCC* numbers often add "Video" to their classification numbers to remind users that the items are videorecordings. In such libraries, items in the closed stacks will be arranged by classification numbers. But closed stacks tend to encourage arrangement by accession number, size, or type, resulting in libraries creating full bibliographic records for videorecordings but assigning special numbers (e.g., Video A12) to them. The reason is that shelving by accession number is more efficient for inventory control and retrieval, but wastes space. Shelving by size, on the other hand, saves space and supports quick retrieval if the catalog is good.

Some libraries arrange items by format, so videocassettes, videodiscs, and films are stored in separate areas, and items within each group are arranged with its own sequence of accession numbers. This approach also requires strong support from the catalog.

Shelving by Format, Type, Etc.

Many public libraries encourage browsing by storing videorecordings in an area separate from the other materials. The video collection is still fully searchable in the catalog. These libraries put a special term (e.g., video, videocassette) on top of the call number to identify them, and use some kind of classification number to subarrange them. Depending on the nature and size of the collection, some libraries use standard classification schemes such as *DDC* and *LCC*, while others devise their own categories (e.g., "B" for biography; "F" for feature films), and subarrange materials by Cutter numbers. This method collocates materials and supports browsing.

A variation to this approach is to arrange videorecordings by their type. That means documentaries, videos of feature films, juvenile videos, and topical videos are arranged separately. This method is appropriate if a library has many items of each type. But if the videos are not classified and items of each category are arranged by title, as in some libraries, browsing becomes somewhat limited. For example, although it is fine to browse feature-film videos by title, it is not easy to browse topical videos by title—*Saving Our Environment* and *Green Earth* cover the same subject but are far apart alphabetically. Users will have to rely on the catalog to collocate these videos. One may wonder if public libraries would take this approach a step further and subarrange feature film videos by genre. A common response to this inquiry is that the videos public libraries purchase are selected to meet the needs of their community and they have no intention to compete with video stores. Indeed, many videos in public libraries are educational and topical videos.

Other Possibilities

The method of "intershelving with dummies" discussed in Chapter 3 is also a possibility for arranging videorecordings because the size of videorecordings is fairly standard. The same benefits and drawbacks also apply. Interested readers may turn to Chapter 3 for a discussion of this method.

Cataloging Examples

Figure 4.1. *Richard Scarry's best sing-along Mother Goose video ever*

SONY
WONDER

Random House
Home Video

[Title screen]
RICHARD SCARRY'S
BEST
SING-ALONG
MOTHER
GOOSE
VIDEO EVER

[closing credits]
Based on books and characters
created by
Richard Scarry

Produced by
Jumbo Pictures, Inc.

Director
Tony Eastman

Producer
Melanie Grisante

Written by
Ellen Weiss

Original music composed
and arranged by
Rich De Rosa

For Random House
Executive Producer
Sharon Lerner
... [assistants, technicians, etc.]
Random House
Home Video

Copyright© 1994 Random House Inc.
Based on characters and art

Type	g	ELvl	I	Srce	d	Audn	a	Ctrl		Lang	eng
BLvl	m	Form		GPub		Time	030	MRec		Ctry	nyu
Desc	a	TMat	v	Tech	a	DtSt	p	Dates	2000, 1994		

007		v $b d $d c $e v $f a $g i $h z $i q
020		0738923273
028	42	LVD 51306 $b Sony Wonder
090		PZ8.3$b .M85
092		398.8
245	00	Richard Scarry's Best sing-along Mother Goose video ever! $h [videorecording] / $c produced by Jumbo Pictures ; director, Tony Eastman ; written by Ellen Weiss ; music composed and arranged by Rich DeRosa.
246	30	Best sing-along Mother Goose video ever!
260		New York, N.Y. : $b Sony Wonder : $b Random House Home Video, $c [2002], c1994.
300		1 DVD (30 min.) : $b sd., col. ; $c 4 ¾ in.
538		DVD, Dolby digital.
546		Closed captioned.
500		Based on books and characters created by Richard Scarry.
520		Huckle looks for his friend Lowly Worm through Mother Gooseland and meets many new friends. Sing along with classic nursery rhymes.
650	0	Children's songs.
650	0	Nursery rhymes.
650	0	Children's films.
650	0	Animated films.
650	0	Video recordings for the hearing impaired.
700	1	Scarry, Richard.
700	1	Eastman, Tony.
700	1	Weiss, Ellen.
700	1	DeRosa, Rich.
710	2	Jumbo Pictures.
710	2	Sony Wonder (Firm)
710	2	Random House Video.

Discussion for Figure 4.1

- Fixed field: Code "g" for type of resources (Type) indicates this is a video. Type of material (TMat) has code "v" for video; technical information (Tech) has code "a" because this is a fully animated video; running time (Time) is thirty minutes. The item does not contain specific statement on target audience, but preschoolers are the obvious intended audience, so code "a" is used for Audn. The DVD version provides the same content as the 1994 version, so date type (DtSt) is coded "p", the latest release date entered as Date 1 and the earlier publication date as Date 2 for the DATES element.

- Field 007: Category of material ($a) has code "v" for a videorecording; specific material designation ($b) has code "d" for videodisc; color ($d) has code "c" for multicolored item; videorecording format ($e) has code "v" for DVD; sound on medium or separate ($f) has code "a" to indicate the sound is on the same medium as the film; medium for sound ($g) has code "i" for videodisc; dimensions of the videotape ($h) has code "z" that is used for all videodisc; configuration of playback channels ($i) has code "q" for surround sound.

- 020 and 028: The ISBN is recorded in the 020 field without hyphens. In the 028 field the first indicator is "4" for videorecordings, the second indicator is "2" to generate a note for this number, subfield $a is for the publisher's number, and subfield $b is for the publisher's name.

- 245 and 246: Because the title proper includes a possessive form, the title after that form is capitalized. Statements of responsibility come from the closing credits. An option is to record this information in the 508 field, instead of the subfield $c of the 245 field. A variant title is provided through the 246 field to make the title following the possessive form searchable.

- 260: Sony Wonder and Random House Home Video are entered in separate subfield $b and traced, using the authorized forms from the Library of Congress name authority file. The year of publication is not on the item and is found through research, so it is entered in brackets.

- 300: The 2004 updates of *AACR2r* give catalogers the option of using conventional terminology such as CD-ROM or DVD as the specific material designation for the physical carrier. It is followed by the total running time recorded in parentheses. Information on sound and color is entered in subfield $b, but details about the sound are recorded in field 538. If the cataloger chooses to use "videodisc" in the 300 field, the DVD format information will be entered in the 538 field as "DVD, Dolby digital."

- 538: If catalogers choose to use common terminology for the carrier, they will still need to record the format of the item, that's why the 538 field includes "DVD" with the sound and sound tracks.

- 546: If a video is closed-captioned, the information goes into the 546 field.

- 500: This note clarifies how Richard Scarry is related to this work.

- 520: A brief, objective summary gives users a good idea of the content of a work. It is generally a good practice to provide a 520 note for nonprint materials.

- 650s: The first two subject headings indicate the subject nature of this video, while the other subject headings focus more on the genre.

- 700s and 710s: Scarry is traced to alert his readers of the existence of this work. The director, producer, writer, and composer are traced for their contribution. In a public library or a school library setting, catalogers may choose not to trace so many individuals. The three companies are traced for their role in the production and distribution of this video.

Figure 4.2. My first green video

SONY KIDS' VIDEO
MY FIRST GREEN VIDEO

[End Credits]
Dorling Kindersley Vision
Demonstrator
EVA MARIE BRYER
Script
ANGELA WILKES . . .
Director
DAVID FURNHAM
© 1993 SONY Music Entertainment, Inc.

Type	g	ELvl	I	Srce	d	Audn	c	Ctrl		Lang	eng
BLvl	m	Form		GPub		Time	040	MRec		Ctry	nyu
Desc	a	TMat	v	Tech	l	DtSt	s	Dates	1993		

007		v $b f $d c $e b $f a $g h $h o $i s
020		1564066908
090		TD170.15
092		363.7
245	00	My first green video $h [videorecording] / $c Dorling Kindersley Vision ; script, Angela Wilkes ; directed by David Furnham.
246	1	$i Subtitle on cassette and container: $a Kids' guide to ecology and environmental activities
260		New York, N.Y. : $b Sony Kids' Video, $c c1993.
300		1 videocassette (40 min.) : $b sd. , col. ; $c 1/2 in.
546		Closed-captioned.
511	0	Demonstrator: Eva Marie Bryer.
538		VHS Hi-fi stereo, Dolby system on linear tracks.
521		For ages 5 years and older.
520		Step-by-step instructions for carrying out experiments and activities that deal with the environment.
500		"LV 49572"—Cassette label.
650	0	Video recordings for the hearing impaired.
650	0	Pollution $x Experiments
650	0	Conservation of natural resources
650	0	Environmental protection
650	0	Ecology
700	1	Wilkes, Angela.
700	1	Furnham, David.
710	2	Dorling Kindersley, Inc.
710	2	Sony Kids' Video (Firm)

Discussion for Figure 4.2

- Fixed field: In addition to the typical codes for videorecordings, the codes for Audn and Tech are added. Code "c" for Audn indicates the item is intended for young people in grades four through eight; code "l" for Tech (technique) indicates live action.

- 090 and 092: TD170.15 is for juvenile works on environmental protection, and 363.7 is for environmental protection. *DDC* does not have a category for juvenile works under this number.

- 245: The statement of responsibility is taken from the end credits. Only people with overall responsibility for the work are included in this area, and the demonstrator is entered in field 511.

- 246: A variant title is recorded in field 246. Subfield $i indicates the source and subfield $a, the variant title. The first indicator "1" means a note and an added entry will be produced.

- 546: If a video is closed-captioned, the information is recorded in field 546. A subject heading needs to be assigned to reflect this fact.

- 511: Demonstrator's name is taken from the end credits. Since she is not well known, the demonstrator is not traced.

- 538: The format of the video and the sound quality are entered in a note. This note complements the information in field 300.

- 521: The intended audience is listed on the container and transcribed in field 521. With the first indicator blank, a print constant "Audience" will precede this information.

- 650s: A form heading is assigned to indicate the film is closed-captioned for the hearing impaired. Because "juvenile videorecordings" is not a form subdivision, the topical headings are not subdivided.

- 700s: People who made significant contributions to the video are traced.

- 710s: The corporate bodies listed in the statement of responsibility area and the publication area are traced.

Figure 4.3. Emily Dickinson

a
mystic fire
video
VOICES
&
VISIONS
A
NEW YORK
CENTER FOR VISUAL HISTORY
PRODUCTION

Emily Dickinson

[END CREDITS]
Director
Veronica Young
Producer
Jill Janows
Editor
Lisa Jackson . . .

For Voices & Visions
Executive producer: Lawrence Pitkethly.

© 1988 New York Center for Visual History, Inc.

Type	g	ELvl	I	Srce	d	Audn		Ctrl	Lang	eng
Blvl	m	Form		GPub		Time	060	MRec	Ctry	nyu
Desc	a	TMat	v	Tech	l	DtSt	p	Dates	1995, 1988	

007		v $b f $d c $e b $f a $g h $h o
020		156176308X
028	42	MYS-76308 $b Mystic Fire Video
090		PS1541
092		811.4
245	00	Emily Dickinson $h [videorecording] / $c A New York Center for Visual History Production ; director, Veronica Young ; producer, Jill Janows.
260		New York, NY : $b Mystic Fire Video, $c c1995.
300		1 videocassette (60 min.) : $b sd., col. ; $c 1/2 in.
440	0	Voices & visions
500		Executive producer of Voices & visions: Lawrence Pitkethly.
538		VHS.
520		Examines the life and work of American poet Emily Dickinson. Richard B. Sewall, Adrienne Rich, Anthony Hecht, and Joyce Carol Oates discuss her achievement, separating the facts of her life from the myths around her.
600	10	Dickinson, Emily, $d 1830–1886.
650	0	Poets, American $y 19th century $v Biography.
700	1	Sewall, Richard Benson.
700	1	Rich, Adrienne Cecile.
700	1	Hecht, Anthony, $d 1923–
700	1	Oates, Joyce Carol, $d 1938– "$i u"
710	2	New York Center for Visual History.

Discussion for Figure 4.3

- Fixed field: The 008 field for video is used, so Type is coded "g". Code "v" for type of material (TMat) indicates this is a video and code "l" for technique (Tech) indicates live action. Because the program was produced and shown in 1988 and the video contains the same content, but on a different medium, date type (DtSt) is coded "p", 1995 is entered as Date 1, and 1988 as Date 2 for the DATES element.

- Field 007: Category of material ($a) has code "v" for a videorecording; specific material designation ($b) has code "f" for videocassette; color ($d) has code "c" for multicolored item; videorecording format ($e) has code "b" for VHS; sound on medium or separate ($f) has code "a" to indicate the sound is on the same medium as the film; medium for sound ($g) has code "h" for videotape; dimensions of the videotape ($h) has code "o" for ½ in.; configuration of playback channels ($i) has code "u" for unknown.

- 020 and 028: The ISBN and the publisher number are taken from the container.

- 090 and 092: PS1541 is for nineteenth-century American poets; 811.4 is a number for works by and about literary authors. 811.4 is built from 811 (American poetry) and 4 (1861–1899).

- 245: The video has a title screen stating simply "Emily Dickinson." The statements of responsibility are taken from the opening credits and the end credits. Young and Janows are transcribed here because they have overall responsibility for the creation of this work.

- 260: The place of publication is taken from the container. The date of publication requires reconciliation. While the program was produced in 1988, the date on the cassette is 1986, and the videocassette was produced in 1995. Since what we have in hand is the video, the 1995 copyright date is used.

- 440: "Voices & visions" is prominently listed on the container and the item itself. The end credits indicate that this is a series.

- 538: The format of the video is always included in this field. Some libraries include the format information in the first element of field 300, for example: 1 videocassette (VHS). That is a local decision.

- 500: Lawrence Pitkethly is well known for his series, so the fact is noted.

- 520: A brief and objective summary of a video gives users an idea of its content. Information on the container is usually useful for this purpose.

- 600 and 650: Since Dickinson is the subject of this video, she is entered in field 600, and a topical heading for her occupation is also provided and subdivided by Biography.

- 700s: *LCRI* 21.29 recommends that when a production company is an added entry, no added entries are made for producers, directors, writers, and so on. Since the production company is traced in 710, the director and the producer are not traced. If a library chooses to trace the producers and the director, it could justify that decision if the contribution of these people is believed to be significant. The same *LCRI* also recommends that added entries be made for people serving as interviewees, delivering lectures or discussing their ideas. So the four poets are traced in the order in which their names appear in the bibliographic description.

- 710 fields: The production firm and the video distribution firm are traced.

Figure 4.4. Lennon legend

CAPITOL RECORDS
Interactive

[title screen]
      PLAY ALL   LENNON
      TRACKLIST   LEGEND
      EXTRAS
      AUDIO
[disc]

                     LENNON
                     LEGEND
         CAPITOL   DVD
        RECORDS [LOGO]
           C9 7243 5 99002 9 2

[Container]
LENNON
LEGEND
The Very Best of John Lennon

	SPECIAL FEATURES
1. Imagine	· **WORKING CLASS HERO**
2. Instant Karma!	· **SLIPPIN' & SLIDIN'**
3. Mother	· **IMAGINE (LIVE)**
4. Jealous Guy	· **HAIR PEACE**
5. . . . [20 song titles listed]	· **EVERYBODY HAD A HARD YEAR**
	· **IMAGINE**
	· A selection of animated John Lennon line drawings

Executive Producer—Yoko Ono
Director—Simon Hilton
. . .
Lennon Legend also available on CD

Capitol	DVD	Dolby	dts
Records	VIDEO	Digital	

Type	g	ELvl	I	Srce	d	Audn	g	Ctrl	Lang	eng
BLvl	m	Form		GPub		Time	100	MRec	Ctry	cau
Desc	a	TMat	v	Tech	l	DtSt	s	Dates	2003	

007		v $b d $d c $e v $f a $g i $h z $i k
024	1	724359900292
028	42	C9 7243 5 99002 9 2 $b Capitol Records
090		ML3534.6.G7 $b L46 2003
092	0	781.660 $2 22
100	1	Lennon, John, $d 1940–1980.

245	10	Lennon legend $h [videorecording] : $b the very best of John Lennon.
246	30	Legend
260		Hollywood, CA : $b EMI Records, $c c2003.
300		1 DVD (100 min.) : $b sd., col. ; $c 4 ¾ in.
500		Title from container.
538		DVD, DTS 5.1 surround sound, Dolby digital 5.1 surround and LPCM stereo; picture aspect ratio 4:3.
511	0	John Lennon; with Plastic Ono Band (tracks 1–7, 18–20); Flux Fiddlers (track 4); Halrem Community Choir (track 19).
508		Executive producer, Yoko Ono; director, Simon Hilton.
500		A compilation of songs previously released from 1969 to 1984.
505	00	$t Imagine — $t Instant Karma! — $t Mother — $t Jealous guy — $t Power of the people — $t Cold turkey — $t Love — $t Mind games — $t Whatever gets you thru the night — $t #9 dream — $t Stand by me — $t (Just Like) starting over — $t Woman — $t Beautiful boy (darling boy) — $t Watching the wheels — $t Nobody told me — $t Borrowed time — $t Working class hero — $t Happy Xmas (war is over) — $t Give peace a chance.
500		Special features: Working class hero; Slippin' & slidin; Imagine (live); Hair peace; Everybody had a hard year; Imagine (instrumental version); a selection of animated John Lennon line drawings.
530		Also available on CD.
650	0	Rock music $y 1961–1970.
650	0	Rock music $y 1971–1980.
650	0	Rock music $y 1981–1990.
700	1	Ono, Yoko.
700	1	Hilton, Simon.
710	2	EMI Records Ltd.
710	2	Capitol Records, Inc.
710	2	Plastic Ono Band.
710	2	Flux Fiddlers.
710	2	Harlem Community Choir.

Discussion for Figure 4.4

- Fixed field: A music video is cataloged as a video, so the video 008 field is used, with Type coded as "g". Type of material (TMat) has code "v" for video; technical information (Tech) has code "l" for live action; and running time (Time) is 100 minutes. This is a compilation of songs that were previously released, and that is noted in a 500 field later. Code "g" for Audn indicates the work is of general interest and not aimed at an audience of a particular intellectual level. Date type (DtSt) is coded "s" because some of the special features were not released before.

- Field 007: Category of material ($a) has code "v" for a videorecording; specific material designation ($b) has code "d" for videodisc; color ($d) has code "c" for multicolored item; videorecording format ($e) has code "v" for DVD; sound on medium or separate ($f) has code "a" to indicate the sound is on the same medium as the film; medium for sound ($g) has code "i" for videodisc; dimensions of the videotape ($h) has code "z" that is used for all videodisc; configuration of playback channels ($i) has code "k" for "mixed," indicating there is more than one type of sound reproduction channels on this video.

- 024 and 028: The UPC is entered in the 024 field without hyphens or spaces; the publisher's name is presented in the 028 field. Value "4" for the first indicator shows this is a videorecording, and value "2" for the second indicator instructs the system to generate a note from this field.

- 245 and 246: The title information on the container is more complete than that on the title screen, so a 500 note is provided to clarify the decision to take the title from the container. Note that the GMD follows the title proper and other title information is recorded later in this field. A variant title is provided through the 246 field to increase access options for users.

- 300: The 2004 updates of *AACR2r* give catalogers the option of using conventional terminology such as CD-ROM or DVD as the specific material designation for the physical carrier. It is followed by the total running time recorded in parentheses. Information on sound and color is entered in subfield $b, but details about the sound are recorded in field 538. If the cataloger chooses to use "videodisc" in the 300 field, the DVD format information will be entered in the 538 field as "DVD, Dolby digital."

- 538: If catalogers choose to use common terminology for the carrier, they will still need to record the format of the item, that's why the 538 field includes "DVD" with the types of sound provided on the video.

- 511: This note clarifies the extent of these groups' contribution. Value "0" for the indicator means no display constant such as cast or presenter will appear with this note.

- 508: People who are mainly responsible for the creation and production of the video are presented in a 508 note.

- 505: Value "0" for the first indicator specifies this is the complete content, while value "0" for the second indicator indicates this is an "enhanced" note, meaning the parts are segmented into appropriate subfields. An enhanced note gives libraries the option of making the parts searchable in their online catalogs. Since there is much interest in Lennon's music, an enhanced note is prepared for this video.

- 500: Special features are usually presented as a 500 note with parts separated by semicolon. The order of these features on the video is slightly different from that on the container. Since the information on the container is more readily accessible, the information on the container is recorded as the special features. If catalogers prefer to make these features potentially searchable, they can present them as a content note, using the 505 field, entering the features in $t (for title) or $g (for miscellaneous information), with "80" for the two indicators. Value "8" means no display constant will be used and value "0" identifies the note as an enhanced note, as the 505 note above.

- 530: If a work is available in another format, that information is entered in the 530 field. Since the CD format information is on the container, it is so noted.

- 700s and 710s: The producer, director, performing groups, publisher, and producer are traced.

Figure 4.5. The orphan trains

THE AMERICAN EXPERIENCE
with David McCullough

THE ORPHAN TRAINS
Produced & directed by
JANET GRAHAM AND
EDWARD GRAY
Written by
EDWARD GRAY
Narrated by
STACEY KEACH

[end credits]
Edited by
Joshn Waletzky...
A production of Edward Gray Films, Inc.
© 1995 Janet Graham and Edward Gray
For
THE AMERICAN EXPERIENCE
© 1995 WGBH Educational Foundation
A production of WGBH Boston [voice announcement]

Type	g	ELvl	I	Srce	d	Audn	e	Ctrl	Lang	eng
BLvl	m	Form		GPub		Time	057	MRec	Ctry	vau
Desc	a	TMat	v	Tech	l	DtSt	p	Dates	1995	

007   v $b f $d m $e b $f a $g h $h o $i u
028 42 AMEX-804 $b PBS Video
043   n-us ----
090   HV985
092   362.734
245 04 The orphan trains $h [videorecording] / $c produced and directed by Janet Graham and Edward Gray ; written by Edward Gray ; a production of WGBH.
260   [Alexandria, Va.] : $b Distributed by PBS Home Video, $c c1995.
300   1 videocassette (57 min.) : $b sd., col. with b&w sequences ; $c 1/2 in.
546   Closed-captioned.
511 3 Stacey Keach.
500   Originally produced as an episode of the television series: The American experience.
538   VHS.
520   An examination of the results of the Children's Aid Society in New York which from 1853 to 1929 sent over 100,000 unwanted and orphaned children from the city to homes in rural America.
650 0 Orphan trains.
610 20 Children's Aid Society (New York, N.Y.)
650 0 Adopted children $z United States $x History.
650 0 Video recordings for the hearing impaired.
700 1 Graham, Janet.
700 1 Gray, Edward, $q (Edward S.)
700 1 Keach, Stacey.
710 2 WGBH (Television station : Boston, Mass.)
710 2 PBS Home Video.
730 0 American experience (Television program)

Discussion for Figure 4.5

- Fixed field: Code "v" for type of material (TMat) indicates a videorecording; code "l" for technique (Tech) indicates the work includes live action; code "p" for DtSt (date type) indicates the release date of an item previously released work. Because the earlier release date is not known, Date 2 of DATES is left blank.

- Field 007: Category of material ($a) has code "v" for a videorecording; specific material designation ($b) has code "f" for videocassette; color ($d) has code "m" for a mix of black-and-white and multicolored footages; videorecording format ($e) has code "b" for VHS; sound on medium or separate ($f) has code "a" to indicate the sound is on the same medium as the film; medium for sound ($g) has code "h" for videotape; dimensions of the videotape ($h) has code "o" for ½ in.; configuration of playback channels ($i) has code "u" for unknown.

- 028: Publisher's number is entered in field 028, the first indicator "4" indicates video and the second indicator "2" will produce a note for this number.

- 245: The statement of responsibility was taken from the beginning screens and the end credits.

- 300: The playing time on the cassette label is "57 min." but it is described as sixty minutes on the container. Since the cassette label is considered a more preferable source for information, "57 min." is used in this field. The phrase, "b&w sequences," is included with the second element to indicate that the video is not entirely colored. The playing time is encoded in the fixed-field element, Time.

- 500: A note of publishing history indicates this video was originally a television episode. It clarifies the nature of this work, links it to the original series, and provides an explanation for an added entry for the original series.

- 520: The summary states that this video is an examination of the Children's Aid Society's success and failure in relocating orphaned children. It clarifies the nature of the video and justifies the provision of an added entry for the society.

- 700s: Directors, producers, and the narrator are traced in the order they appear in the bibliographic description.

- 710s: The production firm and the corporate body mentioned in Area 4 are traced, according to *LCRI* 21.29.

- 730: A uniform title for the original television series is traced to link this item to the series.

Figure 4.6. *Cats*

Really Useful Films
presents
CATS
Music by
ANDREW LLOYD WEBBER
Based on 'Old Possum's book of practical cats' by
T. S. ELIOT
Starring
ELAINE PAGE
JOHN MILLS
KEN PAGE
Originally produced on the stage by
. . .
Director of photography
NIC KNOWLAND
. . .
Music staging and choreography by
GILLIAN LYNNE
. . .
Produced by
ANDREW LLOYD WEBBER
Directed by
DAVID MALLET

[Disc]

CATS
UNIVERSAL   DVD
VIDEO

1.78:1   NTSC   **NOT RATED**
WIDESCREEN

[CONTAINER]
Front: COMMEMORATIVE
           EDITION
Back:
KEY FEATURES
Widescreen version
The Making of Cats * Interactive Menus

LANGUAGE **English**			1.78:1 WIDE- SCREEN	Dolby Digital soundtracks contain up to 5.1 channels of dis- crete audio. Dolby Surround . . .	
Dolby Digital	5.1 Surround	Dolby Surround			
CAPTION **SUBTITLES**	**Captioned**		**Color**	**Dual** **Layer**	**2 Hours** **1 Minute** 21116

Type	g	**ELvl**	I	**Srce**	d	**Audn**	g	**Ctrl**		**Lang**	eng
BLvl	m	**Form**		**GPub**		**Time**	121	**MRec**		**Ctry**	cau
Desc	a	**TMat**	v	**Tech**	l	**DtSt**	s	**Dates**	2000		

007		v $b d $d c $e v $f a $g i $h z $i q
020		0783249667
024	1	025192111624
028	42	21116 $b Universal Studios
090		M1500 .L56 $b C38 2000
092		782.14
245	00	Cats $h [videorecording] / $c Really Useful Films ; produced by Andrew Lloyd Webber ; directed by David Mallet.
250		Commemorative ed.
260		Universal City, CA : $b Universal Studios, $c c2000.
300		1 DVD (2 hrs., 1 min.) : $b sd., col. ; $c 4 ¾ in.
538		DVD, Region 1; Dolby digital 5.1 surround; dual layer; widescreen aspect ratio: 1.78:1.
546		Closed-captioned.
511	1	Elaine Paige, John Mills, Ken Page.
508		Music by Andrew Lloyd Webber; music staging and choreography by Gillian Lynne; director of photography, Nick Knowland.
500		Based on Old Possum's book of practical cats by T.S. Eliot.
518		Filmed at the Adelphi Theatre, London.
500		Includes The making of Cats.
521	8	Not rated.
650	0	Musicals.
650	0	Cats $v Drama.
650	0	Feature films.
650	0	Video recordings for the hearing impaired.
700	1	Lloyd Webber, Andrew, $d 1948–.
700	1	Mallet, David.
700	1	Page, Elaine.
700	1	Mills, John, $d 1908–
700	1	Page, Ken.
700	1	Eliot, T. S. $q (Thomas Stearns), $d 1888–1965. $t Old Possum's book of practical cats.
710	2	Really Useful Films.
710	2	Universal Pictures (Firm)

Discussion for Figure 4.6

- Fixed field: A musical on video is described as a video, so the 008 field for video is used, with Type coded as "g". Type of material (TMat) has code "v" for video; technical information (Tech) has code "l" for live action; target audience (Audn) has code "g" for general interest; running time (Time) is two hours and one minute; date type (DtSt) is coded "s" because this work includes new materials.

- Field 007: Category of material ($a) has code "v" for a videorecording; specific material designation ($b) has code "d" for videodisc; color ($d) has code "c" for multicolored item; videorecording format ($e) has code "v" for DVD; sound on medium or separate ($f) has code "a" to indicate the sound is on the same medium as the film; medium for sound ($g) has code "i" for videodisc; dimensions of the videotape ($h) has code "z" that is used for all videodisc; configuration of playback channels ($i) has code "q" for Surround Sound.

- 020, 024, and 028: The ISBN and UPC numbers are entered without any hyphens or spaces in the 020 field and the 024 field respectively. Publisher's number is recorded in the 028 field, with indicator "4" specifying this is a videorecording and indicator "2" indicating a note is to be generated from this field.

- 090 and 092: Libraries use 090 and 092 to record local call numbers, using 090 for LC classification number and 092 for Dewey classification number. M1527 and 782.14 are for musicals.

- 245: Only parties responsible for the overall production of the work, such as production company, producers, directors, and writers, are recorded in subfield $c of the 245 field. Other types of contributors are presented in the 508 field.

- 260: The disc label shows a 1999 copyright, the program has a 1998 copyright, but the copyright for the entire work is 2000, so it is recorded in the 260 field.

- 300: A term in common usage, DVD, describes the physical carrier, followed by the playing time as found in the item.

- 538: This note specifies the DVD format, the region for which the video is intended, the sound quality, how data are encoded, and the aspect ratio of the widescreen presentation.

- 546: Information on closed-captioned and subtitles are presented in the language note.

- 511: Indicator " 1" will produce "Cast" as the display constant. Only major cast members are recorded.

- 500 and 518: Information on publication history, such as the basis of the work or the recording of the work, is entered in field 500 and field 518 respectively.

- 500: Special features of the DVD are entered in a 500 note.

- 521: Indicator "8" will produce no display constant.

- 700s: The producer, composer, and major cast members are traced. In addition, a name-title added entry is provided for Eliot and his work.

- 710s: The production companies are traced. The authorized form for Universal Studios, Universal Pictures (Firm), is used as the added entry.

Figure 4.7. *Babe*

Universal Pictures
Presents
A Kennedy Miller
Film
Babe
Based on the book by
Dick King-Smith
James Cromwell
as
Farmer Hoggett
Magda Szubanski
as
Mrs Hoggett
Casting by
. . .
Animatronic characters by
Jim Henson's Creature Shop
. . .
Animation and visual effects by
Rhythm & Hues
. . .
Music composed by
Nigel Westlake
Film editors
Marcus D'Arcy and Jan Friedkin
Production designer
Roger Ford
Director of photography
Andrew Lesnie, A.C.S.
Screenplay by
George Miller & Christ Noonan
Produced by
George Miller
Doug Mitchell &
Bill Miller
Directed by
Chris Noonan

[Container]
Front: WIDESCREEN SPECIAL EDITION
            BABE
         A Little Pig
         Goes A Long Way
Back: presents information on captions and subtitles, sound configura-
tions, aspect ratio, color, dual layer, playing time, publisher's number,
and region 1.

Type	g	ELvl	I	Srce	d	Audn	g	Ctrl		Lang	eng
BLvl	m	Form		GPub		Time	092	MRec		Ctry	cau
Desc	a	TMat	v	Tech	l	DtSt	s	Dates	2003		

007		v $b d $d c $e v $f a $g i $h z $i q
020		0783285094
024	1	025192297229
028	42	22972 $b Universal Studios
041	0	eng $a fre $a spa $b fre $b spa
090		PN1997.5 $b .B334 2003
092	0	791.4372 $2 22
245	00	Babe $h [videorecording] / $c Universal Pictures; produced by George Miller, Doug Mitchell, Bill Miller ; directed by Chris Noonan; screenplay by George Miller & Chris Noonan.
250		Special ed.
260		Universal City, CA : $b Universal Studios, $c c2003.
300		1 DVD (1 hr., 21 min.) : $b sd., col. ; $c 4 ¾ in.
538		DVD, Region 1; Dolby digital, 5.1; dual layer; anamorphic widescreen aspect ratio: 1.85:1.
546		Sound track in English, French or Spanish; closed-captioned; subtitles in French and Spanish.
511	1	James Cromwell, Magda Szubanski.
508		Animation and visual effects by Rhythm & Hues; director of photography, Andrew Lesnie; production designer, Roger Ford; editors, Marcus D'Arcy & Jay Friedkin; music, Nigel Westlake.
500		Based on the book by Dick King-Smith.
500		Originally released as a motion picture in 1995.
521	8	MPAA rating: G.
500		Special features: Commentary and interview with writer/producer George Miller; the making of Babe; games.
520		A piglet adopted by a sheep dog discovers that he can be anything he wants to be—even an award-winning sheepdog.
586		Academy Award for best visual effects, 1995.
650	0	Piglets $v Drama.
650	0	Domestic animals $v Drama.
650	0	Feature films.
650	0	Videorecordings for the hearing impaired.
700	1	Miller, George.
700	1	Mitchell, Doug.
700	1	Miller, Bill.
700	1	Noonan, Chris.
700	1	Cromwell, James.
700	1	Szubanski, Magda.
700	1	King-Smith, Dick. $t Sheep-pig.
710	2	Universal Pictures (Firm)

Discussion for Figure 4.7

- Fixed field: The 008 field for video is used, with Type coded as "g". Type of material (TMat) has code "v" for video; technique (Tech) has code "l" for live action; running time (Time) is one hour and thirty-two minutes, according to the disc; target audience (Audn) has code "g" for general audience; date type (DtSt) is single because this work includes new materials. The fact that the movie was released earlier is presented in a 500 note.

- Field 007: Category of material ($a) has code "v" for a videorecording; specific material designation ($b) has code "d" for videodisc; color ($d) has code "c" for multicolored item; videorecording format ($e) has code "v" for DVD; sound on medium or separate ($f) has code "a" to indicate the sound is on the same medium as the film; medium for sound ($g) has code "i" for videodisc; dimensions of the videotape ($h) has code "z" that is used for all videodisc; configuration of playback channels ($i) has code "q" for surround sound.

- 020, 024, and 028: The ISBN and UPC numbers are entered without hyphens or spaces in field 020 and field 024 respectively. Publisher's number is recorded in field 028, with indicator "4" specifying this as a videorecording and indicator "2" indicating a note is to be generated from this field.

- 041 and 546: The sound track is available in several languages and the movie is closed-captioned and subtitled in two languages. Such information is recorded in a 546 note. The information is also coded in the 041 field, with subfield $a for the language of the sound track and subfield $b for the languages of the subtitles. The source of the language codes is the *MARC Code List of Languages* and each code is entered in a separate subfield. The first subfield $a of the 041 field is to correspond with the Lang element in the fixed field.

- 090 and 092: PN1997.5 is the LC number for animated films and 791.4372 is the Dewey number for single films. Materials in each group may be arranged alphabetically by title of film.

- 245 and 508: Only people or corporate bodies responsible for the overall creation of a work are recorded in the statement of responsibility area. Other types of contributors are selectively presented in the 508 note.

- 538: This note records the format, the region for which the video is intended, the sound configuration, how data are encoded, and the aspect ratio for the widescreen presentation.

- 511: Only major cast members are recorded in the 511 note; indicator "1" will produce "Cast" as the display constant.

- 500s: The publishing history of this work, including the basis of this work and its previous release, is recorded in the 500 notes.

- 521: Indicator "8" produces no display constant, so information in this field will be displayed as is.

- 500: Special features are usually presented in the 500 notes, with features separated by semicolons.

- 586: Award information can be taken from reference sources such as the Internet Movie Database and is presented as a 586 note.

- 700s and 710: Only individuals and corporate bodies that are major contributors to the work are traced, including producers, directors, major cast members, and the production firm. A name-title added entry is provided for King-Smith because his work is the basis of this film.

Figure 4.8. *Yoga for beginners*

[Disc label]

YOGA JOURNAL'S

YOGA

FOR BEGINNERS
with Patricia Walden

GAIAM
total content time:
3 hours
©(p)MMII Gaiam, Inc. All rights reserved.

Title screen

YOGA JOURNAL'S

YOGA

FOR BEGINNERS

Container (front):

**SPECIAL
DVD EDITION**
with Patricia Walden

Container (back):

Special DVD includes:
- Beginner's Pose Guide to begin your workout at any point or receive additional instruction on individual poses
- Putting it All Together to practice the poses in continual succession
- Yoga Practice Guide, a 46-page companion booklet to learn about yoga with a complete description and benefit of each pose
- BONUS 85-minute Yoga for Flexibility workout to take your practice to the next level

Total content time: 3 hours

Executive Producers: Steve Adams and Michael Gliksohn . Producer and Director: Steven Adams

DVD Producer: Chris Besett . Co-Producer: Linda Cogozzo . Director of Photography: Bruce Finn

Editor: Tom Mitchell . Composer: Peter Davison

Type	g	**ELvl**	I	**Srce**	d	**Audn**		**Ctrl**	**Lang**	eng
BLvl	m	**Form**		**GPub**		**Time**	180	**MRec**	**Ctry**	cou
Desc	a	**TMat**	v	**Tech**	l	**DtSt**	s	**Dates**	2002	

007		v $b d $d c $e v $f a $g i $h z $i u
020		1930814828
028	42	120-1263 $b Gaiam
090		RA781.7 $b .Y643 2002
092		613.7046
245	00	Yoga journal's yoga for beginners $h [videorecording] : $b with Patricia Walden.
246	30	Yoga for beginners
250		Special DVD ed.
260		[Broomfield, Colo.] : $b Gaiam, $c p2002.
300		1 DVD (180 min.) : $b sd., col. ; $c 4 ¾ in. + $e 1 booklet (44 p. : ill. ; 19 cm.)

538		DVD.
511	0	Instructor: Patricia Walden.
508		Executive Producers: Steve Adams and Michael Gliksohn; producer and director: Steven Adams; co-producer: Linda Cogozzo; director of photography: Bruce Finn; editor: Tom Mitchell; composer: Peter Davison.
520		An easy-to-follow approach to Hatha yoga, providing instructions on basic moves including standing, seated, inverted and relaxation poses.
500		Special DVD includes Beginner's Pose Guide, Putting it All Together, and Yoga for Flexibility.
650	0	Hatha yoga.
700	1	Walden, Patricia.
700	1	Adams, Steve.
710	2	Gaiam, Inc.

Discussion for Figure 4.8

- Fixed field: The video 008 field is used, so Type has code "g" for video. Type of material (TMat) has code "v" for video; technical information (Tech) has code "l" for live action; running time (Time) is three hours converted into minutes for 180; date type (DtSt) is single because this work includes new materials.

- Field 007: Category of material ($a) has code "v" for a videorecording; specific material designation ($b) has code "d" for videodisc; color ($d) has code "c" for multicolored item; videorecording format ($e) has code "v" for DVD; sound on medium or separate ($f) has code "a" to indicate the sound is on the same medium as the film; medium for sound ($g) has code "i" for videodisc; dimensions of the videotape ($h) has code "z" that is used for all videodisc; configuration of playback channels ($i) has code "u" for no information available.

- 020 and 028: The ISBN is recorded in the 020 field without hyphens. In the 028 field, the first indicator value is "4" for videorecordings, the second indicator is "2" to generate a note for this number.

- 245 and 246: The decision to transcribe the title proper as such is based on the layout and the text on the video and the container. Information in these areas and the accompanying material suggests that "Yoga for beginners" is an important title, so it is entered in the 246 field as a variant title. Because Patricia Walden appears on the disc, that statement is included in subfield $b of the 245 field.

- 250: The edition statement can be taken from the chief source, container, or accompanying material, so the statement on the container is entered in the 250 field.

- 260: The place of publication is supplied by the cataloger, so it is entered in brackets.

- 300: According to the latest *AACR2r* update, catalogers can use conventional terminology for specific material designation, so DVD is used. The total running time is recorded in parentheses following the specific material designation, the item has sound and is multicolored. The accompanying material is recorded in subfield $e. Catalogers have the option of recording details of the booklet, including pagination, illustration, and dimensions. This information is recorded following the punctuation pattern of Area 5, physical description.

- 538: The format of the video still needs to be recorded because the "DVD" in the 300 field refers to the physical carrier, not the format.

- 511: This field is used to clarify the role of Walden.

- 508: People responsible for the production of the work are recorded in the 508 field, but not all of them need to be traced. In this case, only the producer/director is traced.

- 520: A brief, objective summary note helps users understand the content of a video. Catalogers may follow the wording in the package to prepare such a note.

- 500: Additional features on the DVD are recorded to alert users of their existence. If desired, catalogers can provide access to these features by providing analytical added entries through the 740 fields, using "02" for the indicators.

- 700 and 710: The instructor and the publisher are traced.

Figure 4.9. *Blade runner* (DVD version)

WARNER HOME VIDEO

WARNER BROS. PICTURES
A TIME WARNER ENTERTAINMENT COMPANY
The Ladd Company
IN ASSOCIATION WITH SIR RUN RUN SHAW
THROUGH WARNER BROS., A TIME WARNER ENTERTAINMENT
COMPANY

JERRY PERENCHIO
AND
BUD YORKIN
PRESIDENT

HARRISON FORD

BLADE RUNNER

RUTGER HAUER
SEAN YOUNG
EDWARD JAMES OLMOS
M. EMMET WALSH
DARYL HANNAH
WILLIAM SANDERSON
BRION JAMES
JOE TURKEL
AND
JOANNA CASSIDY
SUPERVISING EDITOR
TERRY RAWLINGS

MUSIC
COMPOSED, ARRANGED, PERFORMED AND PRODUCED BY
VANGELIS
ASSOCIATE PRODUCER
IVOR POWELL
PRODUCTION DESIGN BY
LAWRENCE G. PAULL
DIRECTOR OF PHOTOGRAPHY
JORDAN CRONENWETH
SCREENPLAY BY
HAMPTON FANCHER
AND
DAVID PEOPLES

PRODUCED BY
MICHAEL DEELEY
DIRECTED BY
RIDLEY SCOTT

****
END CREDITS

A MICHAEL DEELEY —
RIDLEY SCOTT PRODUCTION

[MANY CREDIT FRAMES: on executive producers Brian Kelly
Hampton Fancher . . .
Special photographic effects supervisor . . . art director, and so on.]
BASED ON THE NOVEL
"DO ANDROIDS DREAM OF ELECTRIC SHEEP"
BY PHILIP K. DICK

© 1991 THE BLADE RUNNER PARTNERSHIP
ALL RIGHTS RESERVED

DISTRIBUTED BY WARNER BROS.
A TIME WARNER ENTERTAINMENT COMPANY

140

Type	g	ELvl	I	Srce	d	Audn	e	Ctrl	Lang	eng
BLvl	m	Form		GPub		Time	117	MRec	Ctry	cou
Desc	a	TMat	v	Tech	l	DtSt	s	Dates	1991	

007		v $b d $d c $e v $f a $g i $h z $i q
020		0790729628
028	42	12682 $b DVD Video
041	0	eng $b eng $b fre $b spa
090		PN1997
092		791.4372
245	00	Blade runner $h [videorecording] / $c Warner Bros., ; Ladd Company ; screenplay by Hampton Fancher and David Peoples ; produced by Michael Deeley ; directed by Ridley Scott.
260		Burbank, CA : $b Warner Home Video, $c c1991.
300		1 DVD (117 min.) : $b sd., col. ; $c 4 ¾ in.
538		DVD; Dolby surround.
546		Subtitles in English, French, and Spanish; closed-captioned.
511	1	Harrison Ford, Rutger Hauer, Sean Young, Edward James Olmos, Daryl Hannah.
508		Music by Vangelis; photography, Jordan Cronenweth.
500		Videodisc release of the 1982 motion picture.
500		Based on "Do androids dream of electric sheep?" by Philip K. Dick.
500		"The director's cut"—Disc.
500		"The original cut of the futuristic adventure"—Container.
521	8	R Rated.
520		Los Angeles, 2019: Deckard, a "blade runner," must identify and execute four replicants, which have illegally returned to earth from their off-world slave duty.
650	0	Science fiction films.
650	0	Feature films.
650	0	Video recordings for the hearing impaired.
700	1	Fancher, Hampton.
700	1	Peoples, David Webb.
700	1	Deeley, Michael.
700	1	Scott, Ridley.
700	1	Ford, Harrison, $d 1942–
700	1	Hauer, Rutger, $d 1944–
700	1	Young, Sean.
700	1	Olmos, Edward James.
700	1	Hannah, Daryl.
700	1	Vangelis.
700	1	Dick, Philip K. $t Do androids dream of electric sheep?
710	2	Warner Bro. Pictures.
710	2	Ladd Company.
710	2	Warner Home Video (Firm).

Discussion for Figure 4.9

- Fixed field: The video 008 field is used, so Type has code "g" for video. Type of material (TMat) has code "v" for video; technique (Tech) has code "l" for live action; running time (Time) is 117 minutes; date type (DtSt) is coded "s" because the DVD contains the director's original cut in addition to the 1982 movie. Because this work is R-rated, code "e" (adults) is used in Audn.

- Field 007: Category of material ($a) has code "v" for a videorecording; specific material designation ($b) has code "d" for videodisc; color ($d) has code "c" for multicolored item; videorecording format ($e) has code "v" for DVD; sound on medium or separate ($f) has code "a" to indicate the sound is on the same medium as the film; medium for sound ($g) has code "i" for videodisc; dimensions of the videotape ($h) has code "z" that is used for all videodisc; configuration of playback channels ($i) has code "q" for surround.

- Field 041: Because this item has several subtitle options, that information is recorded as a language note in the 546 field. The languages are coded in field 041, with subfield $a coding the language of the soundtrack, subfield $b for languages of the subtitles. The languages are entered in separate subfields $b, in alphabetical order.

- 245 and 508: One of the major challenges in cataloging films is to determine which corporate bodies and individuals among the many listed in the credits should be transcribed in Area 1. The practice is to record those with overall responsibility for the work. If there are others whose contribution is important, they are recorded in field 508.

- 300: DVD is the physical carrier of this work and is used as the specific material designation per the option for rule 7.5B1. The presence of sound is recorded in subfield $b, but the quality of the sound and the DVD format are recorded in field 538.

- 546: Two language notes are combined.

- 511: Only lead performers are recorded in field 511. Indicator "1" is for cast members.

- 508: This field records people whose contribution to the film is important but not important enough for them to be recorded in the statement of responsibility in Area 1. Catalogers can exercise their judgment in determining if these persons should be traced.

- 500s: These two notes are about the history of this work. They are typical of videos of feature films.

- 500s: The quotation notes explain how this work differs from the others. Since the quotations are not from the title screens, their sources are indicated.

- 521: Rating information is recorded in field 521, indicator "8" means no display constant will appear with this information.

- 650s: Following *SCM* H2230, a genre heading, a required form heading, and a heading for closed-captioned films are assigned to this work.

- 700s: The writer, producer, director, cast members, and other contributors are traced. They are presented in the order in which their names appear in the bibliographic description. The name-title added entry is the last of this group because of the order of added entries specified by *LCRI* 21.29 (CBS 45).

Figure 4.10. *Mary Poppins*

Walt Disney
Presents

Julie Andrews
Dick Van Dyke
David Tomlinson
Glynis Johns
In
Mary Poppins
co-starring
Hermione Baddeley
Karen Dotrice
Matthew Garber
Elsa Lanchester
Arthur Treacher
Reginald Owen
Ed Wynn

Director of Photography
Edward Colman
Technicolor
Music and Lyrics by
Richard M.   Robert B.
and
Sherman   Sherman
Music Supervised, Arranged and Conducted by
Irwin Kostal . . .
Screenplay by
Bill Walsh
Don DaGradi

Based on the "Mary Poppins" books by
P.L. Travers
Co-producer
Bill Walsh
Directed by
Robert Stevenson

Type	g	ELvl	I	Srce	d	Audn	g	Ctrl	Lang	eng
BLvl	m	Form		GPub		Time	139	MRec	Ctry	cau
Desc	a	TMat	v	Tech	c	DtSt	s	Dates	2000	

```
007        v $b d $d c $e v $f a $g i $h z $i q
020        0788823051
024   1    717951009753
028   42   20221 $b Buena Vista home Entertainment
041   0    eng $a fre $a spa
```

143

Figure 4.10. (*Continued*)

090		PN1997 $b .M37 2002
092		791.4372 $b .M3932
245	00	Mary Poppins $h [videorecording] / $c a Walt Disney Production.
260		Burbank, Calif. : $b Distributed by Buena Vista Home Entertainment, $c [2000?]
300		1 DVD (139 min.) : $b sd., col. ; $c 4 ¾ in.
538		DVD, Region 1; Dolby digital, 5.1 surround (English), 2.0 mono. (French and Spanish); widescreen presentation ratio: 1.85:1.
440	0	Walt Disney gold classic collection
546		Sound track in English, French or Spanish; closed-captioned.
511	1	Julie Andrews, Dick Van Dyke, David Tomlinson, Glynis Johns.
508		Music and lyrics, Richard M. and Robert B. Sherman; music supervisor/conductor, Irwin Kostal; screenplay, Bill Walsh, Don DaGradi; co-producers, Bill Walsh; director, Robert Stevenson.
500		Based on the Mary Poppins books by P.L. Travers.
500		Video release of a 1964 motion picture.
521	8	Rated G.
500		Special features: The making of Mary Poppins; "Hollywood goes to a world premiere"; Mary Poppins trivia game; original theatrical trailer.
520		An irrepressible nanny soars out of the London skies, bringing a carpetbag of magical adventures into the lives of the Banks family on Cherry Tree Lane. Blends live-action and animation.
586	8	Academy Awards, 1964: Best actress, Julie Andrews; Best editing, Cotton Warburton; Best visual effects, Peter Ellenshaw, Hamilton Luske, Eustace Lycett; Best original music score, Richard M. & Robert B. Sherman; Best song, Chim Chim Cher-ee, Richard M. & Robert B. Sherman, music & lyrics.
650	0	Musical films.
650	0	Animated films.
650	0	Fantasy films.
650	0	Children's films.
650	0	Video recordings for the hearing impaired.
650	0	Feature films.
700	1	Andrews, Julie.
700	1	Van Dyke, Dick.
700	1	Tomlinson, David.
700	1	Johns, Glynis.
700	1	Stevenson, Robert, $d 1905–1986.
700	1	Travers, P. L. $q (Pamela Lyndon), $d 1899–1996.
710	2	Walt Disney Company.
710	2	Buena Vista Home Entertainment (Firm)

144

Discussion for Figure 4.10

- Fixed field: The 008 field for video is used, with Type coded as "g". Type of material (TMat) has code "v" for video; technique (Tech) has code "c" for live action and animation; running time (Time) is 139 minutes as stated on the disc; because the film is of interest to many age groups, target audience (Audn) has code "g" for general interest; date type (DtSt) is coded "s" because this work includes new materials.

- Field 007: Category of material ($a) has code "v" for a videorecording; specific material designation ($b) has code "d" for videodisc; color ($d) has code "c" for multicolored item; videorecording format ($e) has code "v" for DVD; sound on medium or separate ($f) has code "a" to indicate the sound is on the same medium as the film; medium for sound ($g) has code "i" for videodisc; dimensions of the videotape ($h) has code "z" that is used for all videodisc; configuration of playback channels ($i) has code "q" for Surround Sound.

- 020, 024, and 028: The ISBN and UPC numbers are entered without hyphens or spaces in field 020 and field 024 respectively. The publisher's number is recorded in field 028, with indicator "4" specifying this as a videorecording and indicator "2" indicating a note is to be generated from this field.

- 041 and 546: The sound track is available in several languages and the movie is closed-captioned. Such information is recorded in a 546 note. The information is also coded in the 041 field, with subfield $a for the language of the sound track. The source of the language codes is the *MARC Code List of Languages* and each code is entered in a separate subfield. The first subfield $a of the 041 field is to correspond with the Lang element in the fixed field.

- 090 and 092: PN1997 is the LC number for motion pictures produced through 2000 and 791.4372 is the Dewey number for single films. Films in each group may be arranged alphabetically by title.

- 245 and 508: Because of the way information is presented in the title frames and the credit frames, only the company, Walt Disney, is recorded in the statement of responsibility area. Contributors such as composers, writers, and director are presented in a 508 notes later.

- 260: The DVD does not include information on the production company, but has distributor information, so that information is recorded in the 260 field.

- 440: The series statement appears on the container. The authorized form is taken from the Library of Congress authority file.

- 538: The format, region specification, sound configuration, and aspect ratio of the film are presented in a 538 note. Because the sound configuration for the French and Spanish soundtracks are different from the English soundtrack, that information is recorded as well.

- 511: Many actors and actresses took part in this film, but only major cast members are recorded. Indicator "1" will produce "Cast" as the display constant.

- 500s: Publishing history, such as the basis of the work and its previous release, is entered in two 500 notes.

- 521: The intended audience note reflects the rating information found on the item. Indicator "8" will produce no display constant.

- 586: Award information is found in reference sources such as the Internet Movie Database.

- 700s and 710s: Only people with overall responsibility for the creation of the film and the lead actors are traced. The original production firm and the distributor of the video are also traced. Travers is traced because the film is based on her works.

References

Ashley, Lowell E. (Ed.). Working Group on Bibliographic Control of Music Video Material, Bibliographic Control Committee. (1996). *Cataloging musical moving image material: A guide to the bibliographic control of videorecordings and films of musical performances and other music-related moving image material with examples in MARC format.* Canton, Mass.: Music Library Association.

Association for Library Collections and Technical Services. Subcommittee on the Revision of the Guidelines on Subject Access to Individual Works of Fiction, Subject Analysis Committee, Cataloging and Classification Section. (2000). *Guidelines on subject access to individual works of fiction, drama, etc.* (2nd ed.). Chicago: American Library Association.

Chan, Lois Mai. (1990). *Immroth's guide to the Library of Congress classification* (4th ed.). Englewood, Colo.: Libraries Unlimited.

Chan, Lois Mai. (1996). *Dewey decimal classification: A practical guide* (2nd ed., rev. for *DDC* 21). Albany, N.Y.: Forest Press.

Differences between changes within: Guidelines on when to create a new record. (2005). Chicago: ALCTS Publishing.

Dillon, Patrick M., and Leonard, David C. (1998). *Multimedia and the Web from A to Z* (2nd ed.). Phoenix, Ariz.: Oryx Press.

Dolby Digital FAQ. (2005). http://www.dolby.com/consumer/technology/dolby_faq_4.html (accessed June 1, 2005).

Intner, Sheila S., and Studwell, William E., with the assistance of Blake, Simone E., and Miller, David P. (1992). *Subject access to films and videos.* Lake Crystal, Minn.: Soldier Creek Press.

The letterbox and widescreen advocacy page. (2005). http://www.widescreen.org/widescreen.shtml (accessed June 1, 2005).

MARC 21 concise format for bibliographic data. (2004). http://www.loc.gov/marc/bibliographic/ecbdhome.html (accessed June 1, 2005).

Miller, David P. (1992). Level of compatibility between moving image materials: Genre terms and Library of Congress subject headings in a general library catalog. In Sheila S. Intner and William E. Studwell (Eds.), *Subject access to films and videos*, with the assistance of Simone E. Blake and David P. Miller, 17–30. Lake Crystal, Minn.: Soldier Creek Press.

OCLC bibliographic formats and standards. (2003). http://www.oclc.org/bibformats/ (accessed June 1, 2005).

OCLC interim support for ISBN 13. (2004). http://www.oclc.org/news/announcements/announcement96.htm (accessed June 1, 2005).

Online Audiovisual Catalogers, Inc. Cataloging Policy Committee, DVD Cataloging Task Force. (2002). *Guide to cataloging DVDs using AACR2r chapters 7 and 9.* http://www.olacinc.org/capc/dvd/dvdprimer0.html (accessed June 1, 2005).

Technical bulletin 249 OCLC-MARC format update 2003. (2003). http://www.oclc.org/support/documentation/worldcat/tb/249/249.pdf (accessed June 1, 2005).

Weihs, Jean. (1987). Access to nonbook materials: The role of subject headings and classification numbers for nonbook materials. In Sheila S. Intner and Richard P. Smiraglia (Eds.), *Policy and practice in bibliographic control of nonbook media*, 53–63. Chicago: American Library Association.

Weitz, Jay. (2001). Videorecording cataloging: Problems and pointers. *Cataloging & Classification Quarterly* 31 (2): 53–83.

Weitz, Jay. (2002). *Videorecordings cataloging workshop*. OLAC Conference, Electronic and Media Cataloging for the 21st Century, St. Paul, Minn., September 27–29. http://elibrary.unm.edu/catdept/training/videorecordings-examples.doc (accessed June 1, 2005).

Whatis.com. (2005). *Streaming video*. http://searchenterprisevoice.techtarget.com/gDefinition/0,294236,sid66_gci213055,00.html (accessed June 1, 2005).

Yee, Martha M. (1988). *Moving image materials: Genre terms (MIM)*. Washington, D.C.: Library of Congress, Cataloging Distribution Service.

Suggested Readings

Ashley, Lowell E. (Ed.). Working Group on Bibliographic Control of Music Video Material, Bibliographic Control Committee. (1996). *Cataloging musical moving image material: A guide to the bibliographic control of videorecordings and films of musical performances and other music-related moving image material with examples in MARC format*. Canton, Mass.: Music Library Association.

Association for Library Collections and Technical Services. Subcommittee on the Revision of the Guidelines on Subject Access to Individual Works of Fiction, Subject Analysis Committee, Cataloging and Classification Section. (2000). *Guidelines on subject access to individual works of fiction, drama, etc.* (2nd ed.). Chicago: American Library Association.

Hartsock, Ralph. (1994). *Notes for music catalogers: Examples illustrating AACR2 in the online bibliographic record*. Lake Crystal, Minn.: Soldier Creek Press.

Intner, Sheila S., and Studwell, William E., with the assistance of Blake, Simone E., and Miller, David P. (1992). *Subject access to films and videos*. Lake Crystal, Minn.: Soldier Creek Press.

Maillet, Lucienne G. (1991). *Subject control of film and video: A comparison of three methods*. Chicago: American Library Association.

Weihs, Jean. (1987). Access to nonbook materials: The role of subject headings and classification numbers for nonbook materials. In Sheila S. Intner and Richard P. Smiraglia (Eds.), *Policy and practice in bibliographic control of nonbook media*, 53–63. Chicago: American Library Association.

Weitz, Jay. (2001). Videorecording cataloging: Problems and pointers. *Cataloging & Classification Quarterly* 31 (2): 53–83.

5

Electronic Resources

Library collections of computer files have grown by type and number since the 1960s, and the development of microcomputers in the 1980s contributed to the rapid proliferation of computer programs and data files (Intner 1991). A 1999 survey found that 100 percent of the academic library respondents collect computer files, and 93 percent of the public library respondents collect computer files (Hsieh-Yee). A 2004 survey of libraries in the Washington Metropolitan Area found 73 percent of responding libraries catalog databases and electronic journals, and 69 percent catalog Web resources (Hsieh-Yee). As computer files become increasingly popular among users, the need to organize them for access becomes more pressing. One of the major challenges in cataloging computer files is the lack of uniformity in the information that comes with the work. Some computer files have extensive documentation or tip sheets, while others keep all information on the files and the cataloger needs to install or decompress the files to locate bibliographic information. Some knowledge of computer applications and file structure will make the description of such resources easier for catalogers. A more serious challenge for catalogers is the treatment of varying information from various sources. The title screen(s), disk label, container, and accompanying material may carry information that is different, and catalogers often need to determine which information to transcribe for the bibliographic record. For instance, a "README" file may list the system requirements of a program, while the container highlights some of the machinery needed to run it. Similarly, a file may carry a publication date, while its documentation carries a different date, and the container has a third date. Cataloging rules cover problems like these, but it is also a challenge to keep up with the changing standards.

Cataloging rules for computer files have evolved with technology. The second edition of the *Anglo-American Cataloguing Rules* was published in 1978, when data and program files were stored and manipulated in mainframe computers. As collections of microcomputer files grew in the early 1980s, catalogers realized the inadequacy of the rules designed for machine-readable data files. In 1984, in response to the need for guidance in cataloging micro-computer files, ALA published the *Guidelines for Using AACR2 Chapter 9 for Cataloging Microcomputer Software* (1984) and the British Library published a report, *Study of Cataloguing Computer Software: Applying AACR2 to Microcomputer Programs* (1984). The recommendations were subsequently debated and revised into Chapter 9 of the 1988 revision of *AACR2*. Olson's report on how the rules were developed and approved by various national and international bodies illustrates the thoughtful process of rule revision (1988). The rationale for the major changes in Chapter 9 is explained by Weihs (1988). In 1990 the first edition of the *ISBD (CF) International Standard Bibliographic Description for Computer Files* was published by its sponsor, the International Federation of Library Associations' Sections on Cataloguing and on Information Technology. It focused on software programs and machine-readable databases (ISBD 1990). Many of its recommendations have been incorporated into the latest *AACR2r*.

Technology in the late 1980s made it possible for creators to combine text, sound, music, graphics, video, and other forms to present their ideas. Multimedia applications have soared in the 1990s, and catalogers, once again, realized rules for microcomputer files could not cover multimedia properly. As a result, in 1994 ALA published the *Guidelines for Bibliographic Description of Interactive Multimedia* (1994). A bigger challenge presented itself in the 1990s when the World Wide Web, thanks to user-friendly graphical interface, became widely popular. The here-today-and-gone-tomorrow nature of Web resources caused serious concerns about their organization. Some have questioned the wisdom in cataloging the Web (Banerjee 1997) while others have affirmed the role of libraries in providing access to information (Mandel and Wolven 1996; Oder 1998). A set of guidelines were developed for the InterCat project, an experiment initiated by OCLC to determine whether cataloging rules and MARC format could adequately describe Web resources, and Olson's *Cataloging Internet Resources: A Manual and Practical Guide* (1997) subsequently became the standard for cataloging Web resources. In the international arena the International Federation of Library Associations' Sections on Cataloguing and on Information Technology decided in 1994 to review *ISBD (CF)* to determine how well it could cover interactive multimedia, remote electronic files, new developments in optical technology, and files in various formats. The result is the 1997 publication of *ISBD for Electronic Resources (ER)*. The *ISBD (ER)* covers the cataloging of direct access and remote access electronic resources equally well, provides an expanded list of terminology for Area 3, "type and extent of resource," and recommends that all physical manifestations of the same intellectual content be recorded in one single bibliographic record (1997).

As more and more users are connected to the Internet, it has become a major channel for disseminating publications for commercial publishers and individual authors. A large number of Web sites, PDF files, electronic books, electronic journals, digital sound files, image files, streaming videos, and so on have become available on the World Wide Web. In addition, advances in technology have led to increased reliance on DVD for storing computer files. Strong user interest in using and creating digital resources have prompted the cataloging community to catalog more electronic resources, and cataloging rules were once again revised in the late 1990s to catch up with changes in computing and network technology. The 2001 amendments to the *Anglo-American Cataloguing Rules* incorporates many recommendations from

ISBD (ER) and presents a complete revision of the rules for describing electronic resources. The amended Chapter 9 for electronic resources has a broader scope, covering direct access, remote access, and interactive multimedia published in single part and multiple parts. Unlike the 1998 rules that emphasize internal sources as the chief source of information, the new Chapter 9 identifies "the resource itself" as the chief source. To make bibliographic data more accessible to catalog users, Chapter 9 gives catalogers the option of using conventional terminology such as CD-ROM, and stipulates the same types of information for the system requirements note. But it rejects the terminology for Area 3 proposed by the *ISBD (ER)* and its recommendation to record multiple physical carriers in one bibliographic record (Weiss 2003).

Web resources have posed considerable challenges for catalogers. The continuing nature of such resources suggests their similarity to serials, and yet, they usually do not carry numeric or chronological designations. Hirons and Graham addressed issues related to seriality (1997) and their effort led to a major revision of Chapter 12, originally for serials. The new Chapter 12, published in 2002, is entitled "continuing resources" and covers serials and integrating resources. Unlike serials cataloging, which is based on the first issue or the earliest available issue, the cataloging of integrating resources is based on the latest entry, and previous changes in titles, publishers, publication frequencies, sponsors, and so on are recorded in notes. The Joint Steering Committee for Revision of the Anglo-American Cataloguing Rules (JSC) has published annual updates to provide the cataloging community the latest changes in cataloging rules. The 2004 update eliminates Area 3, "type and extent of resource," from the amended Chapter 9 on electronic resources.

The new rules reflect several significant changes to how computer files are described or referred to throughout the 2002 revision of *AACR2*. The chapter heading of Chapter 9, "Computer Files," becomes "Electronic Resources" and the general material designation (GMD) for this type of resources changes from [computer file] to [electronic resource]. [Interactive multimedia] is no longer a valid GMD and is replaced by [electronic resource] instead.

In addition, rule 0.24 is revised to reflect a shift in cataloging focus. While the 1998 rule instructed catalogers to use the rules for the class of materials to which an item belongs, the new 0.24 rule stresses the need to "bring out all aspects of the item being described, including its content, its carrier, its type of publication, its bibliographic relationships, and whether it is published or unpublished" (*AACR2*). This rule is especially applicable to electronic resources because they often "include components with characteristics found in multiple classes of materials" (rule 9.0A1) and catalogers will need to consult all relevant chapters to describe the hybrid materials.

The amended *AACR2r* Chapter 9 covers the description of all electronic resources that are accessed locally and remotely. In cataloging electronic resources catalogers first need to determine the "type of issurance" of the resource. Is it a monograph, a serial, or an integrating resource? If a resource is complete in one part or intended to be complete in multiple parts, catalogers should treat it as a monograph and follow Chapters 9, 1, and 2 to describe it. If it is published "in succession of discrete parts, usually bearing numbering, that has no predetermined conclusion" (Appendix D) catalogers will treat it as a serial and follow Chapters 12, 9, and other relevant chapters to create the record. But if it is updated frequently and the updates are integrated into earlier iterations, catalogers will treat it as an integrating resource and follow Chapters 12, 9, and other relevant chapters to catalog it. Chapter 5 of this book focuses on the cataloging of direct access electronic resources. In addition, it covers the description and access of remote access electronic resources that are finite, such as finite Internet resources and electronic books. Chapter 6 concentrates on integrating resources and discusses the treatment of updating databases and updating Web sites. Chapter 7 is devoted to the treatment of remote access electronic serials.

MARC Fields for Electronic Resources

The Library of Congress and OCLC have published several helpful guidelines for cataloging electronic resources:

- Library of Congress. Cataloging Policy and Support Office. *Draft Interim Guidelines for Cataloging Electronic Resources*, http://www .loc.gov/catdir/cpso/dcmb19_4.html

- Library of Congress. Network Development and Standards Office. *Guidelines for Coding Electronic Resources in Leader/06*. Revised December 2003. http://www.loc.gov/marc/ldr06guide.html

- Library of Congress. Network Development and Standards Office. *Guidelines for the Use of Field 856*. Revised March 2003. http://www .loc.gov/marc/856guide.html

- Weitz, Jay. Cataloging Electronic Resources: OCLC-MARC Coding Guidelines. Revised November 9, 2004. http://www.oclc.org/support/ documentation/worldcat/cataloging/electronicresources/

The MARC fields commonly used to encode electronic resources are listed below. The electronic resource 006 field is required if the Type element is not coded "m" (see below for further discussion of the use of field 006). It is also required for electronic serials. In these two scenarios electronic resource field 006 is used to bring out the computer aspect of a material so that the material can be retrieved when a user searches for electronic resources. The electronic resource 007 field records additional physical characteristics and is required for all computer files.

Because this chapter covers direct access electronic resources, finite Internet resources, and electronic books, a few relevant MARC fields for remote access electronic resources are included in the following table.

Common Fields for Direct Access and Remote Access Electronic Resources

Field number	Definition
Leader/06 ("Type")	Fixed field code for specifying the type of 008 field for a record code "m" = computer file 008 field code "a" = language material.

	If BLvl is coded "m" for monograph, the monograph 008 field is used. If BLvl is coded "s" for serial, the serial 008 field is used.	
006	**Fixed field elements for coding resource characteristics not represented by the 008 field specified by Leader/06 ("Type").** Electronic resource 006 field is commonly used for electronic resources that are not coded as Type "m" and for electronic serials.	
007	**Fixed field elements for coding additional physical characteristics.** Electronic resource 007 field is commonly used for electronic resources: $a computer file $b specific material designation $d color $e dimensions $f sound	

Field	Indicators	Subfields
010		LC control number
020		ISBN
022		ISSN
1XX	—	Main entry (for personal name (100), corporate body (110), and conference (111) as main entry, not for title main entry)
245	— —	Title proper $h [electronic resource] : $b other title information / $c statement of responsibility. 245 0 _ for title main entry.
246	— —	Variant title $i for display text : $a for variant title
250		Edition statement.
260		Place of publication : $b Publisher, $c Date of publication.
300		Number of specific material designation : $b sound, illustration ; $c dimensions. + $e accompanying material. (NOT for remote access electronic resources)
4XX	— —	Series statement
500/516		Nature and scope; type of electronic resource.
538		System requirements.
538		Mode of access for remote access electronic resources.
546		Languages.

500		Source of title note (a required note). Add viewing date for remote access electronic resources.
500		Other general note.
520	—	Summary.
505	— —	Contents note.
530		Additional physical form available.
6XX	— —	Subject heading. $x, $y, $z, $v
7XX	—	Non-subject added entry.
730	— —	Uniform title added entry for related resources cataloged separately.
740	— —	Analytical title added entry.
776	— —	Link to other physical formats $a, $x, $w
830	—	Series added entries (often used with 490)
856	— —	Electronic location and access $u, $z

Coding electronic resources in MARC bibliographic format can be challenging, especially when fixed-field elements are concerned. After the completion of format integration in the spring of 1996, catalogers are able to code bibliographic information consistently across formats. OCLC's *Bibliographic Formats and Standards* (http://www.oclc.org/bibformats/) contains changes that resulted from format integration. Two major changes related to computer files deserve attention: the narrow definition of code "m" and the addition of field 006.

Type "m"

In MARC 21 for bibliographic records, the Leader/06 (Type of record) position, presented as "**Type**" in the fixed field, is designed for a one-character alphabetic code that specifies the type of field 008 (Fixed Length Data Element) in a record. The code differentiates records created for various types of resources. In June 1997 the definition of code "m" (Computer file) of Leader/06 was revised to support the coding of electronic resources for the most significant aspect of their content, not their physical form. After the revision, code "m" has a narrower scope and is applied to four categories of electronic resources (LC update no. 3 to *USMARC Format for Bibliographic Data*):

- Computer software (including programs, games, fonts)
- Numeric data
- Computer-oriented multimedia
- Online systems or services

For these categories of materials, if there is a significant aspect that causes it to fall into another Leader/06 (Type of record) category, that other category should be used to code the resource. An example provided in the *Guidelines for Coding Electronic Resources in MARC Leader/06* is vector data that is cartographic is not coded as numeric but as cartographic.

Because the purpose of Leader/06 is to code the most significant aspect of the content, not the form, of a resource, it is important to consider what is being cataloged when choosing the code for Ldr/06. If the cataloger is cataloging a statistics program such as *StatView* that can be used to analyze various types of data and the focus is *not* on data this program can process, code "m" (computer file) should be used. Similarly, a bibliographic record for *Term Tree*, a program for thesaurus building, will be coded "m" for computer software. But the Web site that offers information and options for downloading a demonstration kit should be coded "a" because its content is predominantly textual. Figure 2.1 of Chapter 2 of this book offers a model for selecting the 008 field for record creation, including the code options for Type, BLvl, the 008 field, and 006 fields that are applicable to the main entry or accompanying material.

Computer Files/Electronic Resources 006 Field

Another significant result of format integration is the addition of field 006. Field 006 is an optional field that can be used to code items with multiple characteristics. For example, the most significant aspect of a book accompanied by a CD-ROM is the language material aspect, so field 008 for BOOKS is used and Leader/06 position ("Type" in OCLC fixed field) is coded "a" for "language material." In addition, a field 006 for electronic resources brings out the electronic aspect of the CD-ROM.

```
[on the monograph format] Type: a    Blvl: m    Enlv: I    Desc: a
245    00    Web page design cookbook / $c William
             Horton … [et al.]
300          xx, 649 p. : $b ill. ; $c 28 cm. + $e 1 computer optical
             disc (ill ; 4 3/4 in.).

This item will have an electronic resource 006 field as follows:
T006: m AuDn: g File: d GPub:
```

Code "m" stands for computer file, code "g" for general audience, code "d" for document, and GPub (government publication) is blank because this is not a government publication. The presence of this 006 field will enable searchers who qualify their search statement to computer file format to retrieve this item.

MARC 21 defines field 006 for several types of materials, including books, computer files/electronic resources, continuing resources, maps, mixed materials, music, and visual materials. OCLC's Connexion provides a pull-down menu for easy addition of field 006. After a user specifies the type of 006 field needed, Connexion will provide related code elements for the user to fill in appropriate values. The code elements are hyperlinked to OCLC's bibliographic formats, which provide explanations and examples. An electronic resource 006 field and a serial 006 field from Connexion are provided below to illustrate this helpful feature.

```
006 fields for [Computer Files]
Computer File
Audn    File    u    GPub
```

006 field for Serials [Serial]						
Serial						
Freq	Regl	ISSN	SrTp	Orig		
Form	EntW	Cont	GPub	Conf	Alph	S/L

MARC 21 has defined code values for continuing resources, but many of these values have not been implemented. Until code "i" for Bibliographic Level (BLvl) is implemented, all nonserial publications are coded "m" for monograph, and appropriate 006 fields and 007 fields are added to represent important aspects of an electronic resource. The following table summarizes the use of Type, BLvl, fields 006, 007, and 008 for four types of electronic resources.

Nature of publication	Electronic Resource (Monographic)		Electronic Resources (Integrating)	
Element/Field	Computer Content	Text Content	Computer Content	Text Content
Type	m	a	m	a
Blvl	m	m	m	m
Computer file 008	yes	no	yes	no
Book 008	no	yes	no	yes
Electronic resource 006	no	yes	no	yes
Electronic resource 007	yes	yes	yes	yes
Serial 006	no	no	yes	yes

According to this table, when a direct access electronic resource is a software, contains numeric data, is a multimedia or an online system or service, the "Type" element will be coded "m" and the computer file 008 field will be used to create the bibliographic record. Because electronic resource 007 field is required for all electronic resources, it will be added to the bibliographic description too. But when an electronic resource is primarily textual, then "Type" is coded "a" and the book 008 field is used for record creation. In addition, an electronic resource 006 field and an electronic resource 007 field are added to represent the computer aspects of the work.

Similarly, when an electronic integrating resource is being described, the cataloger will code the "Type" element based on the primary content of the work. If it is one of the four categories of materials represented by code "m", the computer file 008 field is used to created a bibliographic record and an electronic resource 007 field is added because it is required for all electronic resources. But when the content is primarily textual, the cataloger will code "Type" as "a" for language material, use the book 008 field to create a bibliographic record, and add an electronic resource 006 field and an electronic resource 007 field to bring out the electronic aspects of the work being cataloged.

When code "i" is implemented for Bibliographic Level (BLvl), all integrating resources will be coded "i." The current practice is to use code "m" for BLvl and a serial 006 field to indicate the continuing nature of these types of resources.

When coding electronic resources, catalogers should base their decision on the most significant aspect of the resource such as language material, cartographic material, sound, or moving images. For instance, code "a" (language materials) will be used for a Web site that contains mostly textual materials and some photographs. An electronic resource 006 field will represent the computer aspect of this resource, and an electronic resource 007 field will cover the physical characteristics. And if the Web site is continuously updated, a serial 006 field will be added to indicate the continuing nature of the resource. The electronic resource 006 field is mandatory in cases like this to enable this type of resources to be retrieved in OCLC through the "COM" search qualifier.

For example, Electronic Information System for International Law (EISIL) is a Web site designed to provide access to quality primary materials, authoritative Web sites, and helpful research guides to international law (www.eisil.org/). The site is primarily text, so the cataloger will use the following fixed-field elements to encode this item:

Type: a	Elvl: **I**	Srce: d	Audn:	Ctrl:	Lang: eng
Blvl: m	Form: s	Conf: 0	Biog:	Mrec:	Ctry:
	Cont:	GPub:	LitF: 0	Indx: 0	
Desc: a	Ills:	Fest: 0	DtSt: m	Dates:	

In addition, a serial 006 field is used to represent the continuing nature of this item:

006 for continuing resources (serials)							
Freq: u	Regl: x	ISSN:	SrTp: w	Orig: s			
Form: s	EntW:	Cont:	GPub:	Conf:	Alph:	S/L: 2	

An electronic resource 006 field and an electronic resource 007 field are added to represent the computer aspects of this work:

006	Type: m	File: d	AuDn:	Gpub:
007	c $b r $d c $e n $f #			

Electronic resources, such as electronic books, that are the electronic equivalent of their print counterparts should have the same "Type" code as their print versions. Again, the electronic aspects are represented by an electronic resource 006 field and an electronic resource 007 field. But no serial 006 should be used if the electronic resources, like their print versions, are finite in nature. The PDF version of *Child Care Expenses of America's Families* (http://newfedralism.urban.org/pdf/occa40.pdf), a publication from the Urban Institute, would be coded the same way as its print version, except for the addition of electronic resources 006 and 007 fields.

In determining whether code "m" should be used for an electronic resource, catalogers need to keep in mind that the presence of search software does not automatically qualify a resource as a computer file. For example, PubMed is a digital archive of medical research reports. Although it has a search engine, the content of the system is primarily textual, so code "a" (language material) is appropriate for Ldr/06 (Type of record) for this resource.

Coding "File" and "Form" in Fixed Field

"File" and "Form" are two elements in the fixed field that deserve some attention from catalogers. The "File" element takes up the position of computer file 008/26 and 006/09, a one-character alphabetic code for specifying the type of resource being cataloged. If an electronic resource is coded "m" (for computer file), the 008/26 position ("File" in the fixed field) is coded. If Type is *not* coded "m," an electronic resource 006 field is used to represent the electronic aspect and the 006/09 position ("File" in the 006 field) is coded. Thirteen code values are available for this element:

Code	Nature of File	Code	Nature of File	Code	Nature of File
a	Numerical data	f	Font	m	Combination
b	Computer program	g	Game	u	Unknown
c	Representational	h	Sound	z	Other
d	Document	i	Interactive multimedia		
e	Bibliographic data	j	Online system or service		

The Library of Congress's *Guidelines for Coding Electronic Resources in Leader/06* and *Cataloging Electronic Resources: OCLC-MARC Coding Guidelines* offer many examples for coding "Type" and "File." The LC *Guidelines* also state that the file information is to be described in field 516. Examples below illustrate a few typical practices for coding Type and File:

Example	Leader/06 "Type" in Fixed Field	008/26 "File" in Fixed Field	006/09 "File" in Field 006
Electronic numeric data (numeric data can be manipulated), e.g., survey data set	m	a	
Electronic numeric data (numeric data in tabular form equivalent to print document), e.g., NCES statistical tables	m	d	
Electronic full-text databases with search software, e.g., MagPortal and JSTOR	a		d
Electronic journals, e.g., *D-Lib magazine*	a		d

Electronic bibliographic databases, e.g., LC online catalog	a		e
Electronic text files with search software, e.g., Engineering handbook	a		d
Online systems or services, e.g., AOL and Web4Lib	m	j	
Web site heavy with text and links to text contents	a		d
Electronic interactive game, e.g., game on CD-ROM	m	g	
Web site of audio files with search software, e.g., speechbot	i or j		h

As for "Form", if an electronic resource contains a significant aspect in any of the following formats—Books, Serials, Mixed Materials, Scores, Maps, and Visual Materials—the "Form" (Form of item) element should be coded "s" in the fixed field or in the 006 field for that format. Code "s" indicates the item is intended for manipulation by a computer. It may be accessed directly or remotely and may require the use of peripheral devices attached to the computer. For example, a Web site of digitized sound files (such as MP3 files) that is continuously updated will have the following codes

> Type: j (for musical sound file, or "i" for non-musical sound file)
> Electronic resource 006 field with "File" coded as "h" for sound files
> Serial 006 field will be added to indicate the continuing nature of this site, with "Form" coded as "s" to indicate this is an electronic resource that requires the use of a computer.

Electronic Resource 007 Field

This 007 field is another important field for electronic resources. It describes additional physical characteristics of an item. After format integration, field 007 is *required* for all computer files. Five subfields of the 007 field are mandatory or required if applicable, and various code values are defined for them. Examples below illustrate the use of electronic resource field 007. For a full list of the values, please see OCLC Bibliographic Format Web site at http://www.oclc.org/bibformats/en/0xx/007

Subfield	*Nature of item*	*Code values*	*Examples*
a	Category of material	c	c computer file
b	Specific material designation	11 codes	j magnetic disk
			o optical disc
			r remote

d	Color	8 codes	b black-and-white
			c multicolored
			g gray scale
			n not applicable
e	Dimensions	10 codes	a 3 1/2 in.
			e 12 in.
			g 4 3/4 in. (CD or DVD)
			o 5 1/4 in.
f	Sound	3 codes	blank (no sound, silent)
			a (sound)
			u (unknown)

Field 007 examples:

A CD-ROM database with gray scale and sound
type: m   ["m" for computer file]
file: j   ["j" for online system or service; see "Type of File" table above]
007              $a c $b o $d g $e g $f a

A game file on disk with multicolor and sound
type: m   ["m" for computer file]
file: g   ["g" for game; see "Type of File" table above]
007              $a c $b j $d c $e a $f a

Another area that is likely to cause confusion is the treatment of the resource that has several manifestations. For instance, an association may publish its membership directory in print every year while updating members' data on its Web database continuously. The print manifestation, according to *AACR2r*, will be treated as a serial, whereas the Web database will be treated as an integrating resource. Library of Congress, CONSER, and OCLC have decided to follow current *AACR2r* definitions. OCLC provides a useful list of remote access electronic resources that should *not* be treated as serials. They include

- Databases (including directories, A&I services, etc.)
- Electronic discussion groups (e.g., SERIALST)
- Electronic discussion group digests (e.g., AUTOCAT digest)
- Gopher servers (e.g., LC-MARVEL)
- Online public access catalogs (e.g., OCLC, RLIN)
- Online services (e.g., America Online)
- Web sites (e.g., the CONSER home page).

Instead, these resources are treated as "integrating resources" (if they are continuously updated) or "monographs" (if they are finite) (Weitz 2004). In either treatment the bibliographic level ("BLvl") element is coded "m" for monographs for now until the new code "i" for integrating resource is implemented.

Description

Rules for Descriptive Cataloging

9.0A. Scope

AACR2r Chapter 9, "Electronic Resources," provides rules that cover all electronic resources, which are "material (data and/or program(s)) encoded for manipulation by a computerized device" (Appendix D, *AACR2r*). Electronic resources may be "data" that represent numerical information, text, images, sounds, moving images, multimedia, and so on. Or they may consist of "programs" that are instructions for processing data or a combination of data and program. Examples of electronic resources include electronic books, word processing programs, statistical programs, multimedia, Web sites, and electronic serials. When electronic resources consist of several types of materials, catalogers will need to consult several chapters of *AACR2r*. For example, in cataloging an electronic journal, catalogers will follow instructions from Chapters 9 and 12.

Electronic resources can be accessed directly or remotely. When information is encoded on a physical carrier that requires the use of a computerized device (e.g., a computer, a personal digital assistant (PDA), an electronic book reader) or a peripheral directly connected to a computerized device (e.g., CD-ROM drive), the material is categorized as "direct access" material. Physical carriers may be magnetic disks, optical discs, DVDs, cassettes, cartridges, reels, and many others; the physical carrier is described in the bibliographic record (field 300). When no physical carrier is involved and information is accessed from a storage device at a remote site or through a connection to a computer network (e.g., the Internet), the material is categorized as "remote access" material, and no physical description is provided. The 2004 update to *AACR2r* offers an option for providing physical description for remote access electronic resources (see rules 9.5B3 and 9.5C3).

9.0B1. Chief Source of Information

The earlier rule about using title screen as the chief source of information was replaced by the new rule that *the entire electronic resource itself* is the chief source. Catalogers are to take information from "formally presented evidence" such as title screen(s), main menus, program statements, initial displays of information, home pages, file header(s) including the "Subject:" lines, encoded metadata such as meta tags in HTML/XML pages and TEI headers, and the physical carrier or its labels. Footnote 1 of Chapter 9 clarifies that "label" is "any paper, plastic, etc., label permanently affixed to a physical carrier, or information printed or embossed directly onto the physical carrier by the publisher, creator, etc., of the resource." When information in these sources varies in fullness, catalogers should choose the source that contains the most complete information. The source of the title proper is required for all electronic resources (rule 9.1B2) and encoded as a 500 note in MARC.

Disc label:

WAVE-Saver
WATER MANAGEMENT SYSTEM
Version 2.0 for Windows

First screen: **Welcome to WAVE Saver**
Transcribed as
245   00   Wave-saver $h [electronic resource] : $b water
                management system.
246   30   Water management system
246   3   Water saver
246   1 $i Title from title screen: $a Welcome to wave saver
500   Title from disc label.

In this example the disc label has the most complete information for the title, so it is chosen as the source. Title variations are recorded in 246 fields to make them searchable. The use of the 246 field is discussed in detail later.

If the resource itself does not provide the information needed for description, catalogers may take the information from alternate sources, in the order of preference: printed or online documentation or other accompanying material such as the publisher's Web page or information printed on a container issued by the publisher or distributor.

When a work being described includes two or more separate physical parts and the information formally presented in the parts does not include a collective title, but the container or its label does, catalogers should treat the container or its label as the chief source of information.

If the information needed is not found in the chief source or the alternate sources listed above, catalogers may use, in the order of preference: other published description of the file or other sources such as metadata records to describe the item being cataloged.

9.0B2. Prescribed Sources of Information

The prescribed sources of information for the eight areas of description are presented below. Information taken from sources other than the prescribed ones should be enclosed in square brackets.

Areas	*MARC Field*	*Prescribed Sources of Information*
Area 1. Title and statement of responsibilities	245	Chief source of information, information issued by the publisher, creator, etc. container
Area 2. Edition	250	
Area 4. Publication, distribution, etc.	260	
Area 6. Series	4XX	
Area 5. Physical description	300	Any source
Area 7. Note	5XX	
Area 8. Standard number and terms of availability	02X	

9.1. Title and Statement of Responsibility (MARC Field 245)

Title information should be taken from one of the formal sources listed in rule 9.0B1. Title screen, main menu, "README" file, "About this program," and meta tags in HTML documents are a few examples. When a file is open in Macintosh machines the Apple icon has an option for "About [this file]," which often provides the title screen or similar information. If the title information varies in these sources, catalogers will use the source with the most complete information and record the title presented there as the title proper. Rule 9.1B2 states that the source of the title is always given in a note (in the 500 field).

Catalogers will transcribe the title proper according to rule 1.1B1. Words introducing a work and not intended to be part of the title should not be transcribed. With electronic resources, a common situation is the expression "welcome to..." In such cases, the part following the "welcome to" is usually transcribed as the title proper, and the title with the "welcome to" is presented in a note. If necessary, a variant-title added entry is provided for this title.

Title screen: Welcome to Clinical Practice Guidelines on CD-ROM
Transcribed as
245   00   Clinical practice guidelines on CD-ROM $h [electronic resource]
246   3   Welcome to clinical practice guidelines on CD-ROM [indicator "3" will generate a title added entry but no notes from this field. Note that field 246 does not end with a period]
500   Title from title screen.

But when a title is preceded by a phrase that indicates the involvement of a corporate body or a person, that phrase is included in the title proper transcription, according to *LCRI* 7.1B. A variant title is usually provided for the part following this phrase.

Title screen: Microsoft presents Dragon Games
Transcribed as
245   00   Microsoft presents dragon games $h [electronic resource]
246   30   Dragon games
500   Title from title screen.

Catalogers familiar with the cataloging of videos may find this practice inconsistent with the description of videos, in which phrases such as "so and so presents" are usually not transcribed as part of the title proper.

General material designation (GMD): The general material designation for all computer files is now "electronic resource," reflecting the recommendation of *ISBD (ER)*. The GMD "interactive multimedia" is no longer valid. All electronic resources that are coded as Type "m", and those that are not coded as Type "m" but have an electronic resource 006 field on their records, should be assigned the GMD [electronic resource]. For example, a text-heavy electronic journal will be coded Type "a" (for language material) and BLvl "s" (for serial), with an electronic resource 006 field to bring out the electronic aspect. This item will be assigned the GMD [electronic resource]. Similarly, a streaming video from the Web will have code "g" (video) for Type, code "m" for BLvl, and electronic resource 006 field and 007 field to represent the electronic aspects of the work. It will also have a GMD [electronic resource].

GMD is to follow the title proper immediately. If an item has a parallel title or other title information, the general material designation will precede the parallel title and other title information.

Statement of responsibility: The statement of responsibility is recorded only if it is prominently presented in the chief source. Persons or bodies responsible for the content of the file are recorded in Area 1. Persons contributing to the preparation or production of the file and those sponsoring the creation of the file are usually recorded in notes (rule 9.7B6). Such notes are useful in justifying the provision of added entries. Information not taken from the chief source should be enclosed in square brackets.

100	1	Hoffman, J. D. $q (James D.)
245	10	National geochemical data base $h [electronic resource] / $c by J.D. Hoffman and Kim Buttleman.
500		"MAPPER display software by Russell A. Ambroziak"—Container insert.
700	1	Buttleman, Kim.

100	1	Alverson, David P.
245	00	ZTerm $h [electronic resource]
500		Author: David P. Alverson. [Author does not appear on the source of title proper, so it is not transcribed in Area 1. The work is still entered under the author.]

If necessary, catalogers may add a word or phrase to clarify the relationship between a title and the persons or bodies named in the statement of responsibility area (rule 9.1F2).

9.2. Edition (MARC Field 250)

When the intellectual or artistic content of a file changes, a separate bibliographic record is prepared to describe the newer version. The presence of an edition statement is often hinted by the presence of words such as "edition, issue, version, release, level, update" (rule 9.2B2). Appropriate abbreviations and numerals from Appendices B and C in *AACR2r* should be used to transcribe an edition statement.

It is important to distinguish the edition of a computer file from the edition of an operating system needed to run the file. The former is recorded in the 250 field, while the latter is usually recorded in a system requirements note (538 field). Only formal edition statements of computer files are recorded; and multiple edition statements can be recorded in one 250 field. If the source of an edition statement is different from the source of the title proper, a note should be provided (rule 9.2B1). This is necessary because information from the container or accompanying material may be different from the information provided in the chief source. Sometimes publishers update a file without updating the documentation. So if the source of an edition is different from that of the title proper, *AACR2r* recommends a note be given.

250		Version 1.0B3., public Beta test version.
245	00	VendorFACTS $h [electronic resource]
250	00	[version] 1.0
500		Title from title screen; ed. statement from disk label.

Some computer files are available for IBM PCs and Macintoshes. A statement such as "Macintosh version" is considered an edition statement. But if a file simply states "Poetry writing for Macintosh," no edition statement should be inferred.

If an electronic resource consists of several parts and there are edition statements referring to the whole resource as well as parts of the item, catalogers should transcribe *only* the edition statement(s) that cover the whole resource.

9.3. Material Specific Details

Area 3, "file characteristics," in the earlier *AACR2r* became "type and extent of resource" in the 2002 revision to indicate the type of the file(s) being described. This area is no longer used for electronic resources, according to the 2004 update.

9.4. Publication, Distribution, Etc. (MARC Field 260)

Rules for describing the publication data of electronic resources are the same as rule 1.4. Catalogers should look for a formal publishing statement and record the first named place of publication. Rule 1.4D2 instructs catalogers to use the shortest form of a publisher's name as long as it can be identified internationally. But catalogers should not use a shorthand, such as "The Association," in Area 4 even if the full name of the association appears in the statement of responsibility area. Rules 1.4D and 9.4D1 provide an option for catalogers to record the distributor of an electronic resource. *LCRI* 9.4D1 encourages this practice. If several dates are found on a computer file, the date that applies to the item as a whole is used. If several copyright dates are present, the latest one is transcribed. All remote access electronic resources are considered published.

For unpublished files, only the date of creation is recorded; the place of publication and the publisher's name are not recorded, and s.l. and s.n. are not used in such cases.

260	Kirkland, WA : $b Ars Nova, $c c1992.

260	[Reston, Va.] : $b U.S. Dept. of Interior, U.S. Geological Survey ; $a [Denver, Colo. : $b USGS Distribution Branch], $c 1995.

9.5. Physical Description (MARC Field 300)

300	Extent of item : $b other physical details ; $c dimensions + $e accompanying material.

The physical description of direct access electronic resources is recorded in bibliographic records (field 300), but this information is not provided for remote access electronic resources unless the cataloger chooses to apply the option provided by rules 9.5B3 and 9.5C3 in the 2004 update to record such information. Here are two physical descriptions of remote access electronic resources:

```
300     1 electronic text (v, 35 p.) : $b digital, PDF file.
300     3 sound files : $b digital, mp3 file.
```

For direct access electronic resources, the first element of this area records the number of physical units of the carrier, using arabic numerals and one of the specific material designations given in rule 9.5B1: computer chip cartridge, computer disk (for magnetically encoded disks), computer optical disc (for optically encoded discs such as CD-ROM or DVD), computer tape cartridge, computer tape cassette, and computer tape reel. The 2002 revision allows the use of conventional terminology to describe the format of the physical carrier; the option is applied by the Library of Congress (*LCRI* 9.5B1). Terms such as CD-ROM and DVD can be used for the first element of field 300.

In anticipation of new physical carriers for which no specific material designations have been given yet, *AACR2r* instructs catalogers to use the name of the physical carrier "as precisely as possible, preferably qualified by *computer*" (p. 9–12).

Although Area 3, extent of resource, is not used for electronic resources now, some of the earlier rules (9.3B2) are transformed into rule 9.5B4 to allow catalogers to record, in Area 5, the number of files, records, statements, or bytes that constitute the content of an electronic resource, if such information is readily available and considered important. Such information is entered in field 516. For example, the file size of an electronic book to be viewed in a PalmPilot is important to potential users, so the cataloger will enter such information in field 516:

```
516     Electronic text; file size: 1440 kilobytes.
```

If a file has sound or produces sound, "sd" is used; if it displays two or more colors, "col." is recorded. The dimensions of the physical carrier are recorded in imperial units (*LCRI* 9.5D1). The size of floppy disks is either 5¼ in. or 3½ in., while the standard size of optical discs, CD-ROMs and DVDs, is 4¾ in.

```
300     2 computer disks ; $c 3 1/2 in.
300     1 computer optical disc : $b sd., col. ; $c 4 3/4 in.
```

Libraries vary in the amount of information they provide for accompanying materials. Generally, details about an accompanying material are provided if the material is considered important. The following practices are common:

```
300     1 computer disk : $b sd., col. ; $c 3 1/2 in + $e 1 user's manual.
300     1 computer optical disc ; $c 4 3/4 in. + $e 1 user's guide (35
        p. : ill. ; 20 cm.) + 1 installation card.
```

9.6. Series (MARC Field 4XX)

The transcription of this area is straightforward and very similar to that for other types of material. Rule 1.6 provides the general guidelines. Subfield 440 is used if a series title found on the item is to be an added entry. If ISSN is readily available, it is entered in subfield $x. Numbering information is entered in subfield $v, using appropriate abbreviations from Appendix B for "volume" and "number." If a series title is to be traced in a form that is different from the title found on the item, catalogers will use 490 to record the title from the publication and 830 to record the controlled series title.

440	0	U.S. Geological Survey digital data series ; $v DDS-15
440	0	Junior adventures
440	0	Davidson Learning Center series

9.7. Notes

Notes are important to electronic resources because they help users assess the items without running the files. Rule 9.7B stipulate the order of notes and allow a note to be given first if it is considered of primary importance. CONSER guidelines, however, instruct CONSER members to enter notes by field number in numerical order. Libraries can choose the approach that is most helpful to their users. In this section the *AACR2r* prescribed order for notes is followed.

9.7B1. Nature and scope, system requirements, and mode of access (MARC Fields 516, 500, and 538): For electronic resources, the note to be presented first covers the nature or scope of a resource, the system required to run it, and, for remote access electronic resources, the mode of access.

516	Statistical program with graphic capabilities.
516	Electronic text; file size: 1224 kilobytes.

9.7B1b. System requirements (MARC Field 538): This information is critical because it helps users decide if they have the right setup to use a file. This note usually includes the following data elements, separated by a semicolon and given in the order below:

538	System requirements: the make and model of the computer; the amount of memory required; the name of the operating system; the software requirements (including the programming language); the characteristics of any required or recommended peripherals; any required or recommended hardware modifications.
538	System requirements: IBM PC compatible; 4 MB RAM; Windows 3.1 or later; double-drive CD-ROM.

This string of data may seem confusing, but the note is actually fairly easy to construct. Information on system requirements often appears on the container, the user's guide, or in internal sources such as the "README" file. Catalogers may find it necessary to rearrange the elements to conform to the order specified above.

> If the requirements for several platforms are the same, only one note is needed.
> 538   System requirements: Windows or Macintosh; 8 MB RAM; CD-ROM.

> If the requirements are platform specific, a note is provided for each platform.
> 538   System requirements for Windows: 133 MHz Pentium computer; 24 MB RAM; Windows 95 or 98; high color (65,535 colors) capable 2 MB video card; 8x CD-ROM drive ; sound card and mouse.
> 538   System requirements for Macintosh: Power MAC 100 MHz; 32 MB RAM; OS 7.6; thousands of colors/640 x 480 screen resolution.

9.7B1c. Mode of access (MARC Field 538): The mode of access must be specified for remote access electronic resources. Previous cataloging practice included the host site of the files. Current practice records only how the files can be accessed.

> 538   Mode of access: Company intranet.
> 538   Mode of access: World Wide Web.

9.7B2. Language and script (MARC Field 546): The language(s) of the content of a resource is recorded free text in field 546 unless the information is clear from the rest of the bibliographic record. Catalogers should use subfield $a of field 546 as the basis to code the "Lang" element in the 008 field, and code the languages recorded in 546 in field 041. Programming language should be recorded as part of the system requirements note and not part of the language note.

> Lang: eng
> 041 $a eng $a ger
> 546   Screen text in English and German

9.7B3. Source of title proper (MARC Field 500): The source of title proper is always recorded for electronic resources, according to rule 9.7B3. For remote access electronic resources, the viewing date should be recorded in the "description based on" note (9.7B22 and 12.7B23). These two notes can be combined (see the third example below).

> 500   Title from title screen.
> 500   Title from disc label.
> 500   Title from home page (viewed on May 5, 2001).

9.7B4. Variant title (MARC Field 246): Title variants are entered in field 246. Such titles can appear in different parts of the chief source or other parts of an item (such as cover title, spine title, running title, and caption title). In using field 246, catalogers are to drop initial articles and should not conclude the field with a period. The first indicator controls the production of a note and an added entry, and the second indicator specifies the type of variant title and generates a display constant. Catalogers may use subfield $i to generate a special display text for the note. *LCRI* 21.29 instructs catalogers not to use general material designation (subfield $h) with added entries. Commonly used indicator values for field 246 are presented in the tables below.

1st Indicator	2nd Indicator	Subfields
0 Note, no added entry	Blank No type specified	$a Title proper
1 Note, added entry	0 Portion of title	$b Remainder of title
2 No note, no added entry	1 Parallel title	$h Medium (*not* used)
3 No note, added entry	2 Distinctive title	$i Display text
	3 Other title	
	4 Cover title	
	5 Added title page title	
	6 Caption title	
	7 Running title	
	8 Spine title	

245	00	History of ships & navies $h [electronic resources].
246	30	History of ships and navies
246	30	Ships and navies

These two 246 fields will produce no notes for the two variant titles but will generate added entries from them to increase access to this item.

To produce a special display for a variant title, catalogers will enter the source of the variant title in subfield $i and the variant title in subfield $a.

246	1	$i Container title: $a Web publishing with HTML

This 246 field will produce a note:
Container title: Web publishing with HTML.
Present and a title added entry:
Title: Web publishing with HTML.

9.7B6. Statement of responsibility (MARC Field 500): People and corporate bodies involved in the creation of the file, but not recorded in Area 1, are recorded in notes.

```
500     Developed by Pixel Technology.
500     Designed by Iris Magic, Inc.
```

9.7B7. Edition and history (MARC Field 500): The source of the edition statement, if different from that of the title proper, should be presented in a note. This note can be combined with the source of title proper note.

```
500     Ed. statement from container.
500     Title from title screen; ed. statement from container.
```

If a work is based on an earlier work, that information is given as a note (9.7B7).
500   Based on: Possessing the past: treasures from the National Palace Museum, Taipei (1996).

Publishing history of an item is also recorded.
500   Data and program first released in 1997.

9.7B8. Type and extent of resource (MARC Field 516): The 2004 update to this rule instructs catalogers to record the type and extent of an electronic resource if the information is considered important and not recorded in other parts of the record.

```
516     Files available in two formats, a multimedia Macintosh
        file and an NCSA Mosaic hypertext file; all images are in
        GIF format.
516     Electronic text in ASCII and PDF formats.
```

9.7B14. Audience (MARC Field 521): Audience information is recorded in field 521 if the information is formally presented. Information can appear in a formal statement or an image indicating the age groups intended. If the rating source is present, it can be included. Catalogers should not use personal evaluation as audience note.

```
521        Ages 9+
521    8   ESRB rating: ages 13+
```

When the first indicator is blank, "Audience:" is displayed with the data. When indicator "8" is used, no text is displayed.

9.7B16. Other formats (MARC Field 530): If an electronic resource is also available in nonelectronic format, catalogers should use field 530 to note the existence of the other format. This note is often used with field 776. See the discussion of single record approach and separate record approach below to see the role of field 530.

9.7B17. Summary (MARC Field 520): A succinct, objective statement of the contents of a file can be very useful for users of electronic resources. If a description in the file summarizes the contents well, catalogers may quote it as the summary.

520		A shareware telecommunications program for the Macintosh. It supports ZModem, YModem, Xmodem, Kermit and CIS B-Plus/Quick-B file transfers, VT100 & ANSI-BBS emulation, including colors, and an efficient scroll back buffer.

9.7B18. Contents (MARC Field 505): The title of parts of an item can be listed in field 505 if they can help users understand the contents of the item. If there are too many parts, a partial list can be provided. If it is desirable to make the individual titles searchable, a second indicator 0 can be used to create an enhanced content note.

505	0	Disc 1. Reading basics — Disc 2. Reading adventure.
505	0	1. Painting. Drawing — 2. Sculpture. Objects d'art — 3. Near and Middle Eastern antiquities. Egyptian antiquities. Greek and Roman antiquities.

9.7B19. Numbers (MARC Field 500): Numbers on an item can be useful for identification purposes. If a number is a publisher's stock number, it can be entered into field 037. If that is difficult to determine, a quotation note is given. If the source of the quotation is not the chief source, it is indicated in this note.

500	"CD92-TGR-42."
500	"ACPHR no. 95-DP10"—Container.

9.8. Standard Numbers (MARC Fields 020, 022)

The International Standard Book Number (ISBN) is entered in field 020. If different parts of a work carry their own ISBN, field 020 can be repeated to encode the numbers. The International Standard Serial Number (ISSN) is entered in field 022.

Electronic Books

Electronic books (e-books) are a resource that continues to evolve and seems to be better received in recent years. They can be accessed directly or remotely. Direct access e-books are often stored on a hard drive, a floppy diskette, a CD-ROM, a personal digital assistant (PDA), or an e-book reader device. They are available from major bookstores. Remote access e-books are often stored on a server on the Internet to allow downloading and viewing. Web sites such as Project Gutenberg and Children's Classics offer free access to digitized books, while companies such as netLibrary market e-books to libraries and individuals. Publishers often make e-books available in several formats: HTML format, PDF format, SGML (Standard Generalized Markup Language) format, or others. HTML files are easy to access and require an Internet connection and a Web browser. Other formats may require a special viewer such as Adobe Acrobat.

The first task in cataloging an e-book is to confirm that it is an electronic resource "encoded for manipulation by a computerized device" and that, like a monograph, it is "complete in one part or intended to be completed within a finite number of parts" (*AACR2r* Appendix D). If so, catalogers will decide how to catalog the item. One option is to apply the single record approach allowed by CONSER and OCLC to record information about the electronic version on the record for the print version. This option is appropriate when the cataloging agency also owns the print version. Another option is to follow *LCRI* 1.11A and catalog the e-book as if it were a microform. A third option is to follow *AACR2r* Chapters 1, 2, and 9 to create a new record for the e-book.

Single Record Approach Vs. Separate Record Approach

In cataloging electronic resources, catalogers may become aware of the existence of other versions of the items being cataloged. If they wish to link the two versions, *Cataloging Electronic Resources: OCLC-MARC Coding Guidelines* offer two options. The single record approach adds information about the new version to the record of the original version to alert users of the availability of the new one. The separate record approach creates a new record for the new version and adds notes to each record to link the two versions. These approaches are most relevant to the description of electronic books and electronic serials. Many libraries use the single record approach to reduce the cost and time of cataloging, while other libraries choose to create separate records to avoid entering information about two items on one record. OCLC and CONSER accept both approaches.

The same guidelines also point out that catalogers need not follow either the single record approach or the separate record approach. In other words, when they are describing an electronic or nonelectronic resource, catalogers are not obligated to verify the existence of other formats or versions. They may add references to other formats if they feel the information would be useful to users.

The single record approach recommends that data about an electronic version of a work be added to the record for the original work. It typically involves the following steps:

- Add a field 530 to the record for the original work to note the availability of the electronic version.

- Add a field 740 for related work if the title of the electronic version is different from that of the nonelectronic version.

- Add a field 856 for location and access information for remote access electronic resources. Indicator 1 specifies the method of access, be it HTTP, FTP, or others. Indicator 2 specifies the relationship between the item referred to by the URL and the item represented by the bibliographic record. If the URL of an electronic version is added to the record for the print version, indicator 2 should have the value of "1" to clarify that the URL links to a version that is different from the item represented by the bibliographic record. If the two items are related, value "2" should be used for indicator 2. For example, the electronic version of the table of contents of a work can be added to the record for the print copy using the 856 field with the indicator value "2" for the second indicator.

- Add an electronic resource 007 field to bring out the physical characteristics of the electronic resource.

- Do not add an electronic resource 006 field for the electronic version.

- Do not code "Form of item" for the electronic version.
- Do not add any 776 field.

[Title page of the e-book from netLibrary]

Working Knowledge

How Organizations Manage What They Know

Thomas H. Davenport   Laurence Prusak

HARVARD BUSINESS SCHOOL PRESS

Boston, Massachusetts

Since this e-book is very similar to the hard copy, the cataloger may want to take the single record approach instead of creating a separate record for the electronic version. The following record is the result of the single record approach.

Type: a	Elvl: I	Srce: d	Audn:	Ctrl:	Lang: eng
Blvl: m	**Form:**	Conf: 0	Biog:	Mrec:	Ctry: mau
	Cont: b	GPub:	LitF: 0	Indx: 1	
Desc: a	Ills: a	Fest: 0	DtSt: s	Dates: 1998	

007		**c $b r $d c $e n**
010		97010781
020		**0585056560 (eBook)**
020		0875846556 (print)
090		HD58.82 $b .D38 1998
092		658.4/03
100	1	Davenport, Thomas H., $d 1954-
245	10	Working knowledge : $b how organizations manage what they know / $c Thomas H. Davenport, Laurence Prusak.
260		Boston, Mass : $b Harvard Business School Press, $c c1998.
300		xv, 199 p. : $b ill. ; $c 24 cm.
504		Includes bibliographical references (p. 179–187) and index.
505	0	What do we talk about when we talk about knowledge? — The promise and challenge of knowledge markets — Knowledge generation — Knowledge codification and coordination — Knowledge transfer — Knowledge roles and skills — Technologies for knowledge management — Knowledge management projects in practice — The pragmatics of knowledge management.

530		Also available as an electronic book from the netLibrary.
506		Access to the electronic book restricted to authorized users only.
650	0	Organizational learning.
650	0	Information resources management.
650	0	Industrial management.
700	1	Prusak, Laurence.
856	41	$u http://www.netlibrary.com.proxycu .wrlc.org/ $z Search for the title to access the eBook.

Discussion: Six areas of this record deserve our attention. Because information about the electronic version is added to the record for the print version, the "Form" element is not coded as "s" for electronic resource. An electronic resource 007 field is an optional addition, according to LC recommendation. The ISBN for the electronic book is recorded in a new 020 field and clarified with a qualifier. The 530 note alerts users of the existence of the electronic version, and field 506 clarifies that only authorized users can access the e-book from the netLibrary. The URL is entered in subfield $u of the 856 field to link users to the opening screen for the netLibrary within the library system, and access instruction is entered in subfield $z for a public display text. Because the URL does not point to the item represented by the original bibliographic record, the second indicator is coded "1" instead of "0".

In the separate record approach, the record for the original version will be enriched by some notes and a new record will be created for the electronic version. The two will be connected by a number of fields. Here are the steps involved:

In the Existing Record for the Original Version

- No electronic resource 006 field is added.
- No electronic resource 007 field is used.
- Do not code "Form of item"
- A 530 field is added to note the existence of the other format.
- A 776 field will link the two records. If ISSN is available, it is entered in subfield $x.
- Add a 700–730 added entry field for the electronic version when the main entry differs.

In the New Record for the Electronic Version

- Use the primary aspect of the content to determine the code for the "Type" element.
- If "Type" is not coded "m" for electronic resources, add an electronic resource 006 field to bring out the electronic aspects of the work.
- Add an electronic resource field 007 to bring out the physical characteristics of the electronic resource.
- Code "Form of item" as "s" for "electronic".
- Add a 530 field to note the existence of the original format.

- Add a 776 field to link the two records.
- Add 856 field to inform users how to access the work. Indicators value tend to be "40" for Web resources.
- If the two versions have different main entry, use 700–730 for an added entry.

In the example of *Working knowledge*, if the cataloger chooses to create a new record, the 008 field for monographs will be used. The cataloger will follow Chapter 9 to describe the electronic book like the other electronic resources and encode the data in the fields commonly used for electronic resources. The 2004 amendment to *AACR2r* discontinues the use of Area 3 (coded in MARC 256 field) for the description of electronic resources. But if the size of the file is important for access, catalogers may record it in the 516 field (e.g., 516 $a Electronic text; file size: 672 kilobytes). No field 300 is used for remote access e-books. Direct access e-books should have a 300 field describing the number of physical units and the specific material designation (SMD), sound, color, and dimensions of the SMD. Catalogers may use conventional terminology such as CD-ROM or DVD for the SMD (*LCRI* 9.5B1) and will continue to record the dimensions of the SMD in imperial units per *LCRI* 9.5D1 even though the 2004 amendment allows the use of metric units. The record for the e-book will be as follows:

Type: a	Elvl: I	Srce: d	Audn:	Ctrl:	Lang: eng
Blvl: m	**Form: s**	Conf: 0	Biog:	Mrec:	Ctry: mau
	Cont: b	GPub:	LitF: 0	Indx: 1	
Desc: a	Ills: a	Fest: 0	DtSt: s	Dates: 1998	

006	Type: m File: d AuDn: GPub:
007	**c $b r $d c $e n**
020	**0585056560 (eBook)**
090	HD58.82 $b .D38 1998
092	658.4/03
100 1	Davenport, Thomas H., $d 1954-
245 10	Working knowledge : $b how organizations manage what they know / $c Thomas H. Davenport, Laurence Prusak.
260	Boston, Mass : $b Harvard Business School Press, $c c1998.
516	**Electronic text.**
538	**Mode of access: World Wide Web.**
500	**Title from title screen (viewed Jan. 5, 2003)**
504	Includes bibliographical references (p. 179–187) and index.
505 0	What do we talk about when we talk about knowledge? — The promise and challenge of knowledge markets — Knowledge generation — Knowledge codification and coordination—Knowledge transfer—Knowledge roles and skills — Technologies for knowledge management — Knowledge management projects in practice — The pragmatics of knowledge management.

530		Also available in print.
506		Access to the electronic book restricted to authorized users only.
650	0	Organizational learning.
650	0	Information resources management.
650	0	Industrial management.
700	1	Prusak, Laurence.
776	1	Davenport, Thomas H., $d 1954– $t Working knowledge $w (OCoLC) [OCLC control number for the print version]
856	40	$u http://www.netlibrary.com.proxycu. wrlc.org/ $z Search for the title to access the eBook.

Discussion: Since this record represents the electronic version only, "Form" is coded "s" for "electronic" resource. Because the item is text-based, in the fixed field Type is coded "a" for "language material." The cataloger adds an electronic resource 006 field to bring out the computer aspects, with the first position coded as "m" for electronic resource and another position reserved for file format is coded "d" for document. The presence of field 006 enables this item to be retrieved when a user limits the search results to electronic resources. For all electronic resources, the electronic resource 007 field is required. Code "c" for subfield $a identifies this item as an electronic resource, code "r" for subfield $b indicates it is a remote-access file, code "c" for subfield $d indicates the text is in black and white, and code "n" for subfield $e states the dimensions information is not applicable to a remote-access file. Only the ISBN for the e-book is recorded in the 020 and a qualifier is added to clarify it. Most of the variable fields are similar to those on the record for the print version. For remote-access files no physical description is provided, so the 300 field is not included. A mode of access note (538 field) is used to indicate how the e-book can be accessed, and a required source of title note and the viewing date are recorded in a 500 note. Access restriction is presented in the 506 field and the URL is included in the 856 field. This time the URL points to a version represented by the bibliographic record, so the second indicator is coded "0". A 776 field is added to link to the record for the print version. A 776 field will also be added to the record of the print version to link it back to this record for the electronic version.

Enhanced CDs

Many vocal artists have used video or multimedia in their recordings to present background information about their songs, concerts, and personal interests. A common practice is to create an "Enhanced CD," which is a regular audio CD with a multimedia CD-ROM track. To play an Enhanced CD, one needs an audio CD player for the audio portion of the disc and a computer for the multimedia CD-ROM track. Publishers usually label Enhanced CDs prominently on the disc, the case, or the documentation to encourage sale. Because audio CD players cannot access the multimedia CD-ROM track, some publishers include a warning on the disc or the case: "Don't play track one. Track one will play silence or static on audio CD players. Macintosh System 7 or Microsoft Windows 3.1 required (or greater)." Details of the system requirements for the multimedia track and installation instructions are usually included in the "README" file on the enhanced CD. See Chapter 3 for details on how to catalog enhanced CDs.

The cataloging of enhanced CDs is the same as for regular CDs, except for the following:

1. The cataloger usually provides a note to indicate the item is an enhanced CD. It can be a 500 note (e.g., An Enhanced CD), a 520 note (An enhanced CD of ten songs and a CD-ROM multimedia presentation), or a 505 note (1. CD-ROM Multimedia presentation — 2. Elsewhere — 3. Plenty).

2. The cataloger records the system requirements of the multimedia track in a 538 field, following rule 9.7B1b.

3. The cataloger records the characteristics of the multimedia CD-ROM track in an electronic resource 006 field so that the item can be retrieved as a computer file.

4. The cataloger uses an electronic resource 007 field to record the physical characteristics of the multimedia CD-ROM. Field 007 is required for all electronic resources.

Finite Internet Resources (PDF Files, Static Documents, Etc.)

Many Internet resources are "integrating resources" because they are updated frequently and new information is integrated into the original versions. Works that are finite in nature are one type of Internet resource. They are complete in one part or "intended to be completed within a finite number of parts" (*AACR2r*, Appendix D). Examples include born-digital documents, Web versions of existing print documents, and Web sites that are updated over a period of time for a particular event and concluded when the event is over. Chapter 9 is most relevant for the description of these resources. Chapters 1 and 2 and other chapters of *AACR2r* should be consulted if appropriate. The treatment of finite Internet resources is different from that of direct access electronic resources in the following ways:

- Area 5, physical description is usually not provided for finite Internet resources. But catalogers have the option to record type of resource and file size in the 516 field.

- A 538 field for "mode of access" is required for Internet resources.

- If a finite Internet resource has a counterpart in other formats, catalogers will use the 530 field to indicate the existence of those formats. If the separate record approach is used, catalogers may use the 776 field to link related records.

- A 856 field is provided for each access method for a finite Internet resource. The indicator values will be "41" if the cataloger uses the one record approach, and "40" if the cataloger chooses the separate record approach.

Assignment of Access Points

Chapter 21, "Choice of Access Points," applies to the selection of access points for computer files also. If a personal author is responsible for a work, the author is the main entry. If a corporate body meets the requirements of rule 21.1B2, it is selected as the main entry. Since the creation of a computer file often involves many people, most computer files have title as the main entry.

Rules 21.29 and 21.30 provide guidelines for selecting added entries. Corporate bodies named in the publication, distribution, etc., area are usually good candidates for added entries. But no headings should be assigned for the program language, the make and model of computer for which the computer file is designed, or the operating system required for a computer file. Such information is included in the note for system requirements (field 538), which can be made searchable if a library chooses to do so. Earlier records in bibliographic utilities may include 753 fields for these elements, but that practice was discontinued by the Library of Congress in 1996.

Subject Analysis

Library of Congress Subject Headings

The American Library Association published *Guidelines on Subject Access to Microcomputer Software* in 1986 to aid the subject analysis of computer files. The three following principles of the *Guidelines* continue to be valid:

1. The entire record (descriptive cataloging, subject cataloging, and classification) should provide the access needed by the user.

2. Sound practices of subject analysis and classification should be followed to avoid unwieldy files and useless shelf arrangements caused by grouping materials together by form alone.

3. One must ensure that adequate subject headings and linkages exist in *Library of Congress Subject Headings*, and that *Library of Congress Classification* and *Dewey Decimal Classification* have adequate provisions for the subjects covered by microcomputer software. Where standard headings are inadequate, libraries should develop and document their own according to sound principles of subject analysis.

LC's practice reflects many recommendations by the ALA *Guidelines*. *Subject Cataloging Manual (SCM)* instructs that the principles regarding the number of headings assigned and the specificity of headings (H180) should be applied to the subject analysis of computer files. *SCM* H2070 recommends that when cataloging a computer program, catalogers should assign at least one topical heading to indicate the subject or genre of the software and add the free-floating subdivision "—Software" to the topical heading. But catalogers should not assign a heading for the named computer program. For instance,

245	00	Songworks $h [electronic resources].
650	0	Composition (Music) $v Software.

The heading of a program should be assigned only to works about the program. This practice is explained later.

SCM H2070 also advises that catalogers assign no headings for the program language, the make or model of the computer, or the operating systems of a computer file because such information is usually recorded in the descriptive cataloging part of a bibliographic record.

Subdivisions such as "—Computer programs" and "—Software" are frequently used in describing computer files, but there is also confusion over their assignment. According to *SCM*, the free-floating form subdivision "—Software" should be used under each heading assigned to a work. Computer programs intended for children no higher than the eighth grade should be assigned "—Juvenile software." This practice applies to materials with the intellectual level code "a," "b," or "c" in "Audn" and those coded "f" (for special audiences) that are clearly juvenile in nature.

However, catalogers should not assign the subdivision "—Computer programs" to software because this subdivision is not a form subdivision and is used only for works about computer programs.

In cataloging works about software, the practice of Library of Congress is to assign a heading (usually a uniform title) for the named computer program and a topical heading with the subdivision "—Computer programs" to indicate a work is about the named computer program. For instance,

245	00	Beginner's guide to Songworks. [a book about this program]
630	00	Songworks.
650	0	Composition (Music) $x Computer programs.

SCM H2070 offers details on how to establish headings for named computer programs. The subdivision "—Databases" is also frequently associated with computer files. *SCM* H1520 defines a database as "a collection of logically interrelated data stored together in one or more computerized files, usually created and managed by a database management system" (p. 1). Before assigning this subdivision, catalogers need to examine the file to determine if it is truly a database. For instance,

245	00	Solutions T-PRO database $h [computer file].
650	0	Chemicals $v Databases.
650	0	Poisons $v Databases.

If a file cannot be viewed, catalogers should consider if the item has been presented as a database or if accompanying materials indicate the coding and structure of the data. To a work about databases on a subject, "—Databases" is assigned as a topical subdivision (entered under subfield x).

In addition, *SCM* stipulates that for two special categories of material the subdivision "—Databases" should not be assigned. If the computer files are "essentially textual in nature" (H1520, p. 3), catalogers are advised to assign only the subject headings appropriate for the textual material. Conference proceedings, full-text databases, literary works, and articles belong to this category. For instance,

245	00	Poetry in motion $h [electronic resource].
520		Includes original texts of poems by 24 contemporary poets. Also contains the poets' performance and interviews.
650	0	American poetry $y 20th century $x History and criticism.
650	0	Poetry, modern $y 20th century.

The other category includes works for reference, such as "directories, bibliographies, catalogs, dictionaries, encyclopedias, indexes, or other similar types" (H1520, p. 6). Catalogers should assign the appropriate form headings or form subdivision under the subjects. For example,

| 245 | 00 | ACM electronic guide to computing literature $h [electronic resource]. |
| 650 | 0 | Computer science literature $v Indexes. |

Furthermore, for collections of nontextual data that are not encoded for data management, *SCM* also advises against using the subdivision "—Databases."

In assigning subject headings to e-books, catalogers should treat them just like materials of other formats. Subject headings should be assigned based on the content of the item. Form subdivisions such as "Database" or "Software" are not appropriate for e-books. Rather, the form of the item is usually represented by a form/genre term such as "Electronic books." MARC 21 2002 concise edition states that 655 should be used for form/genre terms, and the second indicators of the 655 field should parallel those of the other subject tags. So if a form/genre term is an *LCSH* term, the second indicator will be coded "0"; if it is a local term, the second indicator is "7", and the source of the local term is entered in $2.

| 655 | #0 | $a Electronic books. |
| 655 | #7 | $a Interactive games. $2 local |

If direct access electronic books are shelved with other materials, they are assigned classification numbers. But remote access electronic books may or may not be assigned classification numbers, depending on whether catalogers intend to encourage and support virtual browsing.

Classification Numbers

While many libraries use authority lists such as *LCSH* to assign subject headings, the classification of computer files is less uniform. A recent survey found 70 percent of large academic libraries classify computer files by *LCC*, while 64 percent of large public libraries classify them by *DDC* (Hsieh-Yee 1999). There are many other different arrangements among libraries.

Both *LCC* and *DDC* treat computer files the same as other materials, and files are classed with the area of applications. For instance, a computer program for accounting is classed with accounting instead of with computer science. The practice of the Library of Congress is to class a software "in the same number in which a book about that software would be classed" (*Subject Cataloging Manual: Classification*, F710). If "Special programs, A-Z" is listed under the appropriate number, computer files are classed there. In most cases, computer files are classed in the number for "Data processing" or its equivalent under the appropriate topic. *DDC* has expanded the range for computer science materials and offered instructions for the use of 004–006.

Arrangement

Weihs and Intner both advocate an integrated approach to make computer files browsable (Weihs 1988; Intner 1991). Other benefits include ease of circulation control, aid to collection selection, and support for collection evaluation. The use of the same classification scheme is also useful for closed stacks because the scheme gives users and staff an arrangement pattern to follow. Weihs details procedures to intershelve computer files with the rest of the collection (Weihs 1991) and suggests the use of dummies if libraries prefer to shelve computer files elsewhere. But some libraries choose to shelve them separately from other materials because computer files are subject to climatic and handling problems. For security reasons, some place computer files in closed stacks or treat them much like reserve materials (Beaubien et al. 1988).

Circulation of computer files is a related concern. For books accompanied by electronic materials, public libraries tend to shelve them with the books and circulate them like books. But some academic libraries prefer to place the electronic materials in a separate area to ensure their integrity and security, and patrons need to check out the electronic materials while they check out the books. As for computer files, many large academic libraries load popular files on library computers or networks to encourage access and circulate less popular titles. Some libraries do not circulate computer files at all, and patrons have to make a request for files to be loaded on a network to be used. Similarly, some public libraries allow only in-house use of computer files so that patrons can have expert assistance if needed and the security of the file and the security of the library's network are ensured. Some libraries, however, have found success in circulating software and electronic materials that accompany books (Seaman and Carter 1997).

Cataloging Examples

Figure 5.1. Bookends Pro

<table>
<tr><td>Title screen:</td><td></td></tr>
</table>

Bookends Pro
3.2
Reference Management Software
© 1988–1996
Westing Software
134 Redwood Avenue
Corta Madera, CA94925

Type: m	Elvl: I	Srce: d	Audn:	Ctrl:	Lang: eng
Blvl: m	File: b	GPub:		Mrec:	Ctry: cau
Desc: a			DtSt: s	Dates: 1996	

007		c $b j $d g $e a $f #
090		Z1001.A2
092		011.0028533
245	00	Bookends pro $h [electronic resource] : $b reference management software.
250		Version 3.2 for Macintosh.
260		Corta Madera, CA : $b Westing Software, $c c1996.
300		1 computer disk ; $c 3½ in. + $e 1 user's guide (153 p. : ill. ; 22 cm.)
538		System requirements: Macintosh; at least 2 MB RAM (4 MB for System 7); a hard disk with at least 2.5 MB free; System 7 or later.
500		Title from title screen; ed. statement from disc label.
520		A program for organizing references, citations, and notes. Includes several journal specifications and can generate bibliographies in specified styles.
650	0	Bibliographic citations $v Software.
710	2	Westing Software.

Discussion for Figure 5.1

- Fixed field: Because this item is a computer software, Type is coded "m" and File coded "b" for computer program. No computer file 006 field is needed.

- 007: Computer file 007 is required for all electronic resources. The codes specify that this is a computer file (code "c"), stored on a magnetic disk (code "j"), with text in gray scale (code "g"), and that the disk is $3\frac{1}{2}$ in. in diameter (code "a"), but carries no sound ("blank" for subfield $f).

- 245: Like most computer files this item has a title main entry. The general material designation "electronic resource" follows the title proper immediately and the other title information is recorded in subfield $b after the subfield $h for the GMD.

- 250: This is an example of an edition statement that includes information on the type of computer for which a file is intended.

- 300: The file is on a magnetically encoded disk, so "computer disk" is used to describe the physical carrier. Because the user's guide is substantial, details of this item are provided.

- 538: Information on system requirements is one of the first notes to be presented. The information appears on the container and the user's guide, but these two sources do not have exactly the same information. Since the user's guide provides fuller information, system requirements are taken from there. The source does not list the information in the order specified by *AACR2r,* and the elements are rearranged to conform to that order.

- 500: The source of the title proper is a required note. If the source of an edition statement is different from that of the title proper, it is recorded in a 500 note. In this case these two notes are combined into one.

- 650: *LC Subject Cataloging Manual* advises that when cataloging a software program, catalogers should assign a topical heading for the program with "software" as the form subdivision. No headings for the name of the program should be assigned. Following the latest guidelines in encoding form subdivision, "software" is entered under subfield $v.

- 710: Publisher of the program is traced per 21.1B3.

Figure 5.2. StatView5

Disc label:

StatView 5
for Macintosh & Windows
1992–98 SAS Institute Inc.

Title screen:

Stat View

5.0
3/29/98
Free mem: 95%
PowerPC Version
****
Tell All
****

© 1992–98 SAS Institute Inc.   SAS

Type: m	Elvl: I	Srce: d	Audn:	Ctrl:	Lang: eng
Blvl: m	File: b	GPub:		Mrec:	Ctry: ncu
Desc: a			DtSt: s	Dates: 1998	

007		c $b o $d m $e g $f #
090		QA276.3
092		519.5
245	00	StatView 5 $h [electronic resource] : $b for Macintosh & Windows.
246	3	Stat view 5
250		PowerPC version.
260		Cary, N.C. : $b SAS Institute, $c c1998.
300		1 CD-ROM ; $c 4¾ in. + $e 1 installation instruction + 1 StatView shortcuts + 1 manual (288 p. : ill. ; 23 cm.)
538		System requirements for Windows: Minimum CPU 80486; 8 MB for Windows 3.1 or Windows 95; 12 MB for Windows NT; 16–32 MB RAM recommended; 18 MB hard disk space, 20 MB hard disk space for Win32s; Windows 3.1 (requires Win32s, which is provided), Windows 95, or Windows NT version 3.5 or 4.0.
538		System requirements for Macintosh: Any Macintosh or Power Macintosh (68040 or higher recommended); minimum 4 MB free RAM (8 MB free RAM recommended); System 7.1; fully compatible with Mac OS 8; math coprocessor recommended but not required.
500		Title from disc label; ed. statement from title screen.
520		A statistical graphics program that analyzes data and creates reports and graphs.
650	0	Statistics $v Software.
650	0	Statistics $x Graphic methods $v Software.
710	2	SAS Institute.

Discussion for Figure 5.2

- Fixed field: Because this item is a computer software, Type is coded "m" and File coded "b" for computer program. No computer file 006 field is needed.

- 007: Computer file 007 is required for all electronic resources. The codes specify that this is a computer file (code "c"), stored on an optical disc (code "o"), with text and graphics in black and white and color (code "m"), and the disc is $4\frac{3}{4}$ in. in diameter (code "g") but has no sound ("blank" for subfield $f).

- 245: When a title appears in different forms in different sources, the fuller form is used. On the disc label "for Macintosh & Windows" closely follows the title proper, so it is transcribed as the other title information in subfield $b.

- 250: The edition statement appears on the title screen and is transcribed accordingly. "5.0" on the title screen may be interpreted as an edition statement. But since this information is transcribed as part of the title proper, it is not treated as an edition statement here.

- 260: Publisher information is found in the pull-down menu from the title screen. Because the chief source for electronic resources is the entire resource, this information does not need to be bracketed.

- 300: When there are several accompanying materials, all of them are recorded in one subfield $e. There is no prescribed order for entering accompanying materials.

- 500: The required source of the title note is combined with the source of the edition statement note.

- 538: Since the system requirements are platform specific, two 538 notes are provided. The information is taken from the installation instruction, and the elements are rearranged so that computer type is presented first, followed by memory requirements, operating systems, software requirements, and peripherals. "Recommended" system information is included in the second 538 note.

- 650: Two topics describe the purpose of this program, so two topical headings are assigned, with "software" as the form subdivision.

- 710: Publisher is traced per 21.1B3.

Figure 5.3. Smart games

Disc label:

SMART GAMES
Challenge
1

MAC/PC CD-ROM

© 1996 Smart Games, Inc. Smart Games, Smart Games Challenge 1, the excited nerd cartoon character, and the names and logos of the 20 puzzle categories are trademarks of Smart Games, In. All Rights Reserved. P/N:SGC1CD0001.

Type: m	Elvl: I	Srce: d	Audn: e	Ctrl:	Lang: eng
Blvl: m	File: g	GPub:		Mrec:	Ctry: mau
Desc: a			DtSt: s	Dates: 1996	

007		c $b o $d m $e g $f a
090		GV1493
092		793.73
245	00	Smart games $h [electronic resource] : $b challenge 1.
246	3	Smart games challenge 1
260		Marblehead, MA : $b Smart Games = $b Distributed by RandomSoft, $c c1996.
300		1 CD-ROM : $b sd., col. ; $c 4¾ in. + $e 1 booklet (20 p.)
538		System requirements for Macintosh: Macintosh (030 processor or higher) or Power Macintosh; 4 MB RAM; 5 MB of hard disk space; System 7.0 or higher; CD-ROM drive.
538		System requirements for Windows: 386 SX or higher processor; 4 MB RAM; 5 MB of hard disk space; Window 3.x or above; Sound card; 640 x 480 256-color SVGA graphics; CD-ROM drive.
500		Title from disc label.
500		"MAC/PC CD-ROM."
500		"P/N:SGC1CD0001."
500		"Over 300 games for people with brains!"—Container.
521		Ages 14 to adult.
520		Contains more than 300 games and puzzles of word, mathematics, perception, and strategy, with multiple levels of difficulty and optimization scoring.
650	0	Computer games $v Software.
710	2	Smart Games (Firm)
710	2	RandomSoft (Firm)

Discussion for Figure 5.3

- Fixed field: Because this item is a computer game, Type is coded "m" and File coded "g" for game. No computer file 006 field is needed.

- 007: Computer file 007 is required for all electronic resources. The codes specify that this is a computer file (code "c"), stored on an optical disc (code "o"), with mixtures of text and images in gray scale and color (code "m"). The disc is $4\frac{3}{4}$ in. in diameter (code "g") and includes sound (code "a" for subfield $f).

- 245 and 246: Because "smart games" and "challenge 1" appear in different font sizes, they are transcribed as title proper and other title information. A variant title is provided to enable users to find this item under a similar title.

- 260: Information about Area 4 is found in the file. The distributor's information is added and encoded in the second subfield $b.

- 538: Two notes are provided because the system requirements are specific to the platform. The elements in the source have to be rearranged to follow the order specified by *AACR2r*.

- 500: A 500 note is provided for this "MAC/PC CD-ROM" because it appears on the disc.

- 500: The statement about "over 300 games..." appears prominently on three sides of a container. It is presented as a quotation note to help users identify this item.

- 521: The intended audience is clearly identified on the container, so the statement is recorded in this note. The audience group includes secondary ("d") and adult ("e"), two of the audience groups listed for the Audn element in the fixed field. Following the OCLC input standards, the code for the higher level is used for the Audn element.

- 500: The "P/N..." number is on the disc and seems important, so it is presented in a 500 note. If it can be determined that this number is the publisher's stock number, the information can be presented in field 037. According to 9.7B, the note for this number is one of the last notes in a record.

- 650: This is a software for computer games, so form subdivision "—Software" is used.

- 710: The publisher and distributor are traced per 21.1B3.

Figure 5.4. Poetry in motion

Disc label:

POETRY
in
MOTION

by Ron Mann

COMPACT
DISC
DIGITAL DATA
QT 11
CDRMI176910

VOYAGER

© Software design. The Voyager Company. 1992, 1994.

Type: m	Elvl: I	Srce: d	Audn:	Ctrl:	Lang: eng
Blvl: m	File: m	GPub:		Mrec:	Ctry: nyu
Desc: a			DtSt: s	Dates: 1994	

007		c $b o $d c $e g $f a
020		1559404361
090		PN6101
092		811.5
100	1	Mann, Ron.
245	10	Poetry in motion $h [electronic resource] / $c by Ron Mann.
260		New York, N.Y. : $b Voyager, $c c1994.
300		1 computer optical disc : $b sd., col. ; $c 4¾ in. + $e 1 user's guide (5 p.)
538		System requirements for Macintosh: Any Macintosh; 2,500K of available RAM (at least 4 MB installed); System 6.0.7 or higher; 13-inch (640 x 480 resolution) or greater color monitor; CD-ROM drive (double-speed recommended).
538		System requirements for Windows: 486SX-25 or higher CPU; 4 MB RAM (8 MB recommended); Windows 3.1, DOS 5.0 or later, MSCDEX; 640 x 480 256-color display; MPC-compatible CD-ROM drive; sound card with speakers or headphones.
500		Title from disc label.
520		Presents the performances of twenty-four contemporary poets such as Amiri Baraka, William S. Burroughs and Alan Ginsberg. Features original texts and the poems as performed. Includes some interviews.
500		"CDRM176910."
650	0	American poetry $y 20th century $x History and criticism.
650	0	Poetry, Modern $y 20th century.
650	0	Poets $y 20th century $v Interviews
710	2	Voyager Company.

Discussion for Figure 5.4

- Fixed field: This item includes text and video recordings to illustrate the beauty and power of poetry. Users can select a poet to view and hear the poet reading his work, follow the text as performed, read the text as published, and watch an interview with the poet. Users can play and pause the video clips as desired. The navigation paths are predetermined and linear and provide limited interactivity for users. The CD-ROM includes more than one medium, so Type is coded "m" and File is coded "m" (for combining media) and no computer file 006 field is needed.

- 007: The codes indicate this is a computer file (code "c"), on an optical disc (code "o"), with text and images in multicolor (code "c"), and the disc is $4\frac{3}{4}$ in. in diameter (code "g") and includes sound (code "a").

- 020: More and more computer files have been assigned an ISBN, and the number often can be found on the container, as with this one.

- 245: Ron Mann, the person who developed and directed this project, appears prominently on the disc label and is therefore recorded in subfield $c of the 245 field and assigned as the main access point (field 100). The names of the selected poets appear on the table of contents screen, but such information is not recorded in a 500 note because there are twenty-four of them. Many people associated with the technical production of the work are listed on the "credits" screens but are not recorded in a note because there are too many of them.

- 260: Information on the place of publication and publisher appears at the end of the credits screens. Copyright information on the credits screen includes: ©Text of each poem by its author; ©Motion picture footage, Sphinx Production, 1982, 1992, 1994; ©Software design, The Voyager Company, 1992, 1994. Since the computer file brought the texts and videos together, the latest copyright date for the software design is used as the publication date.

- 300: The common term "CD-ROM" is used as the specific material designation for subfield $a. If desired, the cataloger may use "computer optical disc" to identify the physical carrier. The user's guide is included in this field as an accompanying material.

- 538: Two notes are provided because the system requirements are specific to the platform. The elements in the source have to be rearranged to follow the order specified by *AACR2r*.

- 500: The note for numbers borne by a file is usually one of the last notes given.

- 650: As a collection of literary works, this item is assigned literary form headings.

- 710: The publisher is traced per 21.1B3.

Figure 5.5. Welcome to Japan

[Disc label]

Hybrid CD-ROM for Windows & Macintosh
Welcome to Japan
Meet the Ninja through Japanese Scrolls

Planning & Production
Japan Center for Intercultural Communications

MADE with Macromedia Inc.

^^

[Insert back cover]
Minimum System Requirements
    Windows:
        English language version Windows 95/98
        100 MHz Pentium
        32MB RAM
        4x CD-ROM drive
        640 x 480 display, High Color
        Sound Blaster compatible
    Macintosh:
        English language version MAC OS 8.0
        90 MHz PowerPC
        8MB RAM free
        4x CD-ROM drive
        640 × 480 display, thousands of colors

Your system software must include the QuickTime components in the Extensions folder.

This CD-ROM is recommended for upper elementary school to lower junior high school students.

Type: m	Elvl: I	Srce: d	Audn: j	Ctrl:	Lang: eng	
Blvl: m	File: i	GPub:		Mrec:	Ctry: ja	
Desc: a			DtSt: s	Dates: 199u		

007		c $b o $d c $e g $f a
090		HC461
092		915.2
245	00	Welcome to Japan $h [electronic resource] : $b meet the Ninja through Japanese scrolls / $c planning & production, Japan Center for Intercultural Communications.
246	30	Meet the Ninja through Japanese scrolls
260		[Japan?] : $b Japan Center for Intercultural Communications, $c [199-?]
300		1 CD-ROM : $b sd., col. ; $c 4¾ in. + $e 1 insert guide.
538		System requirements for PC: 100MHz Pentium; 32MB RAM; English language version Windows 95/98; QuickTime; 4x CD-ROM drive; 640 × 480 display, high color; Sound Blaster compatible.
538		System requirements for Macintosh: 90MHz Power PC; 8MB RAM free; English language version MAC OS 8.0; QuickTime; 4x CD-ROM drive; 640 × 480 display, thousands of colors.
500		Title from disc label.
500		"Hybrid CD-ROM for Windows & Macintosh."
520		An interactive CD-ROM that introduces students to Japan. There are discussion questions for students and students will receive scores along the way to assess their learning.
521		For upper elementary school to lower junior high school students.
505	0	Geography — Government & economy — Culture — Society.
651	0	Japan $v Interactive multimedia.
650	0	Educational games $v Interactive multimedia.
710	2	Japan Center for Intercultural Communications.

Discussion for Figure 5.5

- Fixed field: This CD-ROM contains text, sound, and images, and users can interact with its content to assess their knowledge of Japan, so it is treated as an interactive multimedia. Type is coded "m" and File is coded "i" for interactive multimedia. No computer file 006 field is needed.

- 007: Computer file 007 is required for all electronic resources. The codes specify that this is a computer file (code "c"), stored on an optical disc (code "o"), with materials presented in multiple colors (code "c"). The disc is $4\frac{3}{4}$ in. in diameter (code "g") and includes sound (code "a" for subfield $f).

- 245 and 246: The statement of responsibility in the 245 field reflects the wording on the chief source. A variant title is provided in the 246 field for the other title information to make it searchable.

- 260: No place of publication or year of publication is explicitly stated in the item, so the cataloger provides the information with a question mark and in brackets.

- 538s: This file can run on two different platforms, so a 538 field is created for each platform. The requirements are rearranged to follow the order specified by *AACR2r*. Information about QuickTime is incorporated into both 538 fields.

- 500: The statement about hybrid CD-ROM is not a formal edition and should not be recorded in the 250 field. The best strategy is to quote it and present it in a 500 note.

- 521: The formal statement about the intended audience is recorded in the 521 field. When the first indicator is blank, "Audience:" will be displayed before data from this field.

- 651 and 650: "Interactive multimedia" is a form subdivision and is assigned to both topical headings and coded in subfield $v.

Figure 5.6. Talking dictionary

Disc label:

THE
AMERICAN HERITAGE
TALKING DICTIONARY

WINDOWS 95
COMPATIBLE
WINDOWS 3.1

COMPACT
DISC
DIGITAL DATA   **SoftKey**

© 1998 Learning Company Properties Inc., a subsidiary of The Learning Company, Inc., and its licensors. All rights reserved....
AMH744CE-CD

Type: m	Elvl: I	Srce: d	Audn:	Ctrl:	Lang: eng
Blvl: m	File: i	GPub:		Mrec:	Ctry: mau
Desc: a			DtSt: s	Dates: 1998	

007		c $b o $d c $e g $f a
020		0763022713
090		PE1628
092		423
245	04	The American Heritage talking dictionary $h [electronic resource].
246	30	Talking dictionary
260		Cambridge, MA : $b SoftKey, $c c1998.
300		1 CD-ROM : $b sd., col., ; $c 4¾ in. + $e 1 installation sheet.
538		System requirements for IBM: IBM PC or compatible, 386/25 or higher; 4 MB RAM; 2 MB hard disk (18 MB if dictionary resides on hard disk); Windows 3.1 or higher; CD-ROM drive; 8-bit sound card (MPC-compliant).
538		System requirements for Macintosh: Any Macintosh; 2 MB RAM (System 6.x), 4 MB (System 7), 500K hard disk (15 MB if dictionary resides on hard disk); CD-ROM drive.
500		Title from disc label.
520		Contains The American Heritage dictionary of the English language, The dictionary of cultural literacy, and an English electronic thesaurus. Provides definitions, proper usage, hyphenation, idioms, synonyms, homographs, pronunciations and inflections, abbreviation, and sample sentences. Supports random searches, searches by word fragment and retrieval by definition.
500		"AMH744CE-CD."
650	0	English language $x Dictionaries $v Interactive multimedia.
650	0	English language $x Synonyms and antonyms $v Interactive multimedia.
700	12	Hirsch, E. D. $q (Eric Donald), $d 1928– $t Dictionary of cultural literacy.
710	2	SoftKey International, Inc.
740	02	American Heritage dictionary of the English language.

Discussion for Figure 5.6

- Fixed field: This item combines texts, images, and sound, and supports random access to words, phrases, and concepts, so it is cataloged as an interactive multimedia. Type is coded "m", File is coded "i", and no computer file 006 field is needed.

- 007: Computer file 007 is required for all electronic resources. The codes specify that this is a computer file (code "c"), stored on an optical disc (code "o"), with materials presented in multiple colors (code "c"). The disc is $4\frac{3}{4}$ in. in diameter (code "g") and includes sound (code "a" for subfield $f).

- 245 and 246: The title proper is transcribed according to rule 1.1B1. Since "talking dictionary" is more prominent by typography, a variant title is provided for it. Indicator "3" will produce an added entry but not a note for this title, indicator "0" explains this title is part of the title proper.

- 250: Although the copyrights of several parts of this work are found in the "copyrights" page, there is no edition statement that covers the entire work. So no edition statement is provided.

- 260: Place of publication is found on the item under "README" and also on the back of the container. SoftKey is a unit within the Learning Company that produced this file, so it is recorded as the publisher (see rule 1.4D2 and examples). Several parts of this item have their own copyright date, but only the date that covers the entire work is recorded in subfield $c.

- 300: The number of SMD (specific material designation) is recorded in subfield $a, sound and color characteristics in subfield $b, dimensions in subfield $c, and accompanying materials in subfield $e.

- 538: This file can run on two different platforms, so a 538 field is created for each platform. The requirements are rearranged to follow the order specified by *AACR2r*. The original wording, "18 MB of free hard disk space if the dictionary is to reside on the hard disk," is revised for this note.

- 500: The note for the source of the title proper is a required note.

- 520: An objective summary is recorded to indicate the content of the file and its features.

- 500: This number appears on the disc label, so it is presented as a quotation note. If it is verified to be a stock number, it can be entered in field 037 (e.g., 037 AMH744CE-CD $b SoftKey International).

- 650: Subdivision—"Interactive multimedia" is a form subdivision, and is coded as subfield v, according to the latest practice.

- 700: A name-title added entry is provided for related work.

- 710: The corporate body is traced per 21.30E.

- 740: An analytical added entry is provided for the work included in this item. Indicator "2" identifies this entry as an analytic.

Figure 5.7. Enduring vision

Title screen

The
ENDURING VISION
A HISTORY OF THE AMERICAN PEOPLE
INTERACTIVE EDITION, 1993 VERSION
BOYER • CLARK • KETT
SALISBURY • SITKOFF • WOLOCH

DEVELOPED BY
BRYTEN, INC.

Type: m	Elvl: I	Srce: d	Audn:	Ctrl:	Lang: eng
Blvl: m	File: i	GPub:		Mrec:	Ctry: mau
Desc: a			DtSt: s	Dates: 1993	

007		c $b o $d m $e g $f a
020		0669340707 (disc)
020		0669324612 (container)
020		0669340693 (guide)
043		n-us---
090		E173
092		973
245	04	The enduring vision $h [electronic resource] : $b a history of the American people / $c Boyer . . . [et al.] ; developed by Bryten, Inc.
250		Interactive ed., 1993 version.
260		Lexington, MA : $b D.C. Heath, $c 1993.
300		1 CD-ROM : $b sd., col. ; $c 4¾ in. + $e 1 user guide (15 p.) + 1 help sheet.
538		system requirements: Macintosh LC or II series computer; 4 MB RAM; 1.5 MB hard disk available; System 6.0.7 or higher; QuickTime 1.5; 13 in. color monitor; CD-RIM drive.
500		Title from title screen.
500		"Macintosh CD-ROM"—Container.
520		An electronic version of the second edition of The enduring vision by Paul Boyer et al. In addition to the original text, this version includes audio, video, maps, charts, graphics, and a search engine to support users' exploration of the documents and data on this CD.
651	0	United States $x History $v Interactive multimedia.
700	1	Boyer, Paul S. $t The enduring vision.
710	2	Bryten, inc.
710	2	D.C. Heath and Company.

Discussion for Figure 5.7

- Fixed field: This CD contains the text of *The Enduring Vision* and enhances it with audio, video, maps, charts, and graphics. Users can randomly access the text and media resources on this file. This item is therefore treated as an interactive multimedia. Type is coded "m" and File is coded "i" for multimedia. No computer file 006 field is needed.

- 007 field: Computer file 007 is required for all electronic resources. The codes specify that this is a computer file (code "c"), stored on an optical disc (code "o"), with mixtures of resources in black and white, gray scale, and color (code "m"). The disc is $4\frac{3}{4}$ in. in diameter (code "g") and includes sound (code "a" for subfield $f).

- 020s: This item has three ISBNs, so field 020 is repeated to record the numbers and the parts that carry these numbers.

- 043: When a geographic name is used in the subject heading, field 043 can be added to indicate the geographic focus of the item. The seven-character code is taken from the *USMARC Code List for Geographic Areas*.

- 245: The last names of six authors are on the title screen. Following rule 1.1F5 of *AACR2r,* only the first author is recorded in subfield $c. The company that developed this work is separated from the authors by a semicolon.

- 250: Edition statements are transcribed exactly from the title screen.

- 500: For electronic resource the source of title note is required.

- 500: The information about Macintosh appears in different forms. On the disc label "Macintosh" appears below the title proper; on the disc case "Macintosh version" appears at the bottom of the cover; and on the container "Macintosh CD-ROM" appears near the developer's name. It seems that the creators mainly want to convey that this file is intended for Macintosh machines. This quotation note is therefore provided to make that point.

- 520: The basis of this file is incorporated into the summary note to indicate its contents and features.

- 700: A name-title added entry is provided for a related work (rule 21.30G1).

- 710s: The developer and the publisher are traced per 21.1B3.

Figure 5.8. Splendors of Imperial China

Title screens:

SPLENDORS
of
IMPERIAL CHINA

TREASURES from the
NATIONAL PALACE MUSEUM, TAIPEI

---

an electronic catalogue of more than 475 masterworks from the imperial collections of China

COPYRIGHT © 1996 THE METROPOLITAN MUSEUM OF ART, NEW YORK, AND THE NATIONAL PALACE MUSEUM, TAIPEI

Type: m	Elvl: I	Srce: d	Audn:	Ctrl:	Lang: eng
Blvl: m	File: m	GPub:		Mrec:	Ctry: nyu
Desc: a			DtSt: s	Dates: 1996	

007		c $b o $d m $e g $f a
090		N3750$bT32
092		709.510747471
110	2	Kuo li ku kung po wu yuan.
245	10	Splendors of imperial China $h [electronic resource] : $b treasures from the National Palace Museum, Taipei : an electronic catalogue of more than 475 masterworks from the imperial collections of China.
246	30	Treasures from the National Palace Museum, Taipei
260		New York : $b Metropolitan Museum of Art, $c c1996.
300		1 CD-ROM : $b sd., col. ; $c 4¾ in.
538		System requirements for Macintosh: Power PC or 68040 processor; 8 MB RAM (16 MB recommended); System 7 or later; 640 x 480+ color monitor; double-speed CD-ROM.
538		System requirements for Windows: Pentium or 486 processor; 8 MB RAM (16 MB recommended); Windows 95; Windows 3.1 or later; SVGA video card and 640 x 480, 245+ color monitor; Windows-compatible sound card; double-speed CD-ROM.
500		Title from title screens.
500		Produced in conjunction with the exhibition, "Splendors of Imperial China: Treasures from the National Palace Museum, Taipei," organized by the National Palace Museum, Taipei, and The Metropolitan Museum of Art, New York.
500		Based on: Possessing the past : treasures from the National Palace Museum, Taipei.
536		The electronic catalog was funded by a grant from the National Endowment for the Humanities.
520		An electronic catalog of images and details accompanied by essays, glossary entries, artists' biographies, maps, pronunciations of Chinese names and terms and translations.
610	20	Kuo li ku kung po wu yüan $v Exhibitions.
650	0	Art, Chinese $v Exhibitions.
650	0	Art $z Taiwan $z Taipei $v Exhibitions.
710	2	Metropolitan Museum of Art (New York, N.Y.)
730	0	Possessing the past: treasures from the National Palace Museum, Taipei.

Discussion for Figure 5.8

- Fixed field: This CD-ROM includes texts, images, and sound, and hyperlinks for users to explore the resources, but the paths are predetermined and provide users with limited interactivity with the resources. Because this resource includes more than one media, Type is coded "m" and File is coded "m" for combination of media. No computer file 006 field is needed.

- 090, 092: The *LCC* number is for this particular museum. The *DDC* number is built from 709 (art), 51 (China), 074 (museum exhibition), and 7471 (the location of the exhibit, New York).

- 110: This item describes the resources of a corporate body, so the corporate body is designated as the main entry (*AACR2* 21.1B2). The LC Name Authority file lists the authorized form for this body in the romanized form.

- 245: The title screens consist of three screens. The third screen has a more detailed explanation of the file and that information is recorded as the second piece of other title information. An alternative treatment is to present this information in a quotation note.

- 538: The file is designed to run on Macintosh and Windows machines. Since the requirements are platform specific, two 538 fields are provided.

- 500: The exhibition information provides a context for this file.

- 500: This note indicates the source of this file's contents, and the source is presented in a citation format specified by 9.7B7.

- 536: Funding sources are recorded in field 536.

- 710: The Metropolitan Museum of Art is traced for publishing this item. The form is taken from the LC Name Authority file.

- 730: A title entry is added according to rule 21.30G for related works.

Figure 5.9. Small business resource guide

[title screen]
Welcome
to the

IRS Small Business

Resource Guide 2000

Click "Next" to continue **NEXT**
Menu Text-Only Version Acknowledgements
^^^
[user guide cover] **SMALL BUSINESS**
Resource Guide 2000

WHAT YOU NEED
TO KNOW ABOUT
TAXES AND
OTHER TOPICS

[user guide p. 1]
SMALL BUSINESS RESOURCE GUIDE:
What you need to know about taxes and other topics.

[user guide]
"Small Business Resource Guide 2000 (CD 2000) is the second version of the small business CD-ROM. CD 2000 is the result of a cross-government effort to provide new small businesses with information... The Internal Revenue Service and Small Business Administration are providing the leadership and resources to produce this new publication. The U.S. Department of Labor, and the U.S. Social Security Administration have also contributed to the content for CD 2000... The Small Business Resource Guide 2000 (IRS Publication 3207) contains all of the business tax forms, instructions, and publications needed by small business owners."

Type: a	Elvl: I	Srce: d	Audn:	Ctrl:	Lang: eng
Blvl: m	Form: s	Conf: 0	Biog:	Mrec:	Ctry: dcu
	Cont:	GPub:	LitF: 0	Indx: 0	
Desc: a	Ills:	Fest: 0	DtSt: s	Dates: 2000	

006		Type: m File: d AuDn: Gpub:
007		c $b o $d c $e g $f #
043		n-us---
090		HF54.55 $b .S63 2000
092		336.207
245	00	Small business resource guide 2000 $h [electronic resource] : $b what you need to know about taxes and other topics.
246	3	What you need to know about taxes and other topics
246	1	$i Title from title screen: $a IRS small business resource guide $n 2000
260		Washington, D.C. : $b U.S. Small Business Administration, $c c2000.
300		1 CD-ROM : $b sd., col. ; $c 4¾ in. + 1 user guide.
538		System requirements for Windows: Pentium; 32MB RAM; 70MB available hard drive space; WIN95/98/NT 4.0; recommended browser Internet Explorer 4.0+ (version 5.0 included); QuickTime 3.0+ (version 4.0 included); Adobe Acrobat 4.0 Fill In (included).
538		System requirements for Macintosh: Power PC; 16MB available RAM; 70MB available hard drive space; MacOS version 8.1+; recommended browser Internet Explorer 4.51 (included); QuickTime 3.0+ (version 4.0 included); Adobe Acrobat 4.0 Fill In (included).
500		Title from user guide.
500		IRS Publication 3207.
520		Includes all of the tax forms, instructions, and publications needed by owners of small businesses. Also provides helpful information such as how to prepare a business plan, finding financing for your business, and much more.
650	0	New business enterprises $z United States $x Information services.
650	0	Small business $z United States $x Information services
650	0	Small business $x Taxation $z United States $v Databases.
710	1	United States. $b Internal Revenue Service.
710	1	United States. $b Small Business Administration.

Discussion for Figure 5.9

- Fixed field: The content of this CD-ROM is primarily text and this is a finite resource, so Type is coded "a" and Form is coded "s" to indicate it is in electronic form. Computer file 006 and 007 fields are added to bring out the electronic aspects of the item.

- 006 field: This field does not have subfields but OCLC's Connexion offers a template for easy creation of this field. Code "m" identifies this item as an electronic resource, code "d" indicates it is a document. There is no information on the intended audience or whether this is a government publication.

- 007 field: This field is required for electronic resources. It has five subfields. Code "c" for subfield $a identifies this item as a computer file, code "o" for subfield $b identifies optical disc as the physical carrier, code "c" for subfield $d indicates materials are presented in multiple colors; code "g" for subfield $e indicates the disc is 4¾ in. in diameter, and code "#" (blank) for subfield $f indicates the CD-ROM is silent.

- 043: Because the content focuses on the United States, the 043 field is used. The seven-character code comes from the "OCLC-MARC Geographic Area Codes List."

- 245 and 246s: The title screen and the user guide present the title differently, and the source with fuller information is preferred. To make the other titles searchable, two 246 fields are used.

- 538s: This file can run on two different platforms, so a 538 field is created for each platform. The requirements are rearranged to follow the order specified by *AACR2r*.

- 710s: The two government agencies that play important role in the creation and publication of this item are traced.

Figure 5.10. *The Diamond Sutra* (CD-ROM)

[title screen]
BRITISH
LIBRARY

TURNING THE PAGES
The Diamond Sutra

[CD label]

BRITISH   **THE DIAMOND SUTRA**

LIBRARY

COMPACT DISC   ISBN 0-7123-4323-7
DIGITAL AUDIO   **PC / Mac dual format**
                                       Created by
                                       www.armadillosystems.com

Copyright ©
The British Library Board
2004

TURNING THE PAGES™

[back cover]
EQUIPMENT REQUIREMENTS
This CD-Rom disc is dual format and will run on a Windows-based
multimedia personal computer or Macintosh

PC minimum specification
Pentium III processor, 128 Mb of RAM, 24x speed CD-Rom drive,
800×600 resolution on a monitor capable of displaying thousands of
colours, running Windows 98 or higher (2000, XP) and Windows Media 9
or higher/QuickTime Player 4 or higher, with a sound card and internal
or external speakers.

Macintosh minimum specification
Apple Power Macintosh G3, 128 Mb of RAM, 24x speed CD-ROM drive,
800×600 resolution on a monitor capable of displaying thousands of
colours, running OS 9.0 or higher, QuickTime Player 4 or higher, with
internal or external speakers.

Type: a	Elvl: I	Srce: d	Audn:	Ctrl:	Lang: eng
Blvl: m	Form: s	Conf: 0	Biog:	Mrec:	Ctry: enk
	Cont:	GPub:	LitF: 0	Indx: 0	
Desc: a	Ills: a	Fest: 0	DtSt: s	Dates: 2004	

006		Type: m File: d AuDn: Gpub:
007		c $b o $d b $e g $f a
020		0712343237
041	1	eng $a chi $d chi $d eng $h san
090		BQ1990
092		294.3

200

130	1	Tripitaka. $p Sūtrapitaka. $p Prajñāpāramitā. $p Vajracchedikā. $1 English
245	14	The Diamond Sutra $h [electronic resource] / $c British Library.
260		London : $b British Library, $c c2004.
300		1 CD-ROM : $b sd., b&w ; $c 4¾ in.
516		Electronic text.
538		System requirements (PC): Pentium III processor; 128 Mb of RAM; Windows 98 or higher (2000, XP); Windows Media 9 or higher/QuickTime Player 4 or higher; 24x speed CD-Rom drive; 800 x 600 resolution on a monitor capable of displaying thousands of colors; sound card; internal or external speakers.
538		System requirements (Macintosh): Apple Power Macintosh G3; 128 Mb of RAM; OS 9.0 or higher; QuickTime Player 4 or higher; 24x speed CD-ROM drive; 800 x 600 resolution on a monitor capable of displaying thousands of colours; internal or external speakers.
546		The Sanskrit original, Vajracchedikia-prajnaparamita-sutra, was translated into Chinese by Kumarajiva.
500		Title from disc label.
500		Produced by the British Library's Turning the Pages system; PC/Mac dual format created by Armadillo systems.
500		Digital audio.
520		A CD-ROM version of a Buddhist text produced in China in AD 868 and known as the world's earliest, dated, printed book. Users can unroll the scroll from beginning to end, with the option of hearing the chanting of the Sutra, reading or hearing text commentary in English, and zooming in to magnify text and image.
530		Also available on the World Wide Web.
650	0	Buddhism $v Sacred books.
655	0	Electronic books.
700	1	Kumarajiva.
710	2	British Library.
710	2	Turning the Pages (Program)
856	41	$u http://www.bl.uk/collections/treasures/diamond.html

Discussion for Figure 5.10

- Fixed field: Since the most significant aspect of the item's content is text, Type is coded "a" for language material, and a computer file 006 and a computer file 007 field are used to bring out the electronic aspects of the item. In addition, Form is coded "s" to indicate the item is intended for computer manipulation. The copyright date 2004 on the CD-ROM is treated as the publication date, so DtSt is coded "s" for single date, and Dates is coded "2004." The item contains English text commentary and instructions, but the Buddhist text is in Chinese, so Lang is coded "eng" for English. The languages are noted in a 041 field later.

- 006 field: This field does not have subfields but OCLC's Connexion offers a template for easy creation of this field. Code "m" identifies this item as an electronic resource, code "d" indicates it is a document. There is no information on the intended audience or whether this is a government publication.

- 007 field: This field is required for electronic resources. It has five subfields. Code "c" for subfield $a stands for computer file, code "o" for subfield $b represents optical disc, code "b" for subfield $d indicates black-and-white presentation, code "g" for subfield $e indicates the dimensions are 4¾ in., and code "a" for subfield $f indicates the presence of sound data.

- 041: When a text is a translation, the 041 field is used to record the languages. The first indicator is coded "1" because this item is a translation. The text commentary is English, but the digitized text is translated from Sanskrit into Chinese, so "eng" and "chi" are entered into separate subfield $a, and "san" in subfield $h for the original language. The electronic book also includes chants of the *Diamond Sutra* in Chinese and the text commentary in English, so "chi" and "eng" are recorded in subfield $d for the audio portions of this work. The language codes are from the "MARC Code List for Languages" (lcweb.loc.gov/marc/languages).

- 130: The uniform title is used to collocate this item with other versions. The authorized form is from the Library of Congress Name Authority File.

- 245 and 260: The relationship between the title proper, British Library, and "Turning the Pages" is clarified by the Credits screen at the end of this item. The British Library digitized this document and produced a CD-ROM from the digitized version, so the 260 field records the location of the Library and the copyright year for the CD-ROM version.

- 300: A term in common usage, "CD-ROM," is used per the 2004 updates for rule 9.5B1. The electronic book contains chanting of the Buddhist text and audio version of the commentary, and the text and image are presented in black and white, so these physical details are recorded in subfield $b. Subfield $c records the standard dimensions of a CD-ROM. The quality of the sound file is recorded in a separate 538 note.

- 516 and 538: Field 516 clarifies the nature of this publication. Two 538 fields are needed to record the system requirements for the PC and the Macintosh environment. The requirements are rearranged to reflect the order specified by rule 9.7B1b.

- 546: The language information is provided to clarify that the text of the document is translated form Sanskrit into Chinese. This information is coded in the 041 field and justifies the provision of the uniform title and the translator's name as access points.

- 500 notes: The first 500 field is a required source of title note. The second one clarifies the role of "Turning the Pages", the format of the file, and the responsible party. Armadillo Systems however is not used as an access point because it contributes to the technical production of this work.

- 520: A free-text summary explains what the item is about and what functions it offers.

- 530: This field alerts the user of the existence of the same material in another format. As a result, the URL of the Web version is recorded in the 856 field, with the second indicator coded "1" to indicate that the URL points to a work that is not the item represented by the bibliographic record.

- 650, 655, 700, 710s: Subject, translator, the party responsible for the digitization and publication of this item, and the system used are used as access points. The term in 655 is a form/genre term that indicates what the item "is" instead of what it is "about" and catalogers have the option of adding form or genre terms. Because the term is an LC subject heading, the second indicator is coded "0". If an organization uses a list of locally developed terms, the second indicator will be coded "7" and the source of the term will be coded as "$2 local."

References

Banerjee, Kyle. (1997). Describing remote electronic documents in the online catalog: Current issues. *Cataloging & Classification Quarterly* 25 (1): 5–20.

Beaubien, Denise M., Emerton, Bruce, Kesse, Erich, Primack, Alice, and Seale, Colleen. (1988, November). Patron-use software in academic library collections. *College and Research Library News* 49: 661 667.

Guidelines for bibliographic description of interactive multimedia. (1994). Chicago: American Library Association.

Guidelines for using AACR2 chapter 9 for cataloging microcomputer software. (1984). Chicago: American Library Association.

Guidelines on subject access to microcomputer software. (1986). Chicago: American Library Association.

Hirons, Jean, and Graham, Crystal. (1997). Issues related to seriality. In Jean Weihs (Ed.), *The Principles and future of AACR: Proceedings of the International Conference on the Principles and Future Development of AACR, Toronto, Ontario, Canada, October 23–25, 1997,* 180–212. Ottawa: Canadian Library Association. http://www.nlc-bnc.ca/jsc/r-serial.pdf (accessed June 1, 2005).

Hsieh-Yee, Ingrid. (1999, May 30). Organization of nonprint resources in public and academic libraries. Unpublished report.

Hsieh-Yee, Ingrid. (2004, December 20). How libraries provide access to digital resources. Unpublished report.

Intner, Sheila S. (1991, Summer). Intellectual access to patron-use software. *Library Trends* 40: 42–62.

ISBD (CF) Review Group. (1990). *ISBD (CF): International standard bibliographic description for computer files.* London: IFLA Universal Bibliographic Control and International MARC programme.

ISBD (CF) Review Group. (1997). *ISBD (ER): International standard bibliographic description for electronic resources.* Munchen: K. G. Sauer.

Library of Congress. (1992). *Subject cataloging manual: Classification.* Washington, D.C.: Cataloging Distribution Service, Library of Congress.

Library of Congress. Cataloging Policy and Support Office. (2004). *Subject cataloging manual: Subject headings* (5th ed.). Washington, D.C.: Cataloging Distribution Service, Library of Congress.

Mandel, Carol A., and Wolven, Robert. (1996). Intellectual access to digital documents: Joining proven principles with new technologies. *Cataloging & Classification Quarterly* 22 (3/4): 25–42.

Oder, Norman. (1998, October). Cataloging the Net: Can we do it? *Library Journal* 123 (1): 47–51.

Olson, Nancy B. 1988. History of organizing microcomputer software. In Sheila S. Intner and Jane Anne Hannigan (Eds.), *The library microcomputer environment: Management issues,* 22–34. Phoenix, Ariz.: Oryx Press.

Olson, Nancy B. (Ed.). (1997). *Cataloging Internet resources: A manual and practical guide* (2nd ed.). Dublin, Ohio: OCLC. http://www.oclc.org/support/documentation/worldcat/cataloging/internetguide/default.htm (accessed June 1, 2005).

Seaman, Scott, and Carter, Nancy. (1997, June). Do not desensitize: Developing a policy for accompanying electronic materials. *Information Technology and Libraries* 16: 86–92.

Templeton, Ray, and Witten, Anita. (1984). *Study of cataloguing computer software: Applying AACR2 to microcomputer programs*. London: British Library.

Weihs, Jean. (1988). Organizing the collection: State of the art. In Sheila S. Intner and Jane Anne Hannigan (Eds.), *The library microcomputer environment: Management issues*, 35–44. Phoenix, Ariz.: Oryx Press.

Weihs, Jean. (1991). *The integrated library: Encouraging access to multimedia materials* (2nd ed.). Phoenix, Ariz.: Oryx Press.

Weiss, Amy. (2003). Proliferating guidelines: A history and analysis of the cataloging of electronic resources. *Library Resources and Technical Services* 47 (4): 171–187.

Weitz, Jay. (2004). *Cataloging Electronic Resources: OCLC-MARC Coding Guidelines*. http://www.oclc.org/support/documentation/worldcat/cataloging/electro nicresources/ (accessed June 1, 2005).

Suggested Readings

Intner, Sheila S. (1991, Summer). Intellectual access to patron-use software. *Library Trends* 40: 42–62.

Library of Congress. Cataloging Policy and Support Office. *Draft interim guidelines for cataloging electronic resources*. http://www.loc.gov/catdir/cpso/dcmb19_4 .html (accessed June 1, 2005).

Library of Congress. Network Development and Standards Office. (2003). *Guidelines for coding electronic resources in leader/06*. http://www.loc.gov/marc/ ldr06guide.html (accessed June 1, 2005).

Library of Congress. Network Development and Standards Office. (2003). *Guidelines for the use of field 856*. http://www.loc.gov/marc/856guide.html (accessed June 1, 2005).

Sandberg-Fox, Ann, and Byrum, John D. (1998, April). From ISBD (CF) to ISBD (ER): Process, policy, and provisions. *Library Resources and Technical Services* 42: 89–101.

Seaman, Scott, and Carter, Nancy. (1997, June). Do not desensitize: Developing a policy for accompanying electronic materials. *Information Technology and Libraries* 16: 86–92.

Weitz, Jay. 2004. *Cataloging electronic resources: OCLC-MARC coding guidelines*. http://www.oclc.org/support/documentation/worldcat/cataloging/electronic resources/ (accessed June 1, 2005).

6

Integrating Resources

The rapid increase of Web resources has intensified the need to organize these resources. The Pew Internet and American Life Project reports that 67 percent of American adults go on the Internet (about 135 million people) and more than 80 percent use it to search for information (2005a; 2005b). In a related study, Jones (2002) reported that 73 percent of college students surveyed say they use the Internet more than the library for research. An earlier study of faculty and students in a university found that 83.2 percent used the Internet for work related to academic studies, while 73.8 percent used it for nonacademic purposes (Bao 1998). Such strong interest in Internet resources has prompted libraries to change their operating philosophy from ownership to access. Many libraries have incorporated Internet resources into their services and operations and actively collect resources of value to their users. An ALA study of academic libraries, for instance, discovered that 87 percent of respondents from doctorate-granting institutions have provided access to Internet resources from their home pages (Lynch 1996). A survey found that 97 percent of large academic libraries and 59 percent of large public libraries have collected Internet resources (Hsieh-Yee 1999). And a recent survey of libraries in the Washington Metropolitan Area reports that 69 percent of respondents catalog freely available Web resources (Hsieh-Yee 2004).

The uneven quality of Web resources, the sheer number of such resources, and their dynamic nature are three of the many challenges facing information organizers. Most libraries recognize the need to incorporate Web resources into their collections and services. Frequently the staff in charge of collection development handles the content quality issue by evaluating freely available Web resources and selecting those relevant to the needs of the library's constituencies. Some libraries compile subject guides or Webliographies to present such resources to users. Others create a special database to control them. And more and more libraries have chosen to catalog them so that users do not need to use several tools to search for print and Web resources.

Since the early 1990s the cataloging community has made steady progress in controlling Web resources. Libraries and catalogers undertook various projects and developed cataloging guidelines to help make them accessible to users. Nancy Olson's guidelines (1997), the InterCat project, the report on seriality by Jean Hirons and Crystal Graham (1997), changes to Chapter 9 of *AACR2* in 2000, and the CORC project all contribute to the development of better cataloging rules and the integration of Web resources into library collections and catalogs. As an effort to provide cataloging rules that describe characteristics of print serials, electronic serials, and Internet resources more effectively, the Joint Steering Committee for Revision of AACR substantially revised Chapter 12 and renamed it "Continuing Resources" in the 2002 revision. The new rules cover two major types of continuing resources—serials and integrating resources. **Serials** are publications "issued in a succession of discrete parts, usually bearing numbering, that has no predetermined conclusion" and **integrating resources** are resources that are "added to or changed by means of updates that do not remain discrete and are integrated into the whole" (Appendix D). Integrating resources can be continuing, such as updating databases or Web sites. Or they can be finite in that the resources are updated continuously until the predetermined end date of publication. Chapter 12 also covers the treatment of a few types of finite resources, including reprints of serials, finite integrating resources, and resources with serial characteristics but limited duration.

Internet resources can be monographs, serials, or integrating resources. The range of possibilities makes it necessary for catalogers to consult several chapters of *AACR2r* in preparing the description. To avoid unnecessary repetition, three major categories of Internet resources are discussed in separate chapters of this book. Chapter 5 covers direct access electronic resources and Internet resources that are static and finite in nature; electronic books and PDF files are also discussed. Chapter 6 focuses on Internet resources that are updated continuously or over a predetermined period of time. Specifically, updating databases, updating Web sites, and finite Web sites are discussed. Chapter 7 discusses treatments of remote access electronic serials.

Issues for Consideration Before Record Creation

Resource Selection

Before cataloging work begins, resource selection needs to take place. What should be selected and cataloged? Who should make the decisions? Many libraries catalog resources they subscribe to, such as electronic journals. In addition, they also catalog items recommended by users and approved by collection development librarians, and resources recommended by the staff such as bibliographers, subject specialists, collection development librarians, catalogers, and reference librarians. The evaluation criteria are similar to those for print resources, with newer criteria such as network capability and graphic design recommended (Smith 1997).

Aspects for Description and Access

In creating a bibliographic record, *LCRI* 1.0 advises catalogers to consider two issues. First, what aspects of the resource will the record represent? A resource such as an updating Web site may or may not be part of a larger resource. If it is not, the bibliographic record will represent the resource itself. If it is part of a larger resource, a bibliographic record could represent the resource itself and another record could represent the larger resource. For example, catalogers could create a record that represents an academic unit's Web site within a university and another record that represents the university's Web site. The aspect to be represented depends largely on the information contained in each resource and its relevance to the user community. Some libraries follow the "two-click" rule to make sure users do not need to go through several levels of a site's hierarchy to reach a page (Veatch 1999).

Type of Issurance

The second issue raised by *LCRI* 1.0 is that catalogers must consider the *type of issurance* of the aspect that will be represented by a bibliographic record. *LCRI* 1.0 defines "type of issurance" as "how the bibliographic resource is published, distributed, or produced, and, if it is updated, how it is updated." Is the resource a monograph, a serial, or something else? *AACR2r* defines a serial as "a publication in any medium issued in successive parts bearing numeric or chronological designations and intended to be continued indefinitely." Many Internet resources are not treated as monographs because they are updated frequently, and yet, they are also not treated as serials because they do not meet the definition of *AACR2r*. Hirons and Graham explained the complex seriality issue and suggested "ongoing publications" as a better description for Web resources such as home pages and resources that are updated continuously (1997). Hirons completed a report on seriality for the Joint Steering Committee for Revision of AACR (1999), and the recommendations led to the revision of *AACR2r* Chapter 12, and a new taxonomy for sorting resources that includes continuing resources, integrating resources, and finite integrating resources. OCLC's *Cataloging Electronic Resources: Coding OCLC-MARC Guidelines* (Weitz 2004) reminds catalogers that when a resource has several manifestations, catalogers should consider the type of issurance carefully. For example, a print publication may have been cataloged as a serial, but its online counterpart may be treated as an "integrating resource" because the resource is continuously updated. The *Guidelines* identify several types of resources that should be treated as monographs or integrating resources, but not as serials:

- Databases (directories, A&I services, etc.)
- Electronic discussion groups (e.g., SERIALIST)
- Electronic discussion group digests (e.g., AUTOCAT digest)
- Gopher servers (e.g., LC-MARVEL)
- Online public access catalogs (e.g., OCLC, RLIN)
- Online services (e.g., America Online)
- Web sites (e.g., the CONSER home page)

If an Internet resource is static and complete like a monograph, the cataloger will catalog it as a remote access electronic resource by consulting *AACR2r* Chapter 9, "Electronic Resources." A PDF file is an example. If the resource is published in successive issues with no predetermined end of publication in sight and each new issue remains a discrete unit, the cataloger will catalog it as an electronic serial by following the rules of Chapters 9 and 12. And if the resource is updated continuously and the updates are integrated into the resource, the cataloger will treat it as an integrating resource and follow Chapters 9 and 12 to prepare the description. Web databases and Web sites that are continuously updated are examples of integrating resources. Some Internet resources may fall into the category of "finite integrating resources" defined as Web resources that are updated continuously over time but intended to conclude after a certain period of time. The cataloger will treat them as continuing integrating resources as long as they are being updated. When the publication has concluded, the cataloger will change the description to reflect the finite nature of the resource. An example is a Web site created for a special event such as the 2004 presidential election. When the election is concluded and the site is no longer updated, the record will be revised to reflect the conclusion of this event.

Single Record Approach Vs. Separate Record Approach

Another issue for catalogers to consider is whether to take the single record approach or the separate record approach. Some electronic resources have print counterparts, while others are available online only. For the former the cataloger has the options of creating a new record for the electronic version or adding relevant information to the record for the print form. Graham and the CONSER Working Group completed a report on these two approaches (1999). The one-record approach enables libraries to catalog resources quickly and make them available to users with less cost, less staff time, and less record maintenance. It may also facilitate access by informing patrons of the existence of several formats of the same item. A major drawback is patrons may be confused by the print and the electronic versions represented by the same record. The advantage of the separate record approach is that there is less confusion over what a record represents, but the cost of creating a separate record is inevitable. A recent survey found that 72 percent of the responding academic and public libraries have taken the one-record approach (Hsieh-Yee 1999), perhaps for economic reasons. CONSER and OCLC initially encouraged the separate record approach, but have endorsed both approaches. CONSER *Cataloging Manual Module 31* makes explicit when the single record approach is most appropriate (2004), and OCLC guidelines provide detailed explanations for using these two approaches (Weitz 2004).

MARC Fields for Integrating Resources

Encoding bibliographic records for integrating resources is another challenging area for catalogers. Although MARC 21 has defined code values for integrating resources, they have not been fully implemented by bibliographic utilities. As a result, catalogers will need to follow an interim practice in coding these resources. Because of the complexity of MARC encoding, selection of the appropriate 008 for integrating resources and related field is discussed before a detailed discussion of *AACR2* rules and examples. The discussion below draws on major documents on cataloging and coding electronic resources:

- CONSER. *Use of Fixed Fields 006/007/008 and Leader Codes in CONSER Records* (http://www.loc.gov/acq/conser/ffuse.html).

- Library of Congress. Cataloging Policy and Support Office. *Draft Interim Guidelines for Cataloging Electronic Resources* (http://www.loc.gov/catdir/cpso/dcmb19_4.html).

- Library of Congress. Network Development and Standards Office. *Guidelines for Coding Electronic Resources in Leader/06.* Revised December 2003 (http://www.loc.gov/marc/ldr06guide.html).

- Library of Congress. Network Development and Standards Office. *Guidelines for the Use of Field 856.* Revised March 2003 (http://www.loc.gov/marc/856guide.html).

- Weitz, Jay. *Cataloging Electronic Resources: OCLC-MARC Coding Guidelines.* Revised November 9, 2004 (http://www.oclc.org/support/documentation/worldcat/cataloging/electronicresources/).

MARC fields that are commonly used in coding integrating resources are

Field number	Definition
Leader/06 ("Type")	Fixed field code for specifying the type of 008 field for a record
006	Fixed field elements for coding resource characteristics not represented by the 008 field specified by Leader/06 ("Type"). Two commonly used 006 fields are (1) Electronic resource 006: For electronic resources not coded as Type "m" (2) Serial 006: For integrating resources before implementation of Bibliographic Level code "i"
007	Fixed field elements for coding additional physical characteristics. Electronic resource 007 is required for electronic resources: $a computer file $b specific material designator $d color $e dimensions $f sound

Field	Indicators	Subfields
010		LC control number
020		ISBN
022		ISSN
1XX	—	Main entry (for personal name (100), corporate body (110), and conference (111) as main entry, not for title main entry)
245	——	Title proper $h [electronic resource] : $b other title information / $c statement of responsibility. 245 0 _ for title main entry.

246	——	Variant title
		$i for display text : $a for variant title
247	——	Former title
		$a earlier title proper $f \<viewing date\>
250		Edition statement.
260		Place of publication : $b publisher, $c
		Date of publication.
		$c used only when the first date of
		publication is explicit.
310		Current frequency.
362	1	Date of publication when the beginning
		date is not available (i.e., when 260 $c is
		not used).
4XX	——	Series statement
500/516		Nature and scope; type of electronic
		resource.
538		System requirements.
538		Mode of access for remote access
		electronic resources.
546		Languages.
500		Source of title note (viewing date) may
		be combined with the description based
		on note
500		Description based on note (for integrat-
		ing resources). Often combined with the
		source of title note (500).
520	—	Summary.
505	——	Contents note.
530		Additional physical form available.
550		Issuing body.
6XX	——	Subject heading.
		$x, $y, $z, $v
7XX	—	Non-subject added entry.
730	——	Uniform title added entry for related
		resources cataloged separately.
740	——	Analytical title added entry.
776	——	Link to other physical formats
		$a, $x, $w
830	—	Series added entries (often used with
		490)
856	——	Electronic location and access
		$u, $z

Decisions on 008 Field and 006 Fields

The first step of record creation is to select an appropriate 008 field. As the model in Chapter 2 illustrates, this decision depends largely on how the Type element and BLvl element are coded. Chapter 5 has a detailed discussion of the development of 006 fields and their usage. It also covers the use of 007 fields and the coding of the File and Form elements.

USMARC defines field 006 for several types of materials, including books, computer files/electronic resources, continuing resources, maps, mixed materials, music, and visual materials. Field 006 has no subfields and information is coded by character positions. OCLC's Connexion provides a pull-down menu for easy addition of field 006. After the cataloger specifies the type of 006 field needed, Connexion presents the elements for the cataloger to fill in appropriate values.

006 fields for Computer Files
Audn   File   u   GPub

Before code "i" for BLvl (bibliographic level) is implemented by bibliographic networks, the interim solution for coding integrating resources is to use the Type element and BLvl element to select the 008 field. Catalogers should consider *the primary aspect of the content* of a resource and use it as the basis for selecting a code for Type. If there are other aspects of the main item or accompanying material that need to be represented, they can add appropriate 006 fields for that purpose. The following table shows what 008 and 006 fields are used with Internet resources:

	Computer Content	*Text Content*
Type	m	a
BLvl	m	m
Computer file 008	yes	no
Book 008	no	yes
Electronic resource 006	no	yes
Electronic resource 007	yes	yes
Serial 006	yes (for continuing)	yes (for continuing)
	no (for finite)	no (for finite)

An integrating resource such as a Web site that is continuously updated and is heavily text based will have code "a" (language material) for the Type element. As an interim solution, the BLvl element will be coded "m", and these two code values will result in the use of the Book 008 field for record creation. In order to bring out the electronic aspect of this resource, an electronic resource 006 field will be added. Because the electronic resource 007 field is required for all electronic resources, it is added to the record as well. To represent the continuing nature of this resource, an interim solution is to add a serial 006 field.

If an integrating resource is a finite integrating resource and contains mostly text, it will have code "a" (language material) for Type, code "m" for BLvl (because it is finite and complete in one part), and the Book 008 field will be used to create a record for it. Electronic resources 006 and 007 will be added to bring out the electronic aspect of this resource. But no serial 006 will be needed because the resource is not continuing.

If an integrating resource contains numerical data for manipulation, is a computer program, is a computer-based multimedia, or an online service or system, code "m" is used for Type. All integrating resources on the Internet are coded "m" for BLvl for now. Type "m" and BLvl "m" will result in the use of the computer file 008 field. Because the electronic aspect is represented by this 008 field already, no electronic resource 006 is necessary. But an electronic resource 007 field should be used because it is required for all electronic resources. If the resource is continuously updated, a serial 006 field should be used too. OCLC offers a menu for selecting 006 fields. Here is the OCLC screen display for the serial 006 field:

006 fields for Serials						
Freq	Reg	ISSN	SrTp	Orig		
Form	EntW	Cont	Gpub	Conf	Alph	S/L

The elements are hyperlinked to "OCLC's Bibliographic Formats" that provide explanation and examples. The File element in the electronic resource 006 field is often coded "d" because many Internet resources are documents or exhibit many characteristics of documents.

Serial 006 is fairly new and "OCLC's Bibliographic Formats" (http://www.oclc.org/bibformats/) and MARC 21 provide complete information on the code values for these data elements. For remote access electronic integrating resources, the following code values are frequently applied:

Element	*Code*	*Definition*
Frequency	blank	No determinable frequency (irregular)
	k	Continuously updated (more frequently than daily)
Regularity	r	Regular
	x	Completely irregular
SrTp	d	Updating database
(Type of continuing resource)	w	Updating Web site
Form	s	Electronic
S/L		
(Entry convention)	2	Integrated entry

Orig is coded "s" for electronic resource. EntW is an optional element designed to specify the nature of a resource and to code what it is (such as "b" for bibliography and "h" for handbook), instead of what it is about. If a resource contains more than one type of content, Cont is used to code up to three types of content. GPub indicates whether a resource is a government publication. Conf indicates whether the resource is a conference publication. Alph (original alphabet or script of title on which a key title is based) is mandatory for members of the International Serials Data System (ISDS) but optional for non-ISDS records.

Electronic Resource 007 Field

The electronic resource 007 field is required for all electronic resources. It describes additional physical characteristics of an item. Five subfields of the 007 field are mandatory or required if applicable and many code values are defined for them. For a full list of the values see *OCLC's Bibliographic Formats* at http://www.oclc.org/bibformats/en/0xx/007comp.shtm. OCLC also has a useful table of 007 field values available at http://www.oclc.org/bibformats/en/0xx/field007table.shtm. The following table highlights a few codes that are commonly used to describe electronic resources:

Subfield	Meaning	Codes	Examples
a	Category of material	1 code	c Computer file
b	Specific material designation	11 codes	j Magnetic disk o Optical disc r Remote
d	Color	8 codes	b Black and white c Multicolored g Gray scale m Mixed
e	Dimensions	10 codes	a 3½ in. e 12 in. g 4¾ in. o 5¼ in.
f	Sound	3 codes	Blank Silent a Sound u Unknown

For subfield $d, resources with mixtures of text and images in black and white, gray scale, and color should be coded "m." This code is often applicable to Web resources. Code "g" is for black-and-white text documents. Code "c" is for colored images such as photos. For subfield $f, code "a" is to indicate that a resource includes digitally encoded sound; code "u" means it is unknown or very difficult to determine the presence of sound files on a resource; and code "blank" means no sound on the resource at all. Code "u" is applied quite often to Internet resources because some sites are too big or complex for the cataloger to search for the presence of sound files.

"File" and "Form" in Fixed Field or Field 006

"File" and "Form" are two elements that deserve some attention from catalogers. The "File" element takes up the position of computer file 008/26 and 006/09, a one-character alphabetic code that specifies the type of resource being cataloged. If an electronic resource is coded "m" (for computer file), File (the 008/26 position) is coded in the computer file 008 field. If Type is *not* coded "m," catalogers will use an electronic resource 006 field to represent the electronic aspect, and File (the 006/09 position) is coded in the 006 field. Thirteen code values on the following page are available for this element.

"Form" codes the form of the resource being described. The primary aspect of a resource may be one of the following formats—Books, Serials, Mixed Materials, Scores, Maps, and Visual Materials—but as long as the item requires the use of a computer or peripheral devices (like a CD player) connected to a computer, Form should be coded "s" to make clear the item is intended for computer manipulation. The item may be a direct access or remote access

Code	Nature of File	Code	Nature of File	Code	Nature of File
a	Numerical data	f	Font	m	Combination
b	Computer program	g	Game	u	Unknown
c	Representational	h	Sound	z	Other
d	Document	i	Interactive multimedia		
e	Bibliographic data	j	Online system or service		

electronic resource. For example, a Web site of digital sound files (such as MP3 files) that is continuously updated will have the following codes

> Type: j (for musical sound file, or "i" for non-musical sound files)
> Electronic resource 006 field with File coded as "h" for sound files
> Serial 006 field will be added to indicate the continuing nature of this site, with Form coded as "s" to indicate this is an electronic resource.

The DtSt element also has an interim value. Currently all continuing integrating resources are coded "m" for multiple dates. After BLvl code "i" is implemented, this element will be coded "c" for "currently published status." The examples below illustrate the interim solutions and future coding practice.

> **Resource: An updating Web site that is text based, in English, began publishing in 2001 in New York.**
> Current coding practice uses the Book 008 field and other controlled fields to represent the electronic and continuing nature of this resource.

Type:	**a**	Elvl:	I	Srce:	d	Audn:		Ctrl:		Lang:	eng
BLvl:	**m**	**Form:**	**s**	Conf:	0	Biog:		MRec:		Ctry:	nyu
		Cont:		GPub:		LitF:		Indx:	0		
Desc:	a	Ills:		Fest:	0	**DtSt:**	**m**	Dates:	2001,9999		

Code "a" for Type identifies this resource as primarily textual, code "m" for BLvl is an interim solution, code "s" for Form indicates it is electronic, and code "m" for DtSt indicates multiple dates are associated with the resource (2001 is the year it began, and Date 2 is "9999" because the resource is expected to continue indefinitely). In addition, the cataloger will use an electronic resource 006 field to bring out the electronic aspects of the resource (code "d" for File specifies it as a document).

> **Audn: File: d   GPub:**

Field 006 is presented in OCLC records as a string of characters, so the field above will display as (m = computer file; d = document): **006   m d**

A serial 006 (continuing resource) will code the continuing nature of this item:

Freq:		Regl: x	ISSN:	**SrTp: w**	Orig:		
Form:	s	EntW:	Cont:	GPub:	Conf:	Alpha:	**S/L: 2**

Because the frequency of update is unknown, Freq (frequency) is left blank (for irregular) and Regl (regularity) coded "x" for completely irregular. SrTp (type of continuing resource) is coded "w" for updating Web site, and S/L (entry convention) is coded "2" for integrated resource.

And an electronic resource 007 field will code the physical details of the resource.

$a	c	$b	r	$d	m	$e	n	$f	u
Category of material	computer file	Specific material designation	remote	Color	mixed	Dimensions	not applicable	Sound	unknown

When new MARC code values are implemented by bibliographic utilities, the same item will be coded in the 008 field for continuing resource as follows:

Type:	a	ELvl:	I	Srce:	d	GPub:		Ctrl:			Lang:	eng
BLvl:	i	Form:	s	Conf:	0	Freq:		MRec:			Ctry:	nyu
S/L:	2	Orig:		Entw:		Regl:	x	ISSN:			Alpha:	
Desc:	a	SrTp:	w	Cont:		DtSt:	c	Dates:	2001, 9999			

Catalogers will continue to use the computer file 006 field and the computer file 007 field with this new 008 field. But the serial 006 field will no longer be needed. Note that BLvl is coded "i" for integrating resource and DtSt coded "c" for continuing publication. "Frequ", "Regl", "S/L", and "SrTp" from the current serial 006 field will be incorporated into the continuing resource 008 field.

Description

Rules for Descriptive Cataloging

Basis of Description

One of the major challenges in describing updating Web resources lies in the fact that new additions to these resources are integrated into them, making it difficult for catalogers to tell the versions apart unless the older versions are archived and accessible through tools such as the *Wayback Machine* (1996–) or from an archive site. Because of this difficulty, *AACR2r* instructs catalogers to base most of the description of integrating resources on the **current "iteration,"** defined as "an instance of an integrating resource, either as first published or after it has been updated" (Appendix D). Rule 12.0B1 specifies what to use to describe integrating resources.

Area	Basis of Description
Title and statement of responsibility	Current iteration
Edition	Current iteration
Place and publisher	Current iteration
Dates	First and/or last iterations
Physical description	Current iteration (not applicable to remote access integrating resources)
Series	Current iteration
Notes	All iterations and any other source
Standard numbers and terms of availability	All iterations and any other source

Date information, however, should be based on the first or the last iteration, while notes and standard numbers can come from many sources.

An important practice about the cataloging of integrating resources is that, whenever possible, catalogers should maintain these records to reflect changes over time. It is unlikely that catalogers will have time to review these records on a regular basis to maintain their currency. But when changes are brought to their attention by staff or users, catalogers will need to provide information about the changes, often through note fields such as field 247.

Chief Source of Information

Rule 12.0B2b instructs catalogers to consult subrules .0B in the relevant chapter for the resource being cataloged to identify the chief source. For remote access updating databases and updating Web sites, the chief source of information, according to rule 9.0B1, will be the resource itself. Catalogers should take information from formally presented evidence such as title screens, home pages, and encoded metadata such as HTML meta tags. If these sources present similar information in different degrees of fullness, catalogers will prefer the source with the most complete information. If the information needed for description is not available from the resource itself, catalogers may use the following sources, in the order recommended by rule 9.0B1:

> printed or online documentation or other accompanying material (e.g., "about" link, publisher's Web page)
>
> other published descriptions of the resource
>
> other sources

Prescribed Sources of Information

Rule 12.0B3 instructs catalogers to follow the instructions in subrule .0B in the chapter appropriate for the item being cataloged to identify the prescribed sources of information for each area of the description. According to rule 9.0B2, the prescribed sources of information for remote access integrating resources are as follows:

Area	Prescribed Sources of Information
Title and statement of responsibility	Resource itself, information issued by the publisher, creator, etc.
Edition	Resource itself, information issued by the publisher, creator, etc.
Type and extent of resource	Not applicable
Publication, distribution, etc.	Resource itself, information issued by the publisher, creator, etc.
Physical description	Not applicable
Series	Resource itself, information issued by the publisher, creator, etc.
Note	Any source
Standard number and terms of availability	Any source

Area 1. Title and Statement of Responsibility (MARC Field 245)

Rules 1.1B–1.1F and 12.1B–12.1F cover the transcription of the title proper of integrating resources. While rule 1.1B1 instructs catalogers to record the title proper "exactly as to wording, order, and spelling, but not necessarily as to punctuation and capitalization," it also states that introductory words not intended to be part of the title should not be transcribed. A common example for updating Web sites is the presence of "Welcome to" on the resource. Indicator # in the 246 field means "blank."

```
245   00   $a East Ironquoit's middle school health website.
246   3#   $a Welcome to East Ironquoit's middle school
           health website
500        $a Title from home page (viewed March 2, 2004).
```

Sometimes such introductory words appear in other sources such as the browser title bar:

```
245   00   $a Health Canada $h [electronic resource].
246   1#   $i Title on HTML source code : $a Welcome to health
           Canada online
500        $a Title from home page (viewed June 2, 2004).
```

Catalogers have the option of making the variant title an added entry if it is considered a useful access point. *LCRI* 1.1B1 advises catalogers to consider how the title is presented in other parts of the resource to identify the real title proper. If it is difficult to identify the real title proper, *LCRI* encourages catalogers to enter the title as found on the resource in field 245 and record the other title in field 246. Rule 1.1B further instructs catalogers to consult rule 12.1B1 when the title proper of an integrating resource contains errors. In such cases catalogers should "correct obvious typographic errors" and use a note to present the title as found on the resource.

When a title proper is presented in full and in an acronym or initialism, the full title is recorded as the title proper (rule 12.1B2). *LCRI* 12.1B2 and rule 12.1E1 both instruct catalogers to record the acronym or initialism as other title information. It can be used as a title added entry if considered important for access.

245	00	$a Knowledge management resources $h [electronic resource] : $b KMR
246	3#	$a KMR

Rules 9.1B2 and 9.7B3 explain that the source of the title proper should always be provided for electronic resources and a viewing date is typically added. The *Source of Title Notes for Internet Resources,* available at http://ublib.buffalo.edu/libraries/units/cts/olac/capc/stnir.html, and issued by the OLAC group provides helpful examples. Rule 12.7B23b instructs catalogers to provide a note on the latest iteration used for the description and add the viewing date for remote access resources. The source of title proper note and the "description based on" notes are often combined.

Rule 12.1B8 explains that when changes in the title proper occur on a later iteration after a record had been created, catalogers should record the new title to reflect the latest iteration. Unlike serials for which a major change in title proper requires the creation of a new record, rule 21.2B1 specifies that no new record needs to be created. Instead, the earlier title will be recorded in a note and made an added entry as instructed in rule 21.30J1. Catalogers will enter an earlier title in field 247 using subfields $a, $n, $p as appropriate, but not subfield $b or $h. If a record has ISSN in the 022 field, that number is moved to subfield $x of field 247. *LCRI* 12.7B4.1 instructs catalogers to add the range of years when the earlier title was in effect. If such information is not readily available, catalogers may record in subfield $f of field 247 the viewing date from the earlier source of title proper note or the description based on note.

Existing record		
245	00	$a Musical resources for children's plays $h [electronic resource].
500		$a Title from title screen (viewed June 5, 2002).
Revised record reflects the new title in the latest iteration		
245	00	$a Rhymes and songs for children's plays $h [electronic resource].
247	10	$a Musical resources for children's plays $f <June 5, 2002>
500		$a Title from title screen (viewed Feb. 5, 2003).

If the title proper changes several times, multiple 247 fields will be used to track the changes. For complex changes that cannot be explained adequately by the 247 field, catalogers may use field 547.

General material designation (GMD): The general material designation for remote access integrating resources is electronic resource and is entered in $h before $b for other title information. Catalogers should note that "multimedia" is no longer valid as a GMD for *AACR2r*.

Other title information ($b of Field 245): Other title information may clarify the title proper and is recorded in subfield $b of the 245 field. Catalogers may use such information to create a title added entry if necessary.

245	04	$a The body $h [electronic resource] : $b an AIDS and HIV information resource.
246	30	$a AIDS and HIV information resource

Rule 12.1E1 specifies three occasions when catalogers should transcribe other title information of integrating resources. If an acronym or initialism appears with a full title proper, catalogers should record the acronym or initialism as other title information. If a statement of responsibility or the name of a publisher is an integral part of the other title information, it should be transcribed. And if the title proper is the name of a corporate body, catalogers should provide a brief statement as other title information to explain the title. But they should not transcribe words that describe the currency of the contents or update frequency of a resource as other title information. If important changes occur in other title information, catalogers will revise the record to reflect the latest iteration, using field 246. Note that this is different from changes to the title proper, which are recorded in field 247.

245	00	$a UNAIDS $h [electronic resource] : $b the jointed United Nations Programme on HIV/AIDS.
246	30	$a Jointed United Nations Programme on HIV/AIDS

Statement of responsibility ($c of Field 245): Web resources do not always contain statements of responsibility. Because the chief source of electronic resources is the resource itself, catalogers need to examine several places for this information. Although some resources present authors near the title on the title screen, the bottom of a home page is another popular place for such information. "About" links are another potential source because they often explain the purpose of a Web page or Web site and identify the people and corporate bodies that contribute to the resource. Some Web page creators use meta tags to provide metadata such as authors, description, and keywords to describe their Web page. These metadata, if harvested by search engine crawlers, could increase the chances of a Web page/site being found by users. In Netscape, Firefox, Explorer, and other browsers catalogers can view meta tags by pulling down the "VIEW" menu to select "Page Source" or "Source." Meta tags are part of the HTML header and should appear in the top portion of the HTML source code. Information from the source code should be verified within the Web page/site. If the author statement is from the HTML source code, the author is used as the main entry, but the author statement should not be recorded in subfield $c of the 245 field. It is more appropriate to provide a 500 note to explain where the author statement comes from.

If the author statement from the HTML source code turns out to identify the webmaster, it should be clarified in a 500 note. For example, the CATCMB site (http://catcmb.cua.edu/) has this information in the source code:

<meta name = "Author" content = "Bernard A. Lynch">

But the information at the site shows that Lynch is responsible for the markup of the site, not the contents. As a result, the resource is described as follows:

245	00	CATCMB Web-page $h [electronic resource].
246	3#	Welcome to the CATCMB web page
500		Webmaster information from HTML source code: Bernard A. Lynch.
700	00	Lynch, Bernard A.

Libraries vary in whether they provide added entries for webmasters. Some consider webmasters to be editors and trace them, while others do not because they believe webmasters do not contribute to the intellectual content of a work. When the contribution of the webmaster is significant, he or she should be traced. Information on webmasters often appear in the "About" link or the "Developers" link. Here is an example:

100	1	Van Helden, Albert.
245	14	The Galileo Project $h [electronic resource] / $c Albert Van Helden, Elizabeth Burr.
500		Webmaster: Krist Bender.
700	1	Bender, Krist.

[Information on the webmaster is from "Developers" under the "About" link.]

If no information is available on the parties responsible for a Web page/site, no information is transcribed for subfield $c of field 245. This is often the case with Web resources.

Area 2. Edition (MARC Field 250)

For integrating resources, rule 12.2B1 instructs catalogers to follow rule 1.2B to record an edition statement if it is considered important. Rule 9.2B1 clarifies an edition statement for electronic resources as "a statement relating to an edition of an electronic resource that contains differences from other editions of that resource, or to a named reissue of a resource." If the source of the edition statement is different from that of the title proper, it should be noted in a 500 field; this note can be combined with the source of title proper note.

Rule 9.2B1 also states that in cataloging **electronic resources** catalogers may take the presence of words such as *edition, issue, version, release, level,* or *update* as an indication that a statement is an edition statement. However, when cataloging **integrating resources**, catalogers need to keep in mind that words such as *version* and *update* do not necessarily denote an edition statement. Because Web sites often contain version or update statements that change frequently, catalogers will need to determine if a version or update statement is truly an edition statement. In case of doubt, such information is not transcribed in the 250 field. A common practice is to record update information for integrating resources in a note, which is often combined with the source of title proper note or the description based on note.

An edition statement is transcribed in the 250 field
    250     $a Online ed.

Information on update is combined with the source of title note in
the 500 field
    500     $a Title from home page last updated July 10, 2003
            (viewed on March 3, 2004)

Rule 12.2F1 states that when edition information is changed on a later iteration but the change does not require the creation of a new record (such as when the meaning does not change very much), catalogers should make a note of the change, if it is considered important, using a 500 note. But if an edition change results in a resource that is different from the one represented by an existing record, then a new record should be created.

Area 3. Material Specific Details

The 2004 update to *AACR2r* indicates that Area 3 is no longer used for electronic resources (rule 9.3A).

Area 4. Publication, Distribution, Etc. (MARC Field 260)

Rule 12.4B1 instructs catalogers to record the place of publication, the name of the publisher, and the year of publication according to rule 1.4B. For integrating resources, the basis of description for publication place and publisher is the current iteration. The challenge is that many Web resources do not explicitly state the place of publication and catalogers may need to search around the site for such information. If the publisher is known, catalogers may be able to determine the place of publication by following the link to the publisher's page. For example, if a Web site lists Cornell University as the copyright holder and publisher but does not state the place of publication, following the link to the university the cataloger may learn that Ithaca, New York, is the place of publication, which can then be recorded in subfield $a of field 260. But if no place of publication is available, catalogers can use [s.l.] for "sine loco" to record that fact. Catalogers need to coordinate subfield $a information with the Ctry (country of publication) element in the fixed field.

Prior to 2002 catalogers could use a shorthand such as "The Association" to name a publisher if its name appears in the title proper or the statement of responsibility (per old rule 1.4D4). This rule no longer applies and in such a situation catalogers will spell out the name of a publisher. Rule 1.4D2 instructs catalogers to record the publisher's name in the shortest form possible for it to be identified internationally. In case of doubt, catalogers should use the full name of the publisher. If a specific unit and its parent organization are both listed as the publisher, the unit responsible for the content of the resource is recorded as the publisher (rule 1.4D2). Rules 12.4C2 and 12.4D2 state that if changes to the place of publication or the name of the publisher occur on a later iteration, the cataloger will change the areas affected to reflect the latest iteration and provide a note (field 500) of the earlier place and name if considered important.

The basis for transcribing the date of publication for integrating resources is the first and/or the last iteration. Rules 1.4F8 and 12.4F1 instruct catalogers to record the beginning date of the resource followed by a hyphen if the first iteration is available. Such information is usually presented at the bottom of the first screen or in a link such as "About us" and "Project background." If the first and/or last iteration is not available, catalogers will not record the beginning and/or ending date in subfield $c of the 260 field. If the beginning and/or ending date information can be determined from other sources, catalogers will record it in a note, using the 362 field with a first indicator value of "1" for "unformatted note."

When the first or last iteration is available and the beginning or ending date of an integrating resource is stated in the item, catalogers record such information in subfield $c of the 260 field. When an integrating resource has concluded and the beginning date and the ending date are known, catalogers will record both dates in the 260 field. If the first iteration is the basis of the description but no explicit beginning date information is available, catalogers may provide an approximate date in the 260 field.

260	$c 2000-
260	$c –2003.
260	$c 1997-2003.
260	$c [2001?]-

When a range of copyright dates appears in the item, *LCRI* 1.4F8 states that catalogers may infer the probable beginning date from the first copyright date and record it in the 362 field. But the final date of the range should not be interpreted as the ending date because it simply means the copyright is continuously held.

Copyright © 1999–2004 The Jubilee Academy		
362	1	$a Began publication in 1999?

When one copyright date appears in the item, catalogers will not record it as the beginning date unless it is clearly identified as such. If no other date information is available, the copyright date can be treated as a possible beginning date of publication and recorded in a 362 field.

Only Child is published by Only Child Enterprises, Inc. Copyright ©2004 All rights reserved.		
362	1	$a Began publication in 2004?

If the resource contains no date information, subfield $c of field 260 is not used and the field ends with a period (not a comma). If the cataloger provides an approximate beginning date, it is recorded in field 362.

A resource with no date information:
        260            $a Chicago : $b University of Chicago Press.

A resource with a beginning date provided by the cataloger:
        362   1 $a Began publication in 2000.

In short, when the beginning date or ending date of an integrating resource is approximated by the cataloger, field 362 (with a first indicator "1") is used. Field 362 with a first indicator "0" is never used for integrating resources.

The date information is coordinated with the DtSt and Dates elements in the 008 field. For continuing integrating resources DtSt (date type) is coded "m" for now. When new code values for integrating resources are implemented, DtSt will be coded "c" for current publication. The fixed-field "Date 1" element is coded based on information from subfield c of field 260 or the 362 field. "Date 2" is coded "9999" for no predetermined end of publication.

MARC Field 270 (address): Field 270 is for addresses and electronic-access data associated with a resource described by a bibliographic record. Before the 2002 *AACR2* revision, catalogers used this field to record contact information for Internet resources. Such information is usually found on Web pages under links for "Contact us," "Feedback," and other similar terms. The revised *AACR2r* does not explicitly advise catalogers to transcribe this information. If considered important, however, catalogers may include it.

Subfield $m is for electronic-mail address. Multiple addresses are entered under separate $m.

270   Library of Congress ‡a Network Development and MARC Standards Office ‡b Washington ‡c DC ‡d U.S. ‡e 20540-4102 ‡l 1-202-707-0115 ‡m ndmso@loc.gov

Area 5. Physical Description (MARC Field 300)

Rule 9.5A1b states that no physical description should be provided for remote access electronic resources. But the 2004 update provides the option through rules 9.5B3 and 9.5C3.

Area 6. Series (MARC Field 440 or 490)

Rule 9.6B1 instructs catalogers to transcribe series statements according to rule 1.6. Rule 12.6B2b states that if a series is added, deleted, or changed on a later iteration, catalogers should update the series area to reflect the current iteration. If the earlier series title is considered a useful access point, it should be recorded in a 500 note. *LCRI* 21.30L states that a series added entry should be provided for a traced series that is recorded in a note.

440	#0	$a Human factors series
500		$a Series title 1998–2000: Cognition and human factors series.
830	#0	$a Cognition and human factors series

Area 7. Notes (MARC Fields 310, 546, 500, 538, 530, 520, 505, Etc.)

The basis of description for Area 7 includes all iterations and any other source, so no information is entered in square brackets. Because integrating resources may experience many changes over time, catalogers often find it necessary to make notes of changes and maintain the records to reflect the latest iteration. Such notes are recorded in specific fields. For instance, field 247 is used to record earlier title proper, field 246 is for changes in parallel titles and other title information, field 550 for changes in statements of responsibility of a corporate body, and field 500 for changes in persons involved in the creation of a resource and other changes. Field 500 is often used to record changes in place of publication, publisher, publishing history, and so on. OCLC has changed how it validates a number of MARC fields that used to be used mainly in serials cataloging. Now catalogers can use fields 022, 222, 247, 310, 321, 362, and 547 when describing integrating resources.

Rules 12.7 and 9.7 provide guidance for preparing notes for remote access integrating resources. The current frequency of updates to the integrating resource is given in a note (field 310), according to rule 12.7B1. If the frequency of updates is not known, no 310 field is given. Catalogers should note that "continuously updated" means a resource is updated more frequently than daily and is applicable to news Web sites or blogs, but probably not applicable to a large number of updating Web sites. Catalogers need to coordinate the Frequency and Regularity elements in the fixed field with the 310 field. If no frequency information is available and no 310 field is given, Frequency will be coded "u" for "unknown" and Regularity also coded "u" for "unknown."

```
Freq: m      Regl: r
310          $a Updated monthly.
```

If frequency changes on a later iteration, catalogers will record the former frequency in field 321 and the current frequency in field 310 to reflect the latest iteration. In addition, subfield $b is used to record the beginning date of the new frequency. Because the exact beginning date is usually difficult to discern, such information is recorded in angle brackets. When a record contains a note on current frequency (field 310), no subfield $b is used. But when it contains notes on current and former frequency (310 field and 321 field), the subfield $b is added. Catalogers will need to change the code values for Frequency and Regularity when frequency changes occur.

```
The first time when a resource was viewed: Feb. 10, 2002.

    Freq: d    Regl: r
    310            $a Updated daily

The same resource viewed on Oct. 10, 2002, and frequency
changed.

    Freq: w    Regl: r
    310            $a Updated weekly $b <Oct. 10, 2002>
    321            $a Updated daily $b <Feb. 10, 2002>
```

Notes on nature and scope, system requirements and mode of access (Fields 500, 538): Rule 9.7B states that for electronic resources notes on the nature and scope, system requirements, and mode of access should be given first. Rule 9.7B1b specifies the order in which system characteristics should be recorded: the make and model of the computer on which the resource is designed to run; the amount of memory required; the name of the operating system; the software requirements; the kind and characteristics of any required or recommended peripherals; the type of any required or recommended hardware modification. If the remote access integrating resources being described have special system requirements such as plug-ins, special printers or special viewers like Adobe Acrobat, catalogers will record such information in a 538 field beginning with the phrase "System requirements." Rule 9.7B1c states that for remote access electronic resources, a note should be provided for each primary method of access using the 538 field and beginning with the phrase "Mode of access:". If a description contains both types of notes, the system requirements note should be given first.

538	$a System requirements: Real player; PostScript printer.
538	$a Mode of access: World Wide Web.

Language (Field 546): When updating databases or Web sites are available in more than one language at one URL, catalogers should prepare a 546 note to name the languages involved and coordinate the information with field 041. In addition, catalogers should code the Lang element in the fixed field from subfield $a of the 041 field. Added entries for the variant title in other languages will be recorded in field 246.

A Web site with text available in English and French.		
Lang:	eng	
	041	$a eng $a fre
	546	Materials in English and French.

Source of title proper (Field 500): Rule 12.7B3 instructs catalogers to follow subrule .7B3 in the chapter that covers the type of material being cataloged. Rule 9.7B3 states that catalogers should always record the source of the title proper for electronic resources. For remote access electronic resources, the viewing date is added in parentheses in the 500 note field. If update information is available, it can be combined with this note:

A resource viewed on March 2, 2003, that has a statement "last updated Dec. 21, 2002", will have the following note:	
500	$a Title from home page last updated on Dec. 21, 2002 (viewed on March 2, 2003).

Changes in title proper (Field 247): If changes in title proper in integrating resources occur, catalogers must change the record to reflect the latest iteration. *LCRI 12.1B8b* instructs catalogers to record the new title proper in field 245 and the earlier title in field 247 with date identification entered in subfield $f in angle brackets. Field 247 will generate a note and an added entry. If changes in title proper are minor, a 500 note ("Title varies") would be sufficient. But if the changes are too complex for field 247 to explain, *LCRI* 12.7B4.2 instructs catalogers to use field 547 for that purpose. If field 547 is used, catalogers should code the second indicator of field 247 "1" so that no note is generated from the field.

Variant titles (Field 246): Remote access integrating resources may contain titles that are different from the title proper and these variant titles may appear in the browser title bar, in the navigation menu, or other sources within the resource. Catalogers will use field 246 to generate notes and added entries for variant titles. The first indicator specifies whether a note and an added entry are generated from this field. The second indicator specifies the type of title recorded in subfield $a. If standard display constants do not adequately describe the nature of a variant title, catalogers may use subfield $i to provide other display texts. First indicators "1" (note, title added entry) and "3" (no note, title added entry) are commonly used for integrating resources. LC practice is not to use first indicator "2" (no note, no title added entry) in its records. *LCRI* 21.29 states that general material designation is not used in added entries, so subfield $h of field 246 is not used.

When changes to parallel titles or other title information occur in integrating resources, catalogers will note the changes in field 246 if the changes are considered important. They should use subfield $f to identify the iteration in which the changes occurred. If there are many changes over time, a general statement such as "Subtitle varies" would be appropriate (rules 12.7B5.2 and 12.7B6.2).

A resource first viewed on June 3, 2002, shows a change in other title information when viewed again in November 20, 2002:

245	00	$a Parenting only children $h [electronic resource] : $b family dynamics and personal growth.
246	1#	$i Earlier subtitle: $a Strategies for healthy family dynamics and personal growth $f <June 3, 2002>
500		$a Title from title screen (viewed on Nov. 20, 2002).

Notes on statements of responsibilities (Fields 500, 536, and 550): Catalogers should provide notes on statements of responsibility not recorded in the title and statement of responsibility area (rule 12.7B7.1). Information on sponsors is recorded in field 536.

500	Authors: Lou Bernard and Richard Light.
536	Funded by the New York State Library.
536	Sponsored by the AT&T Fund.

If important changes to statements of responsibility occur—such as when statements of responsibility do not appear on the latest iteration or when they appear in a different form on earlier iterations—catalogers should make notes of the changes (rule 12.7B7.2), using field 500 for changes in persons and field 550 for changes in corporate bodies.

Other formats notes (Fields 530 and 776): Rule 12.7B16 instructs catalogers to note the existence of the same resource in other physical formats.

| 245 | 10 | Access to multimedia technology by people with sensory disabilities. |
| 530 | | Also available on CD-ROM and on the Web. |

This rule probably applies more often to electronic books and serials that have nonelectronic counterparts than to updating databases or updating Web sites. In such cases catalogers can choose the single record approach or the separate record approach. In the separate record approach, catalogers will use the 530 field to note the existence of other formats and 776 field(s) to link the versions. Chapters 5 and 7 offer more examples on the use of 530 and 776 fields. *Cataloging Electronic Resources: Coding OCLC-MARC Guidelines* and CONSER *Cataloging Manual Model 31* discuss these two approaches in detail. The two approaches are summarized in the following:

Single Record Approach

a. Add a 530 field to the print record to indicate the availability of the online version.

b. Add a 856 field to indicate the location of the online version.

c. Add a 740 field if the title of the online version differs from that of the print version.

d. Optionally, an electronic resource 007 field may be added for the online version.

245	00	Management of digital resources.
530		Also available in online version.
856	41	$u http://www.mdr.com/

[Explanation: The second indicator ("1") of 856 indicates the URL is for an electronic version of the item (the print one) represented by the record.]

Separate Record Approach

a. Create one record for the online version.

b. To the online record add a 530 field to indicate the availability of the print version and a 776 field to link to the record of the print version.

c. To the print record add a 530 field to indicate the availability of the online version, a 776 field to link to the online version, and an 856 field to indicate the location of the online version.

d. Add a 730 field if the title of the online version differs from that of the print version.

```
Record for the online version:

130   0              Management of digital resources (Online)
245   1    0         Management of digital resources $h
                     [electronic resource]
530                  Also available in print version.
776   1              Management of digital resources.
856   40             $u http://www.mdr.com/
```

[Explanation: Because the online version and the print version have the same title, a uniform title with a qualifier is used for the new title. The second indicator ("0") in 856 indicates the URL is for the item (the online one) represented by the record.]

```
Record for the print version:
245   00   Management of digital resources.
530        Also available in online version.
776   1    Management of digital resources (Online).
856   41   $u http://www.mdr.com/
```

[Explanation: The title 776 refers to is the online version, and the second indicator ("1") of 856 indicates the URL is an electronic version of the print publication.]

Type and extent of resource notes (Field 516): Rule 9.7B8 states that important information about the type and extent of the resource should be given in a note (a 516 field) if not found elsewhere in the record. CONSER Module 31 states that CONSER practice is to use this field only for "unusual information about file formats" (p. 32).

Summary notes and content notes (Fields 520 and 505): Rules 9.7B17 and 12.7B18 instruct catalogers to provide brief objective summary notes for remote access integrating resources about the purpose and content of a resource. Rule 9.7B18 instructs catalogers to list the parts of a resource. These types of notes help users understand the scope, purposes, and contents of a resource without accessing the actual item and should be provided, especially for nonprint resources.

Summary notes are presented in field 520 and content notes in field 505. To create a formal summary note with field 520, the first indicator is "blank" to generate a display constant "Summary." If an informal note is desired, value "8" is used for the first indicator. When an item has a clear statement of its objectives, it is acceptable to create a quote note with it.

```
245   00   Developmental Biology Cinema $h [electronic resource]
520        DBC's mission is "to get video sequences of developing
           embryos (organisms), and experimental techniques,
           from the developmental biologist's lab to the
           eyeballs of interested individuals in a user-friendly
           and inexpensive form."
```

The 505 note complements the summary note. It informs users of the contents of a resource by listing the main headings from a Web page. The first indicator value "0" will produce a display constant "Contents:".

245	10	The fitness files $h [electronic resource]
505	0	Fitness fundamentals — Get active — The injurenet — Fuel for fitness.

If desired, the cataloger may provide an enhanced content note in field 505 (second indicator "0"), using subfield $t to mark each part or section.

505	00	$t / $r author — $t / $r author 2 — $t / $r author 3.

Access restriction notes (Field 506): Rules 9.7B20 and 12.7B21 both instruct catalogers to make a note of restrictions on use. These rules are applicable to updating databases and electronic serials, though less so to updating Web sites. Field 506 is used for this purpose.

506	Restricted to users with authenticated username and password.
506	Access limited to members only.

Item described notes (Field 500): Rules 9.7B22 and 12.7B23b both instruct catalogers to make a note of the date when the resource was viewed. Field 500 is used for this purpose and the note is often combined with the source of title proper note. If update information is available, it is combined in the note as well.

Separate notes for source of title proper, item described, and last update.	
500	$a Title from home page.
500	$a Description based on contents viewed on April 9, 2002.
500	$a Last updated Jan. 5, 2002.
These notes can be combined as follows:	
500	$a Title from home page last updated Jan. 5, 2002 (viewed on April 9, 2002).

Bibliographic relationships with other resources (linking Fields 76X–78X): Rule 12.7B8 instructs catalogers to provide notes on important relationships between the resource being cataloged and its immediate predecessor, successor, or other resources that are published simultaneously. The rule explains seven types of relationship between resources, most of them applicable to serials. *LCRI* 21.28 states that linking notes should be provided between integrating resources and related works; links can be made between integrating resources and serials, integrating resources and monographs, and integrating resources and other integrating resources. *LCRI* 21.28 also states added entries will be provided only for relationships specified by rules 21.8–21.27. Accordingly, most linking relationships will be recorded in linking notes but no added entries will be provided for related works. Linking fields frequently used for integrating resources are

- 776 Additional physical form entry (often used with a 530 note)
- 780 Preceding entry
- 785 Succeeding entry
- 787 Nonspecific relationship

Electronic location and access (Field 856): The location of an integrating resource and the primary mode of access are recorded in the 856 field. Many online catalogs present this field as a hyperlink to facilitate easy access to remote access resources on the Internet. *Guidelines for the Use of Field 856* (http://lcweb.loc.gov/marc/856guide.html), from the Network Development and MARC Standards Office of the Library of Congress, provides detailed instructions on the use of field 856. *OCLC Bibliographic Formats and Standards* (http://www.oclc.org/bibformats/en/8xx/856.shtm) also offers helpful notes. The table below presents indicator values and subfields that are often used on Internet resources.

First Indicator: Access Method	*Definition*
#	No information provided
0	Email
1	FTP
2	Remote login (Telnet)
3	Dial-up
4	HTTP
7	Source specified in subfield $2
Second Indicator: Relationship	*Definition*
#	No information provided
0	Resource
1	Version of resource
2	Related resource
8	No display constant generated

The first indicator specifies the access method (gopher, ftp, telnet, http, etc.), while the second indicator indicates the relationship between the file listed in field 856 and the item represented by the bibliographic record. Many subfields are allowed, and there is **no prescribed order** for entering subfields. Several subfields of the 856 field are often used:

$u: Uniform resource identifier (URI) such as a URL or URN

$z: Public note

$2: Source of access

$3: Specific parts represented by the record

If the file in field 856 and the item represented by the record are the same, which is usually the case when the item is an electronic resource, the second indicator value "0" is assigned. Subfield $u presents the Uniform Resource Locator in a standard syntax and can be repeated if necessary.

245	00	Guidelines for the use of field 856 $h [electronic resource].
856	40	$u http://lcweb.loc.gov/marc/856guide.html

But when the file in 856 is an electronic version of a print item described by the bibliographic record, catalogers will use "1" for the second indicator to make clear the file is not the same as the item represented by the record. This practice is appropriate in the single record approach.

245	04	The opera quarterly.
530		Also available online.
856	41	$u http://muse.jhu.edu/journals/opq/

Value "1" is also used when the file in 856 refers to a part of the item described by the record. Subfield $3 records the part of the described material.

856	41	$3 Table of contents $u http://www.apa.org

[The file in 856 is the electronic version of the table of contents of the item described by the bibliographic record.]

Value "2" specifies the file in 856 is related to the item described by the bibliographic record. Catalogers should use subfield $3 to clarify the relationship between the electronic resource and the item described by the record. A display constant "Related electronic resource:" can be used. Value "2" should be limited to electronic resources with a specific relationship with the item being described by the record.

245	10	Borrowed heaven $h [sound recording] / $c the Corrs.
856	42	$3 Web site of the music group $u http://www.thecorrswebsite.com/index2.htm

When a resource located at the URL is not longer accessible, another 856 field should record the new URL. This practice applies to integrating resources that experience changes in location over time.

856	4#	$z This address was not accessible as of June 1, 2003. $u http://www.verbatim.com
856	40	$z Valid address as of Aug. 7, 2003. $u http://www.newaddress.com

Some libraries use PURLs (permanent URLs) to maintain the currency of URLs. If the PURL and the URL of a resource are available, catalogers will enter them in one 856 field but record the PURL in the first subfield $u and the URL in the second $u.

Some resources have mirror sites. Catalogers can decide whether to include mirror sites in the bibliographic record. If several are included, they should be entered in separate 856 fields. Because the contents on mirror sites are the same as the original, indicator values will be "40".

245	00	The Linux Documentation Project $h [electronic resource].
856	40	$u http://tldp.org/index.html
856	40	$z Access from Japan $u http://tldp.attrition.jp

Special characters in uniform resource identifiers or locators: URIs and URLs may contain special characters such as the underscore (_) and the tilde (~). Because some local online catalogs cannot recognize these characters, the current practice is to enter the hexadecimal notation for diacritics and special characters. *Cataloging Electronic Resources: Coding MARC-OCLC Guidelines* has a useful table for this purpose.

Character	*Enter*
Spacing circumflex (^)	%5E
Spacing underscore (_)	%5F
Spacing grave (')	%6O
Vertical bar (|)	%7C
Spacing tilde (~)	%7E

Area 8. Standard Numbers (MARC Fields 020, 022, 024)

While not all Web resources carry international standard numbers, some resources such as electronic books and electronic journals do. There are speculations that standard numbers such as ISBNs may be assigned to Web resources in the future. If international standard numbers such as ISBNs and ISSNs are found in Web resources, they are recorded in field 020 or field 022. The ISBN organization has decided to expand ISBN to thirteen digits, and major changes to the ISBN will take place in 2007. The new system will use the first three digits to identify the industry, followed by a nine-digit number, and a check digit at the end. The new thirteen-digit ISBN will be identical to the EAN (International Article Number) code. Details of the implementation plan are available at http://www.isbn-international.org/en/revision.html and http://www.isbn-international.org/en/download/implementation-guidelines-04.pdf. The Library of Congress planned to begin recording the thirteen-digit ISBN in the 020 field in October 2004. OCLC's interim solution is for catalogers contributing original records to record thirteen-digit ISBN in the EAN field––024 field with value "3" for the first indicator (OCLC Interim 2004).

Assignment of Access Points

Rules 21.0 and 21.1 identify the sources of information for access points and explain when personal author and corporate body should be used as the main access points. Rules for the selection of access points apply to print and electronic resources alike. Personal names, corporate bodies, and titles can serve as main entries if the criteria are met. Web pages created by individuals often have their creators as the main entry, and compilers of subject guides are considered authors. Resources issued or hosted by a corporate body that belongs to one of the six categories enumerated in rule 21.1B2 will have the corporate body as the main entry. Title becomes the main entry when authorship is diffuse or unknown, when a work is under editorial direction, when a work is the sacred scripture of a religious group, or when a work is issued by a corporate body but the corporate body is not the main entry.

Rules 21.29 and 21.30 guide the selection of added entries. Individuals or corporate bodies that are named prominently and contribute to the creation, publication, and access to a remote access file can be selected as added entries. Webmasters or Web page creators, for example, can be added entries if their contribution is significant. This information is often found in an "About this page" link or similar links. Some webmasters include their name in the meta tag as "author" (meaning author of the Web page), which should not be interpreted as the person responsible for the intellectual content of the work. The corporate body that hosts a Web page is often made an added entry. Title is usually an added entry when it is not the main entry. In addition, added entries are made for related works. For instance, if a work is the electronic version of a print publication, besides indicating that in a note, the cataloger will want to provide an added entry for the original work. If a personal author is known, it will be a 700 entry; if the item has a title main entry, a 730 entry will be used. Analytical added entries can also be made.

500		Based on Interactive SGML by Mark Smith.
700	1	Smith, Mark. $t Interactive SGML.
500		Based on the Cambridge companion to Galileo.
730	0	Cambridge companion to Galileo.

Changes in Responsibilities and Titles in Later Iterations

Changes of persons or bodies responsible for a work are treated differently for serials and integrating resources. Rule 21.3B1a identifies three conditions when a new record should be created for a serial: (1) if a serial is entered under a corporate body and the body's heading changes, (2) if the person or corporate body used as the main entry for a serial is no longer responsible for the serial, and (3) if a serial is entered under a uniform title that uses a corporate heading as a qualifier and the corporate heading changes or the body is no longer responsible for the serial. But if any of these changes occur to integrating resources, catalogers should not create a new record, according to rule 21.3B1b. Instead, they should revise the record to reflect the latest iteration of a resource.

Web resources may experience several title changes. According to rule 21.1, when a title change occurs, catalogers should record the earlier title in a note (using rules 12.1B8b and 12.7B4) and make a title added entry. Field 247 is used for these purposes. More complex situations can be explained using the 547 field. But catalogers should not create any new records. *LCRI* 21.3b identifies two occasions when new records are appropriate: when the edition statement changes indicate a new resource exists, and when the URL leads to a new resource that is not the same as the one described by the bibliographic record.

Subject Analysis

Subject analysis of integrating resources is the same as that of resources in other formats. In assigning subject headings, catalogers should treat Internet resources the same as other types of material. Principles regarding the specificity and the number of headings to be assigned also apply to Internet resources (see *SCM* H180). Subject information for these resources can often be found from the title, subtitle, table of contents, "About" link, hyperlinks, and metadata in the source code. Because new materials are integrated into integrating resources, broad headings tend to be assigned to accommodate new materials. Regardless of how resources are accessed (by gopher or by FTP, for instance), the same headings should be assigned to resources on the same subject. *LCSH* and MeSH are often the authority lists used by libraries. Neither of them have "Internet resources" or "Web resources" to identify these materials. *LCSH*'s subdivision "—Computer network resources" (H1095) is a topical subdivision, not a form subdivision, and should not be assigned automatically to indicate that an item is an electronic resource. It is often used under a topical heading for a collection of electronic resources on a topic. Library of Congress does not have a form subdivision such as "electronic resources" to describe Internet resources, but it has "electronic journals" now for remote access electronic serials. Databases (H52) and Software (H2070) may be appropriate for electronic integrating resources. See Chapter 5 for usage of these subject terms.

The decision to classify Internet resources was controversial because classification numbers tend to be associated with the location of a work. Since libraries do not physically own Internet resources, some catalogers are reluctant to classify them. But many catalogers and researchers have pointed out the importance of classification for browsing and searching, and the benefit for collection development and management (Richard 1998; Wilson 2001). The DESIRE (Development of a European Service for Information on Research and Education) project analyzed several classification schemes for their retrieval power and concluded that classification could be an efficient way for searching electronic resources (Koch and Day 1997).

Classification of Internet resources is the same as that of other resources. After the cataloger determines the main thrust of a work, the most specific number is assigned, including building a number that is not listed in the selected classification schedule. Many libraries add "Internet" to their call numbers to alert users that these resources are online, while others list "Internet" in their location field for it to be displayed right next to the call number. Some have used terms such as "electronic journal," "Web site," and "Online U.S. document" to sort search results.

Cataloging Examples

Figure 6.1. Usability.gov

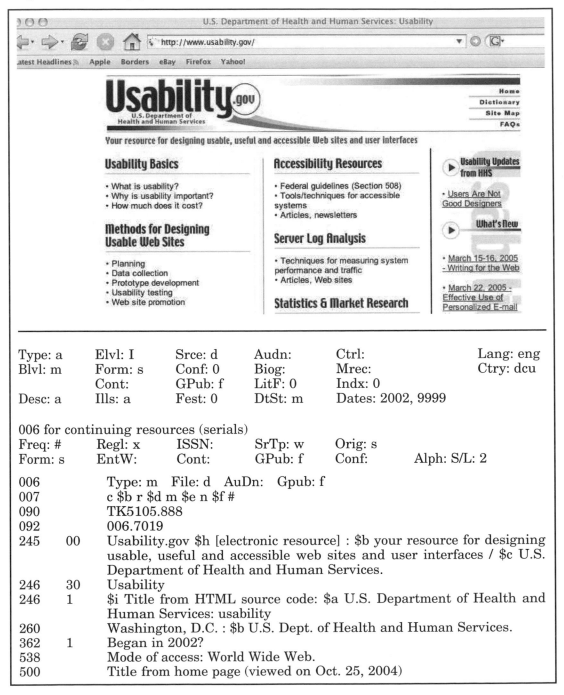

Type: a	Elvl: I	Srce: d	Audn:	Ctrl:	Lang: eng
Blvl: m	Form: s	Conf: 0	Biog:	Mrec:	Ctry: dcu
	Cont:	GPub: f	LitF: 0	Indx: 0	
Desc: a	Ills: a	Fest: 0	DtSt: m	Dates: 2002, 9999	

006 for continuing resources (serials)

Freq: #	Regl: x	ISSN:	SrTp: w	Orig: s	
Form: s	EntW:	Cont:	GPub: f	Conf:	Alph: S/L: 2

006		Type: m File: d AuDn: Gpub: f
007		c $b r $d m $e n $f #
090		TK5105.888
092		006.7019
245	00	Usability.gov $h [electronic resource] : $b your resource for designing usable, useful and accessible web sites and user interfaces / $c U.S. Department of Health and Human Services.
246	30	Usability
246	1	$i Title from HTML source code: $a U.S. Department of Health and Human Services: usability
260		Washington, D.C. : $b U.S. Dept. of Health and Human Services.
362	1	Began in 2002?
538		Mode of access: World Wide Web.
500		Title from home page (viewed on Oct. 25, 2004)

520		"This site is designed to provide current and accurate information on how to make health-related information Web sites and other user interfaces more usable, accessible, and useful. The site also links to a variety of quality Web sites and resources on usability, accessibility, and related topics that exist in the field" — About this site.
505	0	Usability basics — Methods for designing Web sites — Guidelines & checklists — Lessons learned — Links to other usability sites — Accessibility resources — Server log analysis — Statistics & market research — Events & meetings — Newsletters & current publications — Usability updates from HHS — What's new — Dictionary — Site map — FAQs.
650	0	Web sites $x Design.
650	0	Web site development.
710	1	United States. $b Dept. of Health and Human Services.
856	40	$u www.usability.gov

239

Discussion for Figure 6.1

- Fixed field: Because the content of this site is primarily text, Type is coded "a" for language materials. Form is coded "s" because this is an electronic resource, GPub is coded "f" for a resource issued by a federal agency. DtSt is coded "m" because the item is a continuing resource. The first date is "2002", the estimated beginning date recorded in the 362 field below, and the second date is coded "9999" to indicate the resource will continue indefinitely.

- 006 for continuing resources: Before new codes for integrating resources are implemented, an interim solution is to use the 006 field for continuing resources to indicate the nature of this type of publication. The Usability site states that resources are reviewed for currency and accuracy and updated as often as monthly, but the update frequency is not regular, so Freq is left blank (marked as "#") for no determinable frequency and Regl is coded "x" for completely irregular. Orig is coded "s" to indicate the form of the original item is electronic, and Form is coded "s" to show the form of the item is electronic. SrTp is coded "w" for updating Web site and S/L is coded "2" for electronic integrating resource.

- Computer file 006: Because Type is coded "a" for this resource, a computer file 006 field is added to bring out the computer aspects of this item. In the 006 field, the first value is "m" that identifies this item as an electronic resource, File is "d" because most of the resources are documents, and GPub is "f" for a publication from a federal agency. The GPub element is coded "f" in the 008 field, the 006 field for continuing resources, and the 006 field for computer file. The redundancy in coding may be removed when new codes for continuing resources are implemented.

- Computer file 007: The computer file 007 field is required for all electronic resources. Code "c" for subfield $a identifies this item as an electronic resource, code "r" for subfield $b indicates it is a remote-access resource, code "m" for subfield $d indicates the site has a mixtures of text and images in black and white, gray scale, and color, code "n" for subfield $e means the dimensions element does not apply to a remote-access resource, and subfield $f is blank because the site is silent.

- 245 and 246 fields: The GMD follows the title proper and is recorded before the other title information. A 246 field for "Usability" is provided to provide access through this variant title. Indicator value "3" means no note will be generated but the title will be used as an access points. Indicator value "0" explains that this title is a part of the title. A second 246 field records the title given in the HTML source code, using subfield $i to generate a display text and subfield $a to record the title. Since this title is displayed on the browser title bar, it is made an additional access point for users. Indicator value "1" will generate a note and an added entry.

- 260: The information on place of publication and publisher is taken from the contact page. Since there is no clear statement of the beginning date of this site, subfield $c of the 260 field is not used.

- 362: When the beginning date of a resource is determined from other sources, the cataloger will enter this information in the 362 field with the first indicator coded "1". This date is used to code the first date of the Dates element in the fixed field.

- 538: Mode of access is a standard note for Web resources.

- 500: The title source note is required and the viewing date is added in parentheses to clarify the basis of this record.

- 520: The summary note is a quotation taken from the "About this site" page because it summarizes well what the site offers.

- 505: The site uses a banner at the top of the home page and presents information in three columns. The best order for recording components of this site is to list the parts column by column. The site also offers a dictionary for terms related to usability, a site map, and a page of frequently asked questions. They are added to the end of the list to show what the site offers.

- 710: The Department of Health and Human Services produces and publishes this page, but it should not be used as the main entry because the site is not about the resources of HHS. Instead, it is provided as a non-subject additional access point.

Figure 6.2. ACLS

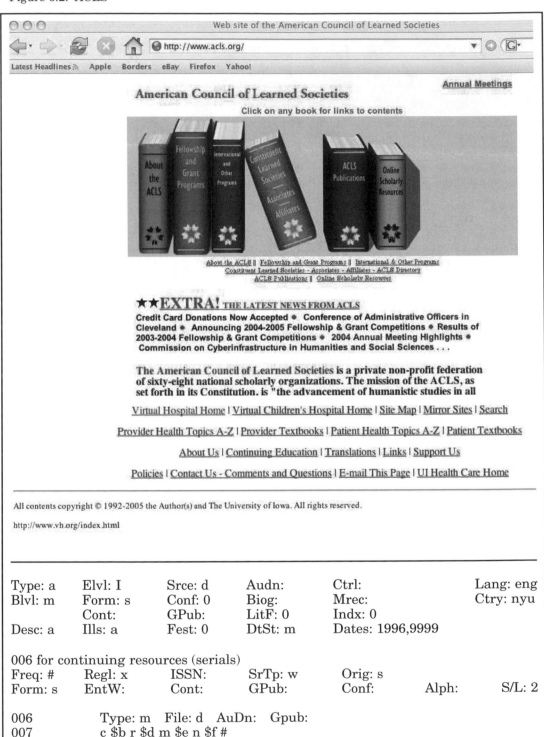

Type: a	Elvl: I	Srce: d	Audn:	Ctrl:		Lang: eng
Blvl: m	Form: s	Conf: 0	Biog:	Mrec:		Ctry: nyu
	Cont:	GPub:	LitF: 0	Indx: 0		
Desc: a	Ills: a	Fest: 0	DtSt: m	Dates: 1996,9999		

006 for continuing resources (serials)

Freq: #	Regl: x	ISSN:	SrTp: w	Orig: s		
Form: s	EntW:	Cont:	GPub:	Conf:	Alph:	S/L: 2

006	Type: m File: d AuDn: Gpub:
007	c $b r $d m $e n $f #
043	n-us—
090	AS911.A45 $b A53

092		001.3
110	2	American Council of Learned Societies.
245	10	American Council of Learned Societies $h [electronic resource].
246	0	$i Title from HTML source code: $a Web site of the American Council of Learned Societies
247	10	ACLS website $f <Apr. 2, 1997-Apr. 25, 1998>
260		New York, NY: $b American Council of Learned Societies.
270		$m cfrede@acls.org
362	1	Began in 1996?
538		Mode of access: World Wide Web.
500		Title from home page (viewed Jan. 6, 2004).
520		Provides access to ACLS resources, including its programs, grants and fellowships, publications, memberships, meetings and committees.
505	0	About the ACLS — Fellowship and grant programs — International & other programs — Constituent learned societies — Associates — Affiliates — ACLS directory — ACLS publications — Online scholarly resources.
610	20	American Council of Learned Societies.
650	0	Learned institutions and societies $z United States.
856	40	$u http://www.acls.org/

Discussion for Figure 6.2

- Fixed field: Because the content of this site is text, Type is coded "a" for language materials. Form is coded "s" because this is an electronic resource, DtSt is coded "m" because the item is a continuing resource. The first date is "1996", the beginning date derived from earlier information about the Web site. The second date is coded "9999" to indicate the resource will continue indefinitely.

- 006 for continuing resources: Before new codes for integrating resources are implemented, an interim solution is to use the 006 field for continuing resources to indicate the nature of this type of publication. There is no information on how often the site is updated, so Freq is left blank (marked as "#") for no determinable frequency and Regl is coded "x" for completely irregular. Orig is coded "s" to indicate the form of the original item is electronic, and Form is coded "s" to show the form of the item is electronic. SrTp is coded "w" for updating Web site and S/L is coded "2" for electronic integrating resource.

- Computer file 006: Because Type is coded "a" for this resource, a computer file 006 field is added to bring out the computer aspects of this item. In the 006 field, the first value is "m" that identifies this item as an electronic resource, and File is "d" because most of the resources are documents.

- Computer file 007: The computer file 007 field is required for all electronic resources. Code "c" for subfield $a identifies this item as an electronic resource, code "r" for subfield $b indicates it is a remote-access resource, code "m" for subfield $d indicates the site has a mixtures of text and images in black and white, gray scale, and color, code "n" for subfield $e means the dimensions element does not apply to a remote-access resource, subfield $f is blank because the site does not contain sound.

- 043: Because this item has a U.S.-focus, the 043 field is used to indicate that. The code is taken from the OCLC-MARC geographic area codes list.

- 110 and 245: Because the site provides access to the resources of ACLS (American Council of Learned Societies), the corporate body is chosen as the main access point. The title proper in the 245 field is traced, even though it has the same form of the corporate body, because the 245 field will enable users to search this form as a title.

- 246: The title in the source code is displayed in the browser title bar, so it is recorded in the 246 field. The first indicator "0" will generate a note from this field but not an access point. If the cataloger feels it could be a useful access point, the first indicator could be changed to "1" to generate a note and an added entry.

- 247: If the previous title of a Web resource is known, it is recorded in the 247 field to make it searchable. The time period when that title was in effect is recorded in subfield $f.

- 270: In records for Web resources the 270 field is mainly used for information on how to contact the webmaster or site manager. It contains many subfields and catalogers will need to exercise discretion to determine how much information is to be recorded for this field. In this case the Web contact person and her e-mail address are recorded.

- 362: The estimated beginning date is recorded in the 362 field with an indicator "1", and subfield $c of the 260 field is not used because the beginning date is not explicitly stated in the resource.

- 520 and 505: The 520 field provides a free text summary for the site and the 505 field lists components of this site.

- 610 and 650: The site is about the corporate body, so its name is entered in the 610 field to enable users to access it as a subject. The 650 field provides access through a subject term.

Figure 6.3. Virtual hospital

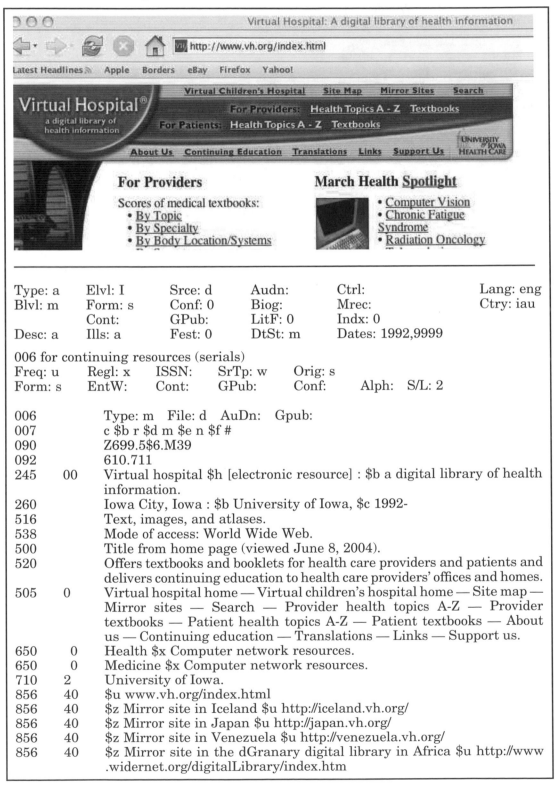

Type: a	Elvl: I	Srce: d	Audn:	Ctrl:		Lang: eng
Blvl: m	Form: s	Conf: 0	Biog:	Mrec:		Ctry: iau
	Cont:	GPub:	LitF: 0	Indx: 0		
Desc: a	Ills: a	Fest: 0	DtSt: m	Dates: 1992,9999		

006 for continuing resources (serials)

| Freq: u | Regl: x | ISSN: | SrTp: w | Orig: s | | |
| Form: s | EntW: | Cont: | GPub: | Conf: | Alph: | S/L: 2 |

006		Type: m File: d AuDn: Gpub:
007		c $b r $d m $e n $f #
090		Z699.5$6.M39
092		610.711
245	00	Virtual hospital $h [electronic resource] : $b a digital library of health information.
260		Iowa City, Iowa : $b University of Iowa, $c 1992-
516		Text, images, and atlases.
538		Mode of access: World Wide Web.
500		Title from home page (viewed June 8, 2004).
520		Offers textbooks and booklets for health care providers and patients and delivers continuing education to health care providers' offices and homes.
505	0	Virtual hospital home — Virtual children's hospital home — Site map — Mirror sites — Search — Provider health topics A-Z — Provider textbooks — Patient health topics A-Z — Patient textbooks — About us — Continuing education — Translations — Links — Support us.
650	0	Health $x Computer network resources.
650	0	Medicine $x Computer network resources.
710	2	University of Iowa.
856	40	$u www.vh.org/index.html
856	40	$z Mirror site in Iceland $u http://iceland.vh.org/
856	40	$z Mirror site in Japan $u http://japan.vh.org/
856	40	$z Mirror site in Venezuela $u http://venezuela.vh.org/
856	40	$z Mirror site in the dGranary digital library in Africa $u http://www.widernet.org/digitalLibrary/index.htm

Discussion for Figure 6.3

- Fixed field: As a digital library of health information this site's materials are predominantly text, so Type is coded "a" for language material. Form is coded "s" to indicate this is an electronic resource, DtSt is coded "m" because the resource began publication in 1992 and will go on indefinitely. The beginning date is entered as Date 1 and "9999" is used as Date 2 for the Dates element.

- 006 for continuing resources: There is little information about the frequency and regularity, so Freq is coded "u" for unknown and Regl, "x" for irregular. SrTp is coded "w" for an updating Web site, and S/L coded "2" for electronic integrating resource.

- Computer file 006: Because Type is coded "a" for this resource, a computer file 006 field is added to bring out the computer aspects of this item. In the 006 field, the first value is "m" that identifies this item as an electronic resource, and File is "d" because most of the resources are documents.

- Computer file 007: The computer file 007 field is required for all electronic resources. Code "c" for subfield $a identifies this item as an electronic resource, code "r" for subfield $b indicates it is a remote-access resource, code "m" for subfield $d indicates the site has a mixtures of text and images in black and white, gray scale, and color, code "n" for subfield $e means the dimensions element does not apply to a remote-access resource, subfield $f is blank because the site does not contain sound.

- 260: The beginning date of publication is clearly stated in the "About us" page, so the date is used in subfield $c of the 260 field and also coded in the fixed field.

- 505: The parts of this site are listed at the top and bottom of the home page. Since the links at the bottom are more informative of the contents of this site, they are used for the 505 notes.

- 856s: The Virtual Hospital has several mirror sites, and they are included in the record, using the second indicator "0" to show they are identical to the item represented by the record.

Figure 6.4. Volunteer service (finite resource)

STATISTICS IN BRIEF December 2003

National Center for Education Statistics

U.S. Department of Education
Institute of Education Sciences
NCES 2004-365

Volunteer Service by Young People From High School Through Early Adulthood

Contact:
Jeffrey Owings
NCES
202-502-7423

Authors:
Mike Planty
Michael Regnier

This Statistics in Brief examines the patterns and characteristics of individual involvement in community service activities from high school through early adulthood. Using data from the National Education Longitudinal Study of 1988 (NELS:88), this Brief describes the characteristics of young adults who volunteered, when they volunteered, why they volunteered, and for which types of organizations they volunteered. Based on data from the NELS:88 1992 sample of 12th-grade students—who were asked about their high school volunteer service for the period 1990–92 and then re-interviewed in 1994 and again in 2000—this Brief also examines whether high school volunteer service was related to volunteering 2 years and 8 years after their scheduled high school graduation.

Major findings include the following:

Type: a	Elvl: I	Srce: d	Audn:	Ctrl:	Lang: eng
Blvl: m	Form: s	Conf: 0	Biog:	Mrec:	Ctry: dcu
	Cont: bs	GPub: f	LitF: 0	Indx: 0	
Desc: a	Ills: a	Fest: 0	DtSt: s	Dates: 2003	

006		Type: m File: d AuDn: Gpub: f
007		c $b r $d g $e n $f #
043		n-us—
088		NCES 2004-365
090		HV1431 $b .P63 2003
092		361.37
100	1	Planty, Mike.
245	10	Volunteer service by young people from high school through early adulthood $h [electronic resource] / $c Mike Planty, Michael Regnier.
260		Washington, DC : $b National Center for Education Statistics, U.S. Dept. of Education, Institute of Education Sciences, $c 2003.
490	1	Statistics in brief
516		Electronic text in PDF format (13 leaves).
538		System requirements: Adobe Acrobat
538		Mode of access: World Wide Web.
500		Caption title (viewed Jan. 20, 2004).
500		"December 2003."
500		"NCES 2004-365."
500		"NELS 88."
520		The brief draws on data from the National Education Longitudinal Study of 1988 (NELS: 88) to describe the characteristics of young adults who performed volunteer service.
504		Includes bibliographical references (leaves 9–10).
650	0	Teenage volunteers in social service $x Training of $z United States $v Statistics.
650	0	Volunteer workers in social service $x Social aspects $z United States $v Statistics.
700	1	Regnier, Michael.
710	2	National Center for Education Statistics.
710	2	Institute of Education Sciences (U.S.)
830	0	Statistics in brief (National Center for Education Statistics)

Discussion for Figure 6.4

- Fixed field: This is a Web resource that is finite in nature. Because this document is primarily text, Type is coded "a" and fixed-field elements appropriate for books are used. Cont is coded "bs" to indicate the item contains bibliographical references and statistics. GPub is coded "f" because it is a document issued by a federal government agency. Form is coded "s" to indicate this is an electronic version.

- 006 and 007: The computer file 006 field is added to bring out the computer aspects of this work. The position for File is coded "d" for document and that for GPub is "f" for federal document. Subfield $a of the 007 field is "c" for computer file, subfield $b is "r" for a remote-access file, subfield $d is "g" because this is a black-and-white PDF text document, subfield $e is "n" because dimensions do not apply to remote access resources, and subfield $f is blank because it does not contain encoded sound.

- 043: Since the subject has a U.S. focus, the geographic code is recorded in the 043 field. The code comes from the OCLC-MARC geographic area codes list.

- 088: This field records the document number.

- 490 and 830: The 490 field records the series title as found in the item, while the 830 field uses the authorized form for the series to provide an access point.

- 516: This note clarifies the nature of the document. The pagination is added because it is readily ascertainable.

- 538s: For all remote access resources, information on system requirements and mode of access should be provided.

- 500s: The first 500 note is a required source of title note. Since it is a remote-access resource, the cataloger includes the viewing date in parentheses. The other three 500 notes record date and numbers found in the item. These notes are provided because they may help users identify this item.

- 520: The 520 field provides a free text summary of the item, spells out what NELS 88 is, and clarifies the relationship between this brief and NELS 88.

- 700 and 710s: The second author and the government agencies involved in the issuing of the report are traced.

Figure 6.5. *Diamond Sutra* (Web version)

The Diamond Sutra:

The World's Earliest Dated Printed Book

British Library, Or. 8210/P.2.

Jin gang ban ruo bo luo mi jing. (The Sanskrit Vajracchedika-prajnaparamitasutra, translated into Chinese by Kumarajiva.) The Diamond Sutra of AD 868.

Frontispiece (detail), showing the Buddha preaching to his aged disciple Subhuti Click for a close up.

This scroll was found in 1907 by the archaeologist Sir Marc Aurel Stein in a walled-up cave at the 'Caves of the Thousand Buddhas', near Dunhuang, in North-West China. It was one of a small number of printed items among many thousands of manuscripts, comprising a library which must have been sealed up in about AD 1000. Although not the earliest example of blockprinting, it is the earliest which bears an actual date. The colophon, at the inner end, reads: `Reverently [caused to be] made for universal free distribution by Wang Jie on behalf of his two parents on the 13th of the 4th moon of the 9th year of Xiantong [i.e. 11th May, AD 868]'.

Frontispiece (detail), showing image and text Click for a close up.

The technique of blockprinting had been known in the Far East for well over 100 years by 868, and the quality of this illustration makes it clear that the blockcutter had a considerable period of experience and skill behind him. It is not known where the printing was carried out, although Sichuan, in south-west China, is known to have been a centre of printing activity at this time.

Turn the pages of the Diamond Sutra online

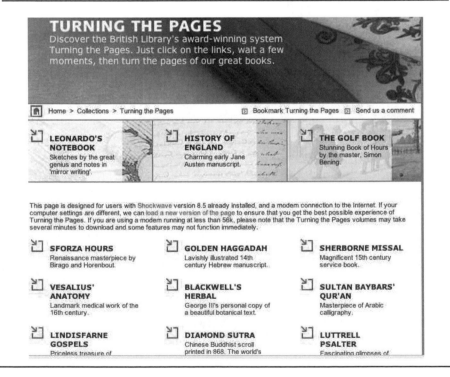

TURNING THE PAGES
Discover the British Library's award-winning system Turning the Pages. Just click on the links, wait a few moments, then turn the pages of our great books.

Home > Collections > Turning the Pages   Bookmark Turning the Pages   Send us a comment

LEONARDO'S NOTEBOOK
Sketches by the great genius and notes in 'mirror writing'.

HISTORY OF ENGLAND
Charming early Jane Austen manuscript.

THE GOLF BOOK
Stunning Book of Hours by the master, Simon Bening.

This page is designed for users with Shockwave version 8.5 already installed, and a modem connection to the Internet. If your computer settings are different, we can load a new version of the page to ensure that you get the best possible experience of Turning the Pages. If you are using a modem running at less than 56k, please note that the Turning the Pages volumes may take several minutes to download and some features may not function immediately.

SFORZA HOURS
Renaissance masterpiece by Birago and Horenbout.

GOLDEN HAGGADAH
Lavishly illustrated 14th century Hebrew manuscript.

SHERBORNE MISSAL
Magnificent 15th century service book.

VESALIUS' ANATOMY
Landmark medical work of the 16th century.

BLACKWELL'S HERBAL
George III's personal copy of a beautiful botanical text.

SULTAN BAYBARS' QUR'AN
Masterpiece of Arabic calligraphy.

LINDISFARNE GOSPELS
Priceless treasure of

DIAMOND SUTRA
Chinese Buddhist scroll printed in 868. The world's

LUTTRELL PSALTER
Fascinating glimpses of

Technical information for Turning the Pages online

We have created different versions of our Turning the Pages volumes to cater for the differing connection speeds of users accessing the Internet via a modem or via broadband.

To view either version, you need the free Macromedia Shockwave plug-in which can take 10 minutes or more to load if you are using a modem.

Where we can detect system settings such as your connection speed, we provide you with a link to the most suitable version for your particular configuration. If you are a broadband user and have your screen set at 800x600 resolution we will offer you the modem version as a first choice as this suits your viewing option.

If we are unable to detect your system settings you need to choose the version of Turning the Pages that best suits your computer.

The broadband/high resolution version is for users with a broadband internet connection (512k cable or DSL) and a screen set to at least 1024x768 screen resolution. You should also set your screen to use 16-bit colour (thousands). You need at least 128mb RAM.

The 56k modem/low resolution version is for users accessing the internet via a modem (ideally 56k) or who prefer to view content at 800x600 screen resolution. Your screen should be set to at least 16-bit colour (thousands). You need at least 64mb RAM.

Type: a	Elvl: I	Srce: d	Audn:	Ctrl:	Lang: eng
Blvl: m	Form: s	Conf: 0	Biog:	Mrec:	Ctry: enk
	Cont:	GPub:	LitF: 0	Indx: 0	
Desc: a	Ills: a	Fest: 0	DtSt: s	Dates: 1997	

006		Type: m File: d AuDn: Gpub:
007		c $b r $d b $e n $f a
041	1	eng $a chi $d eng $h san
090		BQ1990
092		294.3
130	1	Tripitaka. $p Sūtrapitaka. $p Prajñāpāramitā. $p Vajracchedikā. $l English
245	1 4	The Diamond Sutra $h [electronic resource] : $b the world's earliest dated printed book.
246	1	$i Title on home page: $a Diamond Sutra of AD 868
246	1	$i Chinese title from home page: $a Jin gang ban ruo bo luo mi jing
300		London : $b British Library, $c c1997
516		Electronic text.
538		System requirements: Internet Pentium II or Apple Mac G3; Netscape 4.0 or Internet Explorer 4.0 or AOL 4.0; Shockwave version 8.5; a modem connection to the Internet.
538		System requirements (broadband/high resolution version): At least 128 mb of RAM; 1024 x 768 resolution on a monitor capable of displaying thousands of colors.
538		System requirements (56K modem/low resolution version): at least 64 mb of RAM; 800 x 600 resolution on a monitor capable of displaying thousands of colors.
538		Mode of Access: World Wide Web.
546		The Sanskrit original, Vajracchedikia-prajnaparamitasutra, was translated into Chinese by Kumarajiva.

500		Title from home page (viewed Feb. 20, 2004)
500		Produced by the British Library's Turning the Pages system.
520		The Web page for "The Diamond Sutra" provides background information about the text, links for close-up view of image and text, and a link for users to view the online version. The Web version does not offer users the options of hearing the chant or zooming in on text and image when viewing the electronic book.
530		Also available on CD-ROM.
650	0	Buddhism $v Sacred books.
655	0	Electronic books.
700	1	Kumarajiva.
710	2	British Library.
710	2	Turning the Pages (Program)
856	40	$u http://www.bl.uk/collections/treasures/diamond.html
856	41	$u http://www.bl.uk/collections/treasures/digitisation1.html $z Users with Shockwave version 8.5 and an Internet connection can access the Diamond Sutra directly from the Web page of "Turning the Pages"

Discussion for Figure 6.5

- Reason for a separate record: The Web version of this electronic book differs from the CD-ROM version in a number of areas as the following fields illustrate, so a separate record is created. For example, the 538 fields are quite different, therefore it may be confusing to include the system requirements for these two versions in one record.

- Fixed-field elements, 006, 007: The fixed-field elements are identical to those for the CD-ROM version, except for the copyright date, 1997. Computer file 006 and 007 are used to bring out the electronic aspects, and the coding of these two fields are similar to that for the CD-ROM version, except that subfield $b of the 007 field is coded "r" for remote access and subfield $e is coded "n" for "not applicable" because we do not record the dimensions of a remote-access resource.

- 041: The English text and the Chinese text are recorded in two subfield $a; the audio portion is in English and coded in subfield $d; the original language is recorded in subfield $h. The Web version does not offer the chant in Chinese.

- 130, 245, and 246s: The Web page explains the original text is in Sanskrit and presents the Chinese title for this document. So a uniform title is used to collocate it with other versions; the title proper is recorded in the 245 field; a variant title is noted through the 246 field and the Chinese title is also presented in a 246 field. Subfield $i of the 246 field will generate a display text to go with the title entered in subfield $a. Information about the languages is coded in the 041 field and recorded in free text in the 546 language field.

- 516: This field serves to clarify the nature of this file. If the size of the file is known and important for downloading purposes, the cataloger may include file size information.

- 538s: The chief source of an electronic resource is the entire resource, so it is appropriate to go beyond the home page for the document to find needed information. System requirements come from the page that contains technical information for Turning the Pages online. Separate 538 fields are used to record requirements for users with different computer settings. The last 538 field indicates the mode of access.

- 546: The language field follows the notes on system requirements and mode of access, as rule 9.7B2 stipulates.

- 500s: The title source note is required and the date of viewing is recorded for the Web version. The second 500 note clarifies the relationship between the British Library and Turning the Pages.

- 520: A summary explains the content of the Web page, the way to access the electronic book on the Web, and the features offered by the Web version.

- 530: This field notes the existence of the work in a different format.

- 655: Catalogers should treat electronic books like other types of materials when they assign subject headings. One form/genre heading that has become popular for this type of material is "electronic books." Since this is an *LCSH* term, the second indicator is coded "0."

- 856s: The first 856 field contains the URL of the Web page that is represented by the bibliographic record. The second 856 field contains the URL of a related page, so the second indicator is coded "1" and an explanation is provided in $z.

Figure 6.6. SAILOR

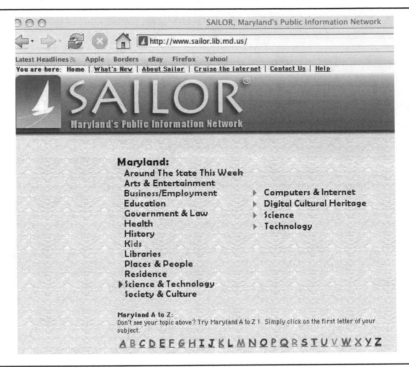

Type: a					
	Elvl: I	Srce: d	Audn:	Ctrl:	Lang: eng
Blvl: m	Form: s	Conf: 0	Biog:	Mrec:	Ctry: mdu
	Cont:	GPub:	LitF: 0	Indx: 0	
Desc: a	Ills: a	Fest: 0	DtSt: m	Dates: 1995,9999	

006 for continuing resources (serials)

Freq: u	Regl: x	ISSN:	SrTp: w	Orig: s		
Form: s	EntW:	Cont:	GPub:	Conf:	Alph:	S/L: 2

006		Type: m File: d AuDn: Gpub:
007		c $b r $d m $e n $f #
043		n-us-md
090		Z674.82$b .S3
092		025.04
245	00	Sailor $h [electronic resource] : $b Maryland's public information network.
246	30	Maryland's public information network
260		Baltimore, Md. : $b Sailor Operations Center, $c 1995-
270		$m askus@sailor.lib.md.us
538		Mode of access: World Wide Web.
500		Title from home page (viewed June 12, 2004).
520		An online reference source for information in Maryland and about Maryland, tailored to youth and adult audiences. Includes information published online by government agencies and public libraries, the Sailor Kids Pages, the Maryland A to Z links, and the links to Sailor commercial databases. Subject categories include Around the State This Week, Arts & Entertainment, Business/Employment, Education, Government & Law, Health, History, Kids, Libraries, Places & People, Residence, Science & Technology, and Society & Culture.
610	2 0	Sailor (Computer network)
650	0	Computer network resources $z Maryland.
710	2	Enoch Pratt Free Library. $b Sailor Operations Center.
856	4 0	$u www.sailor.lib.md.us/

Discussion for Figure 6.6

- Fixed field: The site's materials are predominantly text, so Type is coded "a" for language material. Form is coded "s" to indicate this is an electronic resource, DtSt is coded "m" because this is a continuing resource. The beginning date is entered as Date 1 and "9999" is used as Date 2 for the Dates element.

- 006 for continuing resources: There is little information about the frequency and regularity, so Freq is coded "u" for unknown and Regl "x" for irregular. SrTp is coded "w" for an updating Web site and S/L coded "2" for electronic integrating resource.

- Computer file 006: Because Type is coded "a" for this resource, a computer file 006 field is added to bring out the computer aspects of this item. In the 006 field, the first value is "m" that identifies this item as an electronic resource, and File is "d" because most of the resources are documents.

- Computer file 007: Computer file 007 field is required for all electronic resources. Code "c" for subfield $a identifies this item as an electronic resource, code "r" for subfield $b indicates it is a remote-access resource, code "m" for subfield $d indicates the site has a mixtures of text and images in black and white, gray scale, and color, code "n" for subfield $e means the dimensions element does not apply to a remote-access resource, subfield $f is blank because the site does not contain sound.

- 260: The chief source of electronic resource is the entire resource. Information for this field is taken from "About Sailor" and "Sailor Web Site History" pages. Since the site began in 1995, it is recorded in subfield $c of the 260 field.

- 520: 520 provides a free text summary of what the site is about. Because it is fairly complete, the 505 field is not needed.

- 710: Sailor Operations Center is established within the Enoch Pratt Library, so the authorized form is established with the library as the entry element.

Figure 6.7. MagPortal

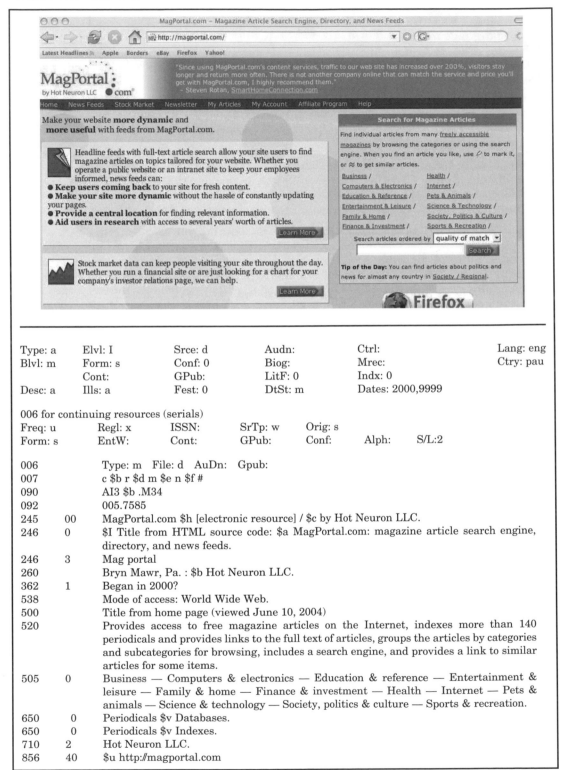

Type: a	Elvl: I	Srce: d	Audn:	Ctrl:		Lang: eng
Blvl: m	Form: s	Conf: 0	Biog:	Mrec:		Ctry: pau
	Cont:	GPub:	LitF: 0	Indx: 0		
Desc: a	Ills: a	Fest: 0	DtSt: m	Dates: 2000,9999		

006 for continuing resources (serials)

Freq: u	Regl: x	ISSN:	SrTp: w	Orig: s		
Form: s	EntW:	Cont:	GPub:	Conf:	Alph:	S/L:2

006		Type: m File: d AuDn: Gpub:
007		c $b r $d m $e n $f #
090		AI3 $b .M34
092		005.7585
245	00	MagPortal.com $h [electronic resource] / $c by Hot Neuron LLC.
246	0	$I Title from HTML source code: $a MagPortal.com: magazine article search engine, directory, and news feeds.
246	3	Mag portal
260		Bryn Mawr, Pa. : $b Hot Neuron LLC.
362	1	Began in 2000?
538		Mode of access: World Wide Web.
500		Title from home page (viewed June 10, 2004)
520		Provides access to free magazine articles on the Internet, indexes more than 140 periodicals and provides links to the full text of articles, groups the articles by categories and subcategories for browsing, includes a search engine, and provides a link to similar articles for some items.
505	0	Business — Computers & electronics — Education & reference — Entertainment & leisure — Family & home — Finance & investment — Health — Internet — Pets & animals — Science & technology — Society, politics & culture — Sports & recreation.
650	0	Periodicals $v Databases.
650	0	Periodicals $v Indexes.
710	2	Hot Neuron LLC.
856	40	$u http://magportal.com

Discussion for Figure 6.7

- Fixed field: This site's materials are predominantly text, so Type is coded "a" for language material. Form is coded "s" to indicate this is an electronic resource, DtSt is coded "m" because this is a continuing resource. The estimated beginning date is entered as Date 1 and "9999" is used as Date 2 for the Dates element.

- 006 for continuing resources: There is little information about the frequency and regularity, so Freq is coded "u" for unknown and Regl "x" for irregular. SrTp is coded "w" for an updating Web site and S/L coded "2" for electronic integrating resource.

- Computer file 006: Because Type is coded "a" for this resource, a computer file 006 field is added to bring out the computer aspects of this item. In the 006 field, the first value is "m," which identifies this item as an electronic resource, and File is "d" because most of the resources are documents.

- Computer file 007: The computer file 007 field is required for all electronic resources. Code "c" for subfield $a identifies this item as an electronic resource, code "r" for subfield $b indicates it is a remote-access resource, code "m" for subfield $d indicates the site has a mixtures of text and images in black and white, gray scale, and color, code "n" for subfield $e means the dimensions element does not apply to a remote-access resource, subfield $f is blank because the site does not contain sound.

- 246s: In the first 246 field indicator "0" is used so that a note will be generated from this field but no additional access points will be generated. The second 246 field enables users to access this title in a different form.

- 260 and 362: The publication information comes from the "Contact us" page and subfield $c is not used because the beginning date is not explicitly stated on the site. Instead, the estimated date is presented in a 362 field with a first indicator value of "1".

- 505: The site lists several components to market its services to users, including news feeds, stock market, newsletter, and so on. Because the site is mainly known for and used for its database of free articles on the Internet, the subject categories are more appropriate for the 505 field than the other links.

Figure 6.8. Galileo

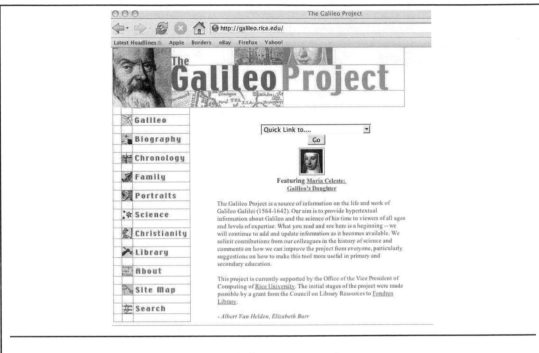

Type: a	Elvl: I	Srce: d	Audn:	Ctrl:		Lang: eng
Blvl: m	Form: s	Conf: 0	Biog:	Mrec:		Ctry: txu
	Cont:	GPub:	LitF: 0	Indx: 0		
Desc: a	Ills: a	Fest: 0	DtSt: m	Dates: 1995,9999		

006 for continuing resources (serials)

Freq: u	Regl: x	ISSN:	SrTp: w	Orig: s		
Form: s	EntW:	Cont:	GPub:	Conf:	Alph:	S/L: 2

006		Type: m File: d AuDn: Gpub:
007		c $b r $d m $e n $f #
090		QB36$b .G2
092		520.92
100	1	Van Helden, Albert.
245	14	The Galileo Project $h [electronic resource] / $c Albert Van Helden, Elizabeth Burr.
260		Houston, TX : $b Rice University, $c 1995-
516		Text and images.
538		Mode of access: World Wide Web.
500		Title from home page (viewed June 5, 2004).
500		Webmaster: Krist Bender.
536		Initial funding provided by the Council on Library Resources; currently supported by the Office of the Vice President of Computing of Rice University.
520		The Project provides information on the life and work of Galileo and the science of his time.
505	0	Galileo — Biography — Chronology — family — Portraits — Science — Christianity — Library — About — Site map — Search.
600	10	Galilei, Galileo, $d 1564–1642 $x Computer network resources.
700	1	Burr, Elizabeth.
700	1	Bender, Krist.
710	2	Rice University.
856	40	$u http://galileo.rice.edu/

Discussion for Figure 6.8

- Fixed field: The site's content is predominantly text, so Type is coded "a" for language material. Form is coded "s" to indicate this is an electronic resource, DtSt is coded "m" because this is a continuing resource. The beginning date is entered as Date 1 and "9999" is used as Date 2 for the Dates element.

- 006 for continuing resources: There is little information about the frequency and regularity, so Freq is coded "u" for unknown and Regl "x" for irregular. SrTp is coded "w" for an updating Web site and S/L coded "2" for electronic integrating resource.

- Computer file 006: Because Type is coded "a" for this resource, a computer file 006 field is added to bring out the computer aspects of this item. In the 006 field, the first value is "m," which identifies this item as an electronic resource, and File is "d" because most of the resources are documents.

- Computer file 007: The computer file 007 field is required for all electronic resources. Code "c" for subfield $a identifies this item as an electronic resource, code "r" for subfield $b indicates it is a remote-access resource, code "m" for subfield $d indicates the site has a mixtures of text and images in black and white, gray scale, and color, code "n" for subfield $e means the dimensions element does not apply to a remote-access resource, subfield $f is blank because the site does not contain sound.

- 100 and 245: The authors are prominently listed in the chief source, so the first author is selected as the main entry.

- 260: The chief source of electronic resource is the entire source, so other pages of this site were consulted to identify the place of publication and date of publication.

- 516: This field clarifies the types of materials on this site.

- 500: Webmaster information is from the "developers" link. The description there indicates his role is important, so he is provided as an added entry.

- 536: Funding information is recorded in the 536 field to justify the provision of this corporate body as an added entry.

- 700s and 710: The other author and the webmaster are traced, the publisher and sponsor, Rice University, is also traced. The Council on Library Resources is not traced but its contribution at the early stage of this project is recorded in a 500 note.

Figure 6.9. Lii.org

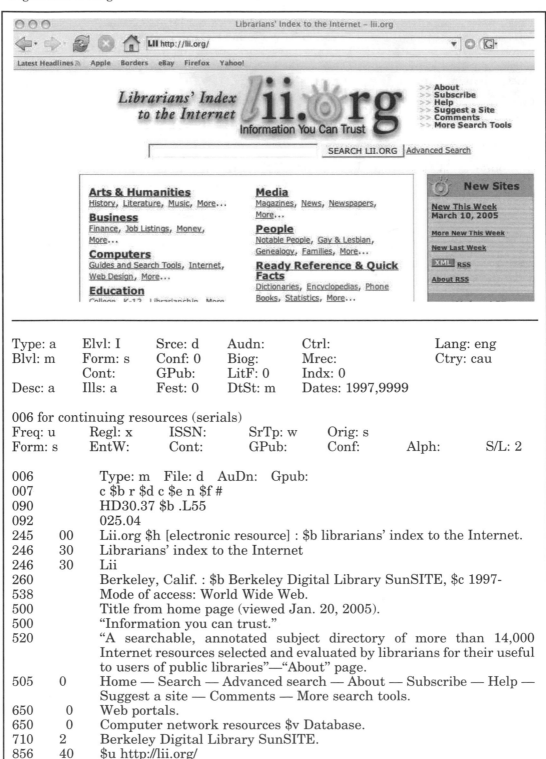

Type: a   Elvl: I   Srce: d   Audn: Ctrl: Lang: eng
Blvl: m   Form: s   Conf: 0   Biog: Mrec: Ctry: cau
           Cont: GPub: LitF: 0   Indx: 0
Desc: a   Ills: a   Fest: 0   DtSt: m   Dates: 1997,9999

006 for continuing resources (serials)
Freq: u   Regl: x   ISSN: SrTp: w   Orig: s
Form: s   EntW: Cont: GPub: Conf: Alph: S/L: 2

006		Type: m File: d AuDn: Gpub:
007		c $b r $d c $e n $f #
090		HD30.37 $b .L55
092		025.04
245	00	Lii.org $h [electronic resource] : $b librarians' index to the Internet.
246	30	Librarians' index to the Internet
246	30	Lii
260		Berkeley, Calif. : $b Berkeley Digital Library SunSITE, $c 1997-
538		Mode of access: World Wide Web.
500		Title from home page (viewed Jan. 20, 2005).
500		"Information you can trust."
520		"A searchable, annotated subject directory of more than 14,000 Internet resources selected and evaluated by librarians for their useful to users of public libraries"—"About" page.
505	0	Home — Search — Advanced search — About — Subscribe — Help — Suggest a site — Comments — More search tools.
650	0	Web portals.
650	0	Computer network resources $v Database.
710	2	Berkeley Digital Library SunSITE.
856	40	$u http://lii.org/

Discussion for Figure 6.9

- Fixed field: The content of this site is text, so Type is coded "a" for language material. Form is coded "s" to indicate this is an electronic resource, DtSt is coded "m" because this is a continuing resource. The beginning date is entered as Date 1 and "9999" is used as Date 2 for the Dates element.

- 006 for continuing resources: There is little information about the frequency and regularity, so Freq is coded "u" for unknown and Regl "x" for irregular. SrTp is coded "w" for an updating Web site and S/L coded "2" for electronic integrating resource.

- Computer file 006: Because Type is coded "a" for this resource, a computer file 006 field is added to bring out the computer aspects of this item. In the 006 field, the first value is "m", which identifies this item as an electronic resource, and File is "d" because most of the resources are documents.

- Computer file 007: The computer file 007 field is required for all electronic resources. Code "c" for subfield $a identifies this item as an electronic resource, code "r" for subfield $b indicates it is a remote-access resource, code "m" for subfield $d indicates the site has a mixtures of text and images in black and white, gray scale, and color, code "n" for subfield $e means the dimensions element does not apply to a remote-access resource, subfield $f is blank because the site does not contain sound.

- 246s: The two 246 fields provide access to this site by two variant forms of the title. Indicator value "3" means no note will be generated but an added entry will be, and indicator value "0" means the variant title is part of the title proper.

- 520 and 505: The 520 field summarizes the content of the site and the 505 field lists major components of this site. The subject categories of this site are too numerous to list.

- 710: The corporate body that hosts and maintains the site is traced.

Figure 6.10. Biological control

Welcome to this Cornell University World Wide Web site! This guide provides photographs and descriptions of biological control (or biocontrol) agents of insect, disease and weed pests in North America. It is also a tutorial on the concept and practice of biological control and integrated pest management (IPM). Whether you are an educator, a commercial grower, a student, a researcher, a land manager, or an extension or regulatory agent, we hope you will find this information useful. The guide currently includes individual pages of approximately 100 natural enemies of pest species, and we envision continued expansion. On each of these pages you will see photographs, descriptions of the life cycles and habits, and other useful information about each natural enemy.

Researchers are encouraged to contribute their expertise to this biological control Web site. Credit is given. Contact Yaxin Li (YL236@cornell.edu).

- Table of Contents
- **SEARCH** (this site)
- Index
- About the Editors
- Other WWW Biological Control Sites

Suppliers of Beneficial Organisms in North America (off site): A list of suppliers and a list of organisms sold in North America. Compiled by Charles D. Hunter, California Enviornmental Protection Agency.

No endorsement of named or illustrated products is intended, nor is criticism implied of similar products that are not mentioned or illustrated.

This project was funded, in part, by the National Biological Control Institute and Communication Services and the Department of Entomology at Cornell's New York State Agricultural Experiment Station. Funding is welcome from other sources who will also be recognized for their contributions.

Type: a	Elvl: I	Srce: d	Audn:	Ctrl:		Lang: eng
Blvl: m	Form: s	Conf: 0	Biog:	Mrec:		Ctry: nyu
	Cont:	GPub:	LitF: 0	Indx: 0		
Desc: a	Ills: a	Fest: 0	DtSt: m	Dates: 1999,9999		

006 for continuing resources (serials)

Freq: u	Regl: x	ISSN:	SrTp: w	Orig: s			
Form: s	Ent W:	Cont:	GPub:	Conf:	Alph:	S/L: 2	

006		Type: m File: d AuDn: Gpub:
007		c $b r $d m $e n $f #
043		n——
090		SB975.5.N7 $b B56
092		632.96
245	00	Biological control $h [electronic resource] : $b a guide to natural enemies in North America / $c C.R. Weeden ... [et al], editors.
260		Ithaca, N.Y. : $b Cornell University.
362	1	Began in 1999?
538		Mode of access: World Wide Web.
500		Title from home page last updated Nov. 22, 2004 (viewed Dec. 10, 2004).
536		Funded in part by the National Biological Control Institute and Cornell's New York State Agricultural Experiment Station.
500		The site indicates it has been translated into Spanish, Biocontrol: Guia de los Enemigos Naturales. But the link leads to a site still under construction.
520		Includes photos and descriptions of biological control agents of insect, disease, and weed pests in North America. It is also a tutorial on the concept and practice of biological control and integrated pest management,
505	0	Table of contents — Search — Index — About the editors — Other WWW biological control sites.
504		Includes bibliographical references and index.
650	0	Biological pest control agents $z North America.
650	0	Insect pests $x Biological control $z North America.
650	0	Plant parasites $x Biological control $z North America.
650	0	Phytopathogenic microorganisms $x Biological control $z North America.
650	0	Plant diseases $z North America.
650	0	Weeds $x Biological control $z North America.
700	1	Weeden, Catherine R.
710	2	Cornell University.
710	2	National Biological Control Institute (U.S.)
710	2	New York State Agricultural Experiment Station.
856	40	$u http://www.nysaes.cornell.edu/ent/biocontrol/

Discussion for Figure 6.10

- Fixed field: The site presents photos and descriptions of biological control but the primarily content is text, so Type is coded "a" for language material. Form is coded "s" for electronic resource, DtSt is coded "m" because this item is continuously updated. Date 1 is the estimated beginning date, 1999, and Date 2 is 9999 for a continuing resource.

- 006 for continuing resources: There is little information about the frequency and regularity, so Freq is coded "u" for unknown and Regl "x" for irregular. SrTp is coded "w" for an updating Web site and S/L coded "2" for electronic integrating resource.

- Computer file 006: Because Type is coded "a" for this resource, a computer file 006 field is added to bring out the computer aspects of this item. In the 006 field, the first value is "m", which identifies this item as an electronic resource, and File is "d" because most of the resources are documents.

- Computer file 007: The computer file 007 field is required for all electronic resources. Code "c" for subfield $a identifies this item as an electronic resource, code "r" for subfield $b indicates it is a remote-access resource, code "m" for subfield $d indicates the site has a mixtures of text and images in black and white, gray scale, and color, code "n" for subfield $e means the dimensions element does not apply to a remote-access resource, subfield $f is blank because the site does not contain sound.

- 245: Four editors are listed on the home page. According to rule 1.1F only the first one is transcribed.

- 260 and 362: Because the beginning date of the site is not explicitly stated, subfield $c of the 260 is not used. Instead, the information is recorded in a 362 field with value "1" for the first indicator.

- 500: The source of title note is required. The statement incorporates the latest update date and includes the viewing date in parentheses.

- 536: Funding information is provided to identify the sponsors and justify the selection of these two organizations as access points.

- 500: The site indicates a Spanish translation is available, so it is noted. But the site is under construction and the Spanish translation is not available, so this is recorded in a 500 field.

- 700 and 710: Because only the first editor is named in subfield $c of the 245 field, she is the only editor traced. The publisher and the sponsors are traced in the 710 fields.

References

Bao, Xue-Ming. (1998, November). Challenges and opportunities: A report of the 1998 library survey of internet users at Seton Hall University. *College and Research Libraries* 59: 535–543.

CONSER. (2004). *CONSER cataloging manual module 31: Remote access electronic serials (online serials).* http://www.loc.gov/acq/conser/Module31.pdf (accessed June 1, 2005).

"CORC project." http://www.oclc.org/research/projects/archive/default.htm (accessed June 1, 2005).

Graham, Crystal, and the CONSER Working Group. (1999). *CONSER WG: Single v. separate records, draft report.* http://www.test.library.ucla.edu/libraries/cata loging/sercat/conserwg/conserwg.draft.htm (accessed June 1, 2005).

Hirons, Jean. (1999). *Revising AACR2 to accommodate seriality: Report to the Joint Steering Committee on the revision of AACR.* http://www.collectionscanada.ca/jsc/docs/ser-rep.pdf (accessed June 1, 2005).

Hirons, Jean, and Graham, Crystal. (1997). Issues related to seriality. In Jean Weihs (Ed.), *The Principles and Future of AACR: Proceedings of the International Conference on the Principles and Future Development of AACR, Toronto, Ontario, Canada, October 23–25, 1997,* 180–212. Ottawa: Canadian Library Association. http://www.nlc-bnc.ca/jsc/r-serial.pdf (accessed June 1, 2005).

Hsieh-Yee, Ingrid. (1999, May 30). Organization of nonprint resources in public and academic libraries. Unpublished report.

Hsieh-Yee, Ingrid. (2004, December 20). How libraries provide access to digital resources. Unpublished report.

"InterCAT project." www.oclc.org/research/projects/archive/intercat.htm (accessed June 1, 2005).

Jones, Steve. (2002). *The internet goes to college: How students are living in the future with today's technology. Pew Internet and American Life.* www.pe winternet.org/pdfs/PIP_College_Report.pdf (accessed June 1, 2005).

Koch, Traugott, and Day, Michael. (1997). *The role of classification schemes in Internet resource description and discovery.* http://www.ukoln.ac.uk/metadata/desire/classification/ (accessed June 1, 2005).

Lynch, Mary J. (1996). *Electronic services in academic libraries: ALA survey report.* Chicago: American Library Association.

Olson, Nancy B. (1997). *Cataloging Internet resources: A manual and practical guide* (2nd ed.). Dublin, Ohio: OCLC. http://www.oclc.org/support/documentation/worldcat/cataloging/internetguide/default.htm (accessed June 1, 2005).

Pew Internet and American Life Project Web Site. (2005). *Internet activities.* http://www.pewinternet.org/trends/Internet_Activities_5.18.05.htm (accessed June 1, 2005).

Pew Internet and American Life Project Web Site. (2005). *Usage over time.* http://www.pewinternet.org/trends.asp#usage (accessed June 1, 2005).

Richard, Robert C. (1998). *Adding classification numbers to bibliographic records for Internet resources: Summary of listserv responses and annotated bibliography.* http://www.colorado.edu/LAW/lawlib/ts/classnet.htm (accessed June 2001).

Smith, Alastair. (1997). *Criteria for evaluation of Internet information resources.* http://www.vuw.ac.nz/~agsmith/evaln/index.htm (accessed June 1, 2005).

Veatch, James R. (1999, January). Insourcing the Web. *American Libraries* 30: 64–67.

"Wayback Machine." (1996). http://www.archive.org/web/web.php (accessed June 1, 2005).

Weitz, Jay. (2004). *Cataloging electronic resources: OCLC-MARC coding guidelines*. http://www.oclc.org/support/documentation/worldcat/cataloging/electronic resources/ (accessed June 1, 2005).

Suggested Readings

Elrod, J. McRee. (2000). Classification of Internet resources: An AUTOCAT discussion. *Cataloging & Classification Quarterly* 29 (4): 19–38.

Herrera, Gail, and Aldana, Lynda. (2001). Integrating electronic resources into the library catalog: A collaborative approach. *Portal: Libraries and the Academy* 1 (3): 241–256.

Lam, Vinh The. (2000). Cataloging Internet resources: Why, what, how. *Cataloging & Classification Quarterly* 29 (3): 49–61.

Library of Congress. Cataloging Policy and Support Office. *Draft interim guidelines for cataloging electronic resources*. http://www.loc.gov/catdir/cpso/dcmb19_4.html (accessed June 1, 2005).

Weber, Mary Beth. (1999). Factors to be considered in the selection and cataloging of Internet resources. *Library Hi Tech* 17 (3): 298–303.

Weitz, Jan. (2004). *Cataloging electronic resources: OCLC-MARC coding guidelines*. http://www.oclc.org/support/documentation/worldcat/cataloging/electronic resources/ (accessed June 1, 2005).

Wilson, Mary Dabney. (2001). Flying first class or economy? Classification of electronic titles in ARL libraries. *Portal: Libraries and the Academy* 1 (3): 225–240.

Zhang, Allison B. (2000). Cataloging Internet resources using the Voyager system. *OCLC Systems and Services* 16 (3): 107–117.

7
Remote Access Electronic Serials

Serial publications have appeared in CD-ROM and computer disk formats, and a popular trend is to publish them as remote access serials on the Internet. Several types of electronic serials are provided to libraries. One category includes new journals that are digital and available only online (e.g., *D-Lib Magazine*). Journals that have transitioned from print to online format are another type. A third category involves the digitization of back issues to make them available online (e.g., *JSTOR*). Journals available both in print and online (e.g., the *Journal of the American Society for Information Science and Technology*) are a fourth type. But the most common type of electronic serials in libraries these days are probably the ones provided through aggregators or aggregated databases. An aggregator is a vendor or publisher that provides access to the content of many electronic serials (such as Project Muse and Emerald), while an aggregated database consists of electronic resources (full-text articles, reports, etc.) from various serial publications (such as ProQuest and OCLC's Electronic Collections Online). These materials pose many challenges for librarians because aggregators may not have complete full-text for each serial title; serial titles in aggregated databases may come and go pending the agreement between the aggregator and serial publishers, and database owners may not notify librarians of changes to the databases.

The 2000 edition of *Directory of Scholarly Electronic Journals and Academic Discussion Lists* reports that peer-reviewed electronic serials grew from seven journals in 1991, to 1,049 in 1997, to 3,915 by 2000. Statistics from members of the Association of Research Libraries show serial expenditures increased by 712 percent between 1994/95 and 2001/02, and more and more libraries have shown interest in canceling print serials to control costs (Case 2004). The complexity of serial acquisition and access has been discussed in numerous articles, especially on *Serials Librarians*. Licensing negotiation, subscription costs, access methods, and long-term access are some of the complex issues facing librarians. To provide access to electronic serials librarians have quite a few options. Cataloging electronic serials is an ideal solution because this approach integrates these resources into the collection and enables users to access all manifestations of the same work. Standards for description and access, authority work, and controlled vocabulary result in collocation of related resources and help users to evaluate and select the most appropriate resources. Direct access to electronic serials, whether they are free or fee-based, can be provided through the online catalogs by the 856 field for electronic location and access. The drawbacks include the costs of record creation, time lags in record creation, and necessary maintenance of these records in the cataloging department. If catalogers take the single record approach, however, the cost and time involved in recording information about electronic serials may be less. But some titles may still require original records because they do not have print counterparts, and the maintenance issue remains a challenge. A related solution is for aggregators to provide libraries with records for their titles. Librarians will then need to consider how to integrate those records into the online catalog and maintain them as the contents of an aggregator service change. The tradeoffs of using vendor-provided records, especially in terms of cost, will need to be assessed.

Presenting alphabetic lists of electronic serial titles on a library's Web site is a popular solution among academic libraries. Such lists facilitate browsing, to some extent. But as the list grows, it becomes unwieldy for users to use. Furthermore, serials that are related in subjects will not be collocated (Hoffmann and Schmidt 1999). But if a library is unable to catalog its electronic serials, title lists present a viable, though not ideal, option for user access. Another solution is to create a separate database for aggregator serial titles. Minimal bibliographic data is provided through the locally created database without heavy involvement of catalogers. But users will have to search the database to identify serial titles of interest and consult the online catalog for holdings information; subject access may be limited as well.

A study in 2004 found 73 percent of the responding libraries catalog their electronic journals, 51 percent provide access through title lists on the Web site, and 16 percent offer a separate database for access (Hsieh-Yee). Vendors have tried to contribute to the control of electronic serials by offering title and holdings data, record sets, or management information. Strong interests in controlling electronic resources, especially electronic serials, have led to the development of electronic resources management systems. The Digital Library Federation offers a model of specifications to guide developers in integrating the management and access modules of such systems (2004). North Carolina State University has made good progress in developing its own E-matrix system (Pace 2004). Many vendor systems are in the works, with many of them using OpenURL and link resolvers to facilitate user access to electronic serials (e.g., SFX and Metalib).

If a library intends for its online catalog to be the major information portal for users, it will take the cataloging approach to control electronic serials. The literature on the cataloging of electronic serials reflects the range of strategies for addressing the challenges posed by them. While some urged the cataloging community to consider alternatives for cataloging electronic serials (Reynolds 1995), and some have compared directories and catalogs for providing access (Ford and Harter 1998), many have affirmed the value of cataloging these materials (CONSER 2004; French 1998; Hill 1996; Hruska 1995; Jones 1995; Sleeman 1995), and several researchers have listed the benefits and drawbacks of cataloging remote access resources

(Jul 1996; Vizine-Goetz 1994). Two literature review articles ably chronicle efforts in controlling electronic serials in the 1990s (Copeland 2002; Williams 1997). Several developments with long-term impact are worth noting. First of all, the *CONSER Cataloging Manual Module 31*, "Remote Access Electronic Serials (Online Serials)," has become the authoritative guideline for creating records for this type of resource (2004). The creation of MARC field 856 in 1994, Electronic Access and Location, has enabled catalogers to provide direct access to remote access electronic resources. CONSER's survey in 1995 led to the acceptance of the single record approach (Hirons 1997). The inadequacy of *AACR* and a thorough examination of the seriality of Web resources (Hirons 1999) have resulted in a new taxonomy for resources (Hirons and Reynolds 1998) and the revision of the serials Chapter 12 into a chapter on continuing resources, as well as CONSER's implementation in July 2003 of the policy for creating aggregator-neutral records that can be easily adapted for local access (FAQ 2003).

This chapter focuses on the cataloging of remote access electronic serials. The discussion and examples illustrate the creation of bibliographic records for these resources with reference to the cataloging of print serials. Electronic serials are often confused with integrating resources. To avoid that confusion, this chapter contrasts the differences in the description of these two types of resources; the cataloging of integrating resources is covered in depth in Chapter 6 of this book.

Issues for Consideration Before Record Creation

Serials Vs. Integrating Resources

Chapter 12 of *AACR2r* was substantially revised in 2002 and the chapter title changed from "Serials" to "Continuing Resources," defined as bibliographic resources that are "issued over time with no predetermined conclusion" (Appendix D). The revision was prompted by dissatisfaction with earlier rules for cataloging Web resources, and built on the study of seriality by Jean Hirons and Crystal Graham (1997). The revised chapter reflects the research team's recommendations and harmonizes the changes with standards from the International Standard Bibliographic Description (ISBD) and the International Standard Serial Number (ISSN) communities.

The new chapter covers the treatment of two types of continuing resources: (1) "**serial**," which is "a continuing resource issued in a succession of discrete parts, usually bearing numbering, that has no predetermined conclusion," and (2) "**integrating resource**," which is "a bibliographic resource that is added to or changed by means of updates that do not remain discrete and are integrated into the whole" (Appendix D). Examples of the former include journals, newspapers, magazines, and electronic serials. Examples of the latter include updating loose-leaf publications, remote access databases, and updating Web sites.

The basis for describing a serial is *the first issue or the earliest available issue* of a serial title. In contrast, the basis for cataloging an integrating resource is *the latest iteration*, except for date of publication. (See Chapter 6 of this book for examples.)

In deciding how to describe a resource, catalogers must first determine the "type of issuance" of a work. The practice is endorsed by *LCRI*. The chart below is derived from a taxonomy of resource types proposed by Hirons

Figure 7.1. Taxonomy of information resources

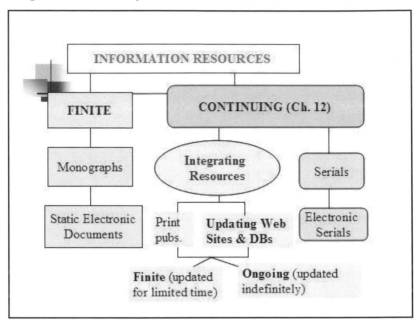

and Graham (1997). If a resource is published in discrete parts and has no predetermined end date of publication, it is considered a serial. But if a resource's updates are integrated into the work and users cannot tell the new iteration from the older ones without careful examination, then it is considered an integrating resource. Integrating resource may be finite or continuing. An example of a finite integrating resource is a resource that is created for a special event such as the Olympics. Before the event takes place the Web site is continuously updated but the site is complete and no longer updated when the games are concluded. During the time leading up to the event, the bibliographic record for this site should reflect the continuing nature of the site (i.e., as an integrating resource), but when the event is completed, the record is revised to reflect the conclusion of the event (changing the resource into a finite integrating resource).

Serials can appear in various media (print, sound recording, etc.) and some of them may become available online over the Internet or other networks. Catalogers need to keep in mind that when a serial is published in an online format, it should not automatically be treated as an electronic serial. Rather, catalogers need to focus on how new issues or updates are published. If they are issued in discrete parts, the online version will be treated as a remote access electronic serial. Otherwise, the online version will be treated as an integrating resource. For example, an association may issue its membership directory on an annual basis in print, but maintain a database of membership on the World Wide Web and update it continuously. In this case, the print version will be treated as a serial, while the online version should be cataloged as an integrating resource. OCLC's guidelines for coding electronic resources specify that the following types of resources should be treated as "integrating resources," not serials (Weitz 2004):

- Databases (including directories, A&I services, etc.)
- Electronic discussion groups (e.g., SERIALST)

- Electronic discussion group digests (e.g., AUTOCAT digest)
- Gopher servers (e.g., LC-MARVEL)
- Online public access catalogs (e.g., OCLC, RLIN)
- Online services (e.g., America Online)
- Web sites (e.g., the CONSER home page).

ISSN and Remote Access Electronic Serials

Although ISSN is often assigned to serials, catalogers need to know that it is likely that Internet resources will be assigned ISSN in the future, so they should not use ISSN alone to determine whether a title is a serial. The main criterion to identify a serial is how updates are published. If they are issued in discrete parts and not integrated into the title, the work is a serial. Catalogers can check the archives for back issues to determine how updates have been published. They should also check the masthead for information on publisher, frequency, ISSN, and so on, and consult the "About us" page or the "About this journal" page for the history and purpose of a publication.

Decisions on Creating New Records

One of the first decisions catalogers need to make about an electronic serial is whether to create a new bibliographic record for it. When a serial experiences "major title changes" (see rule 21.2A), a new record is warranted. Rule 21.2C instructs catalogers to create a new record for issues under the new title and link the earlier record with the new one through a linking field such as 780 (for a preceding title) and 785 (for a succeeding title). To determine if a title change has occurred, catalogers should examine the preface or introduction for a publisher's statement about a title change and review several, or even all, issues in the collection. Rules 21.2A1, 21.2C1, and 21.3B, and LCRIs on these rules, are to be consulted. Examples of major title changes include the following:

- a completely different title;
- a change within the first five words of the title, except for an article, preposition, or conjunction;
- a change in the title that changes the meaning or scope of a serial;
- the order of the first five words changes;
- the name of the issuing body that is part of the title changes;
- the name of an issuing body is added or dropped from the beginning of the title;
- the form of the name of an issuing body that appears at the beginning of the title changes.

Rule 21.3B of *AACR2r* instructs catalogers to create new records in the following situations even when the title proper remains the same: (a) when the serial has a corporate body main entry and the corporate body experiences changes; (b) when personal author or corporate body main entries are no longer responsible for the serial; and (c) when the uniform title for the serial includes a corporate body and that body changes or is no longer responsible for the serial. *LCRI* 21.3B identifies three other occasions when new records are appropriate: (1) when the physical medium of the serial has changed, (2) when the edition statement reflects changes in subject or format (e.g., professional edition vs. student edition), and (3) when "the title of a serial used as the uniform title heading on an entry for a translation changes."

Single Record Approach Vs. Separate Record Approach

According to the guidelines for new records, when a print serial such as *Library Quarterly* becomes available online, a new record for the online version will be justified because of the format change. In such cases the cataloger will have two options for representing the online version: the separate record approach and the single record approach. The separate record approach means the original serial and the electronic version are represented by two separate records but the records are linked through the 530 field (for availability in different formats) and linking fields such as the 760 field. Characteristics of the original version and the online version are recorded separately and users are not likely to mistake one record for another. This approach is ideal in bibliographic terms but less so in economic terms because of the cost and time involved in creating a new record. For this reason, many libraries prefer the single record approach by which some characteristics of the online version are added to the record for the original serial to alert users of the existence of the online version. Typically, a 530 field will make clear the serial is also available online and an 856 field will provide the URL of the online version, but the cataloger can use indicators of the 856 field and the subfield $z to display a text to alert the user that the URL points to a version of the online serial, not the original one. The obvious benefit of this approach is savings in cost and time, and the drawback is the risk of confusing users when a record contains information about the original and the online versions. OCLC and CONSER initially encouraged libraries to take the separate record approach but have accepted both approaches in recent years. *CONSER Module 31* recommends the single record approach a) when the online serial is the equivalent of the original serial and b) when the online version is not an "adequate substitute" of the original because it does not have as much content. When the online version's content is significantly different from that of the original, *CONSER Module 31* recommends the separate record approach.

Steps for Cataloging Remote Access Electronic Serials

When a resource is determined to be a remote access electronic serial, catalogers will follow these steps to prepare bibliographic records:

1. Search for existing records. If a record exists, a record can be created through copy cataloging. If a record for the nonelectronic format of the serial title exists, the cataloger will need to consider how to record the relationship between the earlier format and the online format. For example, the cataloger may need to decide whether to use the single record approach or the separate record approach to alert users of the existence of the serial title in two formats.

2. Choose format and fixed fields. The cataloger will select the 008 field for the serial based on the primarily content. For most serial, Type is likely to be coded "a" for language material; BLvl is coded "s" for serial; and if a serial is electronic, the electronic resources 006 field and 007 field will be added.

3. Identify the chief source for title and other information needed for a bibliographic record. Title page, publisher's page, and other places are likely sources for bibliographic information. The cataloger will need to decide which sources to use.

4. Select a main entry and determine if a uniform title needs to be used. Most serials have title or corporate body as the main entry, but when the title is the same as other existing titles, a uniform title may be needed to identify the new work clearly.

5. Record bibliographic information according to *AACR2r*, including various important notes.

6. Provide added entries as needed.

7. Perform subject analysis and assign subject headings and classification number.

8. Record the URL for the serial and related URLs if necessary.

Major Tools for Serial Cataloging

Basic cataloging standards and tools important to serial catalogers include

- *Anglo-American Cataloging Rules*, 2nd ed., 2002 revision, 2004 updates.
- *CONSER Cataloging Manual*
- *CONSER Cataloging Manual, Module 31*, "Remote Access Electronic Serials (Online Serials)" (http://www.loc.gov/acq/conser/Module31.pdf)
- *Library of Congress Rule Interpretations*
- *MARC 21 for Bibliographic Format* (http://www.loc.gov/marc/)
- *OCLC's Bibliographic Formats and Standards* (http://www.oclc.org/bibformats/)
- *Cataloging Electronic Resources: OCLC-MARC Coding Guidelines* by Jay Weitz (Revised November 9, 2004) (http://www.oclc.org/support/documentation/worldcat/cataloging/electronicresources/)
- *Field 856 (Electronic Location and Access) Guidelines* (Revised March 2003) (http://www.loc.gov/marc/856guide.html)
- Online Audiovisual Catalogers Cataloging Policy Committee. *Source of Title Note for Internet Resources* (Draft, 2nd revision, 2005) (http://www.uwm.edu/People/mll/stnir-2.html)
- ISSN International. Home page of the ISSN International Network (http://www.issn.org/)

- *Tools for Serials Catalogers* by Ann Ercelawn (http://www.library .vanderbilt.edu/ercelawn/serials.html)

MARC Fields for Remote Access Electronic Serials

When creating a new record, the cataloger will begin the description by choosing an appropriate 008 field and workform for the record. The following table presents MARC fields often used for remote access electronic serials.

Field	Instruction & Examples
Serial 008	Based on the most significant content of the work Type: a (language material) is common BLvl: s (serials) Form: s (electronic)
Electronic resource 006	Code the electronic aspects of the resource Audn: File: GPub:
Electronic resource 007	Code physical details of the electronic resource $a computer file $b specific material designator $d color $e dimensions $f sound

Field	Indicators	Subfields
022		ISSN. $a for the ISSN of the electronic version. Record ISSN of the earlier format of the serial in $y
130	__	Enter a serial under a uniform title if appropriate (see LCRI 25.5B). Do not use the name of an aggregator as a uniform title qualifier.
245	__ __	Title proper $h [electronic resource] : $b other title information / $c statement of responsibility. 245 0 _ for title main entry. Record title proper from the first or the earliest available issue. The GMD is "electronic resource".
246	__ __	Variant title $i for display text : $a for variant title
247	__ __	Former title $a earlier title proper $f <viewing date>
250		Edition statement.

260		Place of publication : $b Publisher, $c Date of publication.
		Subfield $a records the first named place and publisher from the first or earliest available issue online.
		Subfield $b: The place/publisher should be appropriate for all online versions and should not reflect the provider of an aggregation.
		Subfield $c is used only when the first or last date of publication is known.
310		Current frequency.
362	0	Formatted note to indicate the beginning or closing date of publication taken from the first or last issue.
	1	If the first issue is not the basis of description, give the beginning date in a 362 1 note (i.e., when 260 $c is not used).
4XX	_ _	Series statement
500		Source of title proper note (a required note).
		Also for "Description based on" note (required if the first issue is not in hand). These two notes are often combined.
		Last issues consulted note is also recorded in field 500 but it should not be combined with other 500 notes.
516		Nature and scope; type of electronic resource.
		Record unusual file characteristics. Not to use "Text (electronic journal)" for this note, per CONSER.
530		Additional physical form available.
538		System requirements.
538		Mode of access for remote access electronic resources.
546		Languages.
550		Issuing body.
6XX	_ _	Subject heading.
		$x, $y, $z, $v
7XX	_	Non-subject added entry.
776	_ _	Link to other physical formats
		$a, $x, $w
856	_ _	Electronic location and access
		$u, $z

The practice for coding electronic serials has evolved over time. From March 1996 to February 1998 all electronic serials were coded "m" for Type. After the definition of code "m" was revised in 1998, catalogers code Type by the primary content of the serial. As catalogers search bibliographic networks for records, they are likely to come across records for textual electronic serials that reflect the practice between 1996 and 1998.

Catalogers should select the bibliographic format for a serial based on the code for the "Type of record" element. Most remote access electronic serials are textual, so Type is coded "a" for language material, and a serial 008 field is used to record serial characteristics. In addition, an electronic resource 006 field records the electronic aspects of the serial, and an electronic resource 007 field represents the physical details of the electronic serial. Form is coded "s" for electronic form intended for computer manipulation. The following table summarizes this practice:

Element/Field	Computer Content Serial	Textual Content Serial
Type	m	a
BLvL	s	s
Computer file 008	yes	no
Serial 008	no	yes
Electronic resource 006	no	yes
Electronic resource 007	yes	yes
Serial 006	yes	no
Form	s	s

In addition, catalogers should be cautious in describing a resource that has several manifestations. For instance, an association may publish its membership directory in print every year while updating members' data on its Web database continuously. The print manifestation, according to *AACR2*, will be treated as a serial, whereas the Web database will be treated as an integrating resource. OCLC provides a useful list of remote access electronic resources that should *not* be treated as serials. They include

- Databases (including directories, A&I services, etc.)
- Electronic discussion groups (e.g., SERIALST)
- Electronic discussion group digests (e.g., AUTOCAT digest)
- Gopher servers (e.g., LC-MARVEL)
- Online public access catalogs (e.g., OCLC, RLIN)
- Online services (e.g., America Online)
- Web sites (e.g., the CONSER home page).

These resources are treated as "integrating resources" (if they are continuously updated) or "monographs" (if they are finite). In either treatment the bibliographic level (BLvL) element is coded "m" for monographs for now until the new code "i" for integrating resource is implemented.

Description

Rules for Descriptive Cataloging

Basis of Description

CONSER Module 31 reminds catalogers of the need to exercise judgment and be flexible in deciding the appropriate sources of information. It states that the objective is to create records to identify and provide access to resources and it is often necessary to provide notes on the sources of information used.

In cataloging serials, the cataloger follows rule 12.0B1 to select the basis of description. For serials the basis is *the first issue or part or, lacking this, the earliest available issue or part*. For numbered serials, the lowest numbered issue or part is the first issue or part. For unnumbered serials, the issue or part with the earliest publication date is the first issue or part. The following table summarizes the basis of description for each of the eight areas of a bibliographic record for a serial.

Area	Basis of Description
Title and statement of responsibility	First or earliest issue or part
Edition	First or earliest issue or part
Numbering	First and/or last issues or parts for each system or sequence
Publication, distribution, etc.	
Place and publisher, distributor, etc.	First or earliest issue or part
Place and manufacturer	First or earliest issue or part
Dates	First and/or last issues or parts
Physical description	All issues or parts
Series	All issues or parts
Note	All issues or parts and any other source
Standard number and terms of availability	All issues or parts and any other source

Chapter 12 and *Module 31* both stress the importance of using the first issue or part to record title, edition, numbering, and publication information. *Module 31* also instructs catalogers to prefer a source associated with the first or earliest issue over a source associated with the whole serial (*Module 31.3.1*). When the first issue does not have all the necessary information, catalogers are allowed to use a home page, the "About" file or similar pages as the source for description.

When a print serial becomes available online and there is an archive of back issues, the publisher may not necessarily digitize the entire run of the print serial. A more common practice is to digitize recent issues only. In such a case, the basis for description will be the earliest issue available online. The earliest issue of the online version of *Library Quarterly,* for example, is vol. 74, no. 1 (January 2004), so the record will be recorded as follows:

130	0	Library quarterly (Online)
245	1 0	Library quarterly $h [electronic resource]
260		Chicago : $b University of Chicago Press
362	1	Print began with: Vol. 1 (Jan. 1931).
500		Based on: Vol. 74, no. 1 (Jan. 2004); title from table of contents screen (viewed April 10, 2004).

Another situation the cataloger is likely to experience is an electronic serial with multiple providers or aggregators. In the past, multiple versions of the same serial were treated as different versions and aggregator-specific bibliographic records were created. But the 2004 *CONSER Cataloging*

Manual Module 31 recommends the creation of an aggregator-neutral record. In choosing a version as the basis for creating an aggregator-neutral record, catalogers will want to consider *the list of preference* offered by *Module 31*:

- Publisher's site when it contains the full text.
- Host or archiving site. Prefer this site over the publisher's site when it contains the first issue and the publisher's site does not. A host site usually preserves the original publisher's content (e.g., publisher logos and statements are preserved); examples include Ingenta. An archive site such as JSTOR (Scholarly Journal Archive) also preserves the original publisher's contents.
- Record for the print version.
- Aggregations and databases that are article based and do not main issue integrity.

In addition, catalogers should consider the local policies for access, the needs of the user community, and the ways the distributors present the title. The cataloger should name the selected version in the required source of title note for electronic serials.

Chief Source of Information

The cataloger follows rule 12.0B2 to identify the chief source of information. For print serials the title page or its substitute is the chief source. For direct access electronic serials, rule 12.0B2b states that the cataloger should prefer the physical carrier (such as a CD-ROM) or its labels as the chief source. For other nonprint resources, rule 12.0B2b instruct the cataloger to follow the subrule .0B in the relevant chapter to identify the chief source of information. A video serial, for instance, will require the use of Chapter 7 of *AACR2* ("Motion Pictures and Videorecordings") to identify the chief source and prescribed sources of information and the use of Chapter 12 to cover the serial aspects.

Following this instruction, the cataloger will consult rule 9.0B1 to identify the chief source for a remote access electronic serial and learn that the entire electronic serial is the chief source. The prescribe sources of information for each of the bibliographic areas for remote access electronic serial are

Area	*Prescribed Sources of Information*
Area 1. Title and statement of responsibility	Chief source, information issued by the publisher, creator, etc.
Area 2. Edition	Chief source, information issued by the publisher, creator, etc.
Area 3. Numbering (per rule 12.3)	See "Basis of description" above
Area 4. Publication, distribution, etc.	Chief source, information issued by the publisher, creator, etc.
Area 6. Series	Chief source, information issued by the publisher, creator, etc.
Area 7. Notes	Any source
Area 8. Standard number and terms of availability	Any source

The cataloger will record information from formally presented sources that are preferably associated with the first or earliest issues. For remote access electronic serials such sources include

- table of contents of the first or earliest issue or contents page listing available volumes
- journal home pages
- navigational menu bars or screens
- HTML header title (as presented in the title bar of Web browsers)
- titles presented in conjunction with the issue as with graphic "cover" images, or caption titles as with a PDF newsletter (*Module 31.3.2*).

When information in these sources varies in fullness, the cataloger will prefer the source with the most complete information. Other formally presented sources named in rule 9.0B1 are title screens, main menus, initial displays of information, home pages, file headers (such as TEI header) and information from meta tags embedded in HTML documents.

Module 31 states that when different information is found in different sources the cataloger should review the earliest issue and other files that contain formal presentations of bibliographic information and record the title proper from "the most complete source of information associated with the first or earliest issue." Variations in bibliographic information and their sources should be explained in a note.

Area 1. Title Proper (MARC Field 245)

Chapters 1, 9, and 12 of *AACR2r* and *Module 6* of *CONSER Cataloging Manual* provide guidance for the transcription of title proper for electronic serials. The cataloger will record the title proper from information formally presented in the chief source of the first or earliest available issue. Rule 1.1B1 instructs the cataloger to transcribe the exact wording of the title, except for capitalization or punctuation. It also states that introductory words not intended as part of the title, such as "Welcome to," should not be transcribed as title proper. But such wording may be presented as a variant title (rules 1.B1 and 1.7B4).

245	00	$a Journal on human factors $h [electronic resource].
246	1#	$i Title from table of contents page: $a Welcome to journal on human factors
500		Title from HTML header (viewed Aug. 7, 2002).

General material designation (GMD): The cataloger will use "electronic resource" as the GMD for electronic serials and present it in $h following the title proper. Other title information should follow $h if it appears in a publication. If considered important, an added title entry can be provided for other title information using the 246 field.

245	00	$a MIS quarterly $h [electronic resource] : $b management information systems.
246	30	$a Management information systems

Statement of responsibility: The cataloger will use $c of the 245 field to record a statement of responsibility that is prominently presented in an electronic serial. Statements of responsibility presented in other parts of the serial can be recorded in field 550. If an electronic serial does not have a formal statement of responsibility, the cataloger needs not provide one. The cataloger may select individual authors or corporate bodies for added entries and make notes of their contribution if appropriate.

Variant titles (MARC Field 246): Acronym, initialism and full title are likely variant titles for serials. Electronic serials may have varying titles appearing in several parts of the work. Variant titles may include caption title, running title, acronym, title in HTML source code, and so on. The cataloger records variant titles in field 246, using the first indicator to specify whether a note will be generated and whether a title added entry will be provided. Indicator "1" will produce a note and a title added entry. Indicator "3" will produce a title added entry but no note. These two indicator values are more frequently used than the others. The second indicator identifies the type of title recorded in field 246. The values entered will generate a display constant preceding the variant title, such as "Cover title:", and "Caption title:". If the standard display constants do not adequately specify the type of title, the cataloger can use $i to indicate the source of the variant title.

245	00	$a MIS quarterly $h [electronic resource] : $b management information systems.
246	13	$a MISQ
246	30	$a Management information systems

["1" will produce a note and a title added entry for "MISQ". "3" produces a title added entry but no note. "0" identifies the title as "portion of title". Note that there is no period at the end of field 246 and that LCRI 21.29 specifies general material designation ($h) is not used in added entries.]

| 245 | 00 | $a Winemaking and marketing $h [electronic resource]. |
| 246 | 1# | $i At head of title: $a Welcome to winemaking and marketing |

| 245 | 00 | $a Families with gifted children newsletter $h [electronic resource]. |
| 246 | 1# | $i Title in HTML source code: $a FGC newsletter |

Area 2. Edition (MARC Field 250)

Edition statements of serials are recorded according to rule 12.2, and the source of the edition statement, if different from the source of title, is recorded according to rule 9.2B1.

Remote access electronic serials, just like print serials, can be issued in different languages, for various geographic areas or for targeted audience groups. *CONSER Cataloging Manual Module 9* instructs the cataloger to consider such editions as serial editions. The treatment of such editions depends on how the publisher presents them on the Web. If each edition has its own Web page, URL, and its own chief source of information, it would be appropriate to create multiple records for the editions. But if the editions were available only through one Web page and URL, one record for the site would be more appropriate. The cataloger may find it helpful to consult print versions of the editions to determine whether they are truly separate works. CONSER cautions that *when a serial is available in different document formats (PDF, HTML, SGML, etc.), the formats should not be interpreted as separate editions*. Instead, only one record should be created for the serial and a note should be provided to indicate the formats available. File upgrades should not be considered an edition statement. If the edition statement is taken from a source different from the source of the title proper, catalogers should give a 500 note for the source of the edition statement.

Area 3. Material Specific Details

Computer file characteristics (Field 256): The 2004 update to *AACR2r* 2002 has removed this area for electronic resources. CONSER advises catalogers not to include this information. If catalogers need to provide special information about file formats, CONSER recommends the use of field 516.

516	8	Bit-mapped images; PDF, PostScript, and TIFF formats available for printing.

Numbering area (Field 362):

362	0	$a Numerical/chronological designation-
362	1	$a Information on the beginning or ending year of publication.

If the first issue of an online serial is available, the cataloger will transcribe numbering information in field 362 as a formatted note. Otherwise, a "Description based on" note in field 500 is used. Numbering information can be taken from the source of title proper or anywhere within a resource. If numbering is peculiar or difficult to locate, a 515 note can be used to explain the source of the numbering information.

362	0#	$a Vol. 1, no. 1 (Spring 2002)-
515	##	Numbering taken from README file.

CONSER's previous practice of providing a "coverage as of" note was discontinued in 2003 when *LCRI* 12.7B10 was removed.

In coding the date information in the fixed field the cataloger needs to coordinate it with the information in the 260 field and the 362 field. Here are a few examples:

When the first issue is the basis of description.		
Dates: 2004, 9999		
260		...$c 2004-
362	0	$a Vol. 1 (2004)-

> When the first issuing date is not known but the last date of publication is known from other sources.
> Dates: uuuu, 2002
> 260   . . . $c −2002.
> 362   1 $a Ceased publication in 2002.

> When the first or last issue is not available and the description is based on the earliest available issue.
> Dates: uuuu, 9999
> 500 $a Description based on: Vol. 7 (1997); title from table of contents page (viewed May 2, 1998).
> [Subfield $c of field 260 and the 362 field (with "0" for the first indicator) are not used when the first or last issue is not available.]

> When the earliest available issue is the basis for description and the beginning date of publication is known from other sources, the date is recorded in 362 1 as an unformatted note. Note that $c of field 260 is *not* used.
> Dates: 2001, 9999
> 362   1 $a Began in 2001.
> 500 $a Description based on: No. 3 (2003); title from HTML header (viewed July 15, 2003).

Latest issues consulted note: If more than one issue of an electronic serial has been consulted in preparing the description, the cataloger should provide a latest issues consulted (LIC) note in field 500 (rule 12.7B23). This note is provided whenever more than one issue or part of a serial has been consulted. The first example below illustrates the case when the first issue is the basis for description. The second example illustrates the use of this note when the earliest available issue is the basis for description and a DBO (description based on) note is required. *LC Rule Interpretations* 12.7B23 instructs catalogers to combine the DBO note with the source of title note, but to always present the *LIC note as a separate note*.

> 362   0# $a Spring 1998-
> 500 $a Title from HTML header (publisher's Web site, viewed Dec. 5, 1998)
> 500 $a Latest issue consulted: Fall 1998 (viewed Dec. 5, 1998)

> 500 $a Description based on: Vol. 4 (1996); title from table of contents screen (publisher's Web site, viewed Aug. 7, 2000).
> 500 $a Latest issue consulted: Vol. 8 (2000) (viewed Aug. 7, 2000).

Area 4. Publication, Distribution, Etc. (MARC Field 260)

AACR2r considers all remote access electronic resources "published." The cataloger transcribes publishing information from a formal presentation on the first or earliest issue if available, and should prefer the chief source (the source of title) to other sources if possible. If such information is not available, the cataloger may consult other sources to locate publishing information. If internal sources show an electronic serial to be emanated from an organization, the cataloger will interpret that organization to be the publisher and the location of the body to be the place of publication. If such information comes from external sources, the cataloger will enter such information in brackets. If no publishing information is found, the cataloger will use "[S.l. : $b s.n.]". In aggregator-neutral records, aggregator names are *not* included in the publishing statement.

130	0#	$a Occupation compensation survey (Online)
245	10	$a Occupation compensation survey $h [electronic resource].
260		$a Washington, DC: $b U.S. Dept. of Labor, Bureau of Labor Statistics, 1960-

130	0#	$a Opera quarterly (Online)
245	14	$a The Opera quarterly $h [electronic resource].
260		$a Chapel Hill, N.C. : $b University of North Carolina Press, $c c1983-
550		$a Digitized and made available by: Project Muse, 2002- [Note that Project Muse is not transcribed as the publisher.]

Area 5. Physical Description (MARC Field 300)

No physical description information is provided for remote access electronic files. Information on sound or images in the serial can be presented in a note and coded in field 007.

Area 6. Series Statement (MARC Field 4XX)

CONSER Cataloging Manual Module 12 summarizes rules and LC rule interpretations on transcribing series statement and making an added entry. If an electronic serial appears on a Web site that includes other serial titles, the Web site should not automatically be treated as a series. For example, ProjectMuse's Web site should not be treated as a series. Aggregators or distributors of electronic serials are not treated as series titles, either. JSTOR and Ingenta, for instance, should not be recorded as series titles. Furthermore, electronic serials may have phrases associated with them that suggest the serial is part of a series—for example, Emerald library. Such information should be recorded but catalogers need to determine whether such phrases are truly series title or intended as marketing or identifying devices. In general it is not a good idea to trace these phrases as true series statements because marketing statements may change quickly. If such phrases are to be used as access points, catalogers should consult authority files first.

Area 7. Notes

Rules 1.7B, 9.7B, and 12.7B instruct catalogers to prepare notes for remote access electronic serials. According to *Module 31*, "notes on a record for an online version appearing in multiple e-serial packages should contain information that is applicable to all online versions" (p. 31). CONSER practice is to enter notes in numeric tag order. The following section highlights notes often provided for remote access electronic serials and presents them in tag order.

Variant title notes (Field 246): Titles that are different from the title proper and are potential access points are transcribed in field 246 to generate appropriate notes and additional title entries.

Frequency (Field 310): If the frequency of a serial is known, it is recorded in field 310. Information on former frequency is recorded in field 321.

Beginning and/or ending dates of publication: If the first or the last issuing date is known, a formatted note (field 362 0) is used. Otherwise, date information obtained from other sources is recorded in an unformatted note (Field 362 1).

Source of title proper (field 500): According to rule 9.7B3, the note of the source of title is required for electronic resources. In the case of remote access electronic serials, if the first or the earliest available issue has a source that presents title formally it can be used as the chief source of information. *Module 31* recommends that the cataloger use specific terms to describe the source (such as "title from table of contents screen") and avoid general terms such as "title from title screen." If the cataloger uses a printout of an online file for description, that should be noted (e.g., "title from printout of publisher's home page"). *Module 31* recommends that when creating new records, the cataloger include the date when a resource is viewed in the source of title note. This is helpful because the serial title may change and individual issues may not carry the same information. *Module 31* does not recommend adding view date to existing records.

500	$a Title from table of contents screen (viewed July 10, 2002).
500	$a Title from PDF title page (publisher Web site, viewed Jan. 3, 2003).

In addition, when the cataloger chooses to use a particular aggregator version and/or a particular file format for description, such information should be included in the source of title note.

500	$a Title from volume contents page (JSTOR, viewed April 9, 2001).

Description based on (DOB) note (Field 500): When the first issue is the basis for cataloging an electronic serial, the publication date and numbering information are recorded in the 260 field and the 362 field (a formatted note) respectively.

```
245    00    Office management quarterly.
260          ...$c 1982-
362    0     Vol. 1, no. 1 (spring 1982)-
```

If the first issue is not available and the earliest available issue is used instead, $c of the 260 field is not used and a "description based on" (DOB) note is provided in the 500 field. The DOB note is often combined with the source of title note.

```
500    $a Description based on: Vol. 7 (2002); title from
       HTML header (viewed Aug. 2002).
```

If the cataloger learns about the beginning date or ending date of an electronic serial from other sources, such information should be noted (rule 12.7B11.1). The cataloger will make an unformatted note in field 362 with value "1" for the first indicator.

```
245    00    Youth development monthly.
362    1     Began in July 1986.
500          Description based on: Vol. 6, no.1 (January,
             1991).
```

Latest issue consulted (LIC) (Field 500): When more than one issue or part of a serial is consulted for description, the LIC note is added. It should not be combined with the DOB note or the source of title note.

Access restrictions (Field 506): When access to an electronic serial is limited to subscribers or selected user groups, many libraries use a "restrictions on access" note (field 506) to inform users. *CONSER Module 31* advises the cataloger to use field 506 only when access restrictions apply to "all versions and formats of the serial" (p. 31) such as when a document is classified. It also recommends that catalogers use $z of field 856 for specific access restrictions. But many libraries routinely use the 506 field to indicate only authorized users may access electronic serials they have subscribed to.

Numbering peculiarities (Field 515): When a serial has unusual numbering patterns, a 515 note should record the unusual patterns.

Type of computer file or data (Field 516): Field 516 is designed to indicate the nature and type of remote access electronic serial; CONSER limits its usage of this field to when unusual information about file formats needs to be included in a record.

```
516    $a Abstracts in HTML; full text articles in PDF and
       Gzip compressed Postscript file formats.
```

System requirements (Field 538): If a remote access electronic serial requires the use of special software, hardware, or peripheral devices, a system requirements note (field 538) is provided. The note will begin with "System requirements:" as the display constant.

Mode of access (Field 538): For remote access electronic serials the mode of access must be recorded. The note begins with the phrase "Mode of access:". If a system requirements note is present in a record, the mode of access note will follow it.

538	$a Mode of access: World Wide Web.

538	$a System requirements: PostScript printer needed for printing.
538	$a Mode of access: Email via electronic mailing list subscription.

Language (Field 546): If a remote access electronic serial is available in more than one language, it should be noted in a 546 field and coded in the 041 field as well.

Issuing bodies (Field 550): Rule 12.7B7.1 instructs catalogers to record statements of responsibility that do not appear in Area 1, the title and statement of responsibility area, in a note if they are considered to be important. Changes in statements of responsibility that occur after the first issue, if considered to be important, should be given in a note, according to rules 12.1F5 and 12.7B7.2a. This type of notes is especially useful if a corporate body is to be used as an added entry.

245	0 0	Wireless technology
260		Chicago : $b Ryan Press.
550		Published under the auspices of the University of Chicago.
710	2	University of Chicago.

If a serial is available through a particular provider, a 550 field is used.

550	Digitized and available through: ProjectMuse.

Linking relationships (77X–78X): Rule 12.7B8 identifies important bibliographic relationships between resources being described. *CONSER Cataloging Manual Module 14* provides guidelines for treating linking relationships. A common practice is to use linking fields to identify earlier titles (field 780), later titles (field 785), supplements (fields 770 and 772), and other related works (787). The following table summarizes linking entry fields for various relationships:

Relationship (AACR2 rule)	MARC linking entry field
Continuation (12.7B8a)	780
Continued by (12.7B8a)	785
Merger (12.7B8b)	580 (as a note), 780, indicators 14
Split (12.7B8c)	780, indicators 01
Absorption (12.7B8d)	780, indicators 05
Translation (12.7B8e)	765, 767
Supplements (12.7B8g)	770, 772
Editions (12.7B8f)	580 (as a note), 775
Other physical format (12.7B16)	530 (as a note), 776
Other nonspecific relationships	787

130	0	$a Quarterly publication of the American Statistical Association (Online)
245	10	$a Quarterly publication of the American Statistical Association $h [electronic resource].
780	00	$a Publications of the American Statistical Association (Online) $x 1522–5437 $w(DLC)sn 99023375 $w(OCoLC)41125188
785	00	$t Journal of the American Statistical Association (Online) $x0162-1459 $w(DLC)sn 99023377 $w(OCoLC)41125238

[Comments: In this example, the bibliographic record represents a serial title that has a predecessor (recorded in 780) and a successor (recorded in 785).]

Other physical formats (fields 530, 776): When remote access electronic serials have counterparts in print or other formats and the cataloger decides to take the single record approach (i.e., adding information about the online format to the record for the original format), a 530 field should be added to indicate the availability of the online version, and a 856 field will be added to provide online access, with value "1" for the second indicator to clarify that the item represented by the URL is not the same as the item represented by the bibliographic record.

Single record approach

245	0 0	Library quarterly.
530		Also available on the World Wide Web.
856	4 1	$u http://www.journals.uchicago.edu/LQ/journal/home.html

If the cataloger chooses to create a separate record for the online version, catalogers will provide a 530 note in the new record to indicate the existence of the other formats, and a 776 field to link to the records for other formats. Alternatively, instead of using the 530 field, catalogers may use $i of the 776 field to provide a note. Catalogers will also use the 530 field and the 776 field from the record for the other format to link back to the record for the online format. Here is the field structure of the 776 field:

---

776 field

First indicator: 0 = a note, 1 = no note
Second indicator: blank (#) = display constant. 8 = no display constant
776   1 # $a main entry $b edition $t title $w record control
number $x ISSN $z ISBN

Separate record approach

Record for the online version:
    130   0# $a Opera quarterly (Online)
    245   14 $a The Opera quarterly $h [electronic resource].
    530   ## $a Also available in print.
    776   1# $t Opera quarterly $x 0736-0053 $w
                  (OCoLC)9068655

Record for the print version:
    245   04 $a The Opera quarterly.
    530   ## $a Also available online.
    776   1# $a Opera quarterly (Online) $x 1486-2870

Electronic location and access (Field 856): The location of the serial and each primary mode of access are recorded in an 856 field, which is designed to help users connect, subscribe or access an electronic serial. Many online catalogs present this field as a hyperlink to facilitate easy access to the serial. Because the electronic location of the serial may change, the information should be transcribed from the most recent issue of the serial. *Guidelines for the Use of Field 856* (http://lcweb.loc.gov/marc/856guide.html) from the Network Development and MARC Standards Office of the Library of Congress provide detailed instructions on the use of field 856. The following three subfields of 856 are often used:

$u: it records a uniform resource identifier (URI) such as a URL or URN.

$z: it provides information on how to access the serial or the status of a URI.

$3: it provides information on a part of the serial represented by the bibliographic record.

The first indicator of field 856 specifies the method for access. Code "4" is commonly used for Web resources, indicating access via HyperText Transmission Protocol (HTTP). The second indicator specifies the relationship between the location in $u and the work represented by the bibliographic record. The following three code values are used:

Code "0": The work located in $u is the same as the work represented by the bibliographic record.

Code "1": The work located in $u is not the same as the work represented by the bibliographic record. Code "1" is used on the record for a print serial to indicate the location of its online version. It is also used when the resource located in $u is a part of the resource represented by the bibliographic record.

Code "2": The resource located in $u is related to the serial represented by the bibliographic record, but it is not its online version or a part of it.

---

856   40 $u http://www.africa.ufl.edu/asq/
[Comment: Code "0" for the second indicator clarifies that the item represented by the URL is the same as the serial represented by the bibliographic record.]

856   00 $z Email subscription $u mailto: listserv@loc.gov
                     $i subscribe $f CONSRLIN

[Comment: First indicator "0" specifies the access method is "email" and second indicator "0" explains the e-mail address presented in $u is for subscription to the serial represented by the bibliographic record.]

856   40 $z Link no longer valid as of June 5, 2002 $u
                     http://www.invalidlink.com
[Comment: Code "0" for the second indicator explains the URL in $u is no longer a valid URL for the serial represented by the bibliographic record.]

856   41 $3 Abstracts available from the publisher's Web site
                     $u http://www.publishersite.com
[Comment: Code "1" for the second indicator explains the URL refers to a part of the serial represented by the bibliographic record. The relationship is clarified in $3.]

245   04   The Opera quarterly.
530   ##   Also available online.
856   41 $u http://muse.jhu.edu/journals/opq/

[Comment: This example illustrates the one-record approach by which the online version of this serial is noted by a 530 field and provided access to by the 856 field. Code "1" for the second indicator specifies the item linked to by the URL is not the same as the serial represented by the bibliographic record.]

Remote access electronic serials may have several URIs associated with them. Publishers of serials that require local subscriptions usually provide each subscribing institution with institution-specific unique URIs for access. The cataloger will provide such information in field 856. *Module 31* recommends that catalogers use widely accessible 856 fields on OCLC/CONSER records. If a URI for free access to the serial is available, it is recorded in a separate 856 field.

856	40	$z Catholic University holdings $u http://libraries.cua.edu/ . . .
856	40	$u http://purl.access.gpo.gov/GPO/LPS16239

If a publisher provides tables of contents, sample pages, or summaries of its journal on its Web site and that URI does not require login identification number or password, such information should be recorded in field 856.

856	42	$a Tables of contents of several titles available at Haworth's Web site: $u http://www.haworth.com [Comment: Code "2" for the second indicator clarifies that the content represented by the URL is related to the serial represented by the bibliographic record, but it is not the online version of the serial or a part of the serial.]

When an electronic serial can be accessed via several providers (aggregators), URIs of all the providers are recorded as separate 856 fields in the aggregator-neutral record.

856	40	$z Access requires an authorization number and password through ProjectMuse at: $u http://muse.jhu.edu/journals/
856	40	$z Access requires an authorized IP address through OCLC FirstSearch Electronic Collections Online $u http://firstsearch.oclc.org/

According to *Module 31*, if the serial is available at mirror sites, the cataloger is not obligated to record all of them. Instead, the cataloger will select several and record them in separate 856 fields to facilitate user access to the serial.

245	00	$a D-Lib magazine $h [electronic resource]
856	40	$z Access from UKOLN, University of Bath, Bath, England: $u http://mirrored.ukoln.ac.uk/lis-journals/dlib/
856	40	$z Access from Academia Sinica, Taipei, Taiwan: $u http://dlib.ejournal.ascc.net/

Link maintenance is essential for all resources accessible on the Internet, especially remote-access electronic serials. Some libraries use link-checking systems to identify broken links. Some serials management services include link maintenance as part of their services for managing subscription information. Another approach is to use persistent identifiers or handle systems such as PURL (persistent uniform resource locator). For example, participants of the CONSER PURL Project use a PURL server hosted by OCLC to maintain URLs. When updates are needed, they change URIs on the PURL server without changing the URLs in individual bibliographic records. On CONSER records the PURL is recorded in the first subfield $u and the URL in a subsequent subfield $u. Information on the CONSER PURL Project is available at http://lcweb.loc.gov/acq/conser/purl/main.html.

> Example of PURL and URL
> 856   40 $u http://bibpurl.oclc.org/web/6022 $u http://web
>   .africa.ufl.edu/asq

Area 8. Standard Numbers: International Standard Serial Number (ISSN)

Most serials are assigned an International Standard Serial number by the centers of the ISSN Network. In the United States, the National Database Project (NDBP) assigns ISSN to serials. While the general practice is to assign separate ISSN to print and electronic versions of a serial, not all electronic versions receive separate ISSN. An electronic serial may display the ISSN for its electronic version only, or present the ISSN for both the print and online version, so catalogers will need to exercise caution in recording ISSN. An ISSN consists of eight digits presented in two four-digit groups linked by a hyphen. The information is entered in the 022 field in the MARC format. First indicator shows whether a serial is of international interest (0 = yes, 1 = no), but these indicators are for the National Serials Data Program (NSDP) and ISSN Canada. *OCLC's Guidelines* instructs catalogers in other organizations to use "blank" for the first indicator when they use the 022 field. If the ISSN for the print and online versions are available, the ISSN for the online version is recorded in $a, while the ISSN for the print version in $y. If only the ISSN for the print version is available, it is recorded in $y of the 022 field.

CONSER Policy for Creating Aggregator-Neutral Records

According to *CONSER Module 31*, an aggregator is "a company that provides digitized access to the content of many different serials and other resources, often from a variety of different publishers" and it often provides access through a searchable database. There are two types of aggregators—one type, such as JSTOR, tends to provide access to the full serials, while the other, such as ACM Digital Library, includes the text of selected articles from serials. Since a common trend in online serials publishing is to provide access to the same serial through multiple aggregators, CONSER used to have a policy for creating a separate record for each aggregation. But the maintenance of aggregator-specific records becomes time-consuming and difficult when aggregators merge or when publishers change what they offer through aggregators often. As a result, CONSER now has a policy for creating aggregator-neutral records, which is intended to represent "all versions of the same online serial on one record" (FAQ on the

Aggregator-neutral record, 2003). The approach is sensible in that each aggregator-neutral record will contain information applicable to all aggregations and less maintenance of the record will be necessary. CONSER applies this policy to online serial packages that "present whole issues of digitized serials rather than to databases that are focused on article delivery" (*Module 31*). The needs of users and policies of the parent institutions nevertheless should always be taken into account when catalogers select titles for this treatment. If an institution needs to create an aggregator-neutral record for an article database to meet the needs of its users, that would be appropriate.

Aggregator-neutral records may be different from records for other online serials in a number of ways. First, an aggregator-neutral record will represent several manifestations of a serial but there is usually only one URL, and variant titles may be provided for the manifestations if necessary. If several packages provide access to the complete serial, catalogers should record these URLs in separate 856 fields (but no access restrictions, format information or system requirements that are specific to aggregators should be recorded). Second, if a record has a uniform title, the word "online" will be part of the qualifier but the aggregators will not be part of the qualifier. Third, catalogers will include the publisher and dates of the original serial as found in the version being described but not the information about the dates of digitization or the digitizers. Fourth, aggregator-neutral records may have fewer notes than records for other online serials. The version used as the basis for description will be given in a title source note or a DOB note. But no notes or added entries will be given for specific packages or aggregations. In these records field 538 is often used for mode of access and seldom for system requirements. *CONSER* implemented this policy in July 2003. Currently WorldCat still has aggregator-specific records for online serials but OCLC has committed to clean up existing records to reflect the new policy. The Web site of CONSER offers information on the rationale, development, and implementation of this approach. In addition to the FAQ cited above, "Record Creation and Modification" (http://www.loc.gov/acq/conser/guidelines.pdf) provides helpful advice, and *CONSER Module 31* includes a section on creating aggregator-neutral records and consolidating existing records.

Assignment of Access Points

Decisions on Main Entry and Added Entries

The principles of *AACR2r* Chapter 21 apply to the choice of main entry for serials. If a personal author is "chiefly responsible for the creation of the intellectual or artistic content of a work" (rule 21.1A1), that individual is chosen as the main entry. But most serials are not entered under personal authors because many authors usually contribute to the contents of serials. Instead, the title of a serial and a corporate body are used more often as the main entry of serials. For example, it is appropriate to use the corporate body as the main entry for the newsletter of the Chinese American Librarians Association because the newsletter focuses on the activities of the corporate body and its members (see rule 21.1B2 for when to use corporate bodies as main entry). But when a newsletter of a corporate body covers many topics in addition to updates of the organization's activities, then it may be more appropriate to use the title as the main entry. Most remote access electronic serials are entered under title but some serials such as annual reports are entered under the corporate body. The cataloger will select the main entry based on the nature of the publication and the roles of the corporate bodies involved.

If personal authors or corporate bodies contribute to the intellectual content of a publication, the cataloger will select them for added entries. If corporate names do not appear in the first six areas of description, the cataloger will provide a note, in the 500 field (for "issuing body") to explain their contribution to the serial. But in aggregator-neutral records, the cataloger will not provide an added entry for aggregators.

Uniform Title (Rule 25.5B1)

Many serials have title as the main entry. *LCRI* 25.5B states that a uniform title should be created for a remote access serial in the following situations:

(1) When the title proper is the same as that of another unrelated serial in the database or catalog:

```
New record:
    130  0#  $a American cultural quarterly (Hamilton, N.Y.)
    245  10  $a American cultural quarterly $h [electronic
             resource].
Existing record:
    245  00  $a American culture quarterly.
    260      $a Chicago : $b University of Chicago Press,
             $c 1967-
```

(2) When the title proper is the same as that of its print (or other format) counterpart

```
New record:
    130    0#    $a Journal of optics. $n B, $p Quantum and
                 semiclassical optics (Online)
    245    10    $a Journal of optics. $n B, $p Quantum and
                 semiclassical optics $h [electronic resource].
    530          Also issued in print.
    776    1     $a Journal of optics. B, Quantum and
                 semiclassical optics $w (OCoLC) 41013469
    [Comments: The uniform title with the qualifier "online"
    uniquely identifies the online version of this serial. The 776
    field links this new record to the record for the print version.]
```

(3) When the serial is published in various editions

```
New record:
    130    0#    $a Environmental policy and debates
                 (California ed.)
```

```
         245      10      $a Environmental policy and debates $h
                          [electronic resource].
Other edition:
         130      0#     $a Environmental policy and debates (Texas ed.)
         245      10     $a Environmental policy and debates $h
                         [electronic resource].
```

(4) When the serial was published in print or other format and became available online

```
New record:
         130      0#     $a MIS quarterly (Online)
         245      10     $a MIS quarterly $h [electronic resource] :
                         $b management information systems.
         530             $a Online version of the print publication.
         550             $a Digitized and made available by JSTOR.
         776      1      $t MIS quarterly $x 0276-7783 $w
                         (OCoLC)3681309
                         [This 776 links the new item to its print
                         counterpart.]
```

As the examples illustrate, uniform title usually consists of the title proper with a qualifier in parentheses and is entered in the 130 field. Qualifiers could be the place of publication of the first issue, a corporate body, the year of the first issue, or others. *LCRI* 25.5B states that the uniform title should be added only to the record for a resource being cataloged (not to the record of an existing serial with the same title). It also specifies that the name of the issuing corporate body should be used as the qualifier if the title proper consists "solely" of words indicating the type of publication (bulletin, newsletter, journal, etc.), and/or periodicity (occasional paper, quarterly journal, weekly newsletter, etc.), and if there is another serial with the same title.

CONSER considers most electronic versions of print serials to be simultaneous editions instead of electronic reproduction, so it recommends that the cataloger use a uniform title with the physical medium as the qualifier. *LCRI* also states that uniform titles should not be applied to reproductions. For most electronic serials the term "online" may distinguish the electronic version from its counterpart in another medium. If the print serial has its own uniform title, a second qualifier indicating the medium could be added.

```
Print version:
         130  0#   $a Economic forecasting (Midwest ed.)

Electronic version:
         130  0#   $a Economic forecasting (Midwest ed. : Online)
         245  10   $a Economic forecasting $h [electronic
                   resource].
```

Module 31 instructs the cataloger to use the uniform title of the print version to formulate the online version's uniform title, even when the online version's place of publication is different from the place qualifier in the print version's uniform title. It also states that the name of a provider (an aggregator, a database, etc.) should *not* be used as a uniform title qualifier. For example, uniform titles such as ERIC (Online: OCLC) are no longer used.

When the print and online versions of a serial are entered under a corporate body or a conference name, the uniform title is presented in the 240 field as follows:

New record for the online version:
    110   2# $a American Farmers Association. $b Legislative
                Research Div.
    240   10 $a Quarterly summary (Online)
    245   10 $a Quarterly summary $h [electronic resource] /
                $c Legislative Research Division, American
                Farmers Association.

Record for the print version:
    110   2# $a American Farmers Association. $b Legislative
                Research Div.
    245   10 $a Quarterly summary / $c Legislative Research
                Division, American Farmers Association.

Subject Analysis

Subject Headings

Subject analysis of remote access electronic serials is similar to that of print resources. A major difference in the subject analysis process is catalogers usually need to scan several issues to have a better understanding of the range of topics covered by a serial. The assignment of subject headings to electronic serials is the same as that for print resources. Cataloger will use terms from authority lists such as *Library of Congress Subject Headings* (*LCSH*) and *Medical Subject Headings* (*MeSH*) to summarize the subject content of a resource. While *MeSH* used "electronic journals" as a form subdivision from 1999 to 2001, *LCSH* does not use "electronic journals" as a form subdivision at all. *Subject Cataloging Manual* (2004) H1580.5 instructs catalogers to use authorized headings to represent the subjects of a serial and subdivide it with a form subdivision "—Periodicals." Catalogers should not use a subdivision "—Databases" to indicate that a serial is an electronic serial. The benefits and problems of such usage were analyzed by Shadle and Davis (Cargille et al. 1998).

SCM H1580.5 instructs catalogers when to apply "databases" as a topical or form subdivision for electronic serials. If a database is issued serially, catalogers will use "[topic]-Databases" to indicate the subject of the database. The subdivision "-Periodicals" is *not* used to indicate the item is published serially. For example,

> Title: Biology database [a database published every six months on CD-ROM]
> 650   0 $a Biology $v Databases.

If an electronic serial is about databases in general, catalogers will use the following subject heading to represent the subject:

> 650   0 $a Databases $v Periodicals.

If an electronic serial is about databases in a particular field, catalogers will use the following subject heading to indicate the topics:

> 650   0 $a Psychology $x Databases $v Periodicals.

But for electronic serials that are reference works such as bibliographies, catalogs, collections of abstracts, directories, dictionaries, indexes, or other similar reference-type works, catalogers *should not* use the subdivision "—Databases". The following example from H1580.5 illustrates this point well:

> Title: Index to legal periodicals [computer file]
> [a quarterly cumulative index to U.S. and foreign law periodicals]
> 650   # 0 $a Law $z United States $x Periodicals $v Indexes $v Periodicals.
> 650   # 0 $a Law $x Periodicals $v Indexes $v Periodicals.

Classification

Subject access to electronic journals is important to users and libraries have provided such access through subject headings, but classification of electronic journals is not common in libraries. This is probably because classification number has long been associated with call numbers, which has been used as a shelving device in libraries. Since electronic journals cannot be shelved, there is less interest in assigning classification numbers to them. Wilson reported that when journals are available in print and electronic format, 70 of the 122 ARL (Association of Research Libraries) (57 percent) classify them; but when electronic journals do not have print counterparts, 79 percent of the respondents do not classify them (2001). This situation is lamentable because classification numbers complement subject headings. Since classification is discipline-based, classification numbers enable users and librarians to browse for resources by discipline, provide a means for collection evaluation and development, and facilitate the design of personalized interfaces like "My Library" that are based on classification numbers (Wilson 2001). Module 31 encourages libraries that classify their print serials to classify their electronic serials as well so that electronic serials are integrated into the collections in the online catalog and users can search or browse them through classification numbers. In classifying electronic serials the cataloger will use the subject as the basis. Neither the Dewey Decimal Classification system nor the Library of Congress Classification scheme provides a number under subjects for electronic serials.

Cataloging Examples

Figure 7.2. *African studies quarterly*

African Studies Quarterly
The Online Journal for African Studies

■Home ■Current Issue ■Previous Issues ■Submission Guidelines ■Books for Review

UNIVERSITY OF
FLORIDA
Center for African Studies

Advisory Board
Editorial Committee

Search

ASQ is indexed in Public Affairs
Information Service (PAIS) and by
the Gale Group.

ASQ Alerts

ASQ is available only in electronic
format. There is no print version.
To receive an email when a new
issue of the journal is published
click the "subscribe" button.

Articles from Current Issue

Volume 8, Issue 1
Fall 2004

SPECIAL ISSUE: TRUTH & RECONCILIATION COMMISSIONS IN AFRICA

Guest Editor: Kimberly Lanegran

Printing Suggestions   Get Acrobat® Reader®

INTRODUCTION

Truth, Justice, and Reconciliation in Africa: Issues and Cases
Lyn S. Graybill and Kimberly Lanegran

ARTICLES

Reconciling South Africa or South Africans? Cautionary Notes from the

---

African Studies Quarterly
The Online Journal for African Studies

■Home ■Current Issue ■Previous Issues ■Submission Guidelines ■Books for Review

African Studies Quarterly: Volume 1, Issue 1 (1997)

Articles

Livelihoods and Security in Africa: Contending Perspectives in the New Global Order
Goran Hyden

Judicial Responses To Genocide: The International Criminal Tribunal For Rwanda And The Rwandan Genocide Courts
Paul J. Magnarella

Creating Peace In An Armed Society: Karamoja, Uganda, 1996.
Michael Quam

Type	a	ELvl	I	Srce	d	GPub		Ctrl		Lang	eng
BLvl	s	Form	s	Conf	0	Freq	q	MRec		Ctry	flu
S/L	0	Orig	s	EntW		Regl	r	ISSN		Alph	
Desc	a	SrTp	p	Cont		DtSt	c	Dates 1997, 9999			

006	m d	
007	c $b r $d m $e n $f u	
090	DT19.8	
092	0	960.0705$2 22
245	00	African studies quarterly $h [electronic resource] : $b the online journal for African studies.

298

246	1#	ASQ
260		Gainesville, FL : $b University of Florida, Center for African Studies, $c 1997-
310		Quarterly
362	0	Vol. 1, issue 1 (1997)-
500		Title from table of contents screen (viewed Dec. 6, 2004)
500		Latest issue consulted: Vol. 8, issue 1 (fall 2004) (viewed at publisher's website, Dec. 6, 2004)
500		Indexed by the Gale Group.
510	0	Public Affairs Information Service (PAIS)
516	8	All issues in HTML format, the more recent issues also available in PDF file format.
520		ASQ publishes articles and book reviews, is available only in electronic format, and offers current and previous issues online.
538		System requirements: Adobe Acrobat reader.
538		Mode of access: World Wide Web.
651	0	Africa $x Study and teaching $v Periodicals.
710	2	University of Florida. $b Center for African Studies.
856	40	$u http://web.africa.ufl.edu/asq/

Discussion for Figure 7.2

- Fixed field: Type of record is coded "a" for textual material, so the serial 008 fixed field is used. BLvl is coded "s" for serial. Form is "s" for electronic form intended for computer manipulation. Freq (frequency of publication) is coded "q" for quarterly. Ctry (country of publication) is coded "flu" for Florida. S/L (entry convention) is "0" for successive entry. Orig (form of original item) is coded "s" for a form intended for machine manipulation. Regl (regularity) is "r" for regular, Desc is "a" for a record created according to *AACR2*, SrTp (type of continuing resource) is "p" for periodical. DtSt (date type) is "c" for current and Date 1 is 1997, the beginning year of the serial, and Date 2 is 9999 for a publication that will continue indefinitely.

- Electronic resource 006: This field is required to bring out the electronic aspect of an electronic serial. Code "m" indicates a computer file, code "d" stands for document. The 006 field has no subfields and specific positions are reserved for coding the resource type, audience information, file type, and type of government publication.

- Electronic resource 007: This field is required whenever an 006 field for electronic resource is included in a record. Code "c" for subfield $a specifies this item as computer file. Code "r" for subfield $b identifies a remote access file. Code "m" for subfield $d indicates mixtures of text and images in black and white and in color. Code "n" for subfield $e indicates no dimension information is applicable and code "u" for subfield $f indicates it is unknown whether the item has sound.

- 245: The title proper is transcribed as found, except for capitalization, and is followed immediately by the general material designation in subfield $h, which is followed by the other title information in subfield $b. Because this journal is not about the Center for African Studies, the title is chosen as the main entry and the Center is selected as a corporate body added entry, using the 710 field.

- 246: The journal's home page refers to this serial as *ASQ*, so it is recorded in the 246 field to provide an access point for the variant title.

- 260: The place of publication and publisher appear on the journal home page. The record is based on the first issue of the serial, so subfield $c is used.

- 310: This is a frequency note.

- 362: Since the first issue is available, it is used as the basis for the description and the numbering information is recorded in the 362 field as a formatted note (with indicator value "0")

- 500s: Title of source note is required of all electronic resources, viewing date is included. The note on the latest issue consulted is presented as a separate per *LCRI* 12.7B23.

- 500 and 510: The journal is indexed by PAIS and the Gale group. The provision of this type of note is optional. Field 510 is used when the name of the index is known. Value "0" for the first indicator will generate a display constant "Indexed by:" Because The Gale Group is a company name and cannot be entered in 510, a 500 note is used.

- 516: The journal is available in two file formats, and the information is given in a 516 note, with indicator value "8" to specify that no display constant is to be generated.

- 520: A summary note indicates the journal's format, contents, and availability of current and previous issues.

- 538: A system requirements note informs users they need a special program to view the PDF files.

- 538: All remote access electronic serials should have a 538, mode of access note, to indicate the access method.

- 651: The heading reflects the subject focus of this serial. The form subdivision, "periodicals", is used because *LCSH* does not have "electronic journals" as a subdivision. *LCSH* has a subject heading, "electronic journals", that is for works about electronic serials and cannot be used to specify the format of a publication.

- 710: The publisher is traced and not provided as a subject heading because the journal is not about the Center for African Studies.

- 856: The URL is entered in subfield $u.

Figure 7.3. *ALCTS newsletter online*

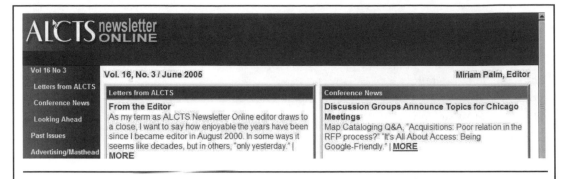

ALCTS Newsletter Online (ISSN 1523-018X) is published six times a year by the Association for Library Collections & Technical Services, American Library Association, 50 E. Huron St., Chicago, IL 60611. It replaced the *ALCTS Newsletter* (ISSN 1047-949X) in December 1998.

Carol Pitts Diedrichs, ALCTS President;
Charles Wilt, Executive Director, ALCTS;

ALCTS Newsletter Online is published free of charge to anyone with Web access.

ALCTS Newsletter Online is indexed in H. W. Wilson's Library Literature.

All materials in this newsletter subject to copyright by the American Library Association may be downloaded for the noncommercial purpose of scientific or educational advancement granted by sections

•Publications

•ALCTS Newsletter Online

•Vol 16 No 1

•Past Issues

•Vol 15 No 6

•Vol 15 No 5

•Vol 15 No 4

•Vol 15 No 3

•Vol 15 No 2

•Vol 15 No 1

•Vol 14 No 6

Volume 15, Number 2
Volume 15, Number 1

2003

Volume 14, Number 6
Volume 14, Number 5
Volume 14, Number 4
Volume 14, Number 3
Volume 14, Number 2
Volume 14, Number 1

2002

Volume 13, Number 4
Volume 13, Number 3
Volume 13, Number 2
Volume 13, Number 1

Type	a	ELvl	I	Srce	d	GPub		Ctrl		Lang	eng
BLvl	s	Form	s	Conf	0	Freq	b	MRec		Ctry	ilu
S/L	0	Orig	s	EntW		Regl	r	ISSN	1	Alph	a
Desc	a	SrTp	p	Cont		DtSt	c	Dates	1998, 9999		

006		m d
007		c $b r $d m $e n $f u
022		1523-018X
090		Z688.5 $b .A43
092	0	020 $2 22
245	00	ALCTS newsletter online $h [electronic resource].
246	3	ALCTS online newsletter
246	3	Association for Library Collections and Technical Services newsletter online
260		Chicago, IL : $b Association for Library Collections & Technical Services, American Library Association, $c c1998-
310		Six times a year.
362	0	Vol. 10, no. 1 (Dec. 1998)-
500		Title from title screen (viewed Jan. 5, 2005).
500		Latest issue consulted: Vol. 15, no. 6 (Dec. 2004).
510	0	Library Literature
520		"The Newsletter keeps members and those interested in ALCTS issues aware of current association news, events, updates, practice and developments in the field, and other relevant issues"—ALCTS Publications page.
538		Mode of access: World Wide Web.
610	20	Association for Library Collections & Technical Services $v Periodicals.
650	0	Technical services (Libraries) $v Periodicals.
650	0	Cataloging $v Periodicals.
650	0	Information retrieval $v Periodicals.
710	2	Association for Library Collections & Technical Services.
780	00	$t ALCTS newsletter $x 1047-949X $w (DLC) 91649699 $w (OCoLC)20820888
856	40	$u http://www.ala.org/ala/alcts/alctspubs/alctsnewsletter/alctsnewsletter.htm

Discussion for Figure 7.3

- Fixed field: Type of record is coded "a" for textual material, so the serial 008 fixed field is used. BLvl is coded "s" for serial. Form is "s" for electronic form intended for computer manipulation. Freq (frequency of publication) is coded "b" for works that are published six times a year. Ctry (country of publication) is coded "ilu" for Illinois. S/L (entry convention) is "0" for successive entry. Orig (form of original item) is coded "s" for a form intended for machine manipulation. Regl (regularity) is "r" for regular, Desc is "a" for a record created according to *AACR2*, SrTp (type of continuing resource) is "p" for periodical. DtSt (date type) is "c" for current and Date 1 is 1998, the year when the print version stopped and the new online version began, and Date 2 is 9999 for a publication that will continue indefinitely.

- Electronic resource 006: This field is required to bring out the electronic aspect of an electronic serial. Code "m" indicates a computer file, code "d" stands for document. The 006 field has no subfields and specific positions are reserved for coding the resource type, audience information, file type, and type of government publication.

- Electronic resource 007: This field is required whenever a 006 field for electronic resource is included in a record. Code "c" for subfield $a specifies this item as computer file. Code "r" for subfield $b identifies a remote access file. Code "m" for subfield $d indicates mixtures of text images in black and white and in color. Code "n" for subfield $e indicates no dimension information is applicable, and code "u" for subfield $f indicates it is unknown whether the item has sound.

- 022: When the ISSN is available, it is recorded in the 022 field. The first indicator specifies whether the work is of international interest. OCLC documentation states that "blank" should be used "by all institutions other than the National Serials Data Program (NSDP) and ISSN Canada when recording the ISSN from an issue or from a bibliography."

- 245: The title proper is transcribed as found, except for capitalization, and is followed immediately by the general material designation in subfield $h. This newsletter contains information about ALCTS and practice and new developments in the field, so ALCTS is not chosen as the main entry. Instead, the journal is entered under title.

- 246s: Added entries are provided for variant titles to increase access to this serial.

- 260: The place of publication and publisher are on the masthead. Since the first issue is the basis for the record, the beginning date is recorded in subfield $c.

- 310: Frequency information is on the masthead and recorded in 310. The information is coordinated with the Freq element in the fixed field, using value "b."

- 362: Since the first issue is available, it is used as the basis for the description and the numbering information is recorded in the 362 field as a formatted note (with indicator value "0").

- 500s: Title of source note is required of all electronic resources, viewing date is included. The note on the latest issue consulted is presented as a separate per *LCRI* 12.7B23.

- 510s: The journal is indexed in H. W. Wilson's Library Literature, so Library Literature is recorded in the 510 with "Indexed by:" as the display constant.

- 520: A summary note indicates the journal's coverage and provides an explanation for using ALCTS as a subject access point and a corporate body access point.

- 538: All remote access electronic serials should have a 538, mode of access note, to indicate the access method.

- 6xx: Because the serial reports on activities of ALCTS committees and events, it is appropriate to use ALCTS as a subject access point. 650 fields are used to indicate other subjects of this serial.

- 710: The publisher is traced.

- 780: The earlier title of this serial is recorded in the 780 field, indicators "00" will generate a note with a display text "Continues:" preceding the title recorded in the 780 field.

- 856: The URL is entered in subfield $u, with first indicator value "4" indicating the access method is HTTP, and second indicator value "0" indicating the item represented by the URL is the same as the item represented by the bibliographic record.

Figure 7.4. *Administrative science quarterly* (online)

ADMINISTRATIVE SCIENCE QUARTERLY

JSTOR Coverage: Vols. 1 - 46, 1956-2001

JSTOR Collections: Arts & Sciences IV, Business

Please read JSTOR's Terms and Conditions of Use before you begin.

Search This Journal | Browse This Journal

Journal Information for *Administrative Science Quarterly*

Publisher: Johnson Graduate School of Management, Cornell University

Moving Wall: 3

Founded in 1956 by James Thompson, the *Administrative Science Quarterly* is a peer-reviewed, interdisciplinary journal publishing theoretical and empirical work that advances the study of organizational behavior and theory. *ASQ* publishes articles that contribute to organization theory from a number of disciplines, including organizational behavior and theory, sociology, psychology and social psychology, strategic management, economics, public administration, and industrial relations. *ASQ* publishes both qualitative and quantitative work, as well as purely theoretical papers. Theoretical perspectives and topics in *ASQ* range from micro to macro, from lab experiments in psychology to work on nation-states. An occasional feature is the "*ASQ* Forum," an essay on a special topic with invited commentaries. Thoughtful reviews of books relevant to organization studies and management theory are a regular feature. Special issues have explored qualitative methods, organizational culture, the utilization of organizational research, the distribution of rewards in organizations, and critical perspectives on organizational control.

ISSN: 00018392
OCLC: 48418629
LCCN: 2001-227349

Type	a	ELvl	I	Srce	d	GPub		Ctrl		Lang	eng
BLvl	s	Form	s	Conf	0	Freq	q	MRec		Ctry	nyu
S/L	0	Orig	s	EntW		Regl	r	ISSN		Alph	
Desc	a	SrTp	p	Cont		DtSt	c	Dates 1956, 9999			

006		m d
007		c $b r $d m $e n $f u
022		$y 0001-8392
090		HD28 $b .A25
092	0	658.005 $2 22
130	0	Administrative science quarterly (Online)
245	10	Administrative science quarterly $h [electronic resource].
246	1#	ASQ
260		Ithaca, N.Y. : $b Graduate School of Business and Public Administration, Cornell University, $c 1956-
310		Quarterly
362	0	Vol. 1, no. 1 (June 1956)-
500		Title from table of contents screen (viewed Jan. 5, 2005).
500		Latest issue consulted: Vol. 49, no. 4 (Dec. 2004) (viewed Jan. 5, 2005)
530		Also available in print.
538		Mode of access: World Wide Web.
550		Published by the Samuel Curtis Johnson Graduate School of Management, Cornell University, Dec. 1984-
650	0	Management $v Periodicals.

650	0	Organization $v Periodicals.
650	0	Public administration $v Periodicals.
710	2	Cornell University. $b Graduate School of Business and Public Administration.
710	2	Johnson Graduate School of Management (Cornell University)
776	1	$t Administrative science quarterly $x 0001-8392 $w (DLC) 57059226 $w (OCoLC) 1461102
856	40	$u http://www.jstor.org/journals/00018392.html $z JSTOR coverage: Vols. 1–46 (1956–2001); available only to users of participating institutions and individual subscribers.
856	40	$u http://www.johnson.cornell.edu/publications/asq/ $z Online issues from 1999 on, available only to subscribers.

Discussion for Figure 7.4

- Fixed field: Type of record is coded "a" for textual material, so the serial 008 fixed field is used. BLvl is coded "s" for serial. Form is "s" for electronic form intended for computer manipulation. Freq (frequency of publication) is coded "q" for a quarterly publication. Ctry (country of publication) is coded "nyu" for New York. S/L (entry convention) is "0" for successive entry. Orig (form of original item) is coded "s" for a form intended for machine manipulation. Regl (regularity) is "r" for regular, Desc is "a" for a record created according to *AACR2*, SrTp (type of continuing resource) is "p" for periodical. DtSt (date type) is "c" for current and Date 1 is 1956 when the journal became available online, and Date 2 is 9999 for a publication that will continue indefinitely.

- Electronic resource 006: This field is required to bring out the electronic aspect of an electronic serial. Code "m" indicates a computer file, code "d" stands for document. The 006 field has no subfields and specific positions are reserved for coding the resource type, audience information, file type, and type of government publication.

- Electronic resource 007: This field is required whenever a 006 field for electronic resource is included in a record. Code "c" for subfield $a specifies this item as computer file. Code "r" for subfield $b identifies a remote access file. Code "m" for subfield $d indicates mixtures of text and images in black and white and in color. Code "n" for subfield $e indicates no dimension information is applicable and code "u" for subfield $f indicates it is unknown whether the item has sound.

- 022: The ISSN on the digitized version is that of the print version, so it is recorded in subfield $y of the 022 field, according to the CONSER guideline. If the cataloger feels this can be confusing to users, this field can be removed. The ISSN for the print version is recorded in the 776 field below.

- 245: The title proper is transcribed as found, except for capitalization, and is followed immediately by the general material designation in subfield $h.

- 246: A variant title added entry is provided to increase access.

- 260: The place of publication and publisher are on the Web site. Since the first issue is available, subfield $c is used.

- 310: Frequency information is indicated by the journal title. It is recorded in the 310 field and coordinated with the Freq element in the fixed field as value "q".

- 362: The first issue is available and the numbering information is recorded in the 362 field, with the first indicator coded "0".

- 500s: The source of the title is recorded with viewing date in parentheses. A separate 500 note is provided for the latest issue consulted note, according to *LCRI* 12.7B23.

- 530: The journal continues to be available in print, so a 530 note is provided to alert the users of this version.

- 538: All remote access electronic serials need to have a mode of access note.

- 550: The name of the publisher changed, so a note is provided to clarify the name change and to provide a justification for the corporate body added entries.

- 650s: Subject headings are assigned to reflect the contents of this journal, with "Periodicals" used as the form subdivision.

- 710s: The earlier and current publishers are traced. No access point is provided for JSTOR.

- 776: This linking field is used to link the online version to its print counterpart. The title is entered in subfield $t, ISSN in subfield $x, and LC record number and OCLC record number are entered in separate subfields $w.

- 856s: The first 856 field presents the URL for the item being cataloged and subfield $z is used to indicate the issues digitized by JSTOR and restrictions about access. Although a 506 field can be used to record access restriction, the CONSER recommendation is to use 506 only for items whose access are truly restricted, such as classified materials. But if the cataloger feels local users would benefit from a 506 field, it could be provided. The second 856 field points to the Web version provided by the publisher. Again, subfield $z is used to indicate coverage and access restrictions.

Figure 7.5. *D-Lib magazine*

D-Lib® Magazine

Search

DOI
10.1045/dlib.magazine

ISSN
1082-9873
•••

RSS D-Lib via RSS

In the Current Issue
Full-length Features

June 2005
Vol. 11 No. 6
Table of Contents
•••
EDITORIAL
Time to Reflect
by Bonita Wilson, *CNRI*
•••
LETTERS
To the Editor
•••
COMMENTARY
**Plenty of Room at the Bottom?
Personal Digital Libraries and
Collections**
Neil Beagrie
doi:10.1045/june2005-beagrie
•••
ARTICLES
**A Standards-based Solution for the
Accurate Transfer of Digital Assets**
by Jeroen Bekaert, *Los Alamos National
Laboratory and Ghent University*; and
Herbert Van de Sompel, *Los Alamos*

Also This Month
Digital Collections

FEATURED COLLECTION

Harva
Open
Progr
Textua
historic
teachin
researc
Harvarc

[The Shelton Looms, ca. 1933
Harvard Business School. Used
permission. Image cropped.]

Digital Library Community A

In Brief
Short items of current awaren

In the News
Recent press releases and an

Clips & Pointers
Documents, deadlines, calls f

Archives
Back Issues and Indexes

Sites for D-Lib Magazine:

Corporation for National Research Initiatives, Reston, Virginia, U.S.A. (originating site)

UKOLN, University of Bath, Bath, England (mirror site)

The Australian National University, Canberra, Australia (mirror site)

State Library of Lower Saxony and the University Library of Goettingen, Goettingen, Germany
(mirror site)

Universidad de Belgrano, Buenos Aires, Argentina (mirror site)

Academia Sinica, Taipei, Taiwan (mirror site)

BN - National Library of Portugal, Portugal (mirror site)

Masthead | Guidelines for Authors | Access Terms
Subscriptions | Privacy Policy | Home

D-Lib Magazine is produced by the Corporation for National Research Initiatives (CNRI), has been
sponsored by the **Defense Advanced Research Project Agency (DARPA)**
on behalf of the Digital Libraries Initiative under Grant No. N66001-98-1-8908,
and is currently being funded by the **National Science Foundation (NSF)**
under Grant No. IIS-0243042.

Please send questions or comments to: dlib@cnri.reston.va.us

doi:march2005-contents

Top | Editorial
First Article

The Magazine of the Digital Library Forum ——————— **July 1995**

editorial

- From the editor: *A Word (or two) of welcome*
- To the editor: *What's needed in future research?*
- News from D-Lib Forum: *Why D-Lib?*
- Participating Organizations

stories & briefings

- Metadata: the foundations of resource description . Stuart Weibel, Office of Research, OCLC Online Computer Library Center, Inc.
- An agent-based architecture for digital libraries . William P. Birmingham, School of Information Science and Library Studies, Electrical Engineering and Computer Science Department, The University of Michigan
- Key concepts in the architecture of the digital library . William Y. Arms, Corporation for National Research Initiatives

Type	a	ELv	l	Srce	d	GPub		Ctrl		Lang	eng
BLvl	s	Form	s	Conf	0	Freq	m	MRec		Ctry	vau
S/L	0	Orig	s	EntW		Regl	r	ISSN	1	Alph	a
Desc	a	SrTp	p	Cont		DtSt	c	Dates	1995, 9999		

006		m d
007		c $b r $d m $e n $f u
022		1082-9873
090		ZA4080
092	0	025 $2 22
245	00	D-Lib magazine $h [electronic resource].
246	3	Digital library magazine
260		Reston, Va.: $b Corporation for National Research Initiatives, $c c1995-
310		Monthly, except for the July and August issues which are combined and released in July.
362	0	July 1995-
500		Title from journal home page (viewed Feb. 7, 2005).
500		Latest issue consulted: Vol. 11, no. 1 (Jan. 2005)
520		"A solely electronic publication with a primary focus on digital library research and development, including but not limited to new technologies, applications, and contextual social and economic issues"—About D-Lib magazine.
538		Mode of access: World Wide Web.
550		"D-Lib Magazine is produced by the Corporation for National Research Initiatives (CNRI), has been sponsored by the Defense Advanced Research Project Agency (DARPA) on behalf of the Digital Libraries Initiative . . . and is currently being funded by the National Science Foundation (NSF)"—Journal home page.
550		1995 issues have subtitle: the magazine of the Digital Library Forum.
650	0	Digital libraries $v Periodicals.
650	0	Electronic publishing $v Periodicals.
650	0	Libraries and electronic publishing $v Periodicals.
650	0	Library information networks $v Periodicals.
710	2	Corporation for National Research Initiatives.
710	1	United States. $b Defense Advanced Research Project Agency.
710	2	National Science Foundation (U.S.)
710	2	D-Lib Forum.
856	40	$u http://www.dlib.org/

Discussion for Figure 7.5

- Fixed field: Type of record is coded "a" for textual material, so the serial 008 fixed field is used. BLvl is coded "s" for serial. Form is "s" for electronic form intended for computer manipulation. Freq (frequency of publication) is coded "m" for works published monthly, including those published eleven times a year like this one. Ctry (country of publication) is coded "vau" for Virginia. S/L (entry convention) is "0" for successive entry. Orig (form of original item) is coded "s" for a form intended for machine manipulation. Regl (regularity) is "r" for regular, Desc is "a" for a record created according to *AACR2*, SrTp (type of continuing resource) is "p" for periodical. DtSt (date type) is "c" for current and Date 1 is 1995 when the journal became available online, and Date 2 is 9999 for a publication that will continue indefinitely.

- Electronic resource 006: This field is required to bring out the electronic aspect of an electronic serial. Code "m" indicates a computer file, code "d" stands for document. The 006 field has no subfields and specific positions are reserved for coding the resource type, audience information, file type, and type of government publication.

- Electronic resource 007: This field is required whenever a 006 field for electronic resource is included in a record. Code "c" for subfield $a specifies this item as computer file. Code "r" for subfield $b identifies a remote-access file. Code "m" for subfield $d indicates mixture of text and images in black and white and in color. Code "n" for subfield $e indicates no dimension information is applicable and code "u" for subfield $f indicates it is unknown whether the item has sound.

- 022: When the ISSN is available, it is recorded in the 022 field. The first indicator specifies whether the work is of international interest. OCLC documentation states that "blank" should be used "by all institutions other than the National Serials Data Program (NSDP) and ISSN Canada when recording the ISSN from an issue or from a bibliography."

- 245: The title proper is transcribed as found, except for capitalization, and is followed immediately by the general material designation in subfield $h. Title is the main entry.

- 246: A variant title added entry is provided to increase access.

- 260: The place of publication and publisher are on the Web site. Since the first issue is the basis for the record, the beginning date is recorded in subfield $c.

- 310: Frequency information appears on the "About" page and is recorded in the 310 field. The information is coordinated with the Freq element in the fixed field as value "m".

- 362: Since the first issue is available, it is used as the basis for the description and the numbering information (in this case, a chronological designation) is recorded in the 362 field as a formatted note (with indicator value "0"). The journal did not begin using volume and issue in its numbering system until 1999, and the numbering continues the original sequence, so it is not necessary to provide a note about any numbering irregularities.

- 500s: Title of source note is required of all electronic resources, viewing date is included. The note on the latest issue consulted is presented as a separate per *LCRI* 12.7B23.

- 520: A summary note quoted from the "About" page explains the coverage of this journal and provides a basis for selecting subject headings.

- 538: All remote access electronic serials should have a 538, mode of access note, to indicate the access method.

- 550s: The 550 field is used to record current and former bodies involved in the issuing of the journal. Information on bodies currently involved is taken from the journal home page. A separate 550 field is used to record the involvement of an earlier body, "Digital Library Forum".

- 650s: Subject headings are assigned to reflect the contents of this journal, with "Periodicals" used as the form subdivision.

- 710s: Bodies that contribute to the issuing of the journal are traced.

- 856: The URL is entered in subfield $u. The journal has mirror sites in England, Germany, Australia, Taiwan, and other countries. *CONSER Module 31* states that catalogers should not feel the need to record all the mirror sites. Instead, they can select a few sites that are useful to their users to record, using separate 856 fields.

Here is an example:
     856   40 $u http://mirrored.ukoln.ac.uk/lis-journals/
                            dlib/ $z Mirror site at Bath, England:

Figure 7.6. *Current cites*

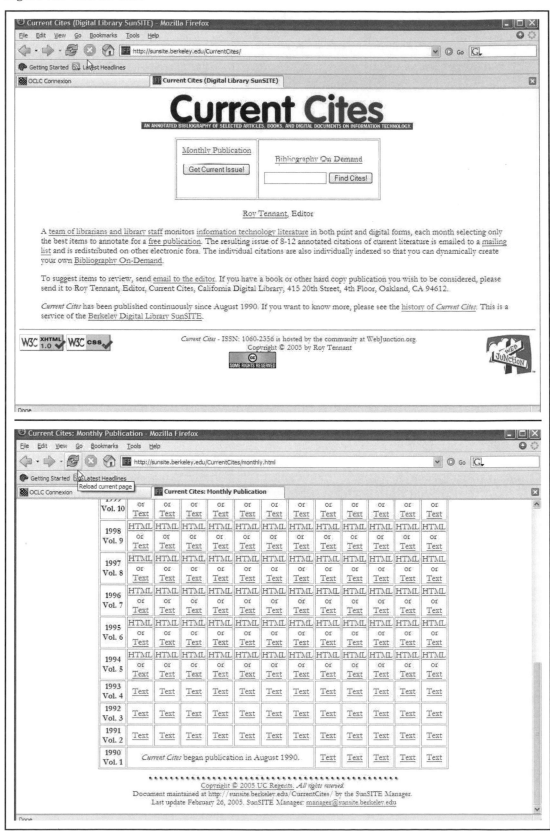

```
                        _Current_Cites_
            I           Volume 1, no. 1
                          August 1990
                Library Technology Watch Program
                University of California, Berkeley
                   Edited by David F.W. Robison
                      ISSN: 1060-2356


                         Contributors:
   Mark Mentges, Teri Rinne, Vivienne Roumani, Lisa Rowlison, Roy Tennant



Optical Disc Technology
```

Type	a	ELvl	I	Srce	d	GPub		Ctrl		Lang	eng
BLvl	s	Form	s	Conf	0	Freq	m	MRec		Ctry	cau
S/L	0	Orig	s	EntW	b	Regl	r	ISSN	1	Alph	a
Desc	a	SrTp	p	Cont		DtSt	c	Dates 1990, 9999			

006		m d
007		c $b r $d a $e n $f u
022		1060-2356
090		Z678.9
092	0	025 $2 22
245	00	Current cites $h [electronic resource].
260		[Berkeley, Calif.]: $b Library Technology Watch Program, University of California, Berkeley, $c 1990-
310		Monthly
362	0	Vol. 1, no. 1 (Aug. 1990)-
500		Title from caption (viewed Jan. 5, 2005)
500		Latest issue consulted: Vol. 15, no. 12 (Dec. 2004).
500		Also distributed in its entirety on *PACS-L* and *PACS-P*
516		Issues in text format, 1990–1993; available in text and HTML formats, 1994-Individual citations are indexed for users to create bibliographies on demand.
538		Mode of access: Electronic mail and World Wide Web.
650	0	Libraries $x Automation $v Bibliography $v Periodicals.
650	0	Library science $x Technological innovations $v Bibliography $v Periodicals.
650	0	Library science $x Data processing $v Bibliography $v Periodicals.
650	0	Internet $v Bibliography $v Periodicals.
650	0	Computers $v Bibliography $v Periodicals.
650	0	Library information networks $v Bibliography $v Periodicals.
650	0	Libraries and electronic publishing $v Bibliography $v Periodicals.
710	2	Library Technology Watch Program.
856	0	$u mail to: listserv@library.berkeley.edu $z To subscribe, send the following text to this address: subscribe cites [yourname]
856	40	$u http://sunsite.berkeley.edu/CurrentCites/

Discussion for Figure 7.6

- Fixed field: Type of record is coded "a" for textual material, so the serial 008 fixed field is used. BLvl is coded "s" for serial. Form is "s" for electronic form intended for computer manipulation. Freq (frequency of publication) is coded "m" for a monthly publication. Ctry (country of publication) is coded "cau" for California. S/L (entry convention) is "0" for successive entry. Orig (form of original item) is coded "s" for a form intended for machine manipulation. Regl (regularity) is "r" for regular, Desc is "a" for a record created according to *AACR2*, SrTp (type of continuing resource) is "p" for periodical. DtSt (date type) is "c" for current and Date 1 is 1990 when the journal became available online, and Date 2 is 9999 for a publication that will continue indefinitely.

- Electronic resource 006: This field is required to bring out the electronic aspect of an electronic serial. Code "m" indicates a computer file, code "d" stands for document. The 006 field has no subfields and specific positions are reserved for coding the resource type, audience information, file type, and type of government publication.

- Electronic resource 007: This field is required whenever a 006 field for electronic resource is included in a record. Code "c" for subfield $a specifies this item as computer file. Code "r" for subfield $b identifies a remote access file. Code "m" for subfield $d indicates the text in one color. Code "n" for subfield $e indicates no dimension information is applicable, and code "u" for subfield $f indicates it is unknown whether the item has sound.

- 022: The ISSN of the electronic journal is entered in the 022 field. The first indicator specifies whether the work is of international interest. OCLC documentation states that "blank" should be used "by all institutions other than the National Serials Data Program (NSDP) and ISSN Canada when recording the ISSN from an issue or from a bibliography."

- 245: The title proper is transcribed as found, except for capitalization, and is followed immediately by the general material designation in subfield $h.

- 260: The place of publication is inferred, so it is recorded in brackets. The publisher and the beginning year of publication are taken from the first issue.

- 310: Frequency information is indicated on the journal Web site. It is recorded in the 310 field and coordinated with the Freq element in the fixed field as value "m".

- 362: The first issue is available and recorded in the 362 field, with the first indicator coded "0".

- 500s: The source of the title is recorded with viewing date in parentheses. A separate 500 field is provided for the latest issue consulted, according to *LCRI* 12.7B23. An optional 500 note indicates two other places the publication is distributed.

- 516: This note indicates the file formats and users' ability to create customized bibliographies from the citations.

- 538: All remote access electronic serials need to have a mode of access note.

- 650s: Subject headings are assigned to reflect the contents of this journal, with "Bibliography" and "Periodicals" used as form subdivisions.

- 710: The publisher is traced.

- 856: The first 856 field provides information for e-mail access in a direct format. If the cataloger chooses to make use of various subfields of the 856 field, the same information can be coded as follows:

856	0	library.berkeley.edu $f CITES $h listserv $i subscribe $z Email subscription information:

- 856: The second 856 field points to the resource that is the same as the item represented by the bibliographic record, so the second indicator is "0". The first indicator is "4" for an item accessed via http.

Figure 7.7. *MIS quarterly executive* (online)

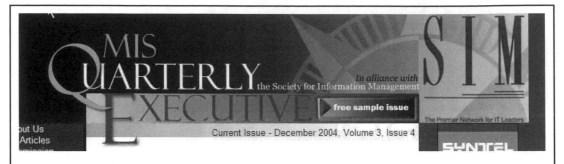

About MISQE

MIS Quarterly Executive is affiliated with MIS Quarterly, one of the leading
academic research journals in MIS. The mission of MISQE is to encourage
practice-based research in the information systems field and to disseminate
the results of that research in a manner that makes its relevance and utility
readily apparent. MISQE will pursue this mission by publishing academic
research in a format targeting senior managers. Executives already have
access to many sources of knowledge about information systems, but
MISQE will differentiate itself from the IS practitioner literature by delivering
articles, case studies, and research reports that are based on in-depth
research and that provide rich stories, unique insights, and useful
conceptual frameworks.

March 2002 (Volume 1, Number 1)

Principles and Models for Organizing the IT Function
Ritu Agarwal, V. Sambamurthy
Abstract

**What IT Infrastructure Capabilities are Needed to Implement
E-Business Models?**
Peter Weill, Michael Vitale
Abstract

Type	a	ELvl	I	Srce	d	GPub		Ctrl		Lang	eng
BLvl	s	Form	s	Conf	0	Freq	q	MRec		Ctry	inu
S/L	0	Orig	s	EntW		Regl	r	ISSN	1	Alph	a
Desc	a	SrTp	p	Cont		DtSt	c	Dates 2002, 9999			

006		m d
007		c $b r $d m $e n $f u
010		2002213593
022		1540-1979
092	0	658 $2 2
090		T58.6
130	0	MIS quarterly executive (Online)
245	10	MIS quarterly executive $h [electronic resource].
246	3	Management information systems quarterly executive
246	13	MISQE
260		Bloomington, IN : $b Accounting and Information Systems Dept., Kelley School of Business, Indiana University, $c 2002-
310		Quarterly
362	0	Vol. 1, no. 1 (Mar. 2002)-
500		Title from table of contents screen (viewed Oct. 15, 2004).
516		Articles in PDF format.
530		Also issued in print.
538		System requirements: Adobe Acrobat Reader.
538		Mode of access: World Wide Web.
580		Companion to: MIS quarterly.
650	0	Management information systems $v Periodicals.
710	2	Kelley School of Business. $b Accounting and Information Systems Dept.
776	1	$t MIS quarterly executive $x 1540-1960 $w (DLC) 2002213592
787	1	$t MIS quarterly (Online)
856	40	$u http://www.misqe.org

319

Discussion for Figure 7.7

- Fixed field: Type of record is coded "a" for textual material, so the serial 008 fixed field is used. BLvl is coded "s" for serial. Form is "s" for electronic form intended for computer manipulation. Freq (frequency of publication) is coded "q" for works published quarterly, including those published eleven times a year like this one. Ctry (country of publication) is coded "inu" for Indiana. S/L (entry convention) is "0" for successive entry. Orig (form of original item) is coded "s" for a form intended for machine manipulation. Regl (regularity) is "r" for regular, Desc is "a" for a record created according to *AACR2*, SrTp (type of continuing resource) is "p" for periodical. DtSt (date type) is "c" for current and Date 1 is 2002 when the journal became available online, and Date 2 is 9999 for a publication that will continue indefinitely.

- Electronic resource 006: This field is required to bring out the electronic aspect of an electronic serial. Code "m" indicates a computer file, code "d" stands for document. The 006 field has no subfields and specific positions are reserved for coding the resource type, audience information, file type, and type of government publication.

- Electronic resource 007: This field is required whenever a 006 field for electronic resource is included in a record. Code "c" for subfield $a specifies this item as computer file. Code "r" for subfield $b identifies a remote access file. Code "m" for subfield $d indicates mixtures of text and images in black and white and in color. Code "n" for subfield $e indicates no dimension information is applicable, and code "u" for subfield $f indicates it is unknown whether the item has sound.

- 022: When the ISSN is available, it is recorded in the 022 field. The first indicator specifies whether the work is of international interest. OCLC documentation states that "blank" should be used "by all institutions other than the National Serials Data Program (NSDP) and ISSN Canada when recording the ISSN from an issue or from a bibliography."

- 245: The title proper is transcribed as found, except for capitalization, and is followed immediately by the general material designation in subfield $h. Title is the main entry.

- 246s: The title added entries are provided for the fuller form of the title proper and the acronym to increase access.

- 260: The place of publication and publisher are found on the first issue, and the beginning year of publication is recorded in subfield $c.

- 310: Frequency of publication is indicated by the journal title and coordinated with the Freq element in the fixed field as value "q".

- 362: Since the first issue is available, it is used as the basis for the description and the numbering information is recorded in the 362 field as a formatted note (with indicator value "0").

- 500: The source of title note is required of all electronic resources and viewing date is included in parentheses.

- 516: This note indicates the format of the articles.

- 530: The online version is identical to the print version, and a 530 note is used to inform users of the existence of the print version. A linking field, 776, is provided later to link the two versions.

- 538s: The first 538 is for system requirements needed for users to view the articles. The second 538 indicates the mode of access. This note is required of all remote access electronic serials.

- 580 and 787: The Web site indicates the journal is "affiliated with" *MIS Quarterly*. The print journal clarifies that this journal is a companion to *MIS Quarterly*. Because the relationship cannot be adequately represented by the 787 field, a 580 note is provided. The 787 field is used to link the two records together.

- 650: The subject heading reflects the contents of this journal, with "Periodicals" used as the form subdivision.

- 710: The publisher is traced.

- 776: This field links this record to the record of the print version. Title is recorded in $t, ISSN in subfield $x, and LCCN in subfield $w.

- 856: Indicator value "4" identifies the access method as HTTP and value "0" means the URL points to the resource that is the same as the one represented by the bibliographic record.

Figure 7.8. *LC cataloging newsline*

Type	a	ELvl	I	Srce	d	GPub	f	Ctrl		Lang	eng
BLvl	s	Form	s	Conf	0	Freq		MRec		Ctry	dcu
S/L	0	Orig	s	EntW		Regl	x	ISSN	1	Alph	a
Desc	a	SrTp	p	Cont		DtSt	c	Dates	1993, 9999		

006		m d f
007		c $b r $d c $e n $f u
022		1066-8829
090		Z693.A15
092	0	025 $2 22
110	2	Library of Congress. $b Cataloging Directorate.
245	10	LC cataloging newsline $h [electronic resource] : $b online newsletter of the Cataloging Directorate, Library of Congress.
246	3	Library of Congress cataloging newsline
246	13	LCCN

260		Washington, D.C. : $b Cataloging Directorate, Library Services, Library of Congress, $c 1993-
310		Irregular
362	0	Vol. 1, no. 1 (Jan. 1993)-
500		Title from title screen (viewed Feb. 20, 2005).
500		Latest issue consulted: Vol. 13, no. 1 (Jan. 2005)
516		Electronic journal in HTML format from vol. 1 to vol. 11, in PDF format starting vol. 12 (Jan. 2004)
538		System requirements: Adobe Acrobat reader.
538		Mode of access: Internet email and World Wide Web.
610	20	Library of Congress. $b Cataloging Directorate. $v Periodicals.
650	0	Cataloging $v Periodicals.
856	40	$u http://lcweb.loc.gov/catdir/lccn/lccn.html
856	0	$u mailto: listserv@loc.gov $i subscribe lccn [firstname lastname]

Discussion for Figure 7.8

- Fixed field: Type of record is coded "a" for textual material, so the serial 008 fixed field is used. BLvl is coded "s" for serial. Form is "s" for electronic form intended for computer manipulation. Freq (frequency of publication) is coded "blank" for irregular frequency. Ctry (country of publication) is coded "dcu" for Washington, D.C. S/L (entry convention) is "0" for successive entry. Orig (form of original item) is coded "s" for a form intended for machine manipulation. GPub is coded "f" because LC is a federal agency. Regl (regularity) is "x" for irregular, Desc is "a" for a record created according to *AACR2*, SrTp (type of continuing resource) is "p" for periodical. DtSt (date type) is "c" for current and Date 1 is 1993, the first year *LCCN* became available online, and Date 2 is 9999 for a publication that will continue indefinitely.

- Electronic resource 006: This field is required to bring out the electronic aspect of an electronic serial. Code "m" indicates a computer file, code "d" stands for document. The 006 field has no subfields and specific positions are reserved for coding the resource type, audience information, file type, and type of government publication.

- Electronic resource 007: This field is required whenever a 006 field for electronic resource is included in a record. Code "c" for subfield $a specifies this item as computer file. Code "r" for subfield $b identifies a remote access file. Code "a" for subfield $d indicates the text is one color. Code "n" for subfield $e indicates no dimension information is applicable and code "u" for subfield $f indicates it is unknown whether the item has sound.

- 022: When the ISSN is available, it is recorded in the 022 field. The first indicator specifies whether the work is of international interest. OCLC documentation states that "blank" should be used "by all institutions other than the National Serials Data Program (NSDP) and ISSN Canada when recording the ISSN from an issue or from a bibliography."

- 245: The title proper is transcribed as found, except for capitalization, and is followed immediately by the general material designation in subfield $h. Other title information follows in subfield $b.

- 246s: Added entries are provided for variant titles to increase access to this serial.

- 260: The place of publication and publisher appears at the end of each issue. Since the first issue is the basis for the record, the beginning date is recorded in subfield $c.

- 310: Frequency information is found on the item and recorded in 310. The information is coordinated with the Freq element in the fixed field, using "blank" value for irregular frequency.

- 362: Since the first issue is available, it is used as the basis for the description and the numbering information is recorded in the 362 field as a formatted note (with indicator value "0").

- 500s: The title of source note is required of all electronic resources, viewing date is included. The note on the latest issue consulted is presented as a separate per *LCRI* 12.7B23.

- 516: Issues are available in HTML format and PDF format, so a note is provided to assist users.

- 538: A system requirements note specifies the need of a special program to read the PDF files.

- 538: All remote access electronic serials should have a 538, model of access note, to indicate the access method.

- 6xx: Because the serial reports on cataloging activities throughout the Library of Congress, it is appropriate to use the Cataloging Directorate as the subject access point in addition to other appropriate subject headings.

- 856s: The URL takes users to the *LCCN* home page to access current and back issues. Another 856 field is provided because the journal can also be accessed by e-mail subscription. The subscription information can be presented in a number of ways because the 856 field has many subfields. The method given in the record provides the host address and instructions for subscription. Another option is to produce a public note, using subfield $z as follows:

856	0	$u mailto: listserv@loc.gov $z send the following message to this address to subscribe: subscribe lccn [firstname lastname]

Figure 7.9. *School library media research*

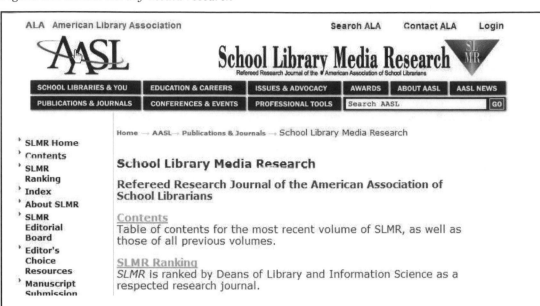

School Library Media Research
Refereed Research Journal of the ♦ American Association of School Librarians

SCHOOL LIBRARIES & YOU | EDUCATION & CAREERS | ISSUES & ADVOCACY | AWARDS | ABOUT AASL | AASL NEWS

PUBLICATIONS & JOURNALS | CONFERENCES & EVENTS | PROFESSIONAL TOOLS | Search AASL | GO

Home → AASL → Publications & Journals → School Library Media Research

- SLMR Home
- Contents
- SLMR Ranking
- Index
- About SLMR
- SLMR Editorial Board
- Editor's Choice Resources
- Manuscript Submission

School Library Media Research

Refereed Research Journal of the American Association of School Librarians

Contents
Table of contents for the most recent volume of SLMR, as well as those of all previous volumes.

SLMR Ranking
SLMR is ranked by Deans of Library and Information Science as a respected research journal.

About SLMR

School Library Media Research (ISSN: 1523-4320) is an official journal of the American Association of School Librarians. It is the successor to *School Library Media Quarterly Online*. The purpose of **School Library Media Research** is to promote and publish high quality original research concerning the management, implementation, and evaluation of school library media programs. The journal will also emphasize research on instructional theory, teaching methods, and critical issues relevant to school library media.

Daniel Callison, Editor
Professor and Executive Associate Dean
School of Library and Information Science
Indiana University, Indianapolis

Type	a	ELvl	I	Srce	d	GPub		Ctrl		Lang	eng
BLvl	s	Form	s	Conf	0	Freq	a	MRec		Ctry	ilu
S/L	0	Orig	s	EntW		Regl	r	ISSN	1	Alph	a
Desc	a	SrTp	p	Cont		DtSt	c	Dates	1999, 9999		

006		m d
007		c $b r $d a $e n $f u
022		1523-4320
043		n-us—
090		Z675 .S3
092	0	027.8 $2 22

245	00	School library media research $h [electronic resource] : $b SLMR : refereed Research Journal of the American Association of School Librarians.
246	30	SLMR
260		Chicago, Ill.: $b American Association of School Librarians, $c 1999-
310		Annual
362	0	Vol. 2 (1999)-
500		Title from journal home page (viewed Jan. 4, 2004).
515		Articles are added continuously as they are approved for publication and compiled on an annual basis.
538		Mode of access: World Wide Web.
650	0	School libraries $z United States $v Periodicals.
650	0	Instructional materials centers $z United States $v Periodicals.
710	2	American Association of School Librarians.
780	00	$t School library media quarterly online $x 1098-738X $w (DLC)sn 98004325 $w (OCoLC)38490845
856	40	$u http://www.ala.org/aasl/SLMR

Discussion for Figure 7.9

- Fixed field: Type of record is coded "a" for textual material, so the serial 008 fixed field is used. BLvl is coded "s" for serial. Form is "s" for electronic form intended for computer manipulation. Freq (frequency of publication) is coded "a" for an annual publication. Ctry (country of publication) is coded "ilu" for Illinois. S/L (entry convention) is "0" for successive entry. Orig (form of original item) is coded "s" for a form intended for machine manipulation. Regl (regularity) is "r" for regular, Desc is "a" for a record created according to *AACR2*, SrTp (type of continuing resource) is "p" for periodical. DtSt (date type) is "c" for current and Date 1 is 1999 when the journal became available online, and Date 2 is 9999 for a publication that will continue indefinitely.

- Electronic resource 006: This field is required to bring out the electronic aspect of an electronic serial. Code "m" indicates a computer file, code "d" stands for document. The 006 field has no subfields and specific positions are reserved for coding the resource type, audience information, file type, and type of government publication.

- Electronic resource 007: This field is required whenever a 006 field for electronic resource is included in a record. Code "c" for subfield $a specifies this item as computer file. Code "r" for subfield $b identifies a remote access file. Code "a" for subfield $d indicates the text is one color. Code "n" for subfield $e indicates no dimension information is applicable, and code "u" for subfield $f indicates it is unknown whether the item has sound.

- 022: The ISSN of the electronic journal is entered in the 022 field. The first indicator specifies whether the work is of international interest. OCLC documentation states that "blank" should be used "by all institutions other than the National Serials Data Program (NSDP) and ISSN Canada when recording the ISSN from an issue or from a bibliography."

- 043: The subject headings contain a geographic term, so a 043 field is used to aid subject access. The code is from *MARC Code List of Geographic Areas* (http://www.loc.gov/marc/geoareas/).

- 245: The title proper is transcribed as found, except for capitalization, and is followed immediately by the general material designation in subfield $h. The acronym is recorded in subfield $b, and the second piece of other title information is recorded after the colon because subfield $b cannot be repeated in the 245 field.

- 246: A variant title added entry is provided for the acronym to increase access.

- 260: The place of publication and publisher are on the Web site. Since the first issue is available, subfield $c is used.

- 310: Frequency information is indicated on the journal Web site. It is recorded in the 310 field and coordinated with the Freq element in the fixed field as value "a".

- 362: The Web site shows that vol. 1 was published under the earlier title and the new title began with vol. 2, so vol. 2 is recorded in the 362 field. This information is recorded in the 362 field, with the first indicator coded "0".

- 500: The source of the title is recorded with viewing date in parentheses.

- 538: All remote access electronic serials need to have a mode of access note.

- 650s: Subject headings are assigned to reflect the contents of this journal, with "Periodicals" used as the form subdivision.

- 710: The publisher is traced.

- 780: This field links this title to its predecessor. The title is entered in subfield $t, ISSN in subfield $x, and LC record number and OCLC record number are entered in separate subfield $w. The indicators will generate a display constant "Continues:"

- 856s: The 856 field points to the resource that is the same as the item represented by the bibliographic record, so the second indicator is "0". The first indicator is "4" for an item accessed via http.

Figure 7.10. *Libres*

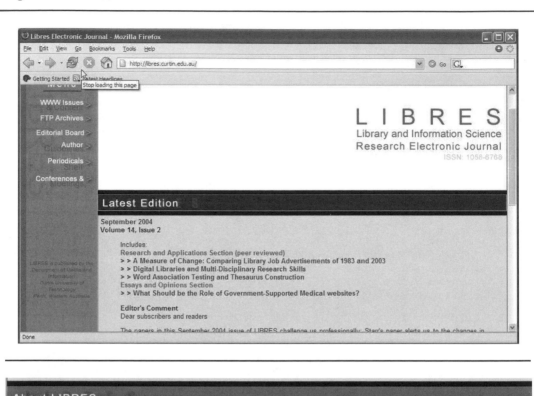

Type a	ELvl I	Srce d	GPub		Ctrl		Lang ent
BLvl s	Form s	Conf 0	Freq f		MRec		Ctry at
S/L 0	Orig s	EntW	Regl r		ISSN 1		Alph a
Desc a	SrTp p	Cont	DtSt c		Dates 1991, 9999		

```
006      m  d  s
007      c $b r $d m $e n $f u
```

```
022            1058-6768
090            Z671 $b.L532
092    0       025 $2 22
245    00      Libres $h [electronic resource] : $b library and information science
               research electronic journal.
246    3       Library and information science research electronic journal
260            Perth, Western Australia : $b Dept. of Media and Information, Curtin
               University of Technology.
310            Semiannual, $b March 1998-
321            Quarterly, $b 1996
362    1       Began in 1990.
500            Description based on: Vol 6, issue ½ (June 1996); title from table of
               contents screen (viewed Oct. 20, 2004)
500            Latest issue consulted: Vol. 14, issue 2 (Sept. 2004) (viewed Oct. 20,
               2004)
510    0       ISA, LISA and Singapore periodicals Index (SPI)
538            Mode of access: Electronic mail, FTP, and World Wide Web.
650    0       Library science $x Research $v Periodicals.
650    0       Library science $v Periodicals.
650    0       Information science $x Research $v Periodicals.
650    0       Information science $v Periodicals.
710    2       Curtin University of Technology. $b Dept. of Media and Information.
856    40      $u http://libres.curtin.edu.au/
856    1       $u ftp://ftp.curtin.edu/au/pub/libres/
856    0       $u mail to: listproc@info.curtin.edu.au $z To subscribe to LIBRES send
               an email message to this address with the text: subscribe libres [your
               first name] [your last name] Listserver subscribers are notified of
               new issues through the distribution of a table of contents to LIBRES,
               LIBREF-L, and any other e-conferences requesting the service.
```

Discussion for Figure 7.10

- Fixed field: Type of record is coded "a" for textual material, so the serial 008 fixed field is used. BLvl is coded "s" for serial. Form is "s" for electronic form intended for computer manipulation. Freq (frequency of publication) is coded "f" for works published semiannually. Ctry (country of publication) is coded "at" for Australia. S/L (entry convention) is "0" for successive entry. Orig (form of original item) is coded "s" for a form intended for machine manipulation. Regl (regularity) is "r" for regular, Desc is "a" for a record created according to *AACR2*, SrTp (type of continuing resource) is "p" for periodical. DtSt (date type) is "c" for current and Date 1 is 1991 when the journal became available online, and Date 2 is 9999 for a publication that will continue indefinitely.

- Electronic resource 006: This field is required to bring out the electronic aspect of an electronic serial. Code "m" indicates a computer file, code "d" stands for document. The 006 field has no subfields and specific positions are reserved for coding the resource type, audience information, file type, and type of government publication.

- Electronic resource 007: This field is required whenever a 006 field for electronic resource is included in a record. Code "c" for subfield $a specifies this item as computer file. Code "r" for subfield $b identifies a remote access file. Code "m" for subfield $d indicates mixtures of text and images in black and white and in color. Code "n" for subfield $e indicates no dimension information is applicable, and code "u" for subfield $f indicates it is unknown whether the item has sound.

- 022: When the ISSN is available, it is recorded in the 022 field. The first indicator specifies whether the work is of international interest. OCLC documentation states that "blank" should be used "by all institutions other than the National Serials Data Program (NSDP) and ISSN Canada when recording the ISSN from an issue or from a bibliography."

- 245: The title proper is transcribed as found, except for capitalization, and is followed immediately by the general material designation in subfield $h. Other title information is recorded in subfield $b. Title is the main entry.

- 246: A variant title added entry is provided to increase access.

- 260: The place of publication and publisher are on the Web site. Since the first issue is not available, subfield $c is not used.

- 310 and 321: Frequency information is found in the publication, recorded in the 310 field and coordinated with the Freq element in the fixed field as value "f". Earlier frequency and the period covered are recorded in a 321 field.

- 362: The first issue is not available but the beginning year of publication can be inferred from back issues, so the information is given as an unformatted note, using the 362 field, with an indicator value "1" for the first indicator.

- 500s: When the first issue is not the basis for the description, a "description based on" note is required. The first 500 field combines the DBO note and the source of title note, with the last viewing date in parentheses. A separate 500 field is used for the latest issue consulted note, according to *LCRI* 12.7B23.

- 510: An optional 91 note is provided for sources that index this journal. Indicator value "0" will generate a display constant "Indexed by:" to precede these sources.

- 538: The journal can be accessed in a number of ways. They are recorded in the 538 field as modes of access. Detailed access information is given in the 856 fields.

- 650s: Subject headings are assigned to reflect the contents of this journal, with "Periodicals" used as the form subdivision.

- 710: The publisher is traced.

- 856s: The first 856 field presents the URL for the item being cataloged. The second 856 records information for FTP. The third one records information for e-mail access. Subfield $z is used to generate a public note. It contains instructions for subscription and how subscribers will be notified of new issues. The 856 field has many subfields, and details on e-mail subscription can be recorded in various subfields. The example below illustrates this approach, but the 856 field in the record above is just as effective and perhaps less confusing to users.

856	0	$z To subscribe to Libres, send the information to: $u mailto:info.curtin.edu.au $f libres $h listproc $i subscribe

Figure 7.11. *Opera quarterly* (online) (two approaches)

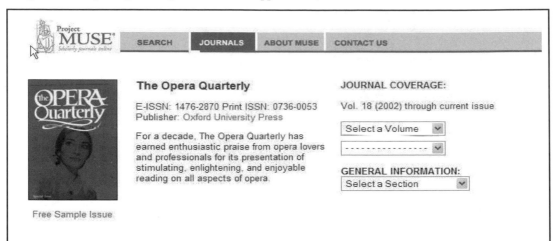

The Opera Quarterly 18.1, Winter 2002

Contents

- Quarter Notes
- Quarterly Quiz: More Singer Anecdotes
- Books Received
- Recordings Received
- Correspondence
- Erratum
- Contributors to This Issue
- Answers to Quarterly Quiz

Articles

Affleck, Edward Lloyd.
- *Forsaken Phantoms of the Opera*
  [Access article in HTML] [Access article in PDF]
  Subjects:
  ◇ Affleck, Edward Lloyd -- Knowledge -- Opera.
  ◇ Opera.

(Separate record approach, a new record is created for the online version.)

Type	a	ELvl	I	Srce	d	GPub		Ctrl		Lang	eng
BLvl	s	Form	s	Conf	0	Freq	q	MRec		Ctry	ncu
S/L	0	Orig	s	EntW		Regl	x	ISSN	1	Alph	a
Desc	a	SrTp	p	Cont		DtSt	c	Dates	1983, 9999		

006		m d
007		c $b r $d m $e n $f u
022		1476-2870
090		ML1699
092	0	782.1 $2 22
130	0	Opera quarterly (Online)
245	14	The opera quarterly $h [electronic resource].
260		Chapel Hill, N.C.: $b University of North Carolina Press
310		Quarterly
362	1	Print began with vol. 1, no. 1 (spring 1983).
500		Description based on: Vol. 18, no. 1 (winter 2002); title from table of contents screen (viewed Oct. 10, 2004).
506		Access restricted to subscribing institutions.
516	8	Issues in HTML and PDF file formats.
530		Also available in print.
538		System requirements: Adobe Acrobat Reader.
538		Mode of access: World Wide Web.
550		Published by: Chapel Hill, N.C.: Oxford University Press, 2001-Digitized and made available by Project Muse, 2002-
650	0	Opera $v Periodicals.
776	1	$t Opera quarterly $x 0736–0053 $w (DLC) 83644370 $w (OCoLC) 9068655
856	40	$u http://muse.jhu.edu/journals/opq/

Discussion for Figure 7.11
(Separate Record Approach)

- Fixed field: Type of record is coded "a" for textual material, so the serial 008 fixed field is used. BLvl is coded "s" for serial. Form is "s" for electronic form intended for computer manipulation. Freq (frequency of publication) is coded "q" for a work published quarterly. Ctry (country of publication) is coded "ncu" for North Carolina. S/L (entry convention) is "0" for successive entry. Orig (form of original item) is coded "s" for a form intended for machine manipulation. Rcgl (regularity) is "r" for regular, Desc is "a" for a record created according to *AACR2*, SrTp (type of continuing resource) is "p" for periodical. DtSt (date type) is "c" for current and Date 1 is 1983, taken from the date entered in the 362 field, and Date 2 is 9999 for a publication that will continue indefinitely.

- Electronic resource 006: This field is required to bring out the electronic aspect of an electronic serial. Code "m" indicates a computer file, code "d" stands for document. The 006 field has no subfields and specific positions are reserved for coding the resource type, audience information, file type, and type of government publication.

- Electronic resource 007: This field is required whenever a 006 field for electronic resource is included in a record. Code "c" for subfield $a specifies this item as computer file. Code "r" for subfield $b identifies a remote access file. Code "m" for subfield $d indicates mixture of text and images in black and white and in color. Code "n" for subfield $e indicates no dimension information is applicable and code "u" for subfield $f indicates it is unknown whether the item has sound.

- 022: When the ISSN is available, it is recorded in the 022 field. The first indicator specifies whether the work is of international interest. OCLC documentation states that "blank" should be used "by all institutions other than the National Serials Data Program (NSDP) and ISSN Canada when recording the ISSN from an issue or from a bibliography."

- 245: The title proper is transcribed as found, except for capitalization, and is followed immediately by the general material designation in subfield $h.

- 260: The place of publication is found from the print journal. Since the first issue is not available, subfield $c is not used.

- 310: The journal title indicates the publishing frequency of this title. Frequency information is recorded in the 310 field and coordinated with the Freq element in the fixed field as value "q."

- 362: The first issue is not available but the beginning year of the print version is found from the print publications, so the information is given as an unformatted note, using the 362 field, with an indicator value "1" for the first indicator.

- 500: When the first issue is not the basis for the description, a "description based on" note is required. The first 500 field combines the DBO note and the source of title note, with the last viewing date in parentheses.

- 506: Access restrictions are typically recorded in the 506 field, even though CONSER encourages catalogers to use the 856 field to record restrictions that are specific to institutions.

- 516: The file formats of the publication are presented in a 516 note, using an indicator value "8" to make sure no display constant is generated.

- 530: The journal continues to be available in print, so a note is provided to alert users of the existence of the print version.

- 538s: The first 538 is a system requirements note indicating the need for a special software for users to view the PDF file. The second 538 is a "mode of access" note that is required of all remote access electronic serials. Detailed access information is given in the 856 fields.

- 550: Corporate bodies involved in the previous and current issuing of the journal are recorded in 550. The first part of the note records a change in publisher and the year of the change, while the second part notes the role of Project Muse. But no added entry will be provided for Project Muse.

- 650: A subject heading is assigned to reflect the contents of this journal, with "Periodicals" used as the form subdivision.

- 776: While 530 provides a natural language note about the availability of the same work in another format, the 776 field links this record to the record for the print version, with title entered in subfield $t, ISSN in subfield $x, and LC and OCLC record numbers in separate subfields $w.

- 856s: The journal is available at two locations, so two separate 856 fields are used. The first indicator "4" specifies the access method is HTTP, and the second indicator "0" means the URL points to a resource that is the same as the one being represented by the bibliographic record.

Figure 7.11 (Single Record Approach)

Type	a	ELvl	I	Srce	d	GPub		Ctrl		Lang	eng
BLvl	s	Form		Conf	0	Freq	q	MRec		Ctry	ncu
S/L	0	Orig		EntW		Regl	r	ISSN	1	Alph	a
Desc	a	SrTp	p	Cont		DtSt	c	Dates	1983, 9999		

007		**c $b r $d m $e n $f u**
022		0736-0053
090		ML1699 $b .O65
092	0	782.1/05 $2 22
245	04	The opera quarterly.
260		Chapel Hill, N.C. : $b University of North Carolina Press, $c c1983-
300		v. ; $c 26 cm.
310		Quarterly
362	0	Vol. 1, no. 1 (spring 1983)-
500		Latest issue consulted: Vol. 17, no. 2 (spring 2001)
530		**Available also to subscribers online via the World Wide Web.**
550		Published by: Chapel Hill, N.C. : Oxford University Press, 2001-
650	0	Opera $v Periodicals.
776	**1**	**$t Opera quarterly (Online) $x 1476-2870 $w (OCoLC) 49558159**
856	**41**	**$u http://muse.jhu.edu/journals/opq/ $z access restricted to subscribing institutions.**

Discussion for Figure 7.11 (Single Record Approach)

- In a single record approach, we add information about a new format to an existing record for the original format of the work. A common practice is to add information about an online version to the record for the print journal. The record above shows that this approach is less time consuming because there are relatively fewer fields to add to the record.

- Fixed field: Nothing in the fixed field is changed. Form remains "blank" and Orig (form of original item) also remains "blank".

- Electronic resource 006: No electronic resource 006 field is added to the record for the print journal.

- Electronic resource 007: This field is optional. Code "c" for subfield $a specifies this item as computer file. Code "r" for subfield $b identifies a remote access file. Code "m" for subfield $d indicates mixtures of text and images in black and white and in color. Code "n" for subfield $e indicates no dimension information is applicable and code "u" for subfield $f indicates it is unknown whether the item has sound.

- 022: The ISSN of the print journal is recorded here, and the ISSN of the online version is not added to this record.

- 245: The title proper remains the same and no subfield $h general material designation is added.

- 260, 310, 362, and 500s: These fields remain the same.

- 516: No file format information is added to the original record.

- 530: A 530 field indicates the journal is available online.

- 538: No system requirements or mode of access notes are added to the record.

- 550: Information on publisher change is recorded as before. But no information about Project Muse is provided.

- 776: While 530 provides a natural language note about the availability of the same work in another format, the 776 field links this record to the record for the online version, with title entered in subfield $t, ISSN in subfield $x, and OCLC record number in subfield $w.

- 856: The 856 field is needed to enable users to access the online version quickly from the record for the print version. The first indicator "4" specifies the access method is HTTP, and the second indicator "1" clarifies that the URL points to a resource that is *not* the same as the one (the print journal) being represented by the bibliographic record. Access restrictions are not recorded in a 506 field. Instead, it is presented in subfield $z to generate a public note for the 856 field.

References

Cargille, Karen, Schaffner, Ann, Shadle, Steve, and Davis, Carroll. (1998). Lost in Cyberspace? Issues in subject access to electronic journals. *Serials Review* 24 (2): 101–109.

Case, Mary M. (2004, July). A snapshot in time: ARL libraries and electronic journal resources. *ARL Bimonthly Report,* 235. http://www.arl.org/newsltr/235/snap shot.html (accessed June 1, 2005).

CONSER. 2004. *CONSER cataloging manual module 31: Remote access electronic serials (online serials).* http://www.loc.gov/acq/conser/Module31.pdf (accessed June 1, 2005).

Copeland, Ann. (2002). E-serials cataloging in the 1990s: A review of the literature. *The Serials Librarian* 41 (3–4): 7–29.

Digital Library Federation. (2004). *Electronic resource management: The report of the DLF initiative.* http://www.diglib.org/pubs/dlfermi0408/dlfermi0408.htm (accessed June 1, 2005).

"Directory of Scholarly Electronic Journals and Academic Discussion Lists." (2000). (1st ed.). Washington, D.C.: Association for Research Libraries. http://db.arl .org/dsej/index.html (accessed June 1, 2005).

FAQ on the Aggregator-Neutral Record Web site. (2003). http://www.loc.gov/acq/ conser/agg-neut-faq.html (accessed June 1, 2005).

Ford, Charlotte E., and Harter, Stephen P. (1998). The downside of scholarly electronic publishing: Problems in accessing electronic journals through online directories and catalogs. *College and Research Libraries* 59 (4): 335–346.

French, Patricia. (1998). Cataloging electronic serials. *The Serials Librarian* 34 (3–4): 385–389.

Hill, Janet Swan. (1996). The elephant in the catalog: Cataloging animals you can't see or touch. *Cataloging & Classification Quarterly* 23 (1): 5–25.

Hirons, Jean. (1997). One record or two? The online discussion and the CONSER interim approach. *Journal of Internet Cataloging* 1 (2): 3–14.

Hirons, Jean. (1999). *Revising AACR2 to accommodate seriality: Report to the Joint Steering Committee on the revision of AACR.* http://www.collectionscanada.ca/ jsc/docs/ser-rep.pdf (accessed June 1, 2005).

Hirons, Jean, and Graham, Crystal. (1997). Issues related to seriality. In Jean Weihs (Ed.), *The Principles and Future of AACR: Proceedings of the International Conference on the Principles and Future Development of AACR, Toronto, Ontario, Canada, October 23–25, 1997,* 180–212. Ottawa: Canadian Library Association. http://www.nlc-bnc.ca/jsc/r-serial.pdf (accessed June 1, 2005).

Hirons, Jean, and Reynolds, Regina. (1998). Proposal to adpot a modified model C. http://www.loc.gov/acq/conser/ModelC.html (accessed June 1, 2005).

Hoffmann, Luise, and Schmidt, Ronald M. (1999). The cataloging of electronic serials in the union catalog of the North Rhine-Westphalian library network. *The Serials Librarian* 35 (3): 123–129.

Hruska, Martha. (1995, Winter). Remote Internet serials in the OPAC? *Serials Review* 21: 68–70.

Hsieh-Yee, Ingrid. (2004, December 20). How libraries provide access to digital resources. Unpublished report.

Jones, Wayne. (1995, Winter). We need those e-serial records. *Serials Review* 21: 74–75.

Jul, Erik. (1996). Why catalog Internet resources? *Computers in Libraries* 16 (1): 8, 10.

Pace, Andrew. (2004). *Dis-integrated library systems and electronic resource management*. http://www.lib.ncsu.edu/presentations/2004ala/IRRT-pace.ppt

Reynolds, Regina. (1995, Winter). Inventory list or information gateway? The role of the catalog in the digital age. *Serial Review* 21: 75–77.

Sleeman, Allison Mook. (1995). Cataloging remote access electronic materials. *Serials Review* 21: 72–74.

Vizine-Goetz, Diane. (1994). Cataloging Internet resources. In *Proceedings of the Seminar on Cataloging Digital Documents, October 12–14, 1994, University of Virginia Library, Charlottesville and the Library of Congress.* http://lcweb.loc.gov/catdir/semdigdocs/goetz.html (accessed June 1, 2005).

Weitz, Jay. (2004). *Cataloging electronic resources: OCLC-MARC coding guidelines.* http://www.oclc.org/support/documentation/worldcat/cataloging/electronicre sources/ (accessed June 1, 2005).

Williams, Jim. (1997). Serials cataloging, 1991–1996: A review. *The Serials Librarian* 32 (1–2): 3–26.

Wilson, Mary Dabney. (2001). Flying first class or economy? Classification of electronic titles in ARL libraries. *Portal: Libraries and the Academy* 1 (3): 225–240.

Suggested Readings

Blosser, John, Hagan, Tim, and Wei Zhang, Yvonne. (2002). Web resources for cataloging electronic serials and continuing resources: An annotated bibliography. *The Serials Librarian* 41 (3–4): 111–126.

Copeland, Ann. (2002). E-Serials cataloging in the 1990s: A review of the literature. *The Serials Librarian* 41 (3–4): 7–29.

Fair, Norma J., and Shadle, Steven C. (2001). Cataloging electronic resources: The practicalities. In Pamela Bluh (Ed.), *Managing electronic serials: Essays based on the ALCTS electronic serials institutes,* 129–142. Chicago: American Library Association.

French, Patricia Sheldahl. (2002). Taming the aggregators: Providing access to journals in aggregator databases. *The Serials Librarian* 41 (3–4): 157–163.

Hirons, Jean, and Graham, Crystal. (1997). Issues related to seriality. In Jean Weihs (Ed.), *The Principles and Future of AACR: Proceedings of the International Conference on the Principles and Future Development of AACR, Toronto, Ontario, Canada, October 23–25, 1997,* 180–212. Ottawa: Canadian Library Association. http://www.nlc-bnc.ca/jsc/r-serial.pdf (accessed June 1, 2005).

Reynolds, Regina Romano. (2001). Seriality and the Web. In Pamela Bluh (Ed.), *Managing electronic serials: essays based on the ALCTS electronic serials institutes,* 1–17. Chicago: American Library Association.

Saxton, Elna L. (2001). Do we catalog these or not? How research libraries are providing bibliographic access to electronic journals. *The Serials Librarian* 40 (3–4): 355–360.

Wilson, Mary Dabney. (2001). Flying first class or economy? Classification of electronic titles in ARL libraries. *Portal: Libraries and the Academy* 1 (3): 225–240.

8

Organizing Information
in the Digital Age

Scholarly Communication

A large part of the information transfer cycle described in Chapter 2 continues to apply in the current information environment, but advanced technology has shortened the distance between the stages. For instance, creators of information previously had to go through an elaborate review and quality control process to publish their works. Now the time between creation and publication is shorter because electronic submission is commonplace, the review cycle is shorter (again due to electronic communication), and electronic editing and production are faster than before. In addition, peer-reviewed e-journals grew from seven titles in 1991 to 3,915 in 2000 (*Directory of Scholarly Electronic Journals* 2000) and researchers now have more channels for publications.

Moreover, Web technology affects the information creation stage because it enables people to communicate through new formal and informal channels. Creators can receive and exchange ideas through e-mail, chat rooms, newsgroups, and listservs, and thus benefit from online discussions as well as completed reports. They can also publish as much as they wish informally because anyone with a Web address is a potential author. Such a free flow of information and the new ease of publishing creates the rapid growth of information on the Web, but exacts a toll on receivers' time and energy. The quantity and the quality of Web information are such that information users find it difficult to search for relevant quality resources or to digest or manage received information.

Furthermore, technology has empowered creators by making it easier for them to communicate by means other than text. Books accompanied by CD-ROMs, sound recordings with "Enhanced CD," and Web sites enriched with sound, video, and images illustrate how creators and publishers have combined formats into new forms of intellectual expression. The emergence of multimedia-embedded electronic journals on the Internet suggests that scholarly communication has entered a new phase. Humanities scholars have recognized that information technology presents new opportunities for research in their fields and many have actively experimented with integrating sound, image, text, and other media into their work (Pavliscak, Ross, and Henry 1997). And the growth of electronic information centers and digital libraries is also likely to stimulate scholars' interest in combining multiple formats for research presentation (Seman 1997; Goldenberg-Hart 1998).

The implications of these changes for catalogers are twofold. First, the increasing volume of Web resources highlights the importance of the selection and evaluation of information. Assessing the accuracy, authority, objectivity, and currency of electronic resources, especially those on the Web, will continue to be challenging and time-consuming. But this filtering effort by information organizers will save users from fruitless searching on the Web and elsewhere, especially when the filtering is performed with a solid understanding of the needs of a user community. Evaluation criteria for print resources have been expanded to cover electronic resources (Smith 1997), and new techniques such as collaborative filtering can alert users of resources used by other users with similar interest (Collaborative Filtering 1996).

Second, the amount of information available and the multiple formats of publications will challenge catalogers to describe file formats adequately and efficiently. Catalogers will need some knowledge of file formats to determine if additional equipment or software is required to run a work that consists of several media. In addition, new ways to organize electronic resources need to be explored. It is also necessary to examine the information creation stage and information organization stage. The University of Virginia, for instance, has established a procedure to generate bibliographic records from information submitted by thesis authors (University of Virginia Library 2003).

Users and Information Environment

Since the 1990s interest in digital resources has grown among users and creators of information. Graphical interface has made the Internet more accessible to the general public, and many individuals, organizations, and libraries have created digital collections for access on the Internet. Users now have many browsers to choose from and can easily find electronic texts, digital audio files, digital video files, multimedia, and resources on various subjects on the Internet. OCLC's study on college students' information choices (2002), a Digital Library Federation study of the information behavior of faculty and students (Healy 2002), and a Pew Research study on college students' Internet use (Jones and Madden 2002) found a tendency among users to use the Internet to search for information. Seventy-three percent of college students in the Pew study, in fact, report they use the Internet more than the library to search for information. A data memo from the Pew Internet and American Life Project found most of the general public choose search engines such as Google as their starting point for searching for information, and many of them report satisfaction with the search results, even though the resources may not be of the best quality and the results are often accompanied by advertisements (Fallows, Rainie, and Mudd 2004).

Another Pew study on search engine use found that at least 80 percent of the users do not understand how search engines work and are not always successful in using these engines, and yet, users have a remarkable tolerance for irrelevant items in the search results and seem willing to make do with whatever they find (Fallows 2005). The study also found users use very simple search statements, making little use of advanced search features such as Boolean operator, and rely heavily on single keyword searches. These characteristics are consistent with a 2000 NPD study (Sullivan).

The popularity of Internet search engines, especially Google, and their power to bring relevant information resources to users should not be ignored. OCLC was wise to collaborate with Google, Yahoo, and others (2005a) to launch the Open WorldCat Project (2005b) so that users of these engines can tap into the rich resources in WorldCat and, through library holdings information, become aware of what their local libraries have to offer. The partnership has brought much visibility to libraries.

On a more ambitious scale, Google has embarked on the Google Print Project with Stanford University, Harvard University, University of Michigan, New York Public Library, and Oxford University to digitize their collections for access. Because of copyright constraints, only materials that are no longer under copyright protection will be freely accessible to users. As for materials that are still under copyright protection, Google plans to display snippets of retrieved items that contain the user's keywords and direct users to purchase those items from booksellers. So far there is no plan to link these search results to any library's holdings, though that remains a possibility. The Google digitization project is laudable in that Google absorbs the costs of digitization and indexing to help make older resources in these highly respected institutions accessible to the public. It is therefore understandable that some people perceive it as an attractive solution for future information organization and access. In a speech in 2005, Deanna Marcum, the associate librarian of the Library of Congress, for instance, cited this project to invite library professionals to consider the future of cataloging. Barbara Forester, on the other hand, questions the effectiveness of this approach (2005). A report in *American Libraries* shows that library leaders have diverse opinions on the benefits and implications of the project ("Google at the Gate" 2005). What many library professionals, and catalogers in particular, probably are most interested in is what will information organization be like in the future? Will cataloging have a role to play in the organization of information in the twenty-first century?

In a way the enthusiasm over the Google digitization project is similar to the early embrace for search engines when they first emerged in the mid-1990. Numerous people thought at the time that there would be no need to organize Internet resources because search engines would make indexing and searching easy. Crawlers or robots would harvest resources on the Internet, provide keyword searches, and everything would be easily retrieved. But soon the limitation of free-text searching of millions of Web resources became clear and many people involved in information organization and retrieval realized searching by keywords was searching by brute force, and the task would become more and more difficult as the number of resources to be searched against increased. While search engines could produce a large number of hits, the precision of search results always suffered because many items were false hits. As a result, search engine designers experimented with normalization of search terms (another way of describing vocabulary control), use of search fields, concept mapping, collaborative filtering (Wiley 1998), and citation indexing (see, for example, CiteSeer and Google Scholar) to improve the performance of their engines. Google's engine has emerged as the winner in the highly competitive search engine industry because of its PageRanking algorithms and other technologies (Google Technology 2005). When Google retrieves a number of hits it examines how each item has been referenced by other Web resources and assigns a weight to it to determine its place in the initial result display; the strength of the algorithms has enabled Google to produce fairly good search results. But materials for the Google Print project have not been referenced on the Web yet, so it remains to be seen whether the same retrieval technologies will work for this project.

Nevertheless, a good lesson librarians can learn from Google is its ability to give users what they want. Because users do not want complexity, Google provides a simple clear search box and gives users the most relevant items it can retrieve without telling them how complicated the algorithms are for producing the search results. Many library information professionals are concerned about Google's relevancy performance, but most users seem to have a "good enough" mentality. It would be interesting to see whether users will respond to Google Print the same way they have responded to the Google's general search engine, and whether their use of Google Print will lead to the actual purchase of items retrieved by this service.

An alternative to free-text searching is to organize resources by metadata, an approach often used by digital collection managers. JStor, for instance, provides access to back issues of important scholarly journals. It supports keyword searches of the full text of articles by using optical-character-recognition technology to digitize the articles. In addition, for each article it creates a metadata record that contains data elements such as author, title, subject, and source to improve the efficiency of searching and browsing (About JStor 2005). This small set of metadata elements serves JStor users well because most users come to JStor looking for known items.

Other digital collections, such as the ACM Digital Library and the EText Center of the University of Virginia, deliver full text to users but provide searching and browsing options through metadata sets such as author, title, subject, format, and so on that will enable users to search for known items and for items on subjects of interest. In addition to providing its own search engine for the collections, the EText Center coordinates with their cataloging staff to create bibliographic records for important items in the center, thus making it possible for users of their online catalog to discover the rich resources of the center.

These examples illustrate that how information is organized depends on the purposes of an information system. If a system is mainly a storage system and most of its users are likely to approach the system with some citation information, the approach used by JStor is appropriate. But if a system intends to help users who need materials on specific topics and users who have some citation information about an item, more data elements will be needed to serve these users well. Technology can certainly enhance searching and browsing, but information organizers still need to approach their task by carefully considering what data elements will be most useful to their users. Most online catalogs contain records created according to the *Anglo-American Cataloguing Rules (AACR)* and presented in MARC format. This is because the data elements recommended by *AACR* and encoded in MARC are considered valuable for describing information resources and providing search options for users. It is true that the dramatic increase of digital resources and the emergence of non-library-based metadata standards since the 1990s have caused some to question the wisdom of cataloging digital resources. The discussion tends to focus on whether to catalog or not to catalog, and what metadata schemas should replace cataloging. But the real issue is not cataloging vs. metadata, but the choice of the most appropriate metadata schemas for an information system, as the next section will illustrate.

Metadata

Metadata has been frequently defined as "data about data" (Weibel 1995). But the simplicity and beauty of this definition often eludes people who are new to this topic. A few more definitions may help:

- "Metadata is data which describes attributes of a resource. Typically, it supports a number of functions: location, discovery, documentation, evaluation, selection and others." (Dempsey and Heery 1998)

- "Metadata includes data associated with either an information system or an information object for purposes of description, administration, legal requirements, technical functionality, use and usage, and preservation." (Baca 2000)

- "'Metadata' is the Internet-age term for structured data about data." (EU-NSF Working Group 1999)

- "Metadata is structured information that describes, explains, locates, or otherwise makes it easier to retrieve, use or manage an information resource. Metadata is often called data about data or information about information." (NISO 2004)

These definitions confirm "metadata" is **structured data** that describe **attributes** of **information-bearing entities**. It can represent intrinsic data (data in an information object) and extrinsic data (data about that object) such as its history, usage, price, and system requirements (Borgman 2000). In a library setting, cataloging data is the best example of metadata because the functions of the catalog are to enable users to find, identify, select, and obtain desired information resources (IFLA Study Group 1998). But metadata can perform functions beyond description and resource discovery. Depending on the needs of users of an information system, these structured data can serve a number of functions, including description, resource discovery, administration and management of resources, technical specifications, information use management, preservation management, and others (Gilliland-Swetland 2000).

According to *Understanding Metadata* (2004), there are three major types of metadata:

- **Descriptive metadata** describes a resource for purposes such as discovery and identification. It can include elements such as title, abstract, author, and keywords.

- **Structural metadata** indicates how compound objects are put together, for example, how pages are ordered to form chapters.

- **Administrative metadata** provides information to help manage a resource, such as when and how it was created, file type, and other technical information, and who can access it. There are several subsets of administrative data. Two that sometimes are listed as separate metadata types are

- rights management metadata, which deals with intellectual property rights, and
- preservation metadata, which contains information needed to archive and preserve a resource.

Different types of metadata serve different functions. The NISO document identifies the major functions of metadata as resource discovery, organization of electronic resources, support for interoperability, digital identification, and archiving and preservation of materials.

Metadata and Cataloging

Another way to understand metadata is to compare and contrast it with cataloging. The dramatic increase of digital resources since the 1990s has led to a strong interest in controlling these resources. Critics of cataloging often regard metadata as a simpler solution, and cataloging and metadata are set up as two opposite approaches to information organization when in reality that is far from the truth.

Descriptive metadata and cataloging data are similar in that both aim to describe information resources so that they can be identified, retrieved, and accessed. Many communities have designed metadata schemas for their own purposes. What is remarkable is that most of these schemas contain elements similar to cataloging data such as name, title, keyword, and date. And the metadata community often turns to the cataloging community for best practices in formulating and presenting content (such as how to handle title variations and how to enter author names) and in deciding what content values should be allowed (such as a particular controlled vocabulary and authority control). Some metadata schemas such as Dublin Core include few data elements, while others such as the FGDC (Federal Geographic Data Committee) Content Standard for Digital Geospatial Metadata can be quite elaborate. Many non-library-based metadata schemas focus on resource description and discovery just like *AACR2* and MARC. But they often include data elements that are unique and important to their user communities. Furthermore, cataloging has standards like *AACR2* that specifies three levels of description and the elements for each level. But implementers of metadata have to address the granularity issue—that is, how much detail should be included in the metadata records for them to be effective.

Metadata and cataloging are different in many ways. Most important of all, metadata encompasses several types of metadata that are designed to serve functions that are not directly related to cataloging data. For example, preservation metadata that specify how resources are to be archived, stored, and maintained for future use are not part of the domain of cataloging. A related difference is that different types of metadata can be provided for information objects during the life cycle of the object by different people, while cataloging data are usually provided after an information object is created, acquired, or identified. For example, descriptive metadata can be provided for a resource after it is incorporated into a system; rights management data can be added later by system administrators to keep track of usage; and when it becomes necessary, preservation metadata may be provided by a preservation specialist at a later stage of the object's life cycle. Different individuals with different background and interests in the object can and will provide different metadata. But cataloging data tend to be provided by catalogers at one point in time, except for occasional update or revision.

Another difference is that many metadata schemas, defined as "sets of metadata elements designed for a specific purpose" by NISO (2004, p. 2), are domain specific, while cataloging schemas are domain free. Various communities have developed metadata schemes for their purposes. Some are domain specific (e.g., Encoded Archival Description for archival finding aids) while others are intended for cross-domain applications (e.g., Dublin Core). Library-centered metadata schemes such as *AACR2* and MARC guide us to manage resources in various formats for users from many disciplines.

Cataloging data are still labor intensive to create, while metadata can be produced manually or by machine—OCLC Connexion, for example, will generate a preliminary record when an URL is submitted at the record creation mode. Similarly, DC-Dot, a Dublin Core metadata editor, will create a record for further edit. While cataloging data are typically stored in an information system for manipulation and are separated from the information objects they represent, metadata can be embedded with an information object or stored in a separate system for access and management purposes. Figure 8.1 shows the metadata embedded in the home page of the National Endowment for the Arts. And Figure 8.2 presents a Dublin Core record generated by DC-Dot for the same Web page.

In terms of encoding system, MARC 21 provides syntax rules for encoding cataloging data elements and their content, and the strong association between the *Anglo-American Cataloguing Rules* and MARC 21 has made it more challenging for cataloging data to be encoded in other syntax. The Network Development and MARC Standards Office at the Library of Congress has provided three XML schemas so far—MARCXML, MODS (Metadata Object Description Schema), and MADS (Metadata Authority Description Schema)—to facilitate the manipulation and management of cataloging data in the XML environment. Metadata, on the other hand, can be encoded in any syntax and most of them use XML.

Cataloging standards and practices are well established and guidelines are available for anyone interested in cataloging their collection. Applications of metadata schemas, however, are usually project specific, and project managers usually need to develop implementation guidelines specific to the project. For instance, the Colorado Digitization Program uses Dublin Core and the project team has to develop its own metadata element set and guidelines for usage for its collections (2005).

Figure 8.1. Embedded metadata in a home page

```
<!DOCTYPE html PUBLIC "-//W3C//DTD HTML 4.0 Transitional//EN"
"http://www.w3.org/TR/REC-html40/loose.dtd">
<html lang="en">
<head>
<title>National Endowment for the Arts</title>
<meta name="description" content="
National Endowment for the Arts">
<meta name="keywords" content="
arts funding, deadlines, organizations, federal funding, arts
education, dance, design, music, musical theater, theater, presenting,
opera, media, film, television, radio, new media, performance,
exhibition, publications, fiction, poetry, magazines, books, community,
youth, youth-at-risk, partnerships">
<meta http-equiv="Content-Type" content="text/html; charset=iso-8859-
1">
```

Figure 8.2. Dublin Core record by DC-Dot

Dublin Core metadata editor

Results for **URL**: http://www.nea.gov/ [summary]

```
<link rel="schema.DC" href="http://purl.org/dc/elements/1.1/" />
<link rel="schema.DCTERMS" href="http://purl.org/dc/terms/" />
<meta name="DC.title" content="National Endowment for the Arts" />
<meta name="DC.subject" content="arts funding; deadlines;
organizations; federal funding; arts education; dance; design; music;
musical theater; theater; presenting; opera; media; film; television;
radio; new media; performance; exhibition; publications; fiction;
poetry; magazines; books; community; youth; youth-at-risk;
partnerships" />
<meta name="DC.description" content="National Endowment for the Arts"
/>
<meta name="DC.date" scheme="DCTERMS.W3CDTF" content="2005-06-02" />
<meta name="DC.type" scheme="DCTERMS.DCMIType" content="Text" />
<meta name="DC.format" content="text/html" />
<meta name="DC.format" content="20367 bytes" />
<meta name="DC.identifier" scheme="DCTERMS.URI"
content="http://www.nea.gov/" />
```

Finally, the cataloging community has a stable infrastructure for record creation and sharing, but the metadata community has to deal with the interoperability issue because there are so many metadata schemas in operation and new ones continue to be developed. Interoperability is "the ability of multiple systems with different hardware and software platforms, data structures, and interfaces to exchange data with minimal loss of content and functionality" (NISO 2004, p. 2). Two common approaches to achieve interoperability are cross-system search using Z39.50 and metadata harvesting such as the Open Archives Initiatives (OAI) (2002).

> Z39.50 implementers do not share metadata but map their own search capabilities to a common set of search attributes. A contrasting approach...is for all data providers to translate their native metadata to a common core set of elements and explore this for harvesting. A search service provider then gathers the metadata into a consistent central index to allow cross-repository searching regardless of the metadata formats used by participating repositories. (NISO 2004, p. 2)

OAI participants map their metadata to Dublin Core for harvesting. Citeseer, for example, has provided its citation data to OAI, and Google has taken advantage of the metadata harvested from major libraries such as the Australian National Library (*OAI News* 2005).

It is worth noting that Google understands the value of metadata and has harvested metadata from organizations such as libraries and OCLC WorldCat to enrich its databases and enhance retrieval. The comparison above illustrates that cataloging data is similar to descriptive metadata. If the purpose of an information system or service is to facilitate searching and access, then some sort of "cataloging" (broadly defined as a way to describe attributes of resources for discovery and access purposes) will be necessary. Cataloging data is a type of descriptive metadata. As far as descriptive metadata is concerned, what distinguishes cataloging practice from providing non-library-based metadata is the choice of metadata schemas. The cataloging approach makes use of standards such as *AACR* and MARC, while the metadata approach involves the use of metadata schemas that are not library based. While some metadata schemas such as Dublin Core may seem easy to understand and use, project managers will need to address issues such as granularity, interoperability, consistency in record creation, and sharing of metadata records.

Selected Metadata Schemas

Metadata schemas have been developed for text, sound, video, geospatial data, visual objects, multimedia, and other resources. They are usually readable by humans and machines. Some are media-specific, many are domain specific, and more domain-specific metadata schemas are likely to be developed as more users take part in the networked information environment (Vellucci 1998). Many publications describe metadata schemas and their applications in depth (Caplan 2003; Eden 2002; Hillmann and Westbrooks 2004; Hudgins, Agnew, and Brown 1999; Milstead and Feldman 1999), and most schemas have their own Web sites or documentation to assist users. To give readers an idea of schemas used more often in library settings, a few schemas are introduced below. The Network Development and MARC Standards Office of the Library of Congress has mapped MODS, Dublin Core, and ONIX to MARC 21 and provided crosswalks with other schemas (see http://www.loc.gov/marc/marcdocz.html).

MARC 21 Formats

MARC (http://www.loc.gov/marc) standards are "**MA**chine-**R**eadable **C**ataloging" standards designed to support the exchange, use, and interpretation of bibliographic and related data between systems. Five formats are defined for bibliographic, holdings, authority, classification, and community information. Developed in the 1960s, MARC became USMARC in the 1980s, and harmonized with CAN/MARC to become MARC 21 in 1997. MARC data elements are the foundation of many online library catalogs. The Library of Congress Network Development and MARC Standards Office offers MARCXML for anyone interested in encoding MARC 21 data elements in XML. Documentation and examples are available at the MARC 21 XML Schema site (http://www.loc.gov/standards/marcxml///).

MODS (Metadata Object Description Schema)

MODS (http://www.loc.gov/standards/mods/) is another XML schema developed by the Library of Congress Network Development and MARC Standards Office to contain a subset of MARC fields and support original resource description. Unlike MARC, MODS uses language tags. In addition to the schema, documentation, and tools, the site includes sample records for book, article, serial, movie, sound recording, and other materials. Figure 8.3 presents a portion of a MODS record for book taken from the MODS

Figure 8.3. Part of a MODS record

```
    <mods version="3.0" xsi:schemaLocation="http://www.loc.gov/mods/v3
http://www.loc.gov/standards/mods/v3/mods-3-0.xsd">
    <titleInfo>
<title>Sound and fury :</title>
<subTitle>the making of the punditocracy /</subTitle>
</titleInfo>
<name type="personal">
    <namePart>Alterman, Eric</namePart>
    <role>
    <roleTerm type="text">creator</roleTerm>
    </role>
</name>
<typeOfResource>text</typeOfResource>
<genre authority="marc">bibliography</genre>
    <originInfo>
    <place>
<placeTerm authority="marccountry" type="code">nyu</placeTerm>
</place>
<place>
<placeTerm type="text">Ithaca, N.Y.</placeTerm>
</place>
<publisher>Cornell University Press</publisher>
<dateIssued>c1999</dateIssued>
<dateIssued encoding="marc">1999</dateIssued>
<issuance>monographic</issuance>
</originInfo>
```

Web site. MODS is highly compatible with MARC 21 and provides more structured data than Dublin Core. For that reason it may be more appealing to information organizers who wish to provide more data for resource description.

Dublin Core

Dublin Core (http://dublincore.org/) is a standard for cross-domain information resource description. It became the NISO Standard 39.85 in 2001 and the ISO Standard 15836 in 2003. Dublin Core Metadata Element Set (http://dublincore.org/documents/dces/) contains definitions of fifteen elements. Elements for describing the content of a resource include Coverage, Type, Resource, Source, Subject, and Title. Elements indicating the intellectual property of a resource include Contributor, Creator, Publisher, and Rights. Elements for instantiation include Date, Format, Identifier, and Language. Each element is optional and repeatable. DCMI Metadata Terms (http://dublincore.org/documents/dcmi-terms/) provides up-to-date specification of all metadata terms used in Dublin Core, including elements, element refinements, encoding schemes, and vocabulary terms (the DCMI Type Vocabulary). "Using Dublin Core" (http://dublincore.org/documents/usageguide/) by Diane Hillmann is a useful guide to Dublin Core.

Several Dublin Core record creation tools are available, including Connexion, DC-Dot, DC-Template, and many others (see "Tools and Software" at http://dublincore.org/tools/). Connexion Dublin Core records can be converted to the MARC 21 format and vice versa. Figure 8.4 shows a Dublin Core record for the National Institute on Aging produced by Connexion. This record is in HTML. Figure 8.5 presents the same data in RDF; and Dublin Core elements and their corresponding MARC fields are presented in Figure 8.6. Note that the mapping between DC and MARC is not necessarily one-to-one. And if DC is extended, through qualifiers, to support

Figure 8.4. Dublin Core record from Connexion in HTML format

```
<meta name="DC.Title" content="NIA Home">
<meta name="DC.Format" scheme="IMT" content="text/html">
<meta name="DC.Description" content="NIA Home U.S. NATIONAL INSTITUTES
OF HEALTH LEADING THE FEDERAL EFFORT ON AGING RESEARCH Health
Information Research Information Grants Training News Events About NIA Health
Information Publications / en Español Alzheimer's Disease Information Clinical Trials
NIHSeniorHealth.gov Research Information NIA Sponsored Research Research
Conducted at NIA Grants and Training Scientific Resources Highlights Cognitive
Emotional Health Project A searchable database of research projects that include
information on">
<meta name="DC.Identifier" scheme="URI" content="http://www.nia.nih.gov/">
<meta name="DC.Language" scheme="ISO639-2" content="eng">
<meta name="DC.Type" scheme="OCLCg" content="Text data">
<meta name="DC.Type" scheme="AACR2-gmd" content="[electronic resource].">
```

Figure 8.5. Dublin Core record from Connexion in RDF format

```
<?xml version="1.0"?>
<rdf:RDF xmlns:rdf="http://www.w3.org/1999/02/22-rdf-syntax-ns#"
xmlns:dc="http://purl.org/dc/elements/1.0/"
xmlns:dcq="http://purl.org/dc/qualifiers/1.0/">
<rdf:Description about="http://www.nia.nih.gov/">
<dc:title>NIA Home</dc:title>
<dc:format>text/html</dc:format>
<dc:description>NIA Home U.S. NATIONAL INSTITUTES OF HEALTH LEADING
THE FEDERAL EFFORT ON AGING RESEARCH Health Information Research
Information Grants Training News Events About NIA Health Information Publications /
en Español Alzheimer's Disease Information Clinical Trials NIHSeniorHealth.gov
Research Information NIA Sponsored Research Research Conducted at NIA Grants
and Training Scientific Resources Highlights Cognitive Emotional Health Project A
searchable database of research projects that include information on</dc:description>
<dc:identifier>http://www.nia.nih.gov/</dc:identifier>
<dc:language>eng</dc:language>
<dc:type>Text data</dc:type>
<dc:type>[electronic resource].</dc:type>
</rdf:Description>
</rdf:RDF>
```

Figure 8.6. Dublin Core and MARC corresponding fields

Dublin Core Elements	MARC Fields
Creator	100, 110, 111; 245 $c
Title	130; 245 $a
Type	245 $h GMD
Title	246 $a
Source, Relation	250
Publisher	260 $b
Date	260 $c
Coverage	500
Description	505 (contents)
Rights	506 (use restrictions)
Format	516 (type of computer file)
Description	520 (summary)
Source, Relation	530 (other formats available)
Format	538 (system requirements; mode of access)
Language	546
Subject	6XX (subject headings)
Contributor	700, 710, 711
Title	730, 740
Source, relation	760–787 (linking entry fields)
Identifier	856 (electronic location and access)

more complex descriptions, the conversion will involve more MARC fields. The Nordic Metadata Project's "d2m: Dublin Core to MARC Converter" (http://www.bibsys.no/meta/d2m/) illustrates the process.

Text Encoding Initiative (TEI)

TEI (http://www.tei-c.org/) guidelines are developed to enable scholars, libraries, museums, and publishers to encode literary and linguistic texts for research, teaching, and preservation. The TEI header portion allows users to embed metadata about the work in the resource itself. The header identifies the object, documents its structure, and records rights information, intended usage, and so on. The header has four sections and only File description is mandatory. Figure 8.7 shows the header's structure. A description of how TEI header elements correspond to MARC fields is available at http://etext.lib.virginia.edu/standards/tei/teip3/tei-usmarc.html/.

Figure 8.7. TEI Header Structure

```
<teiHeader>
<fileDesc> ... </fileDesc>
<encodingDesc> ... </encodingDesc>
<profileDesc> ... </profileDesc>
<revisionDesc> ... </revisionDesc>
</teiHeader>
```

Encoded Archival Description (EAD) Document Type Definition (DTD)

EAD DTD (http://www.loc.gov/ead/) is a standard for encoding archival finding aids. It is written in XML. The standard is maintained by the Network Development and MARC Standards Office in partnership with the Society of American Archivists. The list of EAD sites on the Web includes descriptions of those sites and direct links to them (http://jefferson .village.virginia.edu/ead/sitesann.html).

ONIX for Books

The ONIX (http://www.editeur.org/onix.html) international standard enables publishers to share product and supplier information usable on the Internet. It is developed and maintained by EDItEUR, jointly with the Association of American Publishers, Book Industry Communication, and Book Industry Study Group. It also contains bibliographic data that can be used for resource description. The Network Development and MARC Standards Office has mapped ONIX elements to MARC 21 (see http:// www.loc.gov/marc/onix2marc.html).

For objects of art, Categories for the Description of Works of Art (CDWA) (http://www.getty.edu/research/institute/standards/cdwa/index) and VRA Core Categories version 3.0 (http://www.vraweb.org/vracore3.htm) are good examples. For more metadata schemes, see NISO's *Framework of Guidance for Building Good Digital Collections* (2004) (http://www.niso.org/ framework/framework2.html).

Metadata Schemas Selection and Implementation

A misperception about cataloging and metadata is that cataloging is for print materials and metadata is for digital resources. The truth is these approaches can be applied to resources in all formats. A critical decision for organizing information in the twenty-first century is to select metadata schemas that are appropriate for the purposes and users of an information system. In libraries and other settings, librarians, and catalogers in particular, are often involved in organizing information resources. To select and implement a metadata schema, the organizers will want to begin with the fundamental question: What are the purposes of the information system? More specifically, questions based on the principles of information organization should be addressed.

Purpose and Scope of the System

- Why is the information system created?
- Who are the primary users it intends to serve? What user tasks is the system designed to support?
- Why types of resources will the system contain? How similar are they? Do they come with metadata; and if so, can they be repurposed for the new system?

Answers to these questions will guide the organizers in selecting resources for the system, taking into account user needs, types of resources, intellectual level, language, and many other selection criteria. Then the organizers will address the granularity issue and identify the types of metadata needed, and use that information to select an appropriate metadata schema. The next step is to identify a data element set from the chosen schema and develop guidelines for usage for the system.

Description and Access

- What data elements will be needed to identify the resources adequately and distinguish them from one another?
- What types of collocation are important to the intended users, and what data elements will serve as collocation devices? What data elements will be needed to make these resources searchable and browsable?
- What data elements will enable users to evaluate and select the most appropriate resources for their needs?
- Will all access points be controlled?
- What data elements will support the management of the resources?
- What data elements will control access to the resources?
- What data elements will facilitate long-term access to the resources?
- What are the tradeoffs in providing free-text keyword searching? Will metadata records be needed?
- Who will provide metadata records? How will they be trained? And how will the quality of records be controlled?
- How will indexing be done?

After these tasks are done, the organizers will want to design interface to support users, take steps to ensure the quality of the system, address interoperability issues, and develop a plan to sustain the growth of the system.

Organization of Resources and Surrogates

- What will the search interface be like? What assistance will be provided to users to facilitate known-item searches and subject exploration?
- How will search results be displayed? Will users be able to customize the display? Will there be features for users to narrow or expand a search from a result display?
- How will search results be delivered to users?
- How will the digital objects be delivered to users?
- Will the system support cross-collection searches? How will that be done?
- Can data from the system be easily repurposed if necessary?
- How will the system grow?
- How will the system be maintained?

NISO's *Framework of Guidelines for Building Good Digital Collections* provides helpful explanations and examples for metadata selection and usage (2004); *Getting Miles out of Metadata* discusses the workflow of a metadata project (Hudgins, Agnew, and Brown, 1999); and "Western States Dublin Core Metadata Best Practices" offers a good model for developing guidelines for metadata implementation (2005).

Dublin Core and Cataloging

While many libraries catalog Web resources and even draw on portions of metadata to create bibliographic records, tension exists between people who use non-library-based metadata schemas like Dublin Core and catalogers who provide data by *AACR* and MARC. Many catalogers are concerned whether Dublin Core will replace cataloging and what other implications Dublin Core may have for the future of information organization. On more than one occasion Dublin Core advocates have mentioned the liberation from cataloging rules as a major benefit of having metadata (see, for example, the Nordic Metadata Project report at http://linnea.helsinki.fi/meta/nmfinal.htm). But opponents such as Michael Gorman have pointed out that simplicity is accomplished at the expense of detail and specificity (1999).

Furthermore, the CORC (Cooperative Online Resource Catalog) experience shows that guidelines are needed for the implementation of the Dublin Core standard. To ensure consistent implementation and sharing of metadata, issues such as the levels of description, the definition of chief source of information, and prescribed sources of information, the choice of access points, the semantics of the elements (such as how to record a name or a publication date), interoperability, and many other issues must be addressed. Gorman proposes to control electronic resources by creating records of varying details depending on the importance of resources (1999). His four levels of treatment—full cataloging records, enriched Dublin Core records, minimal Dublin Core records, and keywords—provide a helpful example for specifying the levels of cataloging for electronic resources. What this illustrates is that the cataloging community could and should contribute to the development of metadata guidelines. That is the best approach to ensure appropriate organization of electronic resources.

Catalogers will also want to keep an open mind about metadata's potential. The Metadata Implementation Group's effort at the University of Washington to map data elements from various collections to Dublin Core demonstrates how catalogers can apply their knowledge of cataloging to the creation of metadata dictionaries (2005). The project also makes explicit how services can be enhanced by combining cataloging knowledge with sophisticated tools such as the CONTENT software suite (2005). Electronic resources present opportunities for catalogers to reexamine how they organize information. The efforts by librarians so far suggest many librarians have affirmed the value of systematic human analysis of electronic resources and recognized the benefits of drawing on sophisticated technology and "agents" to enhance services.

The Future of Cataloging and Catalogers

While many catalogers may work in non–library settings in the future, the future of cataloging and catalogers is likely to be tied to the future of libraries. Many believe libraries of the future will be "integrated" in that libraries will integrate new forms of intellectual and artistic expression into existing collections and provide strong bibliographic structures that guide users to resources in any formats, whether they are locally owned or not, and facilitate users' interaction with recorded knowledge and information (Barker 1996; Crawford 1998; Gorman 1997). As libraries evolve, catalogers will need to expand the current bibliographic structures to accommodate resources that combine different media. To prepare for such tasks, catalogers will need to become familiar with cataloging rules for such resources first. Then they can draw on their experience in organizing such resources and their knowledge of the creation, transfer, and use of information to propose ways to improve the cataloging of these resources. By sharing ideas and experience in professional organizations such as ALCTS and IFLA, catalogers will help bring about rule revisions and changes in cataloging practices. When a strong bibliographic structure is in place to support international cooperation in organizing and sharing information resources, the future of cataloging will be further secured (Gorman 1997).

Catalogers also will want to continue to learn about new standards for describing and accessing resources, whether the standards are developed inside or outside the library community. They should know what metadata is, how it relates to cataloging efforts, how to take advantage of non-library-based metadata schemas when necessary, and how to select and implement metadata schemas. The Library of Congress fully realized the challenge in controlling digital resources in the twenty-first century, and held a conference, Bicentennial Conference on Bibliographic Control for the New Millennium, to explore ways to improve description, discovery, and access to Web resources (2000). One of the outcomes of the conference is "Cataloging and Metadata Education: A Proposal for Preparing Cataloging Professionals of the 21st Century," a proposal for providing cataloging and metadata education to prepare future catalogers for the challenges of organizing digital resources (Hsieh-Yee 2002). The proposal led to a workshop for educators and the establishment of a Web clearinghouse, to be hosted by the Cataloger's Learning Workshop, to promote understanding and usage of metadata (2005). Librarians will want to take advantage of resources like these to keep up with new developments in the field and develop new skills.

In addition, catalogers need to work with other professionals to develop or identify appropriate standards and methods for information organization. Digital technology has made it possible for archivists, special collections directors, museum specialists, scientists, and others to present their collections electronically, whether on the Internet or on CD-ROM or DVD. If catalogers are not involved in the planning and implementation of a digital collection, the task of organizing digital objects will become more difficult later. Catalogers have much to offer other professionals. The principles of cataloging are applicable to digital materials, and cataloging concepts such as collocation, access points, authority control, controlled vocabulary, and subject analysis are highly relevant to the organization of digital materials (Mandel and Wolven 1996). Sharing their cataloging expertise with other professionals, catalogers will help others understand critical issues related to resource description and access. Likewise, understanding the purpose and perspectives of other professionals, catalogers will be able to help others in improving standards and accomplishing their objectives through cataloging, metadata, or other methods of information organization.

As more and more digital libraries are taking shape, an inevitable question is Will cataloging and catalogers be needed in digital libraries?

Technology enthusiasts may prefer heavy reliance on technology to create and manage a digital library, but it is humans who make decisions on what technology will do and how technology will carry out instructions. As Levy observed, order is critical for the stability and usability of digital collections, and cataloging efforts, enhanced and facilitated by technology, are critical to bring about order (1995). The organization of digital resources requires that one consider which resources will be cataloged and how much detail should be included in records so that information resources can be identified, discovered, evaluated, and accessed. These goals of cataloging remain the same in the digital environment, but the procedures will evolve. For instance, if future resources have metadata embedded in them, the cataloging process may become simplified. Catalogers will have many areas to apply their expertise. They can, for example, help define how electronic resources, commercially and locally produced, will be described for access; how resources created by different standards and embedded with different metadata will be integrated into the collection; how the collection will be maintained for access; and how to provide interactivity in the system for users to take full advantage of the library's resources.

Conclusion

Cataloging involves technology, yet technology continues to cause concern over the future of cataloging. When bibliographic utilities became available in the 1960s, the fear that machines would replace catalogers loomed large but was never realized. In the 1980s paraprofessionals performed most of copy cataloging, while catalogers were busy preparing data for online catalogs, thus technology seemed less threatening than before. But the economic situation in the first half of 1990s led to reduced support for cataloging and large-scale outsourcing was implemented in some institutions. The growth of the Internet caused further concerns that cataloging might be inadequate for describing dynamic Web resources and that search engines and new initiatives such as Google Print may render cataloging unnecessary. But catalogers drew on the principles of cataloging and the objectives of the catalog, and addressed the challenges directly by developing new guidelines for interactive multimedia, electronic resources, and integrating resources.

The experience of catalogers shows that library information professionals are in fact well positioned to make significant contributions to information organization and management in the twenty-first century. Here are the reasons. First, the LIS field is concerned with the need of users and has insights into user behavior. Second, the principles of information organization are applicable to new resource formats. Third, some cataloging practices and standards such as level of description, controlled vocabularies, and authority control are critical for resource description, discovery, and access of digital resources. Fourth, the library community has experience dealing with a variety of resource formats and has demonstrated it can organize resources of new format. New formats will continue to emerge and we can draw on our experience to manage them. Fifth, librarians have experience in using standards and sharing data and resources. This experience will be valuable because the networked environment has necessitated cooperation and collaboration of different types of information professionals. And finally, the library community has MARC, which provides syntax and structure for bibliographic data, and *AACR2*, which provides semantics for resource description, and both have evolved to accommodate changes in the digital environment. Information organization takes place in many settings and library information professionals are increasingly called on to apply cataloging practices and tools to new resource formats, modify cataloging practices for digital libraries, use non-library-based metadata schemas, or integrate metadata from several sources into an information system. Catalogers' knowledge of information organization and commitment to users will help librarians secure their future in the twenty-first century.

References

About Google Scholar. http://scholar.google.com/scholar/about.html (accessed June 1, 2005).

About JStor. (2005). http://www.jstor.org/about/ (accessed June 1, 2005).

Baca, Murtha (Ed.). (2000). *Introduction to metadata: Pathways to digital information* (version 2). Getty Information Institute. http://www.getty.edu/research/conducting_research/standards/intrometadata/index.html (accessed June 1, 2005).

Barker, Philip. (1996). Electronic libraries of the future. *Encyclopedia of Library and Information Science* 59: 119–153.

Borgman, Christine L. (2000). *From Gutenberg to the global information infrastructure.* Cambridge, Mass.: MIT Press.

Caplan, Priscilla. (2003). *Metadata fundamentals for all librarians.* Chicago: American Library Association.

Cataloger's learning workshop. (2005). http://www.loc.gov/catworkshop/ (accessed June 1, 2005).

CiteSeer.ist. http://citeseer.ist.psu.edu/ (accessed June 1, 2005).

CiteSeer.ist, OAI compliance. (2004). http://citeseer.ist.psu.edu/oai.html (accessed June 1, 2005).

Collaborative filtering. (1996). http://info.berkeley.edu/resources/collab/index.html (accessed June 1, 2005).

CONTENTdm for digital collections. (2005). http://www.oclc.org/contentdm/default.htm (accessed June 1, 2005).

Crawford, Walt. (1998). Paper persists: Why physical library collections still matter. *Online* 22 (January/February): 42–48.

DC-dot: Dublin Core metadata editor. (2005). http://www.ukoln.ac.uk/metadata/dcdot/ (accessed June 1, 2005).

Dempsey, Lorcan, and Heery, Rachel. (1998). Metadata: A current view of practice and issues. *Journal of Documentation* 54 (2): 145–172.

Directory of scholarly electronic journals and academic discussion lists. (1st ed.). (2000). Washington, D.C.: Association for Research Libraries. http://db.arl.org/dsej/index.html (accessed June 1, 2005).

Eden, Brad. (Ed.). (2002, September/October). Metadata and its application. *Library Technology Reports* 38: 5–79.

EU-NSF Working Group on Metadata. (1999). Metadata for digital libraries: A research agenda. http://www.ercim.org/publication/ws-proceedings/EU-NSF/metadata.pdf (accessed June 1, 2005).

Fallows, Deborah. (2005). *Search engine users: Internet searchers are confident, satisfied and trusting—but they are also unaware and naïve.* http://www.pewinternet.org/pdfs/PIP_Searchengine_users.pdf (accessed June 1, 2005).

Fallows, Deborah, Rainie, Lee, and Mudd, Graham. (2004). *Data memo on search engines.* http://www.pewinternet.org/pdfs/PIP_Data_Memo_Searchengines.pdf (accessed June 1, 2005).

Forester, Barbara. (2005, March). Google's digitization project: What difference will it make? *Library Issues*, 25 (password required). http://www.libraryissues.com/pub/LI250004.asp (accessed June 1, 2005).

Gilliland-Swetland, Anne. (2000). "Setting the Stage." In Murtha Baca (Ed.), *Introduction to metadata: Pathways to digital information*, Getty Information Institute. http://www.getty.edu/research/institute/standards/intrometadata/2_articles/index.html (accessed June 1, 2005).

Goldenberg-Hart, Diane Y. (1998). Library technology centers and community building: Yale University Library Electronic Text Center. *Library Hi Tech* 16: 21–26.

Google at the Gate. (2005, March). *American Libraries* 36: 40–43.

Google Print Library project. http://print.google.com/googleprint/library.html (accessed June 1, 2005).

Google technology. http://www.google.com/technology/ (accessed June 1, 2005).

Gorman, Michael. (1997). What is the future of cataloguing and cataloguers. In *The 63rd IFLA General Conference—Conference Programme and Proceedings, August 31–September 5, 1997.* http://www.ifla.org/IV/ifla63/63gorm.htm (accessed June 1, 2005).

Gorman, Michael. (1999). Metadata or cataloguing? A false choice. *Journal of Internet Cataloging* 2 (1): 5–12.

Healy, Leigh Watson. (2002). *The voice of the user: Where faculty and students go for information.* http://www.educause.edu/ir/library/powerpoint/EDU0248c.pps (accessed June 1, 2005).

Hillmann, Diane I., and Westbrooks, Elaine L. (2004). *Metadata in practice.* Chicago: American Library Association.

Hsieh-Yee, Ingrid. (2002). *Cataloging and metadata education: A proposal for preparing cataloging professionals of the 21st century.* http://www.loc.gov/catdir/bibcontrol/CatalogingandMetadataEducation.pdf (accessed June 1, 2005).

Hudgins, Jean, Agnew, Grace, and Brown, Elizabeth. (1999). *Getting mileage out of metadata: Applications for the library.* Chicago: American Library Association.

IFLA Study Group on Functional Requirements for Bibliographic Records. (1998). *Functional requirements for bibliographic records: Final report.* Munchen: G. K. Sauer. http://www.ifla.org/VII/S13/frbr/frbr.pdf (accessed June 1, 2005).

Jones, Steve, and Madden, Mary. (2002). *The Internet goes to college: How students are living in the future with today's technology.* http://www.pewinternet.org/pdfs/PIP_College_Report.pdf (accessed June 1, 2005).

Levy, David M. (1995). *Cataloging in the digital order.* http://csdl.tamu.edu/DL95/papers/levy/levy.html (accessed June 1, 2005).

Library of Congress. (2000). *Bicentennial Conference on Bibliographic Control for the New Millennium.* http://www.loc.gov/catdir/bibcontrol/ (accessed June 1, 2005).

Library of Congress. Network Development and MARC Standards Office. (2005). *MARC standards*. http://www.loc.gov/marc/ (accessed June 1, 2005).

Library of Congress. Network Development and MARC Standards Office. (2005). *MARC 21 XML schema*. http://www.loc.gov/standards/marcxml/// (accessed June 1, 2005).

Library of Congress. Network Development and MARC Standards Office. (2005). *Metadata authority description schema*. http://www.loc.gov/standards/mads/ (accessed June 1, 2005).

Library of Congress. Network Development and MARC Standards Office. (2005). *Metadata object description schema*. http://www.loc.gov/standards/mods// (accessed June 1, 2005).

Mandel, Carol A., and Wolven, Robert. (1996). Intellectual access to digital documents: Joining proven principles with new technologies. *Cataloging & Classification Quarterly* 22 (3–4): 25–42.

Marcum, Deanna. (2005, January 16). *The future of cataloging: Address to the leadership seminar*. Boston, Mass. http://www.loc.gov/library/reports/CatalogingSpeech.pdf (accessed June 1, 2005).

Milstead, Jessica, and Feldman, Susan. (1999, January/February). Metadata projects and standards. *Online* 23: 32–38, 40.

NISO. (2004). *Understanding metadata*. Bethesda, Md.: NISO Press. http://www.niso.org/standards/resources/UnderstandingMetadata.pdf (accessed June 1, 2005).

NISO. Framework Advisory Group. (2004). *A framework of guidance for building good digital collections* (2nd ed.). Bethesda, Md.: National Information Standards Organization. http://www.niso.org/framework/framework2.html (accessed June 1, 2005).

OAI news. (2005). http://www.openarchives.org/news/news2.html#Google (accessed June 1, 2005).

OCLC. (2002). *How academic librarians can influence students' Web-based information choices: OCLC white paper on the information habits of college students*. Dublin, Ohio: OCLC. http://www5.oclc.org/downloads/community/informationhabits.pdf (accessed June 1, 2005).

OCLC. (2005). *Open WorldCat Partners sites*. http://www.oclc.org/worldcat/open/partnersites/default.htm (accessed June 1, 2005).

OCLC. (2005). *Open WorldCat program*. http://www.oclc.org/worldcat/open/default.htm (accessed June 1, 2005).

OCLC Connexion. http://connexion.oclc.org/ (accessed June 1, 2005).

The open archives initiative protocol for metadata harvesting. (2002). http://www.openarchives.org/OAI/2.0/openarchivesprotocol.htm (accessed June 1, 2005).

Pavliscak, Pamela, Ross, Seamus, and Henry, Charles. (1997). *Information technology in humanities scholarship: Achievements, prospects, and challenges: The United States focus*. New York: American Council of Learned Societies. http://www.acls.org/op37.htm (accessed June 1, 2005).

Seaman, David. (1997, July/August). The user community as responsibility and resource: Building a sustainable digital library. *D-Lib Magazine*. http://www.dlib.org/dlib/july97/07seaman.html (accessed June 1, 2005).

Smith, Alastair. (1997). *Criteria for evaluation of Internet information resources*. http://www.vuw.ac.nz/~agsmith/evaln/index.htm (accessed June 1, 2005).

Sullivan, Danny. (2000). *NPD search and portal site study*. http://searchenginewatch.com/sereport/article.php/2162791 (accessed June 1, 2005).

University of Virginia Library. (2003). *Submission of electronic theses and dissertations*. http://viva.lib.virginia.edu/etd/ (accessed June 1, 2005).

University of Washington Libraries. Metadata Implementation Group. (2005). *Dublin Core data dictionaries*. http://www.lib.washington.edu/msd/mig/datadicts/default.html (accessed June 1, 2005).

Vellucci, Sherry. (1998). Metadata. *Annual review of information science and technology*, 33, 187–222.

Weibel, Stuart. (1995, July). Metadata: The foundations of resource description. *D-Lib Magazine*, 1. http://www.dlib.org/dlib/July95/07weibel.html (accessed June 1, 2005).

Western states Dublin Core metadata best practices. (2005). http://www.cdpheritage.org/resource/metadata/wsdcmbp/ (accessed June 1, 2005).

Wiley, Deborah Lynne. (1998, August/September). Beyond information retrieval: Ways to provide content in context. *Database (Weston, Conn.)* 21: 18–22.

Suggested Readings

Baca, Murtha (Ed.). (2000). *Introduction to metadata: Pathways to digital information* (version 2). Getty Information Institute. http://www.getty.edu/research/conducting_research/standards/intrometadata/index.html (accessed June 1, 2005).

Gorman, Michael. (1999). Metadata or cataloging? A false choice. *Journal of Internet Cataloging* 2 (1): 5–22.

Howarth, Lynn C. (2004, January/March). Metadata schemas for subject gateways. *International Cataloguing and Bibliographic Control* 33: 8–12.

IFLA Study Group on the Functional Requirements for Bibliographic Records. (1998). *Functional requirements for bibliographic records: Final report*. Munchen: K. G. Saur. http://www.ifla.org/VII/s13/frbr/frbr.pdf (accessed June 1, 2005).

Library of Congress. (2000). *Bicentennial Conference on Bibliographic Control for the New Millennium*. http://www.loc.gov/catdir/bibcontrol/ (accessed June 1, 2005).

NISO Framework Advisory Group. (2004). *A framework of guidance for building good digital collections* (2nd ed.). Bethesda, Md.: National Information Standards Organization. http://www.niso.org/framework/framework2.html (accessed June 1, 2005).

Bibliography

Cataloging Standards (Print)

Anglo-American cataloguing rules. (2004). (2nd ed. 2002 revision, including 2004 update). Chicago: American Library Association.

Dewey decimal classification and relative index. (2003). (22nd ed.). Dublin, Ohio: Online Computer Library Center.

ISBD (CF) Review Group. (1997). *ISBD (ER): International standard bibliographic description for electronic resources*. München: K. G. Sauer.

Library of Congress. Cataloging Policy and Support Office. (2004). *Subject cataloging manual: Subject headings* (5th ed.). Washington, D.C.: Cataloging Distribution Service, Library of Congress.

Library of Congress. Network Development and MARC Standards Office. (1999). *MARC 21 format for bibliographic data: Including guidelines for content designation*. Washington, D.C.: Cataloging Distribution Service, Library of Congress.

Library of Congress. Office for Subject Cataloging Policy. (2005). *Free-floating subdivisions: An alphabetical Index* (17th ed.). Washington, D.C.: Cataloging Distribution Service, Library of Congress.

Library of Congress. Office for Subject Cataloging Policy. (2005). *Library of Congress subject headings* (28th ed.). Washington, D.C.: Cataloging Distribution Service, Library of Congress.

Library of Congress. Office for Subject Cataloging Policy. (1992). *Subject cataloging manual: Classification*. Washington, D.C.: Cataloging Distribution Service, Library of Congress.

Library of Congress. Subject Cataloging Division. (1996–2005). *Library of Congress classification schedules*. Washington, D.C.: Cataloging Distribution Service, Library of Congress.

Library of Congress rule interpretations. Cumulation: 1989 base text with all updates through 2002 interfiled. (2002). Washington, D.C.: Cataloging Distribution Service, Library of Congress.

OCLC. (1996). *OCLC technical bulletin 212: Format integration phase 2*. Dublin, Ohio: OCLC.

Olson, Nancy B. (Ed.). (1997). *Cataloging internet resources: A manual and practical guide* (2nd ed.). Dublin, Ohio: OCLC.

Cataloging Standards (Online)

ALCTS/CCS/SAC Subcommittee on Form Headings/Subdivisions Implementation. (2000). http://www.pitt.edu/~agtaylor/ala/implem.htm (accessed June 1, 2005).

CONSER. (2004). *Conser cataloging manual module 31: Remote access electronic serials (online serials).* http://www.loc.gov/acq/conser/Module31.pdf (accessed June 1, 2005).

Free-floating subject subdivisions. http://infoshare1.princeton.edu/tsnew/infoshare1/katmandu/subj/subd.html (accessed June 1, 2005).

Guide to the usage of LCSH free-floating form subdivisions. (2000). http://www.itcompany.com/inforetriever/form_subdivisions_list.htm (accessed June 1, 2005).

International Conference on the Principles and Future Development of AACR. (1997). http://www.collectionscanada.ca/jsc/intlconf1.html (accessed June 1, 2005).

ISBD (CF) Review Group. (1997). *ISBD (ER): International standard bibliographic description for electronic resources.* http://www.ifla.org/VII/s13/pubs/isbd.htm (accessed June 1, 2005).

Library of Congress. Cataloging Policy and Support Office. *Draft interim guidelines for cataloging electronic resources.* www.loc.gov/catdir/cpso/dcmb19_4.html (accessed June 1, 2005).

Library of Congress. Cataloging Policy and Support Office. (2005). *Subject headings weekly lists.* http://www.loc.gov/catdir/cpso/cpso.html#subjects (accessed June 1, 2005).

Library of Congress. Network Development and MARC Standards Office. (2003). *Guidelines for coding electronic resources in leader/06.* http://www.loc.gov/marc/ldr06guide.html (accessed June 1, 2005).

Library of Congress. Network Development and MARC Standards Office. (2003). *Guidelines for the use of field 856.* http://www.loc.gov/marc/856guide.html (accessed June 1, 2005).

Library of Congress. Network Development and MARC Standards Office. (2005). *MARC 21 formats.* http://www.loc.gov/marc/marcdocz.html (accessed June 1, 2005).

Library of Congress. Network Development and MARC Standards Office. (2005). *MARC standards.* http://www.loc.gov/marc/ (accessed June 1, 2005).

Library of Congress subject headings: Principles of structure and policies for applications. (1990). Cataloger's Reference Shelf. http://www.tlcdelivers.com/tlc/crs/shed0014.htm (accessed June 1, 2005).

MARC 21 format for bibliographic data. (2000). Cataloger's Reference Shelf. http://www.itsmarc.com/crs/bib0001.htm (accessed June 1, 2005).

OCLC. (2003). *Bibliographic formats and standards.* http://www.oclc.org/bibformats/ (accessed June 1, 2005).

OCLC. (2003). *856 election location and access.* http://www.oclc.org/bibformats/en/8xx/856.shtm (accessed June 1, 2005).

Olson, Nancy B. (Ed.). (1997). *Cataloging Internet resources: A manual and practical guide.* http://www.oclc.org/support/documentation/worldcat/cataloging/internetguide/default.htm (accessed June 1, 2005).

Weitz, Jay. (2004). *Cataloging electronic resources: OCLC-MARC coding guidelines.* http://www.oclc.org/support/documentation/worldcat/cataloging/electronicresources/ (accessed June 1, 2005).

Selected Resources on Cataloging Practices and Metadata Applications

AACR2 and seriality. http://www.loc.gov/acq/conser/serialty.html (accessed June 1, 2005).

AUTOCAT: List of files. (1997). http://ublib.buffalo.edu/libraries/units/cts/autocat/ (accessed June 1, 2005).

AUTOCAT@LISTSERV.ACSU.BUFFALO.EDU-Archives. (2005). http://listserv.acsu.buffalo.edu/archives/autocat.html (accessed June 1, 2005).

Baca, Murtha (Ed.). (2000). *Introduction to Metadata: Pathways to Digital Information* (version 2). Getty Information Institute. http://www.getty.edu/research/conducting_research/standards/intrometadata/index.html (accessed June 1, 2005).

Beyond bookmarks: Schemes for organizing the Web. http://www.public.iastate.edu/~CYBERSTACKS/CTW.htm (accessed June 1, 2005).

Caplan, Priscilla. (2003). *Metadata fundamentals for all librarians.* Chicago: American Library Association.

Cataloger's learning workshop. (2005). http://www.loc.gov/catworkshop/ (accessed June 1, 2005).

Cataloguer's toolbox. (2005). http://staff.library.mun.ca/staff/toolbox/ (accessed June 1, 2005).

DC-Dot, Dublin Core metadata editor. (2005). http://www.ukoln.ac.uk/metadata/dcdot/ (accessed June 1, 2005).

Dublin Core metadata initiative. (2005). http://dublincore.org/ (accessed June 1, 2005).

Dublin Core metadata template. (1998). http://www.lub.lu.se/cgi-bin/nmdc.pl (accessed June 1, 2005).

Duval, Erik, Hodgins, Wayne, Sutton, Stuart, and Weibel, Stuart L. (2002). Metadata principles and practicalities. *D-Lib Magazine,* 8 (4), http://www.dlib.org/dlib/april02/weibel/04weibel.html (accessed June 1, 2005).

Gaynor, Edward. (1996). *From MARC to markup: SGML and online library systems.* http://xml.coverpages.org/gaynorMARC96.html (accessed June 1, 2005).

Gilliland-Swetland, Anne. (2000). Setting the Stage. In Murtha Baca (Ed.), *Introduction to metadata, pathway to digital information.* Getty Information Institute. http://www.getty.edu/research/institute/standards/intrometadata/2_articles/index.html (accessed June 1, 2005).

Gorman, G. E., and Dorner, Daniel G. (Eds.). (2004). *Metadata applications and management.* London: Facet Publishing.

Gorman, Michael. (1999). Metadata or cataloguing? A false choice. *Journal of Internet Cataloging* 2 (1): 5–22.

Graham, Crystal, and the *CONSER* Working Group. (1999). *CONSER WG: Single v. separate records, draft report*. http://wwwtest.library.ucla.edu/libraries/cataloging/ sercat/conserwg/conserwg.draft.htm (accessed June 1, 2005).

Hillmann, Diane I., and Westbrooks, Elaine L. (2004). *Metadata in practice*. Chicago: American Library Association.

Hirons, Jean. (1999). *Revising AACR2 to accommodate seriality: Report to the Joint Steering Committee on the Revision of AACR*. http://www.collectionscanada.ca/jsc/docs/ser-rep.pdf (accessed June 1, 2005).

Howarth, Lynn C. (2004, January/March). Metadata schemas for subject gateways. *International Cataloguing and Bibliographic Control* 33: 8–12.

IFLA Study Group on the Functional Requirements for Bibliographic Records. (1998). *Functional requirements for bibliographic records: Final report*. München: K. G. Saur. http://www.ifla.org/VII/s13/frbr/frbr.pdf; http://www.ifla.org/VII/s13/frbr/frbr.htm (accessed June 1, 2005).

InterCAT project. www.oclc.org/research/projects/archive/intercat.htm (accessed June 1, 2005).

Intner, Sheila S., and Smiraglia, Richard P. (Eds.). (1987). *Policy and practice in bibliographic control of nonbook media*. Chicago: American Library Association.

Library of Congress. (2005). *LC cataloging newsline*. http://www.loc.gov/catdir/lccn/ (accessed June 1, 2005).

Library of Congress. Cataloging Policy and Support Office. (2005). http://www.loc.gov/catdir/cpso/ (accessed June 1, 2005).

Mandel, Carol A., and Wolven, Robert. (1996). Intellectual access to digital documents: Joining proven principles with new technologies. *Cataloging & Classification Quarterly* 22 (3/4): 25–42.

Metadata basics. (2005). http://www.loc.gov/catworkshop/readings/metadatabasics/index.html (accessed June 1, 2005).

Milstead, Jessica, and Feldman, Susan. (1999). Metadata: Cataloging by any other name. *Online* 23: 24–26.

Milstead, Jessica, and Feldman, Susan. (1999). Metadata projects and standards. *Online* 23: 32–38, 40.

NISO. (2004). *Understanding metadata*. Bethesda, Md.: NISO Press. http://www.niso.org/standards/resources/UnderstandingMetadata.pdf (accessed June 1, 2005).

NISO Framework Advisory Group. (2004). *A framework of guidance for building good digital collections* (2nd ed.). Bethesda, Md.: National Information Standards Organization. http://www.niso.org/framework/framework2.html (accessed June 1, 2005).

OCLC. (2005). *OCLC technical bulletins*. http://www.oclc.org/support/documentation/technicalbulletins/default.htm (accessed June 1, 2005).

OLAC: Online Audiovisual Catalogers. (2004). *OLAC*. http://www.olacinc.org/ (accessed June 1, 2005).

The Principles and Future of AACR: Proceedings of the International Conference on the Principles and Future Development of AACR, Toronto, Ontario, Canada, October 23–25, 1997. (1998). Chicago: American Library Association. http://www.collectionscanada.ca/jsc/intlconf1.html (accessed June 1, 2005).

PURLS. (2005). http://purl.oclc.org/ (accessed June 1, 2005).

Sandberg-Fox, Ann, and Byrum, John D. (1998, April). From ISBD (CF) to ISBD (ER): Process, policy, and provisions. *Library Resources and Technical Services* 42: 89–101.

Taylor, Arlene G. (2004). *The organization of information* (2nd ed.). Westport, Conn.: Libraries Unlimited.

User guidelines for Dublin Core creation. (2001). http://www.sics.se/~preben/DC/ DC_guide.html (accessed June 1, 2005).

Western states Dublin Core metadata best practices. Version 2.0. (2005). http:// www.cdpheritage.org/resource/metadata/wsdcmbp/ (accessed June 1, 2005).

Weihs, Jean Riddle. (1991). *The integrated library: Encouraging access to multimedia materials* (2nd ed.). Phoenix, Ariz.: Oryx Press.

Handbooks, Guides, Textbooks, Etc.

Chan, Lois Mai. (1994). *Cataloging and classification: An introduction* (2nd ed.). New York: McGraw-Hill.

Chan, Lois Mai. (1999). *Immroth's guide to the Library of Congress classification* (5th ed.). Englewood, Colo.: Libraries Unlimited.

Chan, Lois Mai. (2005). *Library of Congress subject headings: Principles and application* (4th ed.). Englewood, Colo.: Libraries Unlimited.

Chan, Lois Mai, and Mitchell, Joan S. (2005). *Dewey decimal classification: Principles and application* (3rd ed.). Dublin, Ohio: OCLC.

Downing, Mildred Harlow, and Downing, David H. (1992). *Introduction to cataloging and classification* (6th ed.). Jefferson, N.C.: McFarland.

Fecko, Mary Beth. (1993). *Cataloging nonbook resources: A how-to-do-it manual for librarians.* New York: Neal-Schuman.

Fritz, Deborah A. (2004). *Cataloging with AACR2 and MARC21: For books, electronic resources, sound recordings, videorecordings, and serials* (2nd ed.). Chicago: American Library Association.

Frost, Carolyn O. (1989). *Media access and organization: A cataloging and reference sources guide for nonbook materials.* Englewood, Colo.: Libraries Unlimited.

Furrie, Betty. (2003). *Understanding MARC bibliographic: Machine-readable cataloging* (7th ed.). Washington, D.C.: Cataloging Distribution Service, Library of Congress. http://www.loc.gov/marc/umb/ (accessed June 1, 2005).

Liheng, Carol, and Chan, Winnie S. (1998). *Serials cataloging handbook: An illustrative guide to the use of AACR2 and LC rules interpretations* (2nd ed.). Chicago: American Library Association.

Maxwell, Robert L. (2004). *Maxwell's handbook for AACR2: Explaining and illustrating the Anglo-American cataloguing rules through the 2003 update* (4th ed.). Chicago: American Library Association.

Millsap, Larry, and Ferl, Terry Ellen. (1997). *Descriptive cataloging for the AACR2R and the integrated MARC format: A how-to-do-it workbook* (revised ed.). New York: Neal-Schuman.

Olson, Nancy B. (1998). *Cataloging of audiovisual materials and other special materials: A manual based on AACR2* (4th ed.). Sheila S. Intner and Edward Swanson (Eds.). DeKalb, Ill.: Minnesota Scholarly Press.

Rogers, JoAnn V., with Saye, Jerry D. (1987). *Nonprint cataloging for multimedia collections: A guide based on AACR2* (2nd ed.). Littleton, Colo.: Libraries Unlimited.

Saye, Jerry D. (2000). *Manheimer's cataloging and classification* (4th ed., revised and expanded). New York: Marcel Dekker.

Scott, Mona L. (1998). *Dewey decimal classification, 21st edition: A study manual and number building*. Englewood, Colo.: Libraries Unlimited.

Index

About the Author

INGRID HSIEH-YEE is a Professor in the School of Library and Information Science at the Catholic University of America.